COMPASS POINTS

COMPASS POINTS

Jan Morris introduces a selection from
the first hundred issues of *Planet*

Selected by
Janet Davies

CARDIFF
UNIVERSITY OF WALES PRESS
1993

© The Contributors, 1993

British Library Cataloguing-in-Publication Data.
A catalogue record for this book is available from the British Library.

ISBN 0-7083-1220-9

Jacket design by Design Principle, Cardiff.
Jacket illustration entitled *Paris s'éveille – John Cale*
    by Catrin Williams, Caernarfon.
Printed in Great Britain by Biddles Ltd., Guildford.

Contents

Contents

Foreword

Making a selection from *Planet* for publication in one volume was not an easy task. Poetry is an important part of the magazine's output, but a number of the poems which made their first appearance in *Planet* have by now been published elsewhere in book form; and many of the shorter pieces which appear under the heading 'Matters Arising' would need footnoting to make them intelligible to the reader. It seemed to me that *Planet*'s essential character would best be represented by as wide a selection as possible of full-length articles.

My main concern was to choose articles which would read well. I then sought to select pieces which would give the 'feel' of *Planet*. Just over half the articles fall into one of the three groups which represent what seemed to me, on reading through the published issues, to be *Planet*'s major concerns: Welsh society; minority language cultures and politics; literature and literary criticism. The remainder are on a variety of subjects, reflecting *Planet*'s widely ranging interests.

I decided, however, not to group the articles by topic, but to arrange them in chronological order, thus giving a sense of the changing world and the changing Wales which created and re-created *Planet* and which the magazine in turn helped to create.

The reader of the 1990s may well be struck by the style of earlier periods, and in particular the sexism implicit in the language of some of the articles. The originals have been left unamended, however, as being more truly reflections of their times.

Janet Davies

Introduction

JAN MORRIS

This anthology, besides being a selection of good writing on a
dizzy variety of subjects, is an index to the thinking of an intelligentsia during a particularly interesting period of its history.
When the Welsh magazine *Planet* was founded in 1970 the world
was on the brink of two immense events: the emergence of a new
kind of Europe, the collapse of Communism. Both were to have
incalculable influences upon the smaller nations, the minority
nations in particular, and in Wales they were radically to affect
the way citizens thought about their own country and its future.
The sort of people who best articulated these effects were the sort
who wrote and edited *Planet*, and the pages of this book record
the various states of mind they exhibited in the last three decades
of the twentieth century, and the first 100 issues of the magazine...

Consider, from a long perspective, the Welsh situation when
Planet first appeared. Once a congeries of independent prince-
doms intermittently bonded into unity, Wales had been for almost
700 years subject to the sovereignty of the British Crown, governed by the British government and legislated for by an
overwhelmingly English Parliament in London. About a fifth of
its people still spoke *Cymraeg*, the Welsh language, and the
numbers were declining; perhaps about the same proportion
were consciously dedicated to the principle of Welsh self-
government. Far fewer were active in the chief movements, Plaid
Cymru the political party, Cymdeithas yr Iaith Gymraeg the
extra-Parliamentary body, which represented the nationalist urge.
English governments, both Labour and Conservative, had fairly
effortlessly maintained the status quo; while the young Welsh
activists were indefatigable in their fight to preserve the

nationality of Wales, especially as embodied in its language, people in general were indifferent to the cause.

At the same time the vast mining and steel-making communities of south Wales, which had become in many ways the truest epitome of modern Welshness, were desolated by the precipitate decline of their industries. Chapel Christianity had already lost most of its authority, and now the high-minded socialism of the valleys, which had expressed itself in solidarity and aspiration, and a respect for education and the arts, was losing its moral power too. The old loyalties were being transmuted into nothing more elevating than spectator sport, just as all that was left of the Welsh language, for thousands of Welsh people, was a national anthem most did not understand, and a few hymns sung more or less as mantras before the kick-off.

In 1970 it seemed just possible that this situation might explode into endemic violence, on the Northern Ireland pattern. While an increasing flow of English incomers dangerously shifted the ethnic balance, the Welsh-speaking minority fought back in ever more bitter frustration. *Planet* thus made its appearance upon a scene that was at once volatile and depressing: its very first editorial likened Wales to 'a boisterous and dissident satrapy', and came to the conclusion that whether as a political, a social or even an ethical policy, some kind of Welsh autonomy was essential to the nation's good.

Almost every Welsh political argument since then has revolved about the same assumption – that in one degree or another, whether by accommodation or by challenge, Wales must govern its own affairs. During the twenty odd years since *Planet*'s beginning the idea has sometimes triumphed, sometimes been humiliated.

On the one hand, when in a 1979 referendum the Welsh as a whole overwhelmingly rejected devolution, some observers proclaimed it the end of Welsh history. Economic depression seemed to be attended by political apathy. The nationalists never achieved mass support, the language was apparently in decline. Two months after the referendum the Labour government in London gave way to the Conservative regime, grotesquely unrepresentative of the Welsh electorate, which has been in power ever since, and soon afterwards, with its fiftieth issue *Planet* symbolically ceased publication.

On the other hand in 1981 the activists forced out of Mrs Thatcher's government a Welsh-language channel, seen by some as a vital key to the future of the language. In successive elections Plaid Cymru returned two or three members to Westminster. There was a new surge of interest in the language. Devolution, seen by so many as a dead cause of the 1970s, again became an issue in the 1990s, and though stifled by the election of yet another Tory government in London, seemed to be supported now by a far wider spectrum of Welsh opinion.

Towering above these mixed developments, powerfully influencing them, were those two great political progressions of the time, the end of Marxist power and the rise of the new Europe: and so back into the field once more, in 1985, came the irrepressible *Planet*, with Issue 51. It had been absent for more than five years, and its re-opening editorial was entitled 'As I Was Saying . . .'

Planet is subtitled 'The Welsh Internationalist', and most of the pieces in this collection mirror the magazine's preoccupation with Wales's place in the world at large. In theory that place has been transformed during the magazine's career. Not so long ago it seemed to Welsh patriots that they were almost alone in the world, their national predicament virtually unique, sustained only by the fitful and wistful good wishes of their fellow-Celts in Brittany, Ireland and Scotland, plus the odd Corsican or Croatian. Now it turns out, as one contributor to this book suggests, that Wales stands 'at the dead centre' of a congeries of similar countries, in analagous situations.

At the centre, because its condition overlaps those of states like Latvia or Slovenia on the one side, that of minorities like the Bretons and Basques on the other, while economically it has been neither the passive subject of a larger power – its industries were essential to the rise of Greater Britain – nor an economic machine in its own right. The revival of European nationalisms in the 1980s and 1990s, the new dream of a Wales sovereign within a confederal Europe, the notion of cultural regionalism rather than political autonomy – all these ideas and events, sometimes conflicting, sometimes complementary, are reflected in the pages of this anthology.

A French philosopher, for example, says that the struggle for the identities of the Basques and Bretons is a struggle for France itself, 'the first victim of its own centralism'. We read a Catalan writer's tantalizing view, back in 1977, that 'Catalan culture is bounding back into all aspects of this little nation's life'. A Scot stresses the differences rather than the similarities, between Scottish and Welsh nationalism, and a Welsh historian at an English university, writing in the aftermath of the Communist collapse, makes the point that this is the third occasion in modern history in which the small states of eastern Europe have been emancipated from one empire or another – a third chance, he says, quoting an old Welsh proverb, for Wales to draw the lessons from their example.

These are, so to speak, views from the outside looking in, but the way minds at work within Wales have been affected is chronicled here no less pungently. In the course of the *Planet* decades the Welsh at home have come to think differently about their country. Their prospect of history, scoured by a hard-headed new school of Welsh historians, is clearer than it used to be. Their range of comparisons, stimulated by these great happenings in the world, is wider and perhaps starker. Instead of feeding upon old stereotypes, old yearnings, they are devising more contemporary images for their country, in art, in literature, in business, most potently of all perhaps in popular music. A hunger for modernity and universality has replaced the notorious introspection of this people, and many an old conviction has been turned topsy-turvy.

What kind of a people are the Welsh? More than ever they seem to be wondering, and they wonder it repeatedly in these pages. Welsh visual art, for so long dismissed as non-existent or contemptible, is reappraised. The Welshness of Aneurin Bevan, for many Englishmen the archetypal Welshman, is wryly analysed. The seminal events of 1936, when three Godly Welshmen set the nationalist fireball rolling by burning down an RAF bombing station, are recalled from the viewpoint of a far more violent decade. The significance of rugby football is explored. Black musicians of Mississippi, Albanians of Kosovo, the English themselves are set, as in silhouette, against the background of the Welsh dimension.

Most tellingly the English, perhaps, for implicit throughout the book is the fact that, for now at least, Wales in all its Welshness exists only in reaction to the presence of England. If there were no England there would be no Wales, and even the most thoroughly indigenous of activities is impregnated with English reminders. That *Planet* is written in English is itself a recognition of this truth:

many of the contributors to this book, like many of the magazine's readers, are bilingual in Welsh and English, but as yet no comparable journal, with such a breadth of outlook and concern, is published in *Cymraeg*.

Of course this reflects the profoundest of all the questions the Welsh are still asking themselves: not simply what kind of a people they are, but whether they are truly a people at all. Can there be a nation whose national language is spoken by only a fifth of its people? The nagging sense of alienation which runs through the affairs of Wales shows itself in these pages too. When an eminent learner of the Welsh language here recalls his first immersion in the tongue, his first exposure to 'the rollicking charm' of the *Cymry Cymraeg*, his realization that the language can 'wash over the sores' of the Welsh condition, we may be sure he touches many a nerve of envy and regret among his monoglot readers.

For this is not yet a people at ease with itself. Some of the Welsh feel themselves to be more Welsh than others, some consider themselves British as well as Welsh, some sense themselves to be irreversibly excluded from the innermost chambers of Welsh society, and from the ultimate delights of that rollicking charm. Add to these local discomforts the anxieties and grievances common to all countries, the economic strains and the social doubts, and it is no surprise to find an uncertain and in some ways unhappy comity. 'When was Wales?' asked the most provocative of contemporary Welsh historians, in the title of a book: and in this collection there are sometimes suggestions that even now Wales is really no more than an obsessive figure of the imagination.

Yet the dominant tone of the anthology, assembled from so many years of mingled hope and disappointment, is anything but querulous. On the contrary, it is almost serene. Its authors are as varied in origin as in occupation and outlook. They are dealing with subjects as disparate as sport, portraiture and linguistics from the point of view of a small, poor and deprived country on the western fringes of Europe. Yet there is something grand to the picture they present. It speaks of attitudes tolerant, humorous, self-critical, receptive. There is little cynicism here. The Gypsies of Romania are treated with as much respect as the Ladies of Llangollen.

It is a proud collection, in short, written by people with no illusions about Wales, but with a true and steady affection for the place. The old sentimental gush of Welshness is almost gone, the *hiraeth* and the *hwyl*, to be sustained only by a few obdurate romantics like me. Instead we have here a tone of voice that is modern and without illusions, but none the less loving for that. If I had to choose one passage in the book to stand for it all, I think I would plump for the last paragraph of the late John Tripp's essay about the National Eisteddfod. Having laughed about the misconceptions, the squabbles, the pretensions and mockeries that surround this seminal institution, as he used to laugh about the famous weaknesses of Welshness as a whole, he goes on to remember nevertheless all the generations of decent effort and artistry that have made the Eisteddfod what it is. And he concludes with a lapidary sentence that might well serve as a text for this volume, and an illustration of its approach to the meaning and the future of Wales itself:

May time and our own dignity preserve it.

The George Thomas Era

NED THOMAS

From Planet 1, August/September 1970. This first number appeared soon after a general election had swept Harold Wilson's Labour Government from power in London, and George Thomas from the Welsh Office.

To write about the George Thomas era is not to take the opportunity of knocking a man when he is down or to list the marginal changes in the administration of Wales that took place in his time, some of which may eventually prove important, but to discuss the tone and configuration of Welsh politics which were very different from those of English politics.

It was a more interesting, more exciting sort of politics here, but at the same time a more worrying sort. One's eyes were turned away from the ritual battles of the main British parties over how to interpret the balance of payments situation, to a world of demonstrations and direct action, to a country that at times seemed consumed in endless protest – Pembrey and Cwm Dulas, the farmers and the Rural Development Board, and the many campaigns of the Welsh Language Society. It was also the time of the bombs, the first maimings by explosive charges, and, on the morning of the Investiture of the Prince of Wales, the first deaths, however unintended, in the name of the Welsh national movement. To everyone who noticed it amid the spate of heraldic news, this episode seemed to move us nearer a more tragic kind of national politics.

When it is a case of Negro violence in the United States, or Protestants fighting Catholics in Northern Ireland, our

7

newspapers give us explanations in terms of historical cause and socio-economic conditions. Our own much lesser troubles in Wales have usually been explained away as the antics of a few fanatics. But in the end, here too, no one can escape responsibility for the political climate. There are crimes of omission as well as commission. There can be violence in a bureaucratic disregard for people's rights as well as in acts by individuals. And there is the blindness of pretending there are no conflicts when in fact there are.

The George Thomas era was a remarkably interesting time because many of the conflicts which are built into the structure of our society came right up to the surface. One way of describing conflicts is in terms of situations which frustrate attempts to find a solution. As Welshmen, if we are dissatisfied with the results of economic policy for the regions, there is nothing we can do except protest; there are no democratic institutions which give us an effective say. If the structure of broadcasting in the country is felt to be unsuitable, there is nothing we can do. If Welsh-speakers and non-Welsh speakers seem to be fighting each other for jobs in certain spheres, and jockeying for power, there is again no way of sorting things out between them; no one has responsibility for codifying employment policies. All this, of course, amounts to one very strong argument for devolution which is not merely administrative devolution but puts some power over their own circumstances into the hands of an electorate that has certain interests and problems in common.

But the situation was exacerbated by the fact that people who might have collaborated in finding solutions were thrown into opposition by the political polarization of Wales between social-ists and nationalists. Both the Labour Party and Plaid Cymru have deep roots in Welsh history, and it cannot be said that they include wholly different sorts of people. Indeed it is interesting to note how many of the early members of the nationalist party came from the Independent Labour Party and kept their socialist ideals intact when they moved.

For at least four years the questions most often asked about Wales concerned nationalism: is it a rising tide, a wave of new consciousness, or a protest vote, a flash in the pan? The last elec-tion leaves the question still open to all kinds of interpretation. But there is another question which, with Labour now in opposition, there may be more time for. What has happened to socialism in Wales? Theoretically there was no reason why socialists should be so grudging, graceless and late in their advocacy of devolution. But a party is also an *apparat*, a body concerned with the perpetuation of power, and the George Thomas era showed the Labour Party in Wales as mainly this.

If Wilson's socialism in London seemed a little dull and conservative and uninspired, by the time the perspective moved to Cardiff the effect was one of awful provincial shabbiness. Here, during the Investiture period, was a Labour minister using royalty to bolster his own party's position; here on our television screens a Secretary of State who seemed the quintessential comic stage Welshman wagged his headmasterly finger at the signs of young life in the country and encouraged English-speaking Welshmen to feel threatened by the new liveliness in the Welsh-speaking culture.

Indeed the majority of Welsh Labour MPs seemed content on the language question to play out the parts assigned to them in Mr Saunders Lewis's theories, that is, to act as if the Welsh language were a political threat to them. Mr George Thomas spoke of the language as of a rejected wife – with deliberate goodwill, no love, and periodic complaints about what it was costing him. But second-generation socialism, which has solved the most urgent questions of welfare, should be capable of some imagination in its treatment of the Welsh language and see that cultural rights are one kind of human rights.

All in all the George Thomas era gave one the impression of living in a boisterous and dissident satrapy which an adroit manipulator had been asked to handle.

And, of course, George Thomas *was* adroit. He was also hard-working, and there is no reason to question his own kind of sincerity. The secret nature of the decision-making process in Cardiff and Whitehall, and between the two places, makes it impossible to assess with how much energy he pursued particular Welsh interests. This, by now, is rather beside the point.

What the last years have shown is that the old idea of having a good Welshman working for you inside the governing party is breaking down; it just does not work and it encourages a kind of irresponsibility in everybody else. There are people of all parties who still think in this way. Even those who reject all the British parties can be heard pressing for the appointment of a Welsh-speaker to this or that high post, as if this gave some sort of guarantee to the language. The important thing for the language is a properly codified policy, which, if we had it, could equally well be administered by a non-Welsh-speaker. And for those who do believe in the British parties it gets harder and harder to believe that a Peter Thomas or a George Thomas or even a Lloyd George will see that Wales is all right. The argument again leads us to the concept of devolution in some degree.

But what price devolution, now, with a Conservative government that made no pledges to Wales and which rests, as usual, on a small number of Welsh votes? One hopes for the best and fears the worst, as also in the fields of commercial radio and regional policy. But the short term is rather irrelevant, as indeed is the Conservative Party in Wales, which is best seen as an index of the degree of anglicization, or non-participation in Welsh issues. In the long term it is the interaction of socialism and nationalism that will decide the future of this corner of the world, and what sort of socialism, and what sort of nationalism, are important questions for us. Devolution is a subject that can be phrased either in terms of national rights or socialist rights. It scarcely matters which.

But it is not a vogue word (though a lot of people may have used it that way) any more than De Gaulle's 'participation' has proved to be. Two years after 1968 French students are still in rebellion, and Jean-Jacques Servan Schreiber was recently and unexpectedly elected at Nancy on a programme which was basically one of considerable regional autonomy.

The fossilization of socialism is not something peculiar to Wales or to Britain, nor is the move for a breakthrough to a more participant kind of democracy a local fad taken up for a few years only to be dropped. The majority of people may have little interest in *devolution* as a concept, but they have an interest in all the questions and conflicts it can help to sort out.

Socialism has always stood for a kind of morality and not merely for a kind of power structure. During the George Thomas era the battle for moral leadership in Wales was gradually lost, and the lessons of this time need a lot of thinking over by Welshmen who call themselves socialists. After the June election Mr Leo Abse called for a change in leadership and asked the

Labour Party 'to emancipate itself from the ambiguities and smudged ideals that have blemished our record'. He was thinking of Mr Wilson and of the general record in Britain. Every word he said applies with double truth to Wales.

Why I Write in Welsh

BOBI JONES

From Planet 2, October/November 1970

I write in English like a dead language. This is probably will-power.

When I write Welsh, however, it is not by choice. There is nothing voluntary about that medium. Confronted with the muse (to adopt the usual cliché), I find that it stuffs the Welsh language down my throat.

Language is so totalitarian. How else would many of the most interesting writers in Greek, Hebrew, Latin and Sanskrit have *chosen* to write in a second language, even in a 'dead' language? I suspect that Beckett in his second language, like Conrad in his third, experienced this same compulsion of discovery and *chose* the path of least resistance.

I am not the first to notice this totalitarianism. When imperialist England submerged Wales, the first and last blow at destruction was at the language. Conquer that, and conquer all. A Welshman might henceforth feel a superficial equality in other spheres, but regarding his own country he was permanently condemned. Even inferiority in the economy would now be accepted because the language had inferior status. This was the norm for centuries, the mentality of slant towards London. The language was to be the economy, was politics, was industry, was science: when the language rolled over, they all rolled over.

The key to our dull dark cell was found a long time ago; but the door was not properly opened until about 1936. And Welshmen very slowly and hesitantly, some fearfully, even terrified, began to creep out into the open air: many still cowered in the cupboard. Others slept.

The same thing has been happening over most of the world. Those inbreeding, monoglot, parochial people next door are amazed when they visit the five continents and discover the incomprehensible people everywhere who have been excited by their roots. Why don't they grow up and speak English? Why not die 'internationalists'?

Suddenly, everywhere, we are no longer foreigners standing before our own past. We belong to our land, and are responsible, psychologically and culturally responsible for it before the whole world.

To be born into this is naturally an inspiring experience, as it involves one in the great constructive movement on this globe in this century. In scores of countries there has been a strong affirmation. It is true that there are here and there some very important areas of decadence; but culturally or socially, there has been in many places a positive bid for life. This cultural and psychological movement is something we are very conscious of in Wales, and it is paralleled with a movement towards or into the language.

This affirmation has been my main artistic interest, and its linking through and within the Welsh language in my work is a part of its character. The affirmation, naturally, has reservations: all of us who recognize original sin as an axle point in the human predicament can understand that empty optimism about the language and the universal civilization it symbolizes and enshrines would be pointless. The dangers for the language are a part of the dangers of living in the third third of the twentieth century.

But in moving away from the decadence of our culture towards a renewed vigour, one finds that the old-fashioned Anglo-Welsh masochism, for instance, peels off, and Wales is no longer just a sordid boghouse at the bottom of a coal-tip. Welsh history is no longer just depression. Gradually, the inferiority we felt about Welsh nationhood and identity no longer exists, and the language can wash over the sores. Gradually, the immense parochialism of the 'Englishman', with his negation of all that the world stands for, is replaced by a realization of the essential variety within the unity.

To a dogmatic Calvinist like me, the accidents of life never seem very convincing. In my own personal history, there may appear,

13

on the surface, to be an element of the accidental, and my first real encounter with the Welsh language was all just an unfortunate mistake, and should not properly have happened. So too, I suspect, with the whole society. No doubt those neutralist histor- ians, who discuss history as a series of undirected events, could make out a solid case for this absolutely incongruous movement towards the language as being just an understandable disturbance in the genes of the community. But I would plump for election.

We were a shy band, on a September morning in 1940, standing before a grand old gentleman from Lancashire, Mr J. O. Cheetham. It was his lot to divide us into three streams, two to take Spanish, one to take Welsh. French was – well, compulsory is not the word – a 'natural' subject, like English and the air we breathed.

There were ninety of us, and he asked those who wished to 'do' Welsh to stand forward. Some five quivering schoolboys ventured a step. The rest of us stood our ground, certain that Spanish would be intensely useful for our commercial weekend trips to South America later on. And would we not have chosen Timbuktuish, if such a language existed, rather than degrade our- selves to do that indeed-to-goodness stuff?

But the headmaster had his job to do, and needed a 'stream': at a push, twenty-five might do, but certainly not five. It was wartime, and volunteering was in the air. 'Tell me, my boy,' said he, turning on a fat blushing specimen in the middle of the front row, 'why don't you want to do Welsh?'

'I know enough, sir.'

Had I not done it in the elementary?

'Well, tell me, my boy. What's "good morning" in Welsh?'

This was one of those phrases that had somehow slipped the syllabus of the elementary. The blush reached my knees.

'Tell me, my boy. What's "good night"?'

This too had slipped attention. The blush rattled to the floor.

'Don't you think you'd better reconsider your decision?'

The vision had come.

I was converted. On that sad September day my fate was sealed, and unknown to myself I now slid into the clutches of one who must be amongst the most brilliant Welsh teachers Wales has ever employed – W. C. Elvet Thomas. Quite by accident, of course.

The rot set in.

It is impossible for me to analyse the quality of his teaching, but I have always supposed that the main secret of his gift was that he used the language as an introduction to the whole versatility and contemporary energy of Wales. Language was not just a means of communication, and certainly not a school subject. It was the expression of a complete national life and was linked to place-names, the Urdd, mountains and history, poetry and songs, dances and drama and the Eisteddfod, altars, and lots of enthralling Welsh characters and anecdotes.

My ambitions were, naturally, in Africa at the time. And so they continued into my first year in college. I had, at the bright shining age of nine, decided to be a missionary, and kept my path direct all the way to the university: I thought that I could conveniently shed my Welsh after the first college session, and raise my sights to broader horizons.

However, another collision with the parish-pump occurred during the first term. This accident was in the shape of inspiring university teachers and a new type of ethos amongst Welsh-speaking students never before encountered. Even at that advanced stage in my education, although fully able to read Welsh, and write it less fluently, I was completely socially dumb, due to the artificial examination emphasis on written answers. Now, for the first time, I came in contact with the rollicking charm of the *gwerin*. A tidy anglophile from Cardiff became immersed in the warmth and gaiety of a rural culture hitherto hidden from him, in the form of students, and in a teacher who was as intense about the Latin Element in Welsh as if it were the Day of Judgement.

And it was my day of no return, to say the least.

For an adolescent involved in such a personal upheaval, there had to be a most disconcerting reorientation.

Dreaming in Welsh, lovemaking in Welsh, poems, stories, children, friends, a nation, the whole world: the relationship between peoples, this daily consciousness of international friction and its dangerous but golden possibilities, from the inside, no longer dead or academic or up in the gallery, but here down in the arena. Writing in Welsh means now to be in the middle of the great human struggle – not to have pulled out, not to be superior or neutral or to have one's eyes on the ends of the world as if they were not here; it is to be sensitive to the tingling life of words, to the rhythmic muscles of sentences, to the quiveringness of images, to the possession of great themes. It is to turn the soil in this part of the earth as it should really be turned.

For a middle-aged man I presume there must be a settling down too, although to settle down in the Welsh language today is rather like trying to snatch a nap on the tip of a volcano. But by now, for me, there are so many more cogent reasons for writing in Welsh: quiet ones, old ones, long ones. Welsh has been for many years my first language, and practically speaking, my only language. There is so little time to read any other languages, as the Welsh materials are endless and so tremendously versatile; they are the windows of the whole world. Writing in English or any other foreign language is, for me, a discipline, necessary but almost tedious and irrelevant. I still can't help savouring the salty tang of a Welsh which will always be for me a new-old language. My ancient dynamite.

In his delightful essays, *The Dragon has Two Tongues*, Glyn Jones refers to himself as belonging to a generation or rather a series of generations that had moved away from the Welsh language, or as he says, 'From Taf Carmarthenshire to Taf Glamorganshire, in fact'. A few years previously I had brought out a little book of verse, *Rhwng Taf a Thaf* (Between Taf and Taf), referring to the same two rivers but expressing a completely contrary experience. I suppose I belong to the opposite generation, maybe generations, younger than Glyn Jones; but would agree wholeheartedly with him that a writer's 'mother' tongue, in the literal sense, is not necessarily his best medium for his creative work – but 'the language which captures his heart and imagination during the emotional and intellectual upheavals of adolescence, the language of his awakening, the language in which ideas – political, religious, aesthetic – and an understanding of personal and social relationships first dawn upon his mind'. This is the language that writes him.

During each of the last three centuries, it is worth noting that there has been at least one poet in Wales creating in his second language who must be accounted amongst the two or three greatest poets of his age, namely Iolo Morganwg, Islwyn and Waldo Williams. They have written in the language of their hearts. For me, in a much more minor way, the same has again been true. Why I write in Welsh is partly why I write at all: there is no longer any question to answer.

A Short Walk in the Desert

RAYMOND GARLICK

From Planet 4, December 1970/January 1971

Just as, in the last year or two, young Dutch men and women have conceived and begun to realize an alternative society to the Kingdom of the Netherlands, and called it the Orange Free State, so in Wales – less consciously perhaps, more pragmatically – the outlines of an alternative state have begun to emerge. Unlike Plato's these alternative republics are already being lived in by those who are creating them – rather as, in a great modern block, rooms are moved into as they are completed, while other parts of the building are still being constructed. The image of the house is particularly appropriate to the Netherlands, a country long afflicted by a housing shortage, where young people have brought about the occupation of property which had long stood empty – usually because it was too expensive for those without homes. In Wales the alternative state has sought to occupy corresponding areas of injustice within the existing order – courtrooms, rural schools, valleys threatened with flooding, a countryside threatened with alienation.

A particular concern of the new Wales, however, is the linguistic pattern towards which it is to develop. Three images are available: first, a monoglot Welsh-speaking Wales; second, a monoglot English-speaking Wales; and third, the spectrum of positions projected by the term bilingualism.

To the image of a wholly Welsh-speaking Wales one cannot but be sympathetic. The idealism of its protagonists, their restraint under gross provocation, their responsible use of non-violent techniques, the sincerity of their motives, the sacrifices freely made, the gaiety of spirit in which it is done: all this must stir admiration, however grudging. A time when, in some other societies, their generation is accused of irresponsible, anarchic and decadent behaviour, the poise and social commitment of the same generation in Wales should be a matter of national encouragement. On the other hand, a monoglot Welsh-speaking Wales is an emotive rather than a realistic position, and – though one can sympathize with the way they have been driven to take it up – it is held only by a minority of those working for the Welsh language.

The image of a monoglot English-speaking Wales is a very different matter. It is a measure of the education of public opinion that no responsible voice now wishes to be heard advocating it. Its last, noisy protagonists flourished in the columns of certain newspapers in the fifties. Their motive, far from being idealism, was clearly some personal tension. To wish for the extinction of any language, most delicate and wonderful of human achievements, can never be the expression of a civilized and balanced mind. And indeed it is natural that, in a partially bilingual society, the monoglot – in practice the English-speaker – should feel a sense of regret and disadvantage amounting at times to deprivation. That the distortion of this into an antipathy towards the Welsh language is not now publicly acceptable does not, however, mean that it no longer exists.

The image of a bilingual Wales now commands widespread support – not least, it appears, among the monoglot majority. Unfortunately the protagonists of this image have not always managed to present it in the happiest manner. Influenced too much by insular inhibitions, they have been too ready to see bilingualism as a problem – not as an advantage, not as an education in its own right. This is quite to forget that an imperial civil service, of remarkably flexible outlook, was raised in the eighteenth and nineteenth centuries upon the foundation of a school and university education which was simply bilingualism – in two dead languages, plus the mother tongue. Education consisted almost exclusively of the mastery of Latin and Greek, composition in them, and translation into and out of the vernacular. That the creation of bilingualism as a minimum, plus the achievement of a working knowledge of two other languages, is the very core of education is the assumption of many modern education systems.

In most places of post-primary education in the Netherlands – including agricultural, technical and engineering institutions – the mother tongue plus French, German and English are compulsory throughout. The notion that a mere second language might be too much for the child of average ability is a peculiarly British delusion, and a comparatively recent one.

Many countries, in short, are trying to create a bilingual situation – not without success. Some years ago I was invited to the Speech Day of a large secondary school at Leiden, to give an address – in English – on Dylan Thomas. It was perfectly clear that they understood. How many English secondary schools could invite a Frenchman, to give an address in French, as principal speaker on such an occasion? With much more than the nucleus of a living bilingual situation, Wales is at a huge advantage, and it is in this light that the bilingual image should be presented. England, for example, is likely to find itself in severe linguistic difficulties if it is admitted to the European Common Market. Compared with European education systems – that of the Netherlands, for instance – its own no longer offers that 'rapid and fluent switching between languages' (Gittins Report, page 282) to which theirs give a central position, as an intellectual, cultural and economic necessity.

A second weakness in the image of a bilingual Wales as it has so far been presented is the notion, following Gittins, that this can be an optional affair. It is not only that no responsible society can allow the basic elements of education to be matters of choice: English, Welsh, Mathematics and so forth, lie outside the kingdom of conscience. It is that for some considerable time a whole range of appointments in Wales, particularly at executive level, has required bilingual candidates, and this will increase. No doubt it is desirable that bilingualism should be welcomed, but it is irresponsible to permit parents (conditioned as we all are by a constricting history and education) to disable their children's future in their own country by blocking their entry into a bilingual society. Where there is no natural enthusiasm, the challenge is the teacher's.

Of the various other dangers which can benight bilingualism, there are two which might be watched for in Wales. The first is that, in a society in which two languages exist side by side, there appears to be a point at which – if the centripetal action of bilingualism has not been undertaken – a fiercely centrifugal action

19

supervenes. A time factor seems to be built in (as it is in other dual situations elsewhere, those of colour and religion): it is as though there is a limit beyond which this most sensitive nerve of language cannot be exacerbated by injustice, inequality, and social tensions. A poem of mine, 'Academic Overture', is concerned with what appears to have been this moment in Belgium several years ago, and the wounds which that society continues to inflict upon itself are a sombre warning to others.

The other danger, which I shall try to chart in more detail, is the relation between the two languages in the bilingual situation. The most disastrous forms of it are rivalry and indifference. Landmarks in the defusing of rivalry may be seen to be Harri Webb's letter, signed by almost all Anglo-Welsh writers, supporting the All-Welsh Rule at the National Eisteddfod; the establishment by the Academi Gymreig of an Anglo-Welsh section; the late J. E. Jones's quotation with approval, in *Baner ac Amserau Cymru*, of a foreign critic's judgement that contemporary Welsh and Anglo-Welsh poets speak with one mind; and Mr Dafydd Elis Thomas's address to the 1970 Plaid Cymru Summer School developing this theme. I am inclined to think, in spite of occasional alarums and excursions, that the general adoption of the term Anglo-Welsh – with the relaxing possibilities of execration this offers – instead of the arrogation of the epithet Welsh to writing in English, has also removed a cause of tension.

Much more serious now is the indifference between the two languages, with the honourable exception of a few representatives of each of the language communities. Both sides are guilty. In January and February of last year a television company transmitted an admirable series of seven Welsh-language programmes, each concerned with some aspect of Wales in the sixties. The texts were subsequently published as a pleasant paperback, *Y Chwedegau*. The whole design is, however, distorted by the absence of a programme on the vigorous English-language literary activity of the decade. Wales was not a monoglot Welsh-writing society during the sixties. This was a crucial period in which Anglo-Welsh writing clearly underwent a change of heart and direction and began to burgeon as an integrating force, affecting public opinion, education, politics, and correcting the image of Wales abroad. Moreover it is as desirable that Anglo-Welsh literature should be discussed through the medium of the Welsh language as it is that

Welsh literature should be discussed through the medium of the English language – a responsibility which *Poetry Wales*, itself an important flowering of the sixties, has discharged particularly well.

To be concerned, in a two-language situation, with the minority language in isolation from its fellow is to render its life more precarious. To consider the majority language as though it existed alone is to impoverish its life and to undermine the other. In general, the indifference of the English language to Wales and Welsh is massive. At root this must be a matter of education. English has always been presented in Wales not as a language of Wales, which it has been to some degree for many centuries, but as the language of England (a country which, ironically, has become less and less interested in it as an instrument of its own identity, so that in its original home it has become primarily the medium of admass).

No doubt in recent years there have been some changes in the presentation of English in Wales: the colour and vigour of Welsh accent and intonation are now accepted, and there have been slight incursions of literary material of Welsh relevance at the upper end of the secondary school. But by and large English is presented in the schools as the language of another society, with different personal and place names, a different landscape, different values, customs, criteria, preoccupations – an urban culture, with a very strong sense of class, an imperial view of the world still to be detected, a strange obsession with ceremony and dressing-up, a reverence for military achievement, and so forth. No doubt these impressions come as much through history and geography as through poems and stories, but the vehicle with which they are subconsciously identified is the English language. Its relationship to Wales is unstated, it does not present the child's world of Wales as he perceives and experiences it. The world of the English with which he is presented is different from the world of the English he uses. The tendency of school English is thus deracinating, provincializing, and so the empire of admass expands. No hint is given of the life English has for so long led as a partner of the other language of Wales: like the roads and the railways, it points away.

A vicious circle exists. Although it is to be hoped that the 'O to be in England'/'Our England is a garden' approach is now a matter of the past, since English in school is negative towards Wales the

21

material which could make it relevant is not forthcoming. There is no demand for it. One suspects that a good deal of such support as there is for Anglo-Welsh periodicals and books – the articulation of the life of the English-speaking majority – comes from the Welsh-speaking public. Few school or public libraries stock them. With a handful of distinguished exceptions, such bookshops as exist display no representative stock of the work of Anglo-Welsh writers. There is no demand. The featuring and discussion of their work by the mass media, compared with that of Welsh-language and London writers, is negligible. An interesting example was provided recently by the Welsh-language television news programme *Y Dydd*, which devoted a fair amount of its time to a newly published book of verse by Mrs Harold Wilson – to the extent of reading four or five painful extracts. A new book by R. S. Thomas or any other Anglo-Welsh poet has never received such attention. Such naïve priorities are the essence of provincialism. Even those Welsh folk groups who also sing in English have ignored Anglo-Welsh sources, and it is an American – Pete Seeger – who has discovered Idris Davies's 'Bells of Rhymney' and made a superb setting of it. The vast majority of people in Wales, having passed through the schools, sees no relevance to itself in a verbal culture in English. It leads its own vigorous, distinctive, national life in the English language, but education has stimulated no taste for the verbal icon of its experience, which might make it aware of its richness and individuality, savour it, assess it, criticize it.

So far as the schools, the bookshops and the media are concerned, then, the Anglo-Welsh writer today is a voice crying in the wilderness. What he is crying is relevance, integration, anti-provincialism. He is also crying that the English language is not merely the patois of international admass, and that in enunciating the oneness, the separateness and the identity of Wales it can become an instrument of precision and grace. Those who remember that it is in the desert that alternative societies are always proclaimed are beginning to go out and listen to him.

The Burgos Trials

JEAN-PAUL SARTRE

From Planet 9, December 1971/January 1972

If the newspapers are to be believed the Burgos trials have caused a sensation by bringing to light the grotesque ferocity of the Franco regime. But, really, did we need any fresh proof of fascist savagery? Since 1936 imprisonment, torture and execution have been commonplace throughout the Iberian Peninsula. What the trials have done is to arouse consciences inside and outside of Spain by revealing to many people for the first time the existence of the Basque nation, and established this fact as by no means unique. All big nations contain interior colonies within frontiers they themselves have drawn.

Shackled and muzzled though they were, the men of Burgos, instead of having to fight for their lives, succeeded in turning the trial into a test of decentralization. To take another European example, French children are taught that the history of France consists in the unification of all 'our' provinces, begun by the kings, carried on by the French Revolution and completed in the nineteenth century. When I was at school I was taught to be proud of this. The attainment of national unity, once it had been achieved, explained the perfection of our language and the universality of our culture. Whatever our political views, this was beyond challenge. On this point, socialists and communists were at one with conservatives. Whether reformers or revolutionaries, they all considered themselves heirs of jacobin centralism, they took the Hexagon as a unity to which they wished to bring the benefits of a new regime. Certain things were so and could not be

23

changed. The absolute monarchy had evolved along with the development of roads and means of communication, with the invention of artillery, and the mercantilist needs of the capital. The revolution and jacobinism had enabled the bourgeoisie now in power to further the unification of the economy by levelling feudal and ethnic barriers and to win foreign wars with mass armies levied without regard to ethnic origins. The nineteenth century had completed this work by industrialization and its consequences of rural depopulation, concentration and the new ideology, bourgeois nationalism. The present unity was in fact the historic achievement of the dominant class and had produced everywhere between the Belgian and Spanish frontiers the same type of abstract man defined by the same formal rights – democracy – and the same real obligations, without taking any account of his concrete necessities. Nobody questioned this. Hence the stupefaction of December 1970.

The trial was infamous and ridiculous, but could one reject the validity of the charges brought against the accused without at the same time acknowledging the validity of ETA's objections? Of course, the Spanish government is fascist and this complicated matters. Most people could protest against the Franco regime with a clear conscience. But they then had to support the accused and ETA who said, 'We are not only against Franco, we are first and foremost against "Spain".' This was a bitter pill to swallow. They could not acknowledge that a Basque nation existed on the other side of the Pyrenees without conceding the right of 'our' Basques to integration with them. And after that, what about Brittany, Alsace, Occitania? As Morvan Lebesque recently said, the history of France would have to be written backwards. Du Guesclin, hero of Centralism, would have to figure simply as a traitor to the Breton cause. The Burgos trials drew attention to a new fact, the gradual re-birth everywhere of what centralist governments call 'Separatism'. In the USSR, many republics, especially the Ukraine, are troubled by centrifugal forces. Sicily recently achieved separate status. In Yugoslavia, France, Spain, Northern Ireland, Belgium, Canada and elsewhere, social conflicts have begun to take on an ethnic dimension. Provinces declare themselves nations and more or less openly claim the status of nations. It has become clear that the present frontiers correspond to the interests of the dominant classes and not to popular aspirations, that the unity of which the great powers are so proud is a cloak for the oppression of peoples and for the overt or covert use of repressive violence.

There are two obvious reasons for the revitalization of nationalist movements. First the atomic revolution. Morvan Lebesque tells of a leading Breton nationalist who on hearing of Hiroshima cried out, 'At last the Breton problem exists'. Up till that moment, centralism was reinforced and justified by the threat of one country against another. In the age of the atomic bomb this blackmail has no force. The centralism of the cold war, the power of Washington and Moscow, holds sway over nations, not provinces. Suddenly, while some nations hasten to join one or the other bloc, other smaller nations regain consciousness of their identity and no longer feel integrated. The second reason, related to the first, is the process of decolonization which since the last war has spread over three continents.

Imagine a young man from the department of Finistère in Brittany doing his national service in North Africa in 1960. They tell him that it's to support a police action, to suppress an insane criminal agitation in some overseas departments. Then, behold, the French are routed and abandon these departments. They retreat from them and recognize Algeria as a sovereign nation. What now does it mean to the demobilized soldier that he belongs to Finistère? He has seen in Algeria that the departments are abstract divisions, serving to disguise conquest by force and colonization. Why shouldn't the same apply on this side of the Mediterranean, in 'metropolitan' France? Finistère disappears as an abstraction, a mere administrative convenience. He feels himself to be Breton, no more and no less, and French only by conquest. Is he going to resign himself to being colonized? If not, the examples of Algeria and Vietnam are there to impel him to revolt. The victories in Vietnam, above all, teach him that the colonizers have cleverly narrowed the field of possibilities for him and his brothers. They have made him a deviant. They have taught him that as a Frenchman he has the same right to vote as the inhabitant of any other province, as a Breton he cannot raise a finger, much less fight against the central power, which can annihilate him effortlessly. But in Indo-China, poor peasants threw the French into the sea and have fought successfully against the greatest military power in the capitalist world. This, too, was impossible.

The field of possibilities is suddenly enlarged for him. What if the colonizers are only paper tigers?

Atomic fission and decolonization have rekindled a new patriotism among conquered peoples. Everybody basically realizes this, but there are those in France and Spain and Canada who think that this will to independence is a mere caprice, nourished on false analogies, and that the separatist movements will disappear of their own accord. But now the example of the Basques is here to show us that this rebirth is not a casual thing but a necessity. It could not have taken place if the so-called provinces had not had a national existence which for centuries the conquerors had tried to suppress and obstruct and conceal, but had remained in being, a historic and fundamental tie between the people.

If this link, tacitly acknowledged by the central government, does not justify an inferior status for a conquered land, then that people will wage a fierce struggle for self-determination.

If we read our history without centralist prejudices, clearly the Basque people differ from all surrounding peoples and have never lost the consciousness of their singularity, defined by physical characteristics and preserved by the difference between their language, Euskerra, and all Indo-European languages. In the seventh century the Duchy of Vasconia was the home of a mountain people who defeated the army of Charlemagne at Roncevalles. By the year 1000 it had become the Kingdom of Navarre, but from the twelfth century was in decline. In 1515, Spain took possession. Despite or perhaps because of that conquest, the Basque consciousness increased. It was still largely a feudal age, Spanish centralism was weak and the vanquished retained from the Middle Ages certain rights, the *Fueros*, long to be a bastion of resistance. But people become discontented with this restricted autonomy, and did not lose hope of regaining their independence. When Napoleon was re-fashioning Europe, a deputation from Biscay proposed to him the establishment of an independent Basque state inside the Empire, but in vain. The constitution of 1812 almost abolished the *Fueros* and the nationalist movement wasted itself in a blind attempt to bring back the past. Isabel II was more liberal but still a centralizer in the French style, so that popular forces sided with Don Carlos, the absolutist Pretender, who was more old-fashioned but whose love of the past made him wish to restore the feudal autonomy of Navarre.

Both Carlist wars were lost. In 1879 the *Fueros* were abolished, and there arose a zealot traditionalism, the legacy of the sword.

Six years later Sabino Aranda formed the PNV – the Basque National Party – bourgeois and intellectual. There was now no question of fighting for absolutism and the restoration of the *Fueros*. The PNV was politically progressive, aiming at independence, but socially conservative, even antiquated – one of its slogans was 'God and the old laws'. Basque resistance so shocked the Spaniards that some of them, including the anarchist Pi-y-Margall, proposed a federalist solution for the problems of the Peninsula. Later, during the Republic, the plan was adopted and the central government recognized the principle of regional autonomy on condition that 70 per cent of the inhabitants concerned voted for it in a referendum. Upper Navarre was essentially rural and attached to Carlism. The Carlists promptly took up arms for Franco and the Navarrese voted against autonomy, though what they were really voting against was not autonomy but the Republic. The other three Basque provinces voted overwhelmingly in favour of autonomy.

The Republican government turned out to be more centralist than it had at first seemed, and needlessly held things up until 1936. Autonomy was now conceded but under pressure of events and for essentially practical and military reasons. The Basque country had to be won over for armed resistance to Franco's coup. So the Basque government was established, three socialists, two liberals and one communist. This showed that the influence of the PNV extended to the most diverse strata of society, and that it had modified its initial conservatism. Until April 1937 Basque troops ferociously defended the provinces of Guipuzcoa and Biscay. We know the rest. Franco sends up reinforcements, the reign of terror, the bombing of Guernica, 1,500 dead. August 1937 was the last month of the Republic of Euskadi.

After the war came repression, imprisonment, torture, executions. President Aguirre, leader of the PNV, fled to France. During the Second World War he played the cards of the democracies, hoping that France would follow Hitler and Mussolini into defeat. Today we can see his innocence and our shame. The PNV was played out and has been in constant decline since 1945. However in 1947, hoping to involve its allies, it fomented a general strike. The allies did not move, they stood by while Franco put it down with an implacable repression. It was the end of the road for the PNV, which retains a certain prestige as the 'historic' party which gave birth to the short-lived Basque Republic, but today has no potential for action. Its methods do not correspond to the situation, the exiles are growing old and Aguirre is dead. But none of this matters. ETA has arisen to take the place of the old bourgeois party. Let this brief résumé show that the Basques, a people only *recently* conquered by Spain, have always fiercely rejected integration. If the Basques could vote today I believe that by an overwhelming majority they would choose independence.

Can we say, with ETA, that Euskadi is a colony of Spain? The question is important, for it is in colonies that the class struggle and the national struggle merge. Under the colonial system, the colonized countries supply raw materials and food products for the industrial metropolis, and the workers are underpaid. But the Basque country, especially the provinces of Guipuzcoa and Biscay, have since the beginning of this century been fully developed industrially. In 1960 the consumption of electrical energy per inhabitant per annum was 2,008 kW in these two provinces. In Spain and Catalonia it was 658 kW. The figure for Spain alone would be lower still, but official statistics deliberately take Catalonia jointly with Spain in order to create intentional confusion. Steel production per head of the population is 860 kilos in Biscay, 450 for all Euskadi, 45 in Spain-and-Catalonia. In Guipuzcoa 9.45 per cent of the population work in the primary sector, 56.8 per cent in the secondary sector, 33.75 per cent in the tertiary sector. For Biscay the proportions are 8.6, 57.5, 33.9 per cent. By contrast, in Spain-and-Catalonia the primary sector employs 43.5 per cent of the workers, the secondary sector 27.2 per cent and the tertiary 29.3 per cent. The considerable growth of the last two sectors, plus the fact that in these provinces the rural population is consistently decreasing, shows the enormous potential of the Basque country for industrial development. From this point of view Biscay and Guipuzcoa are the pilot regions of the Iberian Peninsula. And here we come up against the paradox that, if this is a colonial situation, the colonizing country is poor and mainly agricultural while the colonized country is rich and displays the demographic profile of a highly industrialized society.

But at second glance the paradox is more apparent than real. Euskadi may be prosperous but its population is only two million, it had fewer in 1514 and in those days the population was rural. The conquest happened because of the much greater population of the other country. On the other bank of the Bidassoa the French Basque country, similar in structure to Upper Navarre (in Spain), has been systematically pillaged, ruined and depopulated by the French conquerors. Here colonialism is much more apparent. Obviously the lethargy of 'Spain' during the first thirty years of this century allowed Euskadi to ensure for itself a flourishing economy with Bilbao as the focal point. But the question is, who profits by this economy? One answer is that history offers no example of a conquered country which does not pay tribute to the conqueror. But official sources supply a better answer. These prove that 'Spain' is committed to a veritable campaign of fiscal pillage against the Basque country. The workers are crushed by taxes. In Guipuzcoa these are the highest in the peninsula.

And that is not all. In all the 'Spanish' provinces the government puts in more than it takes out in taxes, 150 per cent in Toledo, 151 per cent in Burgos, 164 per cent in Avila, etc. The two industrialized provinces of the Basque country pay to the foreign government that exploits them 4,338,400,000 pesetas. The Spanish state puts into Euskadi 774,000,000 pesetas, stealing 3,000,500,000 pesetas for the benefit of the Castilian desert. Moreover, most of the 774,000,000 pesetas go to maintain the apparatus of oppression (a Spanish or hispanicized administration, army of occupation, police, courts, etc.) or debasquization (the University where only Spanish language and culture are taught). The main problem of Basque industry is that of productivity. To achieve competitive prices in the world markets it must import modern machinery, but the Spanish state is largely autarchic and forbids this. The Madrid money market discriminates against Biscay and favours Castille. The ports of Bilbao and Pasajes need to be adapted and equipped for big ships. A considerable construction programme is essential for them, as for the fishing ports, but nothing has been done. Likewise the 'Spanish' railway system is a serious drawback. The direct road distance between Bilbao and Vitoria is 66 km., the journey by rail is 137 km. But the administration and the INI (the National Institute of Industry), the organ of the oppressor state, is manned by ignorant and stubborn bureaucrats who understand none of the country's needs, largely because they consider it to be, at least in theory, a Spanish province, and obstruct the necessary improvements, while 'Spain' makes no attempt to absorb the uncompetitive products.

Tariffs are inversely preferential, preventing the lowering of certain costs and procuring the privilege of consuming Basque products without correspondingly increased profits to the producer. The consequence is inevitable. Per capita revenue is among the highest in the Peninsula (though that is not saying much), but the income of wage-earners (85 per cent of the active population) is lower than that of those in Madrid, Burgos, Valencia, etc. It must be pointed out that the rates of wage increases between 1955 and 1967 were for Spain 6.3 per cent, for Euskadi 4.1 per cent. So despite the over-industrialization of the country, there are two essential factors in a classical example of colonialism: pillage, fiscal or other, of the colonized country and super-exploitation of the workers.

To these may be added a third, which proceeds from the first two, the rhythm of emigration and immigration. The Spanish government has taken advantage of the necessities of industrialization to direct to Euskadi unskilled labour from the more backward regions. It has offered them such inducements as housing priority. Super-exploited like the Basques, but without an evolved class consciousness, they are peons at the disposal of the bosses. Out of a population of between 1,800,000 and 2,000,000, between 300,000 and 351,000 are estimated to be immigrants. On the other hand there is Basque emigration from the poorer regions, especially Navarre. Between 150,000 and 200,000 Basques live in Madrid of whom about 100,000 are from Navarre. This considerable bloodletting together with the influx of Spanish workers into the industrial regions may be considered as a principle of colonial destruction.

This consistent fascist policy clearly involves the complicity of the large employers of Biscay and Guipuzcoa. Ever since an upper bourgeoisie began to appear in Bilbao after the Carlist Wars, they have always been liberal and centralist. The registered offices of their big companies have moved to Madrid. They can only see advantages in the curbing of modernization by Spanish incompetence and autarchy. The vast Spanish market can absorb their uncompetitive products on a global scale. The management is assured of a high percentage of profit without being obliged to invest heavily. Strangers to the true interests of the nation, these collaborationists, whose centralism spells ruin to the Basque economy, have excluded themselves from the community of the nation, and play the role of what has been called the *comprador*. In the final analysis, and within the framework of the centralist system, they find their advantages in a certain malthusianism.

The conclusion is clear. Despite appearances, the situation of the Basque wage-earner is in all aspects that of a colonialized worker. He is not merely exploited, as the Castilian worker is exploited, who wages a 'chemically pure' class struggle, but deliberately super-exploited, in that he does the same work as the Spanish worker and receives a lower wage for it. There is super-exploitation of the country by the central government with the complicity of the *compradors* who, on the basis of this super-exploitation, themselves exploit the workers. Super-exploitation does not benefit the Basque capitalists, simple exploiters overburdened by taxes and protected by a foreign army which only benefits 'Spain', that is to say a fascist society propped up by American imperialism. The working classes however are not always conscious of this super-exploitation, and many wage-earners dreamed until recently of identifying with the claims of workers of Madrid and Burgos. This would only have led them into a negative centralism. They have to be made to understand that in the case of Euskadi, the economic and social problems are expressed in national terms. When the country no longer pays fiscal tribute to the occupying power, when its true problems are formulated and dealt with in Bilbao and Pamplona, not in Madrid, then the economic structure can be freely transformed.

We repeat, 'Spain' super-exploits the Basques *because they are Basques*. Without ever officially admitting it, they are convinced that the Basques are *distinct*, ethnically and culturally. Do they believe that all memory of the Carlist Wars, the Republic of 1936 and the strikes of 1947 has been expunged? If no such memories were left, would there be such interest in destroying the Basque language? Here clearly is a colonialist technique. For a hundred years the French tried to destroy Arabic in Algeria. They did not succeed, but at least they made literary Arabic into a dead language which is no longer taught. They have done the same thing, relatively successfully, with Basque in Lower Navarre and Breton in Brittany.

Thus on both sides of the frontier there has been an attempt to make an identical people believe that their language is merely a dialect and a dying one at that. In Southern ('Spanish') Euskadi its use is virtually prohibited. No Basque-medium schools are allowed, publication in the language is being eliminated, schools and the University teach the language and culture of the oppressor. Radio, films, television and the Press explain in Spanish the problems of 'Spain'; they are all propaganda organs of the Madrid government. The administrative personnel are all Spanish or hispanicized, chosen by examination organized in Spanish by Madrid bureaucrats. For this reason, for the reason that the foreigner has willed it, one hears it said in Bilbao: 'The Basque language and culture are of no use.' And the Press often repeats an unfortunate remark of Unamuno: 'The Basque language will soon die out.'

But even this is not all. In the schools, children are punished for talking in Basque. Peasants may speak it in the villages, but would never think of doing so in big towns. One of the accused at Burgos was allowed to receive visits from his father while in prison, but permission was withdrawn when he spoke Basque, not out of provocation but because he knew no other language. The forcible suppression of the Basque language is cultural genocide. It is one of the oldest languages in Europe. True, it emerged at a time when the economy of the entire continent was rural, and if it has not adapted itself to the evolution of society, this is because the Spanish conqueror has prohibited its use. In order that it may become a twentieth-century language – and to some extent it already has – it must be spoken.

Hebrew and Breton have had the same difficulties and have solved them. An Israeli can talk about nuclear fission and read the Dead Sea Scrolls as we read Racine and Corneille. Morvan Lebesque claims that Breton has a modern vocabulary formed more regularly than that of French, the 'national' language. An ancient language which has remained young because its development has been arrested will have considerable resources. If Basque were to become the national language of Euskadi it would carry within itself all the riches of its past, a special way of thinking and feeling, and would enrich the present and the future. What the Spaniard wants is for it to disappear, and with it the Basque personality. The inhabitant of Biscay who talks Euskerra makes himself into a Basque, not only because he regains a past that belongs to him, and him alone, but because it leads him, although he may be alone, into the community of all those who speak the language.

In Burgos, the final speeches of the accused were delivered in Euskerra. They rejected the claim of the tribunal to sit in judgment on them when it did not even understand them. In doing so they summoned the entire nation into the hall of judgment. And, although unseen, in that moment it stood there with them.

The official account of the trial records at this point that the accused made unintelligible statements in a language which 'appeared to be Basque'. Marvellous! The judges understood nothing, but they knew what it was about. They could not bring themselves to admit that the Basque nation had invaded the courtroom, so they reduced Euskerra to the status of a 'probable' language, so obscure that no one knew whether the speaker was really using it or was making meaningless sounds. The language is the arrow of Basque culture and the grand preoccupation of the oppressors. If they succeed in destroying the language, the Basque will become the abstract man they want him to be. He will speak Spanish, which is not and never has been his language. But as this does not mean that he will cease to be super-exploited, once he becomes conscious of colonialism, Euskerra revives.

The converse is also true. *For him to speak his own language is a revolutionary act.* The conscious Basque of today goes still further, when he talks about the culture it gives him and that he wishes it to give him. Culture, he will say, is a creation by man for man. But he will add that there cannot be a universal culture while universal oppression remains unbroken. The official culture in Euskadi today is universalist, in that it seeks to make the Basque into a universal man, deprived of all his natural idiosyncrasies, an abstract citizen similar in every respect to the Spaniard, except that he is super-exploited and does not realize it. In this sense, the only universalism he shares is that of oppression. But however exploited men are, they do not become *things*. On the contrary, they fashion themselves into the negation of the contradictions that are imposed on them. Thus the Basque must be the negation of the Spaniard that they have tried to turn him into. Not an abstract negation but a microcosm of all they know that is special to themselves and their environment. In this sense, Basque culture today must be a counter-culture, aimed at the destruction of

Spanish culture and the rejection of the universalist humanism of the centralist powers. It is a strong and continuing effort to win back to Basque reality – the landscape, ecology, ethnic characteristics, literature in Euskerra, which is clearly visible but disguised by the oppressor as harmless folklore for foreign tourists. So they add a third formula, Basque culture is the *praxis* which will get rid of the oppression of man by man in the Basque country. And conversely this work must lead out into a political *praxis*, since Basque man cannot fully express himself until his country is sovereign.

Thus by inexorable dialectic, conquest, centralization and super-exploitation have resulted in the maintenance and strengthening of the Basque claim to independence by the very forces that Spain has used to suppress it. We can now try to determine the precise necessities of the concrete situation, that is, the nature of the Basque people's fight today. There are two different responses to Spanish oppression, both of them inadequate. We may identify them as the Basque Communist Party (PC) and the PNV.

PC regards Euskadi as merely a geographical expression. It takes its orders from the Spanish Communist Party in Madrid and takes no account of local realities. Clinging to centralism, it is socially progressive and politically conservative. It attempts to lead the Basque workers into the 'chemically pure' class struggle. They forget they are dealing with a colonized, super-exploited country.

Despite certain opportunist declarations of support for ETA during the Burgos trials, PC does not understand that the actions it proposes have inadequate objectives and hence cannot succeed. If the Basques merely struggle against exploitation as such, they abandon their own problems in order to help the Spanish workers to eliminate the Franco bourgeoisie. They would thus cease to be Basques. They would be working towards a socialist society for abstract, universalist man who is the product of centralizing capitalism. And when that man is in power in Madrid and controls the means of production, will the Basques be able to count on him to grant them autonomy? Highly unlikely: he saw what it cost the Republic, and socialist countries today are willing colonizers. Against super-exploitation and consequent debasquization, the Basques have to *fight alone*. This does not rule out *tactical* alliances with other revolutionary movements working to undermine the

Franco dictorship. But there can be no common strategy. The fight will be a solitary one. It will be against 'Spain', not the Spanish people, for a colonized nation can only put an end to super-exploitation by making itself sovereign *vis-à-vis* the colonizer.

The PNV is also mistaken. It considers independence as an end in itself. First, they say, let us set up the Basque Republic, then we can change our society any way we like. But if this means setting up a bourgeois Basque state then, although Spanish super-exploitation would be brought to an end, it would not be long before the new state fell into the clutches of American Imperialism. If the state retained the structure of capitalism the *compradors* would sell the country, the USA would rule through the local bourgeoisie, colonialism would be succeeded by neo-colonialism. Super-exploitation, although disguised, would not be lessened. Only a socialist society, because of its rigorous control of the economy, can establish economic relations with other nations, capitalist or communist, and then only at great risk, as the history of relations between Cuba and the USSR clearly shows.

The inadequacy of both PC and PNV responses demonstrates, in the case of Euskadi, that independence and socialism are two sides of the same coin. Thus the fight for socialism and the fight for independence must be the same fight. And if this is so, obviously the working class, who, as we have seen, are in the majority, must assume the leadership of the struggle. The worker, by becoming conscious of super-exploitation, and thus of his nationality, fulfils his vocation as a socialist. Can this be said to have happened? That is something we will deal with later. On the other hand the situation of the colonized country is such that many people in the middle classes reject cultural depersonalization without always realizing the social consequences which this rejection implies. They are, in principle, the allies of the proletariat. A revolutionary movement in a colony, if it is conscious of its task, will not be inspired by the concept of 'class against class' which only makes sense in a metropolitan country, but will accept the lower middle class and the intellectuals, on condition that the revolutionaries sprung from the middle class align themselves under the leadership of the working class. Thus the work to be done consists in a dual and progressive enlightenment. The proleteriat must first become aware of its colonized condition.

The other classes, more committedly nationalist, must understand that for a colonized nation, socialism is the only possible avenue to sovereignty. For these reasons, the independence party has evolved over 150 years, changing its orientation. Instead of its nostalgic striving to re-establish the ancient *Fueros* in the bosom of an absolutist state, it must aim at building a sovereign and socialist society. And it must adjust to another peculiarity of the Iberian Peninsula which gives a special character to the Basque struggle. Centralist unification, as in Italy and Germany, was not completed until the nineteenth century and thus took the form of a fascist dictatorship which reacts, and can only react, to separatist claims by violence and in no other way.

In two of these three countries, fascism is no longer in power, but Franco is still the Caudillo of Spain. That is what a Basque meant when he said to me, 'we have the horrible fate of Francoism'. Horrible it certainly is. But why fate? If Spain were a bourgeois democracy the situation would be more ambiguous. The regime would be dilatory, full of false promises and reforms. This would undoubtedly create an important sector of reformists among the Basques which would be allied to the oppressor and would be content with concessions and a federal status. Since 1937, the blind brutality of Franco has exposed the futility of reformist illusions. Every claim has always met with the same answer: bloody repression. We should not be surprised that the regime should behave in this way. But this regime is the reality of Spain the colonizer. Whatever form it takes, the government of centralist Spain will totally reject Basque claims and will in the last analysis drown every Basque revolt in blood. Spaniards, in that they are themselves the creation of centralist idealism, are abstract men, they believe that all inhabitants of the Peninsula find this logical except a handful of agitators.

Do they really believe it? Obviously not. They know that Euskadi exists, but they prefer to ignore it. They get annoyed when the Basques affirm themselves as such, and end up by hating them as Basques, that is as concrete men. The holders of power also know that the end of the colonial regime in Euskadi would bring greater misery to Castille and Andalusia. A republic would have to do the same thing as Franco. The 'fate' that the Franco regime represents for the Basques is this: it shows clearly the true nature of colonialism. It does not discuss, it oppresses or kills. Since oppressive violence is inevitable the colonials have no choice but to meet violence with violence. Temptations to reformism have no place. The Basque people must be radicalized. They know that independence can only be obtained by armed struggle. The Burgos trial was clear on this point. When they confronted the 'Spaniards' the accused knew that they risked imprisonment, torture and death. They knew it and they fought. Not in the hope of throwing out the oppressor immediately, but to contribute to the build-up of a clandestine army. If PNV is in decline it is because it had only superficially understood fascism. The Basques have no other alternative but a people's war. Independence or death, yesterday's motto in Cuba and Algeria, is today's motto in Euskadi. Armed struggle for an independent and socialist Euskadi is what the present situation demands. Either that or submission, which is unthinkable.

From 1947 to 1959 it was an empty, unanswered demand. But in reality it was at work inside the Basque people, especially the young. In 1953 it all began. A group of intellectuals founded EKIN. Barely conscious of the true reality of the Basque problem in all its tragic simplicity, they yet understood the necessity for recourse to new and radical action. They were soon obliged to merge with the PNV which, although inert, was still important. But they became distinguished for taking up 'extremist' positions, and one of them was soon expelled as a 'communist'. The group promptly left the PNV *en bloc* out of solidarity, convinced by experience that the struggle waged by the old party since 1936 had petered out in mere words. In 1959 the group became the nucleus of a new party, ETA – Euskadi Ta Askatasuna.

At first, before taking up a theoretical position, ETA reflected the two tendencies that divided the country – the nationalist claims and the workers' revolt. From 1960 it came to be understood that in daily practice the two struggles must be united, the one strengthened by the other, and carried on jointly by the same organizations. Slowly and surely the position was clarified. In the 1960s there were violent crises. The 'humanist' right resigned. The 'universalist' left was expelled after trying to abandon the anti-colonialist struggle in order to wage, with the Spanish workers, the 'chemically pure' class war. These defections define the line much more clearly than could the writings of a hundred theorists. Still, after the purges, ETA strove to define its theories until 1968.

On this level its principles are clear, they are the objective struggles with the rightists and left-centralists.

The ETA campaign is waged on four fronts: the workers, cultural, political, military. They function simultaneously and under common leadership, but remain separate. On the workers' front the struggle in 1969 was to get closer to the workers, who were often stubborn, and the organization of a vanguard nucleus inside the working class. On the cultural front, ETA attacked the weakest link, the dehumanizing universalism of the oppressor government. It has created *ikastolas*, nursery and primary schools where the education is exclusively through the medium of Basque; 15,000 children were in these schools in 1968–9. It has launched a literacy campaign among adults, created committees of students who agitate, by demonstrations, strikes and sit-ins, for the creation of a Basque university. It promotes Basque artists, writers, painters, singers and sculptors who go around the villages with exhibitions, popular songs and street performances – direct theatre. In 1966 it began organizing schools where the workers are taught Marxism-Leninism.

On the political front, which works closely with the military front, ETA politicizes the entire Basque people, teaching it the scandal of repression. This is what explains the present direction of the armed struggle. The objective is not as yet to expel the oppressor but to mobilize the Basques towards the gradual build-up of a clandestine army of liberation. Nevertheless since 1970 a new tendency has emerged in favour of the demilitarization of ETA and more emphasis on political action by Basque workers. The militants of this school believe that the commitment of ETA to the armed struggle, and the total secrecy that this must involve, runs the risk of isolating them from the working masses and so works against the ends they seek. The present tactic may be described as a spiral: action–repression–action, each action producing a brutal repression which shows the naked face of fascist centralism, opening the eyes of an ever-increasing section of the people and so facilitating the undertaking of still more important actions.

We cannot give a better example of this form of struggle than the dialectical chain of events which reached a provisional culmination in the Burgos trials. From beginning to end of the proceedings, ETA called the shots and emerged triumphant, thus demonstrating the soundness of its tactics. At first however this was not obvious. After the massacres of 1936 and the repression of 1937, the Basque country lay crushed under Franco's repressive peace. Against this, the PNV, as we have seen, organized the strike of 1947, an action without real substance which provoked the terrible repression that silenced PNV.

But out of this very débâcle the younger generation took over, and began to understand the necessity to go over to the armed struggle. ETA served notice of its existence in 1961 by its first military action. Crude bombs went off all over the place and an attempt was made to sabotage a train. This inexperienced effort brought down a brutal repression; 135 militants were detained. And so the infernal cycle, action–repression–action, was set in motion. But for a few years the 'forces of order' were made fools of. ETA could not be brought under control. Bombs went off throughout the land. Only in the spring of 1968 did the Chief of Police publish a communiqué in the Bilbao press declaring a state of hot war against ETA. The man-hunts began, but a few days later an explosion blocked the route of the 'Tour of Spain' cycle races. ('Let them take another road. They have no business here.') In June a Civil Guard was shot in the street. A few hours later, other Civil Guards on highway patrol fired at random at a suspect and killed him. He was Javier Echebarrieta, one of the leaders of ETA. Repression spread to the clandestine movement and to the general public. Masses for the memory of Echebarrieta were prohibited, alienating the village clergy and the people. Since then intensified repression has provoked a response which could arouse the people fundamentally. Three months later the notorious police torturer Manzanas, active in Euskadi for thirty years, was executed on his own front doorstep.

As had been foreseen this action provoked a vile and savage repression. It brought the people into open opposition to the authorities. The government could not accept the liquidation of its representatives, it had to find guilty men, stage a trial, demand death. But, as the 'victim' had been a hangman, most of the country could not disapprove of this execution which was a just punishment. The government thus fell into a contradiction it could not get out of. According to its point of view, which it could not change, there had to be intimidatory sanctions, but the publicity of the trial made it clear to everybody that it was a travesty of justice. The accused were selected at random from among the detainees or among those thought to be ETA leaders. Under these conditions the trial could be nothing but a farce. Izko was condemned to death although there was no evidence against him. The tribunal was a military one, although many of the 'accused' had already been condemned for the same or similar actions by a civil court. The judges were army officers, ignorant of the law, except for one who had enough juridical knowledge to advise the soldiers. The lawyers were constantly threatened with imprisonment by the president of the tribunal, and had difficulty in expressing themselves.

The accused, chained together, were calm and haughty. They fought continually, not to defend themselves against the accusations of their oppressors, but to proclaim, in the hearing of the press, the tortures to which they had been subjected, to which the president, seeing that he could not silence them, replied, inevitably, 'Irrelevant'. It was clear to the reporters that these soldiers had been mustered not to judge but to kill. They went conscientiously through an absurd ceremony with which they were unfamiliar. 'The accused' laid bare the oppressive violence of 'Spain'. They forbade the lawyers to defend them. They won. Their admirable courage and the obtuse idiocy of the judges made the trial the concern of all Basques. When the workers of the big concerns in Bilbao went on strike ETA knew that it had involved large sections of the working class.

Besides, indignation was so widespread throughout the world that for the first time the Basque question stood before international opinion. Euskadi became known everywhere as a martyred nation, fighting for its independence. The reaction of general anger recoiled on the government. The death penalties were commuted. ETA by this unasked-for but necessary victory for its tactics was publicly confirmed as the spearhead of the working class. The entire nation was mobilized and ETA acquired considerable prestige, as PNV had done twenty-five years previously. The militants know that there is a long struggle ahead, that it could take twenty or thirty years to build up a people's army. No matter. In Burgos, between December 1970 and January 1971, the challenge had been thrown down.

So here we are, we French, who willy-nilly, are always somewhat the heirs of Jacobinism! A heroic people, led by a revolutionary party, has given us a glimpse of the 'other' social-ism, decentralist and concrete, the singular universality that ETA rightly sets up in opposition to the abstract centralism of its oppressors. Is this socialism viable for all? Isn't it only a provi-sional solution for colonized countries? In other terms, can we foresee that this is the end of a stage towards the time when uni-versal exploitations will come to an end and all men will enjoy equally a true universalism by the common operation of all partic-ularisms? This is a problem for the colonialists. We can be sure that the colonials, fighting for independence, have no problem.

What is certain in the eyes of the Basque militants is that the right of people to self-determination, affirmed in the most radical necessity, implies everywhere the revision of all present frontiers, which are the residue of bourgeois expansion, corresponding nowhere to the needs of peoples. And this can only be achieved by a cultural revolution, which will create a socialist man, on the foundations of his land, his language and his renovated customs. It is from this point alone that man will gradually cease to be the product of his product and will at the last become the son of man. Can we concur in these Marxist conceptions? We may note at this point some doubts among the ETA leaders. Some call themselves neo-Marxists, and others, apparently the majority, 'Marxist-Leninists'. The day-to-day realities of the struggle will decide. As Ché Guevara once said to me, 'Are we Marxists? I don't know', adding with a smile, 'it's not our fault if reality is Marxist'. What ETA has shown us is the need of all men to affirm (including the centralists) their particularisms against abstract universalism. For us to listen to the Basques, the Bretons and the Occitans, to fight at their side so that they may affirm their concrete singularity, is, as a direct consequence, to fight for ourselves as French people, for the true independence of France, which is the first victim of its own centralism. For there exists a Basque people and a Breton people, but Jacobinism and industrialization have liquidated our people, today there are only French masses.

Translated from the French by Harri Webb.

Ceri Richards – Root and Branch

JOHN ORMOND

From Planet 10, February/March 1972

Many of Ceri Richards's paintings have to do with roots, beginnings, the surge of life. Many are concerned with music and
musical situations. Some start in myth. His temperament and
style Richards regarded as part of a Celtic, and incidentally Welsh,
heritage. His death on November 9, 1971 (eighteen years to the
day after the death of Dylan Thomas) robbed European art of a
major lyrical painter and the world of a draughtsman whose
talent, especially in dealing with the human form, approached
that of Rembrandt. At best the various themes he took are unified
by unmistakable characteristics of a taut, rhythmic line, of proliferating images that seed and re-seed from each other, sensual,
flowing, exuberant and singing in their colours. Yet, for all this
flux, they are sometimes touched by a living stillness that has
been reached by a paring away of the decorative, so that what is
left is a deep bone, a tension of statement, a transfixed energy
central to Richards's genius. He said: 'Working through from
direct visual facts to a more sensory counterpart of the reality of
my subject, I hope that as I work I can create later on an intense
metaphorical image for my subject.' In this respect, and in others,
his approach was poetic.

Ceri Giraldus Richards was born in Dunvant, near Swansea, on 6
June, 1903, the eldest of the three children of Thomas Coslett
Richards and his wife Sarah. Tom Richards's family had come to the
village from Betws, near Ammanford, and Sarah Jones's from
Dryslwyn, Llandeilo, though originally from Henllan, Cardiganshire.

When Ceri left Gowerton Intermediate School he began work as an electrical apprentice. He had loved drawing from the time he was old enough to hold a pencil; as a boy, had felt disappointed that his father could not describe in drawings his work as a roller-man in the tinplate works in the next village of Gowerton. But the lad had no idea that there was such a thing as a professional artist or that there was an art school in Swansea. Nor did his family. If the firm in which he began work had not ceased to function (it seems that a strike caused the trouble), Ceri Richards would not have enrolled, with the encouragement of local people who knew more about it, after ten months at his trade, at Swansea School of Art.

The Richardses were, and are, a gifted family, much given to music and verbally graphic statement. Tom Richards was a tall, kind, unhurried, big-framed man who could quote Welsh poetry, especially that of Dewi Emrys, by the hour. He conducted three choirs in Dunvant and produced local plays as well as acting in them. As a boy Ceri helped one Alf Phillips – a small man who looked exactly like Toulouse-Lautrec, bowler-hat and all – paint scenery for the productions. But music was the big thing in the Richards household. There was a time when Tom Richards was tutor to anybody in the area who sang. Before eisteddfodau (so the artist said) the three children would sometimes have to have their tea in one of the bedrooms of 'Preswylfa' because of the throng of would-be competitors in the class-room kitchen. Ceri, Owen and Esther Richards all learned the piano. Ceri used to remark, 'If I find myself in a house without a piano I feel a bit miserable.'

One of my vivid recollections of Tom Richards is of his occupying a corner in the Big Seat in Ebenezer. The preacher would open the Welsh Bible to his text:

'Yn y dechreuad yr oedd y Gair.'

Oh, Tom Richards would say, clearly very surprised.

Then, with a clatter of bindings falling off and a whispering of rice-paper, for there were two bibles in the pulpit and both were used:

'In the beginning was the Word.'

I *see*, Tom Richards would add, as though the whole meaning of everything that ever was now struck him, the actual syllables of Gospel, for that matter, never before that second having been uttered. He would draw his left hand (half his thumb, half his index-finger and the top joint of his middle finger missing from an accident in the works) slowly across his brow, clearing his mind for the next revelation. He lived at that moment, like many another there, in a bliss of biblical understanding. He grew, with the years, towards a wide charity of outlook beyond the narrow, literal, Nonconformist attitude.

Going off with a box of oil paints subscribed for by the chapel, in 1924 Ceri Richards left Swansea for the Royal College of Art where Randolph Schwabe introduced him to the work of Picasso. The previous year, attending a summer school at Gregynog Hall, he had seen the Gwendoline and Margaret Davies Collection that had been assembled by Hugh Blaker. Richards had been espe-cially affected by the Monets and Daumiers. Now, in London, with Schwabe revealing to him even more startling things, he also read Kandinsky's *Concerning the Spiritual in Art*, written in 1912. Kandinsky wrote, 'Colours are a keyboard, the artist the hand that plays on them . . . A painter who finds no satisfaction in represen-tation, but who wants to express his internal life, and who envies the ease with which it can be done by music, applies the means of music to his own art. And from this results the modern desire for rhythm in painting, for mathematic abstract construction, for repeated notes of colour, for setting colour in motion.' Richards told me that this passage had had a great influence on him.

There was never any doubt about Richards's earnestness about music. At a Christmas dance at the Royal College of Art in 1928 he got into conversation for the first time with Frances Clayton, from Burslem, Stoke-on-Trent. For two years before winning a major scholarship to the college she had earned her living as a designer in a famous china works. As fellow-students she and Ceri had admired each other's work. Now he asked her out – to a concert. Schoenberg conducted his *Gurrelieder*; Delius, wrapped in his rug, was in the audience; Arnold Bennett sat next to the young couple who were married the following year.

Frances Richards has always been a fine artist in her own right. Her importance to her husband was that for forty years she supported his vision with her enthusiasm, belief, judgement and imagination; for Richards was never a fashionable artist in the sense that, say, John Piper, Graham Sutherland and Francis Bacon have been painters whose work has been bought by many as investments on the international art market. In the early days

Richards had to work as a church organist, and for many years he and his wife had to teach in art schools, Frances bringing up their children as well. It was only from about 1960 on that Richards received anything like his fair share of acclaim. He held himself aloof from art cliques and maintained it was not an artist's job to act as his own public relations man.

In the 1930s his experiments with wood and metal constructions, though limited in number, were a quarter of a century before their time. And by the time British art ran towards abstractionism Richards, long since, had gone back to his own kind of figurative painting – this, too, twenty-five years before the swing that has fairly recently begun. With due acknowledgement to what he learned from Picasso, Matisse and Max Ernst, of the modern masters, Richards committed himself in his own style to his subjects.

He defined a subject as a theme that would work back at him and haunt him. Drawing was always the first stage in his creative process. He would make 'masses of the speediest notes to catch at all sorts of evocations. This foraging is stimulating,' he said, 'because the speed of the drawing spills out a spate of unpredictable images.' These were virtually calligraphic accounts of various reactions to a subject. The problems encountered and thrown up in the drawings brought together and suggested graphic tensions. Transposed and reappraised on a canvas, these presented questions not of scaling-up but of a change of approach in a different medium, and this involved a re-working of design and proportion from what Richards called 'hints' in the drawings. It was at this stage that the creation of a painted metaphor for reality began.

In the early 1930s the figures of London costers, the pearl-button kings and queens, attracted Richards. He said the extravagance of their costumes, especially that of the women, 'became a sort of flower symbol, something like a marvellous bouquet'. In the mid-1940s, out of a commission to do a treatment of Dylan Thomas's 'The force that through the green fuse' for Tambimuttu's *Poetry London*, there grew a grand series of paintings and lithographs that revealed Richards's kinship with the poet; though contrary to many accounts they were not close friends and met on only one brief occasion. Out of this 'Force that through the green fuse' series there was to grow the 'Cycle of

Nature' works in which there is a great sensuality, even sexuality. Congestions and profusions of shapes entwine in a contorted order on the canvases. Parts of the human form protrude from a convoluted, vegetable scheme of things. Stems, stalks, foliage, flowers coil about seed-pods that seem to germinate galaxies. Much later another, not so extended, series of works stemmed from a starting-point in 'Music of Colours – White Blossom' by Vernon Watkins. Watkins and Richards enjoyed a long and close friendship, especially after Richards took a holiday house on Pennard Cliffs in Gower near Watkins's home.

Of other subjects that Richards took up during the years of the 1939–45 war I remember three distinct themes. One was tentatively dealt with and I cannot recall the material being publicly shown. Nevertheless Richards was attempting to come to terms with the time. There were drawings in which scenes of bombing were organized into strange patterns. Falling walls were wilting stems to explosive flowers blossoming in the skies. The second theme was 'Rocks', slabs of stone where human figures were half-hidden, half-emergent. And the third, and to me by far the most important material of the period apart from the work that began in the Dylan Thomas poem, was the subject of tinplate workers. For a short period Richards worked as an official war artist and he chose to go back to the mill in Gowerton where his father had spent nearly all his working life. Mistakenly, no example of these 'Worker' drawings was included in the Ceri Richards Retrospective Exhibition in the Whitechapel Gallery in 1960. The artist regarded the drawings as too documentary. But they go beyond the documentation of an archaic and back-breaking industrial method. For all the grace in the figures of roller-men, furnace-men and doublers there is revealed a concern for people, an expression of what it was like to be a human being caught in the jaws of a machine.

After the war, off and on for a decade or more, Richards had a great outpouring of pictures that had to do with music, music-rooms and pianists. This period covers a major part of his output, a huge wave of creation in which he explores all the possibilities of the particular music theme with an unflagging energy and excitement. The exploration goes on into homages to Beethoven and Saint Cecilia and into what the artist called the 'Hammerklavier' suite. They are all related.

In the late 1940s, for a few years, it was the theme of 'The Rape of the Sabines' that preoccupied Richards's imagination. He had always had a great admiration for Rubens. For this 'Sabine' series he made hundreds of drawings, more than for any other series of paintings. They deal with the human figure with a rhythmic brilliance of invention; and the resultant large paintings are celebrations of energy and movement. There is the same celebratory strength in the 'Trafalgar Square' series that started from a painting made for the 1951 Festival of Britain. In this series Richards lets loose his sense of graphic wit in a firework display of complicated and formally streaming design. The Trafalgar Square fountains soar and spread out like great flingings-upward of glittering coins that keep a constant canopy, fragmented by sunlight, over lions and wheeling pigeons and fussing photographers. Yet the colours in this most English of scenes are in the French and not the English tradition. The same vibrant palette is seen in most of Richards's work.

Many of Richards's admirers think that he discovered his most successful theme when, in the late 1950s, he came to the legend of the submerged cathedral said to lie off the coast at Ys in Brittany. The legend had inspired Debussy's piano work *La Cathédrale engloutie*; and Richards, who all his life went on playing the piano for pleasure and for the inspiration which music gave him, brought together on large and small square canvases the notions of the legend, his response to the Debussy music and his feeling for coastal seascape and weather that had been rekindled in Gower. The rose window of the cathedral drowned under great depths of water is often the focal point of the paintings. Above the window the long arms and fingers of currents stretch out in the tides as they move over the lost buildings. Under the surface of the sea the stones and arches of submarine architecture are eroded by the relentless working of water.

Early on in the series Richards reverted to his experiments of the thirties making wood and metal constructions, and collages, putting in brass bells to suggest the cathedral bells being tolled by the movement of currents; arranging them with miniature keyboards and rosaries, putting in even the shells of small crabs found in Gower pools. The results are diverting, but I believe the works to be more fabricated than felt. The grand effects lie in the painted works, especially where Richards brings in the shape of

47

the round sections of pillars he imagines lying like millstones on the sea-bed – here singly, there grouped in a formal disarray. The works are all part of a rich maturity, all part of the artist's metaphor for ebb and flow, for fixity and transience. He could not discuss his work for long without using that word metaphor.

He talked in little bursts, with a soft voice, his words darting, minute tacits between phrases, never at a loss for a word but naturally quiet and, in company, slightly hesitant in manner. Important matters he seemed sure about without being righteous or ponderous. But smaller things he seemed to note with that old surprise that in him would widen into a smile. He was a compassionate man. Perhaps the least generally known of his big works are the few directly religious paintings that came after a period when he had been in hospital in the 1950s. What he saw then of the human condition opened the way to a number of paintings that culminated in the *Deposition* which hangs in Saint Mary's, Swansea. In this the rejoicing colours are gone. The body of Christ, brought down from the Cross, is at once a particular and universal statement of the vulnerability of the human body. Looking at the distortions and the distended limbs, one's first feeling is of shock but this is overtaken by a spreading sense of pathos. I have the same reaction to the small tender drawing Richards made of his dead father. Grief is transmuted and transcended by art. Yet the grief remains. This is what we shall all come to. The roots of Richards's sensibilities go back through the centuries. The drawing has its ancestors in the drawings that Rembrandt made of his wife Saskia as she was dying in 1642.

Richards's depth of feeling is also seen in the many loving drawings he made of his children and grandchildren; and one hopes that his family can be persuaded to allow these to be shown in the major exhibition of his work that ought now to be mounted in the National Museum of Wales. The Tate Gallery – of which he had been a Trustee – honoured Richards's memory and achievement at his death by devoting a wall to those works of his that are in the National Collection and in the spring there is to be an exhibition of his work in the Municipal Gallery of Milan. Some paintings like the inspired altar-piece *Supper at Emmaus* – with its richnesses of blues and yellows – which Richards painted for Saint Edmund Hall, Oxford, will be unlikely to be available. But at a time when the National Museum of Wales houses such big special exhibitions one hopes that it will take the responsibility of mounting a show that will adequately reflect, on many walls, the themes that Ceri Richards developed out of obsession. Works from his last one-man exhibition in October 1970 have never been seen in Wales.

I never once heard Ceri Richards express pride in his own work. He was never jealous for fame. He had sureness, complete naturalness and a complex nervous energy. As I write that I recall his telling me, a year before he died, not out of bitterness or injury but with the tone of a man underlining one of the facts of life: 'Always remember this,' he said, 'critics are to artists as ornithologists are to birds.'

Fields of Praise

GARETH WILLIAMS

From Planet 14, October/November 1972

During a Wales v. England international at St Helens sometime in the twenties a Welsh player was to be seen at one stage kicking a prostrate Englishman. The English captain, Wavell Wakefield, ran over to break it up, at which the Welshman apologized profusely, saying that he thought it was Wakefield he was kicking.

It is a well-known anecdote, but it matures with age. Whether or not the incident ever took place is basically irrelevant. What is relevant is the enjoyment of the telling, the fact that Welsh rugby created the story about itself, from itself. Rugby football is obviously bound up with Welsh society, particularly with the urban industrial community of the south. It is a subculture, inextricably involved with and prismatically reflecting the modes and rhythms of thought and expression of an entire society, an essential part of that elusive community culture which Richard Hoggart and Raymond Williams have been telling us about for years.

There seems to be an accepted phenomenon called Welsh rugby, though there is recognizably no such thing as Welsh soccer or Welsh cricket. There is soccer in Wales and cricket in Wales, and bowls and baseball: but only Welsh rugby. It is odd that this should be so on several counts. For one thing, club soccer in Wales attracts more people than club rugby. For another, so little has been written, *really* written, about it. Nobody has done for Welsh rugby what Norman Mailer or Budd Schulberg have done for boxing, or Hemingway for bull-fighting, or even David Storey for rugby league. One wishes that someone might do for the Wales v. New Zealand match what Mailer did for the Paterson–Liston fight. Presumably presidential papers are alien to the Welsh literary tradition (the absence of a president is not really an excuse). In Welsh there is Cynan's crowned *pryddest* of 1931, 'Y Dyrfa' ('The Crowd'), which among other things describes an England v. Wales match at HQ; there are also a couple of Islwyn Williams short stories. In English there is less, a quantity of reportage and historical journalism, but no literature to capture the passions, the pathos, the earthiness, gutsiness, chauvinism, parochialism, emotions and aspirations of Welsh rugby. Regrettably there is no Tom Buchanan, who, admirers of Scott Fitzgerald will recall, 'among various physical accomplishments, had been one of the most powerful ends that ever played football at New Haven – a national figure in a way, one of those men who reached such an acute limited excellence at twenty-one that everything afterwards savours of anti-climax . . . Tom would drift on forever seeking, a little wistfully, for the dramatic turbulence of some irrecoverable football game.'

We speak of Welsh rugby, but historically there is nothing particularly Welsh about rugby football. Like most of the opiates which have dulled and diverted Welsh minds away from the realities of life, rugby, like Methodism and marijuana, trickled into Wales from England, via the border country and the eastern valleys of Monmouthshire. Among the first clubs to be formed in Wales were those of Blaenau Gwent and Chepstow. The advance camps of the game in Wales were Monmouth School and Christ's College, Brecon: élitist institutions like Cowbridge, Llandovery and Lampeter Colleges sustained the impetus of the initial drive. For a game that is supposed to be so peculiarly Welsh, we have contributed little to its evolution. That first fine disregard for the rules of football was displayed at Rugby School in 1823; the first club match ever played was between Richmond and Blackheath in the 1860s; the first international between Scotland and England in 1871; fifteen-a-side was an Oxbridge innovation; Adrian Stoop was the first fly-half (or more appropriately stand-off), just as it was Wakefield who pioneered specialist forward play in the 1920s; ten-man rugby was introduced by the 1931 Springboks; forward mobility and back row inventiveness by South African and French teams of the 1950s and the early 1960s. If Wales deserves a mention in this roll-call of technical innovation, all she can claim is the introduction of the differential penalty in 1889; or, perhaps, the specialist hooking of George Travers between 1903 and 1911 (which was crucial to the 'Golden Era' of those years). The fact remains, when the time comes for us to pass through the customs-bay of rugby's hereafter we will have nothing to declare but our genius.

But such genius. Surely that requires no itemizing. One has only to look at those early photos of Dicky Owen and Trew, or recent ones of Clive and Gareth to see faces hypnotized by rugby, the trance-like state of men for whom rugby is the textbook romantic experience – Byronic, Keatsian, Schubertian; men for whom each creative act on the rugby field has meant giving a piece of themselves. Giants of Welsh rugby testify to the romantic syndrome: Cliff Jones had burnt himself out by the time he retired at 24; Owen, Trew, Albert Jenkins, Cliff Davies did not live long after retiring from the game.

Because it is so intensely bound up with Welsh society at the present time, Welsh rugby mirrors a great deal of it. He would be a fool who would deny that, with its new-found optimism, confidence, aggression and self-discipline, Welsh rugby does not reflect much of what has been happening in various fields of activity in Wales during the last six years or so. The forces and currents which have been coursing through the arteries of Welsh rugby recently are also those that have reddened the corpuscles of Welsh life in other directions: they have been part and parcel of a revitalizing of Welsh society on a broad front. Rugby plays an important role in that process, and in the national psyche. On four occasions during the year rugby internationals are stimulants, providing a fix of 'Welshness' to many thousands of people, in Glamorgan and Monmouthshire in particular, for whom Welshness is a sort of underground movement minus the revolution. These occasions make them high on Wales; to many they inaugurate a process of rediscovery, and one suspects that the re-born Lord Chalfont is only the titled sunlit tip of a pretty sizeable iceberg. Equally, internationals bring north and south together: both claim stakes in recent triumphs. The accents of Llŷn and Llanarmon-yn-iâl blow defiantly through Westgate Street these days, just as northern-based papers like *Y Faner* are full of fulsome tributes in verse and prose to Barry and Carwyn and Gareth (particularly deserving of such tributes, of course, as they are Welsh-speaking). At times this sounds false, ingratiating, or simply inappropriate, but as a phenomenon it is significant and to be welcomed, especially when many south Walians, encouraged by some politicians, are too ready to see themselves as a sort of Ulster Defence Association.

The Welshness of the 'atmosphere' generated by international rugby is nevertheless phoney, a fabrication, a shadow without the substance; it is a showpiece of maudlin sentimentality, allowing the music-hall Taff a free run – witty, thirsty, emotional, gregarious, randy. There is much truth in the purists' condemnation of saccharine one-day Welshness, except that many Welshmen are quite content with precisely this sort of glucosity. *Hen Wlad fy Nhadau* (My hen laid a haddock; half the crowd have no idea of the words), *Cwm Rhondda* (which one's that?), *Sospan Fach, Rachie* (which?) or *Calon Lân*, and that's your lot. Otherwise it's likely to be 'You'll never walk alone' from Ninian Park.

It is not without its significance that in J. B. G. Thomas's latest book, the only Welsh words to appear in it are *hiraeth* and *hwyl*, both misspelt. No man has written more about the Game than Bryn Thomas. He is no Neville Cardus, but perhaps that is just as well. Nobody wants to see John Dawes compared to Bruno Walter. But whatever Mr Thomas lacks in style (and he lacks plenty) he makes up for by his infectious enthusiasm, labour, and love for 'the Game'. This is his twenty-first book on the Game, and it must be said that there is little in it that has not been said before, mostly by Mr Thomas himself. His best books remain his earlier ones, *Great Rugby Players, Great Rugby Matches*, and *On Tour*. In books such as these Mr Thomas has done enough to deserve an honorary degree from the University of Wales: he has put the rugby present in the context of the rugby past by reconstructing the past, resurrecting it Lazarus-like from the tomb of newspaper files, yellowing documents and contemporary witness. He has confirmed in print what our fathers and grandfathers told us, about Kershaw and Davies and Corbett of England, of Bannerman and Wilson Shaw of Scotland, Clinch and Sugden of Ireland, of Nepia and Olser and Pamathios. But most important of all, Mr Thomas has told us, and tells us here again, about Gould and Gwyn Nicholls and Percy Bush, of Bassett and Powell and Watcyn Thomas, of Wooller, Tanner and Claude Davey, of Cleaver, Gwilliam, Lewis Jones and Roy John. And of Bleddyn. Mr

Thomas knows more about the epic match of 1905 than any of those who played in it ever did – or was it 1935, or 1951?

In recounting great moments, in quickening our pulse-rates with accounts of legendary tries, Mr Thomas has told us a lot about himself. He is a former navy man, and very British. He has a great fondness for royalty and royal occasions. His view of Wales is the standard Cardiff one (Aberavon is a west Wales club). There was a time when his ideal Welsh XV consisted entirely of players drawn from Cardiff and Newport, for which he was roundly booed when he entered the press-box at Stradey or the Gnoll. But generally he is in the run of progressive thinking on most aspects of the Game – sponsorship, coaching, league competition etc. Also, through his sports editorship of the *Western Mail*, he is fighting a lone battle against the soulless soccer-crazed media, to keep the faith with the past he has done so much to restore. Mr Thomas may have a view of Welshness that is rather superficial, but at least it is less pernicious than the mindless cosmopolitanism of the *Sun*, the *Mirror*, the *Mail* and the television companies, who are indoctrinating a whole generation with the crass trivia of the Texaco cup, Rodney Marsh's shirts and Don Revie's ingrowing toenails. Anything is grist to the soccer mill, from 'Foul of the Month' to the all-encompassing insidiousness of mass advertising. Faced with this brutalizing assault on our sensibility, the survival of rugby is a modern miracle, like the survival of the Welsh language.

However, twenty-one books later, one is reminded of another Thomas, one Dylan, who once read a book about an insect. Dylan said that the book told him everything he could possibly want to know about this insect except – why? Despite the immense work of J. B. G. Thomas, who is after all no sociologist or historian, we still need to know the why of Welsh rugby. Most games are the product of social forces, and it is unlikely that rugby is an exception. What made a game imported from England and spread by students and public schoolboys home for the hols so particularly appealing to the pent-up passions, frustrations and neuroses of the Welsh? Mr Thomas gives ritual acknowledgement to 'the steel and coal towns up and down the scarred valleys, where there was blood and sweat in industry . . . (and) hard men who made champion boxers and fine rugby forwards'. One feels that here is an Alexander Cordell struggling to get out; but obviously the development of rugby does have a lot to do with the industrial expansion of south Wales in the second half of the nineteenth century, and its accompanying population explosion. The traditional games of the old agrarian society, like *cnapan*, that swept the length of the village, often several villages, and which lasted indefinitely were now impossible. Both space and time were in short supply. Rugby and soccer established themselves because they were a form of recreation practicable within a restricted area, and a society that was governed by clock and whistle imported the same dominating influences into its entertainment.

What, one wonders, was the precise relationship between rugby and chapel? Rugby players used pubs as their changing rooms, a deliberate affront to late Victorian Nonconformist morality. Pre-1914 Welsh sides are characterized by a high percentage of publicans, just as policemen dominated the inter-war, and school-teachers the post-1950, sides. Physique was also an important factor. Welshmen tend to be smaller, and were particularly likely to be so before 1914. To avoid being trampled into the ground by the bigger-boned English and Scots, the one way to beat them was to dodge them. The Welsh genius has expressed itself in half-back and three-quarter play for this reason.

We have all passed a lot of water since then, though that genius has once again imposed itself on the Game these last few years. Whereas in the late fifties and most of the sixties an edgy pessimism prevailed, and a 6–3 victory was hailed as it if were 44–0, the mood at the Arms Park nowadays is aggressively optimistic and expectant. But the euphoria, though certainly not misplaced, deludes. There are more important issues at stake in Wales today than whether or not we beat the All-Blacks, and of the various passions they arouse, euphoria is not one of them. It would be a pity if our most constructive energies were dissipated on fifteen men in scarlet. A society that regards success on the sports field as the highest manifestation of being is an unhealthy one: Latin America, South Africa, the U.S., Australia. Wales too would be a healthier place if its rugby men opened their eyes to the wider reality that lies beyond the dead-ball line. There is something rotten in the state of the Union when a man of the integrity and intelligence of Carwyn James, his unimpeachable rugby credentials apart, fails to get elected to one of the five vice-presidential positions in the W.R.U. hierarchy. It looks like a witch-hunt.

55

For this reason alone it is quite ridiculous for the W.R.U., and people like Mr Thomas, to pretend that politics and rugby can be kept apart. Quite ridiculous, when there are concrete examples to show that South Africa *has* relaxed some of its more rigorous apartheid laws under threat of a sports boycott; when Dawie de Villiers stands for Mr Vorter's nationalist party in a by-election, when Clem Thomas is nominated a prospective Liberal candidate for Carmarthenshire, when Carwyn James and David Harries have stood for Plaid Cymru, when Wilfred Wooller has been invited to stand for the Conservatives; when a mere game of table-tennis can bring about the most astounding volte-face in modern diplomacy since the Russo-German pact of 1939. It therefore seems a pity that a great club like Llanelli, with the blessing of the W.R.U., should insist on touring a country where 3 million white supremacists hold 17 million Africans in the most obscene political, economic and educational stranglehold since the Third Reich. It seems silly to pretend that by maintaining contact and exchanging visits we will be better able to influence them. British teams have been visiting South Africa since 1891 but conditions there, for the vast non-white majority, have got steadily worse, not better. There are more important things than even rugby football; though the devil often has the best tunes. Two of the astutest critics of the Game today are Wilfred Wooller and John Reason, though their political stance is somewhere to the right of the Pharaohs. And the fact remains that South Africa has produced the greatest side ever to tour these islands – the 1951 Springboks, just as it has produced the greatest back-row forwards of modern times – Van Wyck, Fry, Muller, Hopwood, Greyling, Bedford and Ellis, and staged the greatest test match of all time (according to Mr Thomas) – the first test against the 1955 Lions. We cannot deny these things, but neither can we deny that since 1948 South Africa has been ruled by a gang of former Nazis who think God speaks Afrikaans. There was a time when jackboot politics would arouse the intense loathing of Welshmen. In the 1930s men from Llanelli went voluntarily to fight fascist tyranny in Spain. In the 1970s their sons go voluntarily to South Africa to condone it.

It is not good enough to say 'Of course we are against racial discrimination, but . . .', just as it is not good enough to say 'Of course we are for preserving the Welsh language but . . .' But me no buts, butty. Morality does not deal in shades of grey: it is yes, or no.

Perhaps Welsh rugby's view of the world would be more in focus if its vision were illuminated by a clearer recognition of its own individuality, its Welshness. Equality, like charity, begins at home. Where stands the W.R.U. on recognition of that language which is spoken by many thousands of its followers? There are many to whom Wales is also *Cymru*, and to whom it is more than just *Dynion* on the convenience in the new North Stand. This is bog Welsh. In *Death in the Afternoon*, Papa tells us of the bullfighter Chaves, and the official recognition he was given by his home town. They named a public building in his honour: *El Urinario Chaves*.

But the Game goes on (one of Mr Thomas's favourite phrases)! Rugby has had a new lease of life, not only because the W.R.U. has initiated a number of forward-looking policies in the schools and on the administrative side in recent years, but also because the Lions' tour gave the Game unprecedented publicity. It has reached a new and wider audience. It has its own superstar. But at what cost? So far, Welsh rugby, despite a massive popular following at international level at least, has been free of the thug element that is increasingly prevalent in soccer. Urban violence takes on different forms in different places. In these islands, a generation that has not been instructed in organized violence has become preoccupied with it. It finds its kicks in wrecking excursion trains and terrifying the high street. In England and Scotland, soccer provides it with the opportunity. For how much longer will Welsh rugby be resistant to the infection of hooliganism? Cardiff is increasingly a rough place on international day: bands of hards, tarts and skinheads roam through St Mary's Street like panzer divisions, making curious stiff-arm gestures that derive from either Harvey Smith or Il Duce, and chanting 'We are the Champions'.

And we are, of course. The magical genius of the men in scarlet sees to that. But one hopes that the rugby revolution will not deprive Welsh rugby of its individuality. Not the cloying Welshness of *hiraeth* and *hwyl* and 'We'll keep a welcome' – it is truly an odd sort of Welshness that welcomes the French with three anthems, but the Irish with two – but hopefully a more vital and resilient Welshness that shows that it is aware of things, in Wales and in the world.

Carl Meyer in Wales

MARY ELLIS

From Planet 14, October/November 1972

Reading the list of guests at the Abergavenny Eisteddfod of 1845 is like reading a page of Jennifer's Diary in the *Tatler*; counts, ambassadors, army officers, distinguished and colourful foreigners and double-barrelled names abound. Miss Maxwell Fraser, in her vivid account, published in the *National Library of Wales Journal*, Vol. 14, states that the Eisteddfod was held under the royal patronage of the Prince of Wales, and on the opening day there were four hundred carriages in the long procession.

The explanation for the presence of so many members of the upper class lies in the name of Lady Llanover. Her enthusiasm for the Welsh way of life knew no bounds. Whatever she undertook, she carried out with all her might. She and her husband usually entertained house-parties for the eisteddfodau, and other country houses in the neighbourhood followed suit. From the beginning, foreign scholars had been attracted to this assembly. Part of the reason for this was the interest which Lady Llanover's sister and her husband, the German scholar Charles Bunsen, later Baron de Bunsen, took in the proceedings. This family introduced the Breton scholar M. Rio to the first eisteddfod meeting in 1833; he afterwards married into the Llanover circle. More Bretons attended in 1838, escorted by 'three wagons full of bards and harpers'. Bunsen, it seems, suggested subjects for prize essays, which attracted competitors from abroad. In 1840 the German professor Albert Schulz, 'San-Marte', won a prize for writing on the influence of Welsh traditions on the literature of Germany,

France and Scandinavia. In 1842 an essay on the Celtic languages written in French gained a prize of sixty guineas for Dr Carl Meyer, another German. The adjudicator was Dr James Cowles Prichard, the author of *The Eastern Origin of the Celtic Nations*, 1831.

Carl Meyer came over to Wales to claim his prize. During the winter of 1843 he was staying at Llanover, as he was anxious to study the Welsh language seriously. Later he took lodgings at Velindre, in the parish of Cwmdu, Breconshire, where the celebrated Carnhuanawc (Thomas Price) was vicar. Meyer was thus able to benefit from his company and make use of the books in his library. He seems to have made rapid progress, so Carnhuanawc suggested to him that he should get to know as many Welsh literary men as possible.

In September 1844 Meyer determined to see north Wales; Carnhuanawc was particularly anxious that he should meet Gwallter Mechain (Walter Davies), the cultured vicar of Llanrhaeadr-ym-Mochnant. In order to do so, he would pass the homes of many other literary clerics, and by calling on them he would obtain both bodily and mental refreshment. Carl Meyer preferred walking to riding; he was a young man of spartan habits and was abstemious in his diet. His first stopping-place was the rectory at Cascob, Radnorshire, the home of W. J. Rees who had devoted many years of his life to eisteddfodic matters, and who still laboured, in his old age, for the Welsh Manuscripts Society. He was a man who liked to have everything 'decent and in order', and it was he who worked out an itinerary for Meyer. He informed Gwallter Mechain:

> I have supplied him with particulars of his route from Cwmdu to Cascob, mentioning the places through which he is to pass, with the distances from each other etc., & the whole distance I make out to be 31 miles. I intend to supply him with a route somewhat similar from here to your residence viz. through Knighton, Llanfyllin, Llanrhaiadr, which may be about double the distance from Cwmdu to Cascob, and take him two days to accomplish as a pedestrian . . .

Carl Meyer did the journey in a day and a half, and spent a week with Gwallter Mechain. Then he went on to Merioneth, staying at Penmaen Dyfi, near Pennal, with Mr and Mrs John Vaughan. He visited Castell y Bere, Abergynolwyn, Craig yr

Aderyn, Tywyn and Ynysmaengwyn before returning to Llanrhaeadr to spend Christmas. He stayed on till the end of January, making good use of Gwallter Mechain's vast library and practising his conversational Welsh with Jane, the daughter of the house. It was a convivial household, and Meyer enjoyed the festivities, the good company and 'all the singing and drinking farmers of New Year's Day', as he recalled in a letter.

Ten years later George Borrow entered the church of Llanrhaeadr-ym-Mochnant, and asking the clerk who admitted him whether any remarkable men had been clergymen there, he was told of Bishop William Morgan, and '. . . then there was the last vicar, Walter D—, a great preacher and writer, who styled himself in print Gwallter Mechain'. But Borrow was not interested in him, as he had never heard of him before. Carl Meyer however was most interested in his host. He regarded his Powysland intonation most suited to the reciting of Welsh poetry, and remarked on his clear enunciation. Meyer also tells us that his hair had not lost its colour even then, when he was over eighty years old.

A former neighbour of Gwallter Mechain, the Reverend Thomas Richards, rector of Llangynyw, near Meifod, called while Meyer was at Llanrhaeadr, and invited him to call at Llangynyw on his way back to Cascob. Richards, a former secretary of the Powys Eisteddfod and a famous schoolmaster, possessed a good library and his household was renowned as a centre for musicmakers and bards. When Meyer arrived, he found a former acquaintance, Arthur Johnes, the future County Court judge, whom he had met at Llanover, and Richards's younger brother, Lewis, the rector of Llanerfyl. Meyer was easily persuaded to stay the night, once Richards had promised him the loan of a pony to take him as far as Kerry the following morning. He set out through the snow at half past seven on a Tuesday morning in late January, riding one of the Llangynyw ponies, accompanied by a boy on another pony. They had only travelled about half a mile, however, before Meyer discovered that both horses were badly shod, 'clogging and stumbling most frightfully, and as I would not undergo the risk of having their legs broken, I sent them both back'. He continued on foot 'through an indescribable chaos of snow, dirt and water, which different elements myself being destined to unite and carry away on my own feet, it took me nearly five hours to cross the Kerry Hills and to reach a place called

Velindre, on the road from Kerry to Knighton (from which place it is still 10 miles and about 13 from Cascob)'. He was determined to reach Llangynllo vicarage as Mr Richards had thoughtfully given him a letter of introduction to the incumbent. It was already dark, but within a quarter of a mile of his destination he took a wrong turning, and for three hours he trudged through snow and slush, finally arriving at the vicarage at ten o'clock when the inhabitants were going to bed. He reports that they 'most civilly dressed again and favoured me with a very kind and graceful reception'. After a night's sleep he was off again the next morning, arriving at Cascob between two and three on Wednesday afternoon, much to the relief of W. J. Rees, who had ben expecting him since the previous Saturday. But he was away again the next morning, between seven and eight, on the road to Crickhowell.

Later on in February he visited Bishop Connop Thirlwall at the Palace, Abergwili, where he enjoyed 'an undisturbed regular tranquility, abundance of books, a fine country to ride over and before all, the conversation of that most excellent Bishop, whom both on account of his learning and his character, of his mind and his heart I find every evening more interesting'. Connop Thirlwall had addressed the gathering at the Abergavenny Eisteddfod of 1840, the year of his appointment, and was busy learning Welsh. In March Meyer proposed going to Nevern to spend some time with the vicar, John Jones (Ioan Tegid) whom he had met in Llanover. Soon, however he was back again at Cascob Rectory where he sat

> at a little writing-table between the chimney and the window . . . chiefly occupied with the study of the Gododdin after a transcript which Mr Rees made of the MSS formerly in the possession of Theophilus Jones, now of Mr Price of Cwmdu, who does not, however, lend it to anybody . . . This manuscript, unknown to the editors of the Myvyrian Archaiology, is certainly superior to all those which they knew, and in fact the only one by which it is possible to make out the real meaning of many passages of that most difficult but at the same time most beautiful old poem . . .

Meyer criticized the English translations of Edward Davies and Dr William Owen Pughe, and goes on:

> Very amusing I found the seriousness with which both translated as though it was an essential part of the heroic poem some old nursery rhymes which some roguish transcriber has inserted there . . . I remember to have heard similar ones from my German nurse . . .

61

When he was not studying, he would be walking the countryside, and sometimes W. J. Rees would accompany him on horseback; one day they accomplished over thirty miles, visiting the reputed battlefield 'between Britania and Caractacus near Brampton Briar . . . the Roman camp on Brandon Hill near Leintwardine and . . . Caer Caradoc . . . above the Vale of the river Redlake about three miles from Clun'.

In June 1845 he set out for Ireland, but he was back by October, and attended the Abergavenny Eisteddfod amongst the distinguished visitors.

Early in 1847 Carl Meyer was appointed Librarian to Prince Albert. Lady Llanover was ecstatic:

> he has apartments in all the Palaces, dines with the Queen every day and moves with the court from place to place . . . he has begun to arrange the Library and he tells me has appropriated one side entirely to Irish and Welsh literature . . .

Although he kept up his connection with his Welsh friends, his visits to Wales after this were rare. He returned to Germany in 1851, but continued his interest in Celtic literature. Fortunately for us Lady Llanover has sketched Carl Meyer in the album of Angharad Llwyd, who was staying at Llanover in November 1843. He was a slim young man with fuzzy brown hair and side whiskers continuing down under his chin. He wore a thick moustache. Sitting on a high-backed chair, in a tight-fitting coat, his serious expression confirms W. J. Rees's appellation, 'the learned German'.

The English at the Eisteddfod

JOHN TRIPP

From Planet 18/19, Summer 1973

In his book of essays, *What Became of Jane Austen?*, Mr Kingsley Amis the well-known humorous novelist, former jovial left-winger and present pessimistic right-winger who seems to believe that only a cheerful benevolent despotism can cure England's ills, wrote a piece about the Eisteddfod called 'Where Tawe Flows' – which I shall come to in a moment.

I must confess a liking for Mr Amis. He taught English literature at Swansea University for a while and got to know the Welsh as well as any visiting Englishman can (he even wrote a novel about them). What I find rather impressive about him is that he backs off panaceas, he propounds no single philosophy and takes nothing for gospel – but he assumes that any creed in which people believe is bound to fade eventually and that the epitaph should be inscribed not in 'sombre respectful sepia', as the mandarin poet Roy Fuller put it, but with a certain gaiety. Let us hope that when Wales eventually comes jolting and complaining to her full stature, the loyal nationalists who rebuilt her will go out with gaiety and not with melancholy, once the job has been done and her position made safe. That day will come, I have no doubt. It is only then, I feel, that Welshmen can afford the luxury of practising a morality of moderation – learning, painfully and uncharacteristically, to view the temperate not merely as a tactical negative but as a crucial positive.

Anyway, just a few years before Kingsley Amis had a press button fixed to his label with 'Y Wasg' on it, at the 1964

Ystradgynlais Eisteddfod, he thought in cobwebbed cliché of Wales as a vast rugby ground with Cader Idris on one side and a slag-heap on the other, populated by pit-caked miners who only stopped singing 'All Through the Night' to bawl 'Look you to goodness whateffer' at one another, and subjected to continuous rainfall. In his essay, after doing his habitual smarty-pants bit and taking the customary unsubtle English piss out of the Welsh – an exercise which even the most intelligent can't seem to resist – Mr Amis is suddenly made aware of our remarkable 'difference' and 'foreignness' by noticing the passage of time when one had to listen to proceedings in an unknown tongue. Probably he would have felt more at home in Paris than in Ystradgynlais. Sweating in a stifling wooden box without a fag or Guinness, he is 'moved' considerably by the singing of our national anthem and 'Men of Harlech'. He is struck by the traditional Welsh respect for scholarship, and the fierce argument going on between a clerk and a shopkeeper in his bank as to whether a bardic adjudicator should or should not be a poet himself.

A discussion of this familiar point, at such an unfamiliar level, momentarily throws him. He reverts to quoting Matthew Arnold: 'When I see the enthusiasm the Eisteddfod can awaken in your whole people, and then think of the tastes, the literature, the amusements of our own lower middle classes, I am filled with admiration for the Welsh.' Mr Amis, slightly sheepish, quickly dismantles Arnold's starry-eyed view, but concedes that 'despite all that clever London stuff' he is a bit starry-eyed himself. Even after relinquishing his 'adopted semi-Welsh citizenship', he never wants to have the Eisteddfod ridiculed.

At least the man is honest, unlike others who slip across the border like thieves in the night to report the supreme event in the Welsh calendar. Year after year, the correspondents of English newspapers write in overblown prose about this institution, laying emphasis on its 'quaintness,' its seemingly archaic and obsolete rituals, and its general air of parochial solemnity, with a touch of flamboyance, as if the participants and visitors formed the last remnant of some peripheral province of Rome, before the barbarians came. At Llanelli, Llandudno, Newtown, Aberavon, Bala, Fflint, Ammanford and Bangor, reporters from glossy magazines have wallowed in purple descriptions of the chaired bard, honoured by his literary establishment, striding in his robe through a huge wood-and-corrugated-iron pavilion between cheering thousands to the strains of a patriotic march, passing beneath heraldic banners and escorted by sagacious pillars of the Gorsedd, as the great assembly rises and the music thunders around him. Etcetera. I remember a headline in an English women's rag that ran: 'CROWNED BIRD IS A PARSON'.

Once, long ago (on the Ebbw Vale field, I think it was), I met an apprenticed lady reporter from one of those posh county periodicals with names like *Hound & Horn* or *Trout & Stream*. She was looking at the London Welsh Association's portrait gallery of eminent hucksters and exiles, and was carrying an empty notebook about as thick as the Shorter Oxford. Her sadistic editor had sent her from the calm of Berkshire to Ebbw Vale to do a piece on the Eisteddfod, and she couldn't have looked more lost if she had been dumped in the middle of Outer Mongolia. I felt sorry for her and bought her a cup of tea. She was surprised to learn that the pavilion was a movable structure and did heavy duty anywhere from Chester to Penarth. I don't know if she ever finished her piece for *Hound & Trout* or whatever it was, but she should never have been sent to an Eisteddfod in darkest Monmouthshire on her first assignment without someone to hold her hand.

Our own reputation for flooding rhetoric and our gift for histrionics are often given a good run for their money by some of the boys from the London journals and the odd 'observer' from the Central Office of Information (I have a private theory that a sprinkling of these pale, chain-smoking Saxons are really lost, romantic Celts in disguise). Phrases like 'voluptuous splendour', 'oratorical glory', and 'blazing pageantry' have been known to run amok through columns of the stuff, or else they wax mock-lyrical about the 'hardy, tweedy country folk' in paragraphs of treacly slush, as if Iago Prytherch had never existed. God knows what their weary sub-editors, surrounded by tapes of disaster and mayhem, mutter to themselves at the other end.

This is the sort of surface copy they file to their home base, but I have heard them later in a bar when they loosen off their cynicism at such sentimental, medieval goings-on. They wear about five hats. The best among them, of course, like those from *The Times*, *Guardian*, and *Observer*, realize that we couldn't care less what they think, that we convince ourselves, if nobody else, that our culture is worth preserving. We leave the sly digs, the thinly-veiled envy and the often-bitter criticism to the anglicized cosmopolitans who want the Eisteddfod riddled with English. These shrieks from various quarters for 'fringe events' in English do not come from Dr Bobi Jones's 'colonial' Anglo-Welsh literati. They are more likely to emanate from uncultivated aldermen, councillors and businessmen sipping Scotch in the Park Hotel in Cardiff, waiting to kiss the hem of a former secretary-of-state or a property million-aire, and blissfully unconcerned about the English-speaking Welshman's vacuum of cultural disinheritance. If they do see an image of separation, it is doubtful whether they look beyond the possibility of making a combined take-over bid for the modern Welsh spirit.

Even among the Welsh-speakers there are churlish and cur-mudgeonly fellows who cavil at the Eisteddfod, their prescriptive misgivings over the years amounting to a programme of action. One whiskered faction would like it shoved well back into the Nonconformist heyday, dragging its black stove-pipe hats and boots behind it; the other, pink-cheeked lot would have it stream-lined and up-dated out of all recognition, a sort of mobile Dafydd Iwan-Lolfa Show (and I am all for gaiety), with Cymdeithas loud-speakers and Plaid Cymru klaxons drowning out the attempts at art. There are places for the publicity of the Welsh truth anywhere throughout Europe, but the Eisteddfod field, where only the con-verted would be preached at, is not one of them. The answer, as usual, probably lies somewhere in the middle, where the Eisteddfod is trying to remain, zealously guarded and unique.

And how unique it can be. At the Barry National in 1968, I met an American of Merioneth stock from Pennsylvania who was fes-tooned with cameras and exposure meters. He was in the company of a Breton, a Basque, a Taff farmer from Patagonia, a Dubliner who knew O'Casey, and a Cornishman who spoke frac-tured Welsh and Spanish (he and the Patagonian got on like a bomb). Both the Breton and the Basque were interested in *cyng-hanedd* and the history of Calvinistic Methodism. I gave them copies of Williams Parry and Euros Bowen, and showed them a couple of good chapels.

In the evening, we all went over to respectable Cold Knap and sat on the sea wall, drinking cheap plonk from bottles and gab-bling like fishwives as we watched the orange sun go down across the water. It was the last day of the Eisteddfod. Later we had fish-and-chips in Barry town and then went our ways. It was a small, lovely gathering of Celts and their allies, brought together by an event where the very essence of a nation was concentrated for a week – an accidental meeting which might happen only once in a lifetime. Someone like Gwyn Thomas, with his warmth and appetite for such unusual occasions, would have enjoyed it hugely.

Also at Barry that year was the editor of a technical journal who gave me the chance to do a well-paid colour piece on the Eisteddfod. He had the expression of a man on his way to the block. I asked him the reason. Apparently someone or something had upset him, and he felt crushed. He was a knowing political animal, with a nice, home-grown line in irony and sardonic wit that does not appeal to all tastes, as well as long, chastening experience of his more corkscrew compatriots. He confided in me that he thought the Welsh possessed almost every virtue except magnanimity. This saddened him. He felt a new, fresh, warm wind when it blew through his country, but he also fully comprehended that the only thing which could ruin our renaissance was *ourselves*, with our singular talent for cutting each other up, while the smug Anglo-Saxon continued to grin through the window.

That day I learned a valuable lesson from my friend, though I had long suspected it was the correct one. It is this: the only enormity that the complacent, pontificating Englishman cannot cope with is utter, articulate rudeness from his apparent inferiors who do not know, or have inconveniently forgotten, their station. If an abusive tirade doesn't work, we may have to resort to deviousness – which should come naturally to us – that would make his Machiavellian ancestors look like dim children. If this fails, too, the final alternative is a swift kick in the groin, without observing the Queensberry rules.

The other type of Englishman to beware of (and there are many lurking about in this present decade) is the wishy-washy, fence-sitting, do-gooder liberal, as personified in countless TV chat-programmes, who has the best interests of all struggling and suffering minorities, everywhere, at heart, from the Angolans to the Basques. He worries so much about us, it's a wonder he finds time for sleep. But when the crunch comes, like the white 'friends' of the American blacks, he is usually out of sight, on his mentally pure, idealistic way to shattered Biafra or underground Greece. (I recall what my old Fusilier sergeant used to tell us: 'You know who your mates are when you're in a foxhole.')

Another species of liberal to watch are those tough, sophisticated TV political anchor-men, a fairly recent breed of death's-head box performers who put the wind up me. They'll have the shirt off your back and your trousers down in five minutes. They have been in the lucrative game of overpaid objectivity for so long that they think a cause or an ideal is something you purchase in a supermarket. I doubt whether Wales, even now, means much more to them than the cradle of Lloyd George, the Depression, Nye Bevan, Cliff Morgan, Richard Burton, and a film-clip of Dylan Thomas in his boathouse – not necessarily in that order. You should take a very long spoon if you sup with one of them.

Such 'experts' spawned by our peculiar time never come to an Eisteddfod, of course. It might unbalance their sense of urgent priorities, of what they consider to be immediately significant, like the drearier aspects of domestic current affairs. Doubtless they are a portent of even worse to come. Last year, for instance, in the churning mud and squelching duckboards of Haverfordwest, several scribes leapt with glee on the storm-in-teacup friction over flags and grants. They must have blessed the people who originally triggered off the fuss. This year, when parsimonious Glamorgan and other bilingual counties jibbed at their contributions to the Eisteddfod, our own English-language press were among the first to send out their ferrets to open up the sore. Most newspapers hook on to bad news and trouble like ghouls at a traffic accident. Grubby, ephemeral sensation captures the attention before any noble celebration of art.

Sometimes, all too humanly, things go dismally wrong for the organizers. The skies open like the wrath of God, the tents and booths collapse, the vehicles are jammed for miles in every direction. All those visitors look so cold and hungry, in the drizzle, with good Welsh muck clinging to their boots, wanting not so much a definition of a *pryddest* or *arweinydd*, or even a sermon on the mechanics of language, as a thick steak and a big mug of tea. But old friends meet here again, leaking affection, perhaps once in the year; old enemies avoid the shifty eye or patch up a trivial scar. The squabbles about dwindling funds and the fluttering Jack having to partner the Dragon are soon forgotten (why not take the 'Royal' out of the National Eisteddfod first?). Some fainthearts drive home from the saturated field swearing never, never to return, and ask 'Where's it going next year?' on the way out.

Truly, how far would we have to travel to find a land that honours its language and its bards so magnificently? Where else does a people insist on such exclusion? Let those English scriveners, with nothing much left to believe in, snidely chuckle as we give them a show of quality, sensitivity and intellect, laced with a contemporary gaiety, panache, arrogance and strut. Let their kinder, wiser brothers be made welcome in the taverns and hotels bursting with a confident goodwill. And let our nostalgic exiles and the open-mouthed, wide-eyed citizens from abroad go away with amazing snapshots for their family albums in Surrey, Nantes, Stockholm and Kiev, with a memory of a people who live with style, wear their ancient pride lightly, and keep their simmering patriotism like a revolver in the cupboard – no longer some obscure enclave overshadowed on England's western flank. They will never see another festival quite like this one.

Behind it are generations of effort, decency, artistry, love and high accomplishment. May time and our own dignity preserve it.

Webb's Progress

HARRI WEBB

From Planet 30, January 1976

At my nativity the front of heaven was full of fiery shapes, but whatever flames flared over Warsaw, Amritsar or Cork, the skies above Tŷ-Coch were quiet. It was then one of Swansea's newer suburbs, the First World War was just over, and my father had returned from a wandering life, from Gallipoli and the Western Front, to get married and go into rooms, as young working-class couples then almost invariably did. Ours, where I was born, were with a Devonshire family called Brown in Tŷ-Coch Road. The upstairs landing window at the back looked out on to a large cemetery. Whenever there was a funeral within earshot – and in those days funerals carried a long way – Mrs Brown, who had obviously gone native, would stand at the window with the lodger's infant in her arms, rocking and weeping to the hymns. I can recollect none of this (though hymns in a minor key still upset me), for before my second birthday we moved into a house of our own in the middle of Swansea, the only home I remember.

A man of quiet temperament and stocky, powerful physique hardened by an upbringing as a farm boy in Gower, and an open-air life in Australia, my father was able to find work soon after his discharge from the Anzac forces. He became a coal trimmer and then a stoker at the Swansea Corporation's Electric Works, a primitive and dirty place on the once-notorious Strand. When this ancient plant was superseded in the 1930s by the new power station at Tir John North on the edge of Crumlin Bog, he became a boiler operator, exchanging shovel and sweat-rag for a white coat and horn-rimmed glasses but doing basically the same job with the same equable patience. My mother had learnt her trade as a dressmaker and continued to work at it with a treadle-operated sewing machine situated under the kitchen window to catch the light. The hours she spent at it brought in a useful supplement to my father's moderate but regular wage, and we were never conscious of want or deprivation.

It was a happy, stable, undramatic background. We belonged to that vast invisible section of the community, the un-unemployed, the class nobody has ever heard of or ever heard from, the people who had no ambitions or standards that were beyond their means, who kept a good table, who were neither abstainers nor driven by despair to drink, whose religious observance was one of social custom and good conduct, devoid of rapture, speculation or controversy, who voted when there was an election, but took little interest at other times, who struck no attitudes and minded their own business. Even in Wales, we formed the majority of the population.

The most distinctive thing about our household was that, although living in the middle of Swansea, we reckoned ourselves to be Gower people. This both my parents and all my relatives undoubtedly were by birth and upbringing. I was the first of our line to be born in a town. My father was a native of Bishopston, son of a smaller farmer who later moved to High Pennard, where my grandmother, Elizabeth Rees, made memorable ham-and-egg teas for visitors, and so pioneered the tourist industry which has since engulfed the peninsula. My mother was the youngest of a large family bearing the well-known Gower name of Gibbs. I heard recently that someone is going around genealogizing the clan and has traced us back to the Netherlands, an exotic origin that does not really register.

My maternal grandmother was Elizabeth Bowen. There is plenty of room for genealogical speculation about the various Bowens of Gower, but I have never pursued it. On some document I once saw she registered her name with the cross of illiteracy. My mother was born in a little house in the corner of Pennard churchyard. It had some ancient features and was later identified as the old Priest's House. When she died, she was laid to rest a few paces from where she was born. But she spent most of her early years in a whitewashed, thatched cottage on the edge of Fairwood Common. It began to look less picturesque some time in the thirties, when the thatched roof was replaced by galvanized, and the last time I saw it (it has probably disappeared by now) it looked like a disgraceful example of substandard rural housing. But it had sheltered a large and lively brood, always well fed and well dressed, high-spirited, quick-tempered, opinionated, talkative, full of self-esteem and usefully employed in the more responsible sort of working-class job.

Between them, my parents provided me with uncles, aunts and cousins beyond counting, and more distant, peripheral and honorary relations and connections in an ever-receding spectrum that seemed to embrace most of Pennard and Ilston parishes, with scattered outposts all over Gower. We spent much time visiting and gossiping. Talking to older relatives my parents' speech would broaden into the full dialect. To their amusement I soon picked this up and can still speak it if there is anybody left to speak it to. It sometimes occurs to me that I must be one of the last people who could, in the appropriate context, use thee and thou without affectation or archaism.

By the inter-war years, many, though by no means all, of the children and grandchildren of farm and cottage had drifted away, not very far geographically, and not at all in any emotional or social sense. Up until the last war, most of my relations were still to be found in Gower, Swansea and the Swansea Valley. (The rare exceptions were spoken of in tones usually reserved for the deceased.) Their various jobs read like a representative cross-section of a census of occupations: the steelworks, the pit, the line, the land, the Forces, the Trade, the docks, the dead-ends, the dole. The prosperous and the not so prosperous, the country people and the townies, mingled together, visited and gossiped as a family. That was all we talked about, that was all that mattered.

Great-Uncle William Webb farmed Ilston Glebe. Every Saturday on his way to market he would detour to our street with his pony and cart, he would tie the reins to the railings and deliver pale butter of a delicate fragrance (I used to think it smelt of the meadowsweet in Ilston Cwm), eggs each wrapped separately in a page of the *Christian Herald*, and other produce in season. His was one of the places I used to go, to turn the separator in the tiny dairy, drive the small herd of diverse cows down from the moor to the evening milking, carry swill to the sow with the piglets plugged into her huge flank, do odd jobs and earn my reward in milk warm and fresh from the cow, or delicious buttermilk straight from the separator.

A stream ran past the door and down the Cwm to Parkmill. The best way to the farm was through the churchyard and over the stone stile, past the graves of many other Webbs at rest under the huge dark tree that was said in its day to have provided yew-wood for the longbows of even more distant ancestors. A hoard of Roman coins was discovered quite near the Glebe. Lloyd George came and dedicated a memorial to the Baptist pioneers who had once worshipped in these solitudes, among the coltsfoot and cowslips, at a well sacred long before their day, and, I would guess, long before the day of the Trinity to which it had once been dedicated. In the next valley, there was a Giant's Grave, and Parc le Breos still retains a name that was part-Norman and a direct link with the crucial manoeuvres for Welsh independence. Pennard Castle loomed over the dunes. One could well believe the legend that it had been overwhelmed in a night of super-natural vengeance.

As a growing lad, I was taken further afield by my father. Together we roamed all Gower. Unlike my mother's side of the family he was not a talkative man. He let Gower speak for itself, the castles, the earthworks, the cliffs, the deep limestone valleys. Bacon Hole and Cefn Bryn with their mysterious relics. Rhossili Beacon from which you could see the width of Wales. The ancient parish churches, the mills and kilns of the last century. The quarry above Pwll Du, with its stone sentinel, Davy Dawkin, and the vestiges of the quay beneath, that had shipped the limestone to Devonshire, and the little pub nearby, left over from that vanished trade, and kept by another uncle. The mass-burial trenches at Gravesend on the same stretch of cliffs, dug by the John Webb of his day for the victims of an eighteenth-century shipwreck, Brandy Cove where another John Webb, revenue officer, had an affray with smugglers. John Webb my grandfather, stern and bearded in his clifftop holding, with his almost legendary reputation as a close-fisted, old-fashioned farmer.

After his time the place was briefly occupied by another great Gower character, the laureate of our community, the poet and raconteur, Cyril Gwynne, also a connection by marriage and I do not know how much of an example and a stimulus to my young imagination. I used to have many of his cheerful, simple rhymes, tales and musings by heart. 'The Giant Mangel-Wurzel', 'The Hungry Lurcher', 'What's in a Name?' 'Feyther Mightn't Like It' – the titles tell you all about them. I retained a fondness for them throughout the years of Ronsard and Baudelaire and all the other giants, a fondness which unfortunately has outlasted all but a few fragments in my memory. And he established in my mind an image of the poet as essentially a social rather than a solitary character, one, moreover, fortunate in his gifts, however humble, and under something of an obligation to spread them around for the pleasure of the people he belongs to, rather than to hoard them in the dank private cellars of introspection and incomprehension.

Cyril was lively and well liked. He had many jobs and moved around a lot. Welsh-speakers would recognize in him a mixture of Pontshaen and Wil Parsel, and might marvel that an Englishry could produce such a 'deryn'. But this was the special magic of old Gower. It was as Welsh as anywhere in Wales, yet used the English language naturally, without strain or shame or awkwardness or guilt or apology. It is a priceless attitude to have inherited just at this juncture. I speak of all this in the past tense, because I believe that the old, self-contained type of society that I remember in the last decades of its solitude and relative isolation, even from Swansea and 'the Works' in north Gower, has passed away altogether by now, like most such societies. I rarely return there, preferring to keep my memories intact. The Area of Outstanding Natural Beauty which it has since officially become is something else again.

Little of this has found its way into my work, and I sometimes wonder why, though without regret, because it is all very much still there, a massive rock that anchors in position a bobbing buoy whose business it is to offer what guiding light it can in a very stormy sea.

An important aspect of this background was our Church membership. Dissent never struck deep roots in Gower Anglicana, as much, I would guess, for reasons of temperament as of language. Obviously the Church had not failed in its duty here for the latter reason. I was baptized so soon after disestablishment that the new baptismal certificates were not available; still I consider myself to be among the founder members of the present Church in Wales. I was early enrolled in Sunday school and have still the most clear recollection of being taken there by the hand. It was before I started day school, and it was my first introduction to any society larger than that of my own family.

Saint Faith's, near the Guildhall, long turned over to secular use, was a bright little place with a pretty blue-and-white reredos of vaguely della-Robbian inspiration. There was a succession of cheerful curates serving under a vintage vicar, one of those short, plump, rosy-cheeked west Wales clerics who I sometimes think must be the fruit of a special tree in the palace grounds at Abergwili. He was the only man I have ever heard who could chant the liturgy with the *hwyl* of a chapel minister. The Bishop of St David's had served under him as a curate, and delighted to come back to his first parish, although it was now in the new diocese of Swansea Brecon. My first ambition (after the stage of wanting to drive a fire engine) was to become a bishop, and to resemble that venerable figure in his full vestments. Various factors have prevented this, but there have been more enduring influences from those days.

The first and most fundamental is the Anglican ethos itself: Arminian, Erastian, near enough Pelagian. There is a touch of Calvin's brimstone in the Thirty-Nine Articles of course, but not very much comes over in practice. Faith, to me, is firmly a matter of good works, good conduct and upright dealing, rather than subjective emotionalism. The Catechism cannot be improved upon as a rule of life. (Like most people I have, of course, broken most of the rules from time to time.) The love of God is best interpreted in terms of charity, humour and tolerance. You can't get away from Calvinism, of course, not in Wales, but my portion of this heritage seems to have transferred itself bodily from the spiritual to the political sphere. *There*, I accept cheerfully, even with gusto, that there are individuals who are damned beyond redemption, and the contemplation of their discomfort in the, I hope, fairly immediate earthly future is going to be a lively augmentation to the pleasures of the redeemed.

Then there is the influence of regular attendance at services with a set liturgy of some magnificence. I don't suppose anybody can be fully literate in Welsh who has not been similarly immersed in the eloquence of the Nonconformist pulpit and the wash of great hymns. Certainly the chances are very much against anyone who has not had an Anglican upbringing being able to write good English. This very point, incidentally, is made by both W. J. Gruffydd and George Orwell, not so much an unlikely duo really. The decline in regular attendance at religious services poses problems for the culture of both languages, which I have been happily spared. Not only the shape of the language, but its sound and presentation, are an integral part of the Church's ministry. I can never read in public without wishing to have in front of me a decent lectern, preferably in the form of the Eagle of the Apocalypse. For the lightest word spoken is an act of pure creation. In all logia is the Logos; to mumble and gobble and make animal noises as some so-called poets do these days is not merely bad manners, it is a very serious sin, like every other abuse of language.

Next in this tale of origins comes school. There was Church influence here too. Instead of going to any of the nearer places I was sent to the National School in Oxford Street, not much further away really, but very much a Church school. The headmaster was People's Warden at the town's parish church, and rugby-playing curates came to open each day's education with judiciously chosen Bible stories of battle and shipwreck. It was a down-town school, cheek by jowl with the market, the Vetch Field, the jail, the Grand Theatre and the Empire Music Hall. We were a mixed lot. Some of the boys wore collars and ties, one or two, briefly, came to school barefoot. But mostly it was jerseys and stout boots. The teachers taught and exercised discipline; there was no bullying or bad violence. Billy Meredith's nephew won a cap for football. I was often in trouble, but it was discovered that I could write. At the age of nine or ten I wrote a thrilling adventure story which ended with everybody becoming rich. I've been writing it ever since.

It was a heavily Imperialist school. We saluted the flag on Empire Day, and a huge map showed 'The Empire in red and all the rest grey' (the same one as Chesterton saw, I'm sure), while John Bull stood somewhere south-east of New Zealand with his bulldog holding a Union Jack in its jaws, and one or the other of them saying 'What I have, I hold'.

Even so, if there is a seed in the air, it will fall to ground somewhere. In Standard One, Miss Lloyd taught a surprisingly healthy and vigorous version of our own history. In the clear light of later years, I was to read Owen Rhoscomyl's *Flame-Bearers of Welsh*

History with becoming detachment. I was to work in Dowlais around the corner from Well Street, where Prytherch, its illustrator, was born, and meet people who had known him, drink in the Church Tavern at Faenor, kept by former servants of the gallant Colonel who had been his model for Prince Llywelyn and Caractacus. It got by, of course, because it ended happily with Henry Tudor winning the Crown of London. Miss Lloyd made us all look out of the classroom window to see the name Tudor on a tailor's shop in Oxford Street – proof indeed.

Catherine Street, where we lived, was at the intersection of many impalpable frontiers. Basically it was respectable working class, with scrubbed doorsteps and ritually polished brass strips on every threshold. My natural playground was the sweep of the sands. Every summer, we took in regular visitors from Rhondda. We went to the Grand Theatre most weeks to see sensational thrillers – which never failed to thrill – and rather less gripping intrigues on a different level, involving gentlemen in evening dress and ladies in long frocks. There must have been at least half a dozen cinemas. We lived so near to St Helen's that we could follow the fortunes of the home team by minute fluctuations in the continuous noise from the ground. Evangelists and agitators of every persuasion raised their rostrums on the sands. Holy Joe and other well-known characters walked the streets, creating the atmosphere of a much smaller place. Tennyson and Gladstone glowered through the gloom of the Public Library. Later, Thomas Taig inspired some remarkable productions at the Little Theatre. It was a many-faceted town of crowds and encounters, a seaport, a market town, a resort and a place of entertainment. It freed one from narrowness of outlook and from the obsessions of a one-industry economy which even today can infect some quite articulate attitudes to Wales, and prevent many people from taking a balanced and optimistic view of the nation as a whole.

Not that the shadows of the depression were absent, or evidence lacking of the grim price of over-dependence on heavy industry. We lived opposite the hospital, our house a port of call on visiting days, an ever-open door, and the kettle always on the hob for relatives and their neighbours and workmates, some of them distressed, shocked or bereaved. I never knew who would be sitting down to tea with us when I came home from school on such days, or what stories I would hear. The flame-bearers kindled a spark of anger. This was not what we were born for. On visits up the Swansea Valley, I played with children ruined before birth by their father's employment in the spelter works. You could tell the 'leaded' children by their rotten teeth and continuous dribbling, and as we romped on a hillside of slag and clinker, the hideous devastated Landore region stretched its ruins beside the poisoned yellow Tawe. In an old encyclopaedia bought from a market stall I read 'Swansea is the non-ferrous metallurgical metropolis of the world'. And this was all that was left, those children, that place. From the hills around the town, and deep into Gower, you could see at night the sky suddenly lit up by a slow lightning, and you knew then that they were tapping the Bessemers at Dowlais, all those miles away, far inland, a place of power that lit up half Wales. That, too, went dark.

In these villages, much Welsh was spoken. There was plenty of it to be heard on the sands during the holiday periods, or in the market and the cinema queues and on big match days, very obviously a living language. Nobody seemed to have any definite attitude to it one way or the other. It was just there, like Kilvey Hill or Mumbles Head. I suppose speakers and non-speakers alike acquiesced in its complete lack of any public recognition or official status. To me, though not understanding more than a few colloquial phrases, it added to the colour and variety of the life around us. The language of home and Church and rural background was English. Welsh excitingly belonged to the industrial places, and crowded streets.

The rewards of the ready verbalizer early came my way. I was destined for 'the scholarship' and passed from the noisy bustle of Oxford Street to a delightful suburban secondary school perched on top of a matchless view of the bay and embowered (a truly appropriate word) in a rose garden, amenities which partly compensated for its rather exiguous housing in wooden buildings left over from the First World War. It was much smaller, and had much less prestige than the other schools, it had no tiresome 'traditions' and was a good place. True, Welsh was not well taught there in my time, though it improved a lot afterwards, but I learnt enough of the grammar to give me a toehold. French was taught superbly, with a good accent and in a lively manner, stimulating an interest that filled my life for many years and is still among my chiefest pleasures. And, as other and greater Welshmen were finding at that very time, acquaintance with Europe's central and seminal culture is in itself a liberation, not least from the hick provincialism that characterizes so many of the claims made for Eng. Lit.

We learnt Spanish too, another window flung open on an unsuspected world, one I could not somehow enter into as fully as the other, but providing, as it happened at that time, a more vivid stimulus. Lorca. Not that he was on the syllabus of course. But the *Romancero Gitano* came into my hands, in a poorly produced commemorative volume brought out soon after his murder. Here now was a poet of my own day, a poet of his own people, killed, as far as I could make out, simply because he was such a poet. His death seemed part of the poetry itself. It meant more to me than anything I had encountered so far in the three literatures with which I was beginning to become acquainted. Later, at Oxford I talked about him with Don Alberto Jimenez. His teacher and mine, a circumstance I still find incredible. *Verde que te quiero verde.*

The Spanish Civil War, of which this was a minor episode, had up till now been a remote, confused business. The burning of Penyberth, which took place on my sixteenth birthday, was equally remote and puzzling. We were not an apolitical generation though. We were in a special position. Hitler had come into power when I was twelve, and all the boys of my age knew, far more clearly than our rulers, that we were the ones who would have to fight him. The thought worried our parents more than it worried us, and they tried to put it out of their heads. For us, it banished all futures.

Ambitious teachers put me on the road to Oxford, frugal parents made the journey possible. In those days one could live reasonably well on remarkably little, if one had it. My time among the dreaming spires was something of a mixture. My first term began just after the Munich betrayal, which jolted me into sudden political awareness, and profoundly influenced my attitude to public morality ever since. My second year began in the early days of the war. Having gone up rather young, I was allowed to stay on and finish my three years, and then I joined the Navy, just in time for Pearl Harbour and the fall of Singapore.

All these years and scenes have been written about by others and my experiences were in no way remarkable. Oxford was a different world in a different country, one I could enjoy without being nobbled by it, unlike some. The war, even if it was full of new experiences, and incidents too stirring to be comfortable, was, on balance, a drag, and has rarely moved my pen. In Cairo, on leave from the Malta convoys, I picked up Aragon's *Le Crève-Cœur*. I knew of him as a surrealist, a communist, a literary manifestant. Here he suddenly was as a poet of action and feeling, of involvement and immediate communication, a man who loved his country deeply, and was scalded by her shame. It was another revelation of what real poetry was all about. *Je n'oublierai jamais les lilas ni les roses*. In Scotland, on the edge of the Burns Country, I became aware of MacDiarmid, and learnt that 'The rose of all the world is not for me'.

I came back to Wales and made up my mind to stay here and slog it out with her enemies, using whatever weapons had been given me. I made a serious effort to learn the language, but could not claim to wear it at all comfortably until I had spent many happy years working in the Dowlais and living in that raffish mini-metropolis Merthyr Tydfil, with all its fascinating paradoxes.

My work since the war scarcely needs any further comment or elucidation. Those years have seen significant and encouraging changes in attitude and direction, and I like to think that what I have written has been part of the process. The last decade has been particularly exciting. Now (I write in the summer of 1975) we are in for a less dramatic trudge, while the machinery of devolution is being assembled. Wales is marching backwards into independence, everybody desperately pretending that we are going somewhere else. It is one of those moments of nice irony, with which the story has so often been scripted. But sooner or later the crunch will come, and I hope that what I have written will be of some help to those who have to take their part in the final confrontation.

The Romantic Parody

D. TECWYN LLOYD

From Planet 31, March 1976

Sometime during 1817 or 1818, Philip Klempferhausen, a young German student, made the usual romantic Tour of the Lake District and, later on, wrote about it thus:

> A strong and deep passion for nature especially when of a sudden revived and gratified to the utmost, seeks to indulge itself in solitude – and on plunging into the manifold recesses of those magnificent mountains, I felt that even the conversation and society of a beloved friend would have been irksome, much more the unsatisfactory talk of some peasant guide, whose provincial dialect I, though well acquainted with the pure English tongue, might have been unable distinctly to have understood. I wished for no guide and in good truth I needed none . . . Why should I ask what the mountains themselves told me in language easily understood. I saw before me the cliff that might not be scaled, and the abyss that might not be descended . . . I felt afraid to enter into conversation with the shepherds and peasants in whose cottages I slept. *I wished them to be what they seemed to my imagination* [my emphasis here] and I was loth to acquire an imperfect knowledge of their character lest the strong interest which their appearance had created in my mind should thereby be destroyed or weakened . . . How should I dare to describe their character, till I have seen into the soul of their lovely, their adventurous, and most peculiar life?

We would do well to preface every discussion of the Romantic tourist, his writings and sketches, with the lines just quoted. Here we find as good a description as any of the romantic True Voice of

81

Nature and of how and where one might hear it. It is also an equally concise portrait of the True Natural Man: the untutored man – shepherd, farm worker, cottage girl, wife – who is as much a part of Nature as the trees, crags, rivers, clouds that surround him. The whole image or notion seems to possess an almost Hindu or Buddhist passivity; the true natural man co-operates with all the natural, unbidden forces around him, he attains a balance between his own contriving and nature's actions, and an outsider, such as an insensitive tourist, can do harm to this 'most peculiar life' by his ill-informed questions and interferences.

Klempferhausen, nevertheless, is aware that he is transfiguring his shepherds and peasants by the power of his own imagination, but yet, he is more than half persuaded that, given a perfect knowledge of their character, the resulting 'real' portrait of them will turn out to be the same as the one his imagination has already prefigured. So that, granted 'real' or 'true' knowledge, the world of actuality will merge into the world of ideal categories created by the romantic imagination; the platonic is reconciled with the actual, timelessness with time and placelessness with place. It seems that the whole romantic pilgrimage or tour is about precisely this; its difficulties, problems, even its frequent absurdities, are those that belong to every attempt at incarnation.

During the last quarter of the eighteenth century and the first half of the nineteenth, a considerable number of literate, middle-class Englishmen 'toured' Wales. Henry Penruddocke Wyndham was one of the earliest of the romantics to do this and George Borrow one of the last. Even before Borrow started on his journey the railway age that was to transmute tourer into tripper was well advanced. *Wild Wales* is the last of its romantic clan; the tour-book thereafter gave way to the factual, impersonal guide that listed all the available trips to seaside resorts.

The Welsh tourers (and I use this word in order to avoid the present-day connotations of 'tourists' and 'tourism'), as I have said, belonged to the English middle and upper middle classes. Many of them were clergymen, some were men of letters, others were engineers, university teachers, lawyers and the like but most of them seem to be steeped in the romantic interpretation of life and to accept it as the normal one.

Wales, before the day of the railroad, was served by abominably bad roads, dangerously rutted in winter, intolerably dusty in summer. Decent hostelries were few and far between and we hear complaints of even the best recommended ones; the fare was indifferently cooked more often than not, parlours were chilly and beds never above suspicion of damp and fleas. Not that Welsh hostelries were at all peculiar in this respect; most European hotels and pensions were the same and few indeed had a clean bill of fare. Then, there was the difficulty of language. At this time, between, say, 1775 and 1850, Wales was Welsh even from beyond the English border in Herefordshire or Gloucestershire to the western coasts; from Holyhead to Chepstow. To the monoglot Englishman this in itself was a totally unexpected discovery and something of a shock. Whence came this strange speech, how explain it, what did it all mean? Explanations indeed are offered but they seem to mystify the matter rather than enlighten it. John Evans writes:

> The Welsh Language lays claim to high antiquity, as being a branch of the Jaspian, or that dialect of the Hebrew spoken by the posterity of Japhet . . . Both in its formation as well as grammatical construction it bears a near resemblance to the Hebrew and its affinity is further traced by the learned Rowlands in his comparative table of three hundred words, similar in sound and meaning, to so many Hebrew ones: whence it appears to be the most primitive and uncorrupt of living languages in the western world.

Bingley is even more emphatic:

> But it is not in single words merely that the Welsh and Hebrew languages agree, they are likewise so nearly allied in their grammatical forms that it would be difficult to adduce even a single article from the Hebrew which is not also to be found in the Welsh grammar, and there are many whole sentences to be found in both languages which in words are exactly alike.

But, for good measure, there seems to be also a dash of Greek in Welsh as well as Hebrew:

> If the Welsh language had its origin in the Hebrew of which, all circumstances considered, there can be little doubt, this analogy betwixt the Welsh and Greek is only what might be expected.

Hebrew, Greek, Jaspian, – which? These notions were not peculiar to the tourers nor, for that matter, to English tourers. In the paragraph we have just quoted Evans refers to Rowlands. He was the Revd Henry Rowlands, rector of Llanidan in Anglesey and author of *Mona Antiqua Restaurata* (1723). Other Welsh writers like the historian Theophilus Evans held similar views. In fact, the idea of tracing all languages back to a few 'primitive originals', of assessing what wealth of 'primitive purity' every language possessed is a debased remnant of the great interest in linguistic studies fostered by the Renaissance. Hebrew, of course, was the first of all languages, the language of Eden and of celestial beings and a language whose very letters and syllables, in the hands of the magi and the hermetic philosophers, became charged with supernatural powers. Needless to say, these ideas accorded well with the romantic disposition, and thus Welsh seemed to be a felicitously near relation of Hebrew, the speech of power and, above all, of mystery. All the romantics loved mysteries.

Certainly, Wales was mysterious. Thus, Wyndham again:

> Tis among the sable mountains that, according to some authors, the genuine British language is spoken with its primitive accent and simplicity . . . The original manners also prevail; they are unadulterated with either ancient or modern civilisation, and the village of Rhos Fair and its inhabitants, would quickly convince a traveller that simplicity in building or cloathing is not partially confined to the wigwams and natives of either the Cape of Good Hope or of Terra del Fuego . . .

Here, too, we see the well-worn romantic clichés: *sable mountains, original manners, primitive accent and simplicity* and the like. Note also the reference to the savages of South Africa and South America. To a person of Wyndham's time, these natives typified the old idea of a people living in a state of nature; they are the hyperboreans of the political philosophers who, by the mid-eighteenth century, were becoming the noble savages of Henry Mackenzie and his followers and imitators. It was in this manner that Wyndham saw the Welsh people; half savages that seem, more often than not, to carry on their persons some romantic (possibly tribal) disfigurement or oddity. Their behaviour is also unaccountable: here is one of their funerals:

> The dismal solemnity of these weeping countenances soon evaporated and the sorrows and senses of the company were quickly drowned in large potations of ale. Such is the general conclusion of a Welsh meeting, whether it begins with mirth or melancholy. I was here informed that a burial was esteemed the most profitable

function of a Welsh clergyman. The relations, and neighbours of the deceased, attend the funeral in large numbers and made considerable offerings to the officiating priest, for they are taught to believe that their respect to their friend's memory is in proportion to the oblations they give.

But for a description of the 'natural state' of Welsh natives it would be hard to come by a better one than this by a Mr Pratt:

> I have seen groups of poor people on the sequestered spots of both North and South Wales, sporting among the precipices or in the glens with a content so absolute as to look on any object less in a state of nature than themselves as unwelcome: at the sight of an unexpected man of the world, they will run into a rocky cavity, like a rabbit into its hole, or plunge into the thickest shade of the valley, as if they were escaping from a bird of prey.

If this be not the 'very bowels' of the state of nature it is difficult to imagine what it is. Mr Pratt's scoops must have been the envy of other romantic fellow travellers. His whole point, nevertheless, is to contrast this primitive innocence with worldly sophistication, and he goes on:

> Were they to know what a snaky train of passions are probably folded up in the bosom of that well-dressed worldling, which never crept into their breasts, they would often have reason to believe he was the most dangerous monster they could encounter, and double their diligence to avoid him.

The natural scenery of Wales had, of course, much to do with all this. We have already seen a reference to 'sable' mountains, but John Evans gives us a much fuller exposition of this romantic-gothic view of the matter. According to him:

> It has been observed that mountain scenery is peculiarly friendly to those aerial and imaginary existences that constitute the objects of *superstition*. The constant variation in their appearance, added to the gloom attendant upon lofty crags, hollow cwms, deep ravines, lakes, dingles, caves, and torrents, must have a strong tendency to affect the imagination: fear is the offspring of ignorance, and unbounded credulity the concomitant of fear ... Hence the spirit of conjuration so prevalent in Lapland, the second sight of the Highlands and the vagaries of the Awenyddion in Wales (a word significant of poetic raptures) were derived from the same origin; these persons, when consulted, become inflamed with a high

degree of enthusiasm, were, to all appearance, carried out of themselves, and seemed possessed of an invisible spirit.

Much later, as we shall see, popular Anglo-Welsh fiction of the
Allen Raine–Edith Nepean brand was to make great play out of
this image of the Welsh poet or 'bard' according to Romantic
usage: it is the same image, of course, as that of Coleridge in
Khubla Kahn: 'And they shall cry, beware beware/ His flashing
eye, his floating hair'. As anyone who can read *Gramadegau'r
Penceirddiaid* can see at once the whole notion is ludicrously inept.
Pictorially, it is well represented by the frontispiece drawing published in Edward Jones's *Musical & Poetical Relicks of the Welsh
Bards* (2nd edn., 1974). This drawing could, indeed, be used after
the manner of Lessing's *Laocoon* to typify practically every aspect
of the English Romantic view of Wales during this period.

A slightly later writer, G. J. Freeman, divides scenery into five
varieties: viz., the 'pleasing or pretty', the beautiful, the romantic,
the magnificent – and the sublime. Space will not allow us to
quote what he has to say about each of these varieties, but in his
view the sublime is the highest and rarest:

> The sublime is altogether of a different order . . . Nothing pleasing,
> merely pleasing, nothing pretty, graceful or elegant or beautiful . . .
> No, nature herself gives evidence in this case of what is becoming.
> Trees, the most beautiful of her ornaments, are no longer to be
> found, or they are decayed, blasted and in ruins. Water, in order to
> be in place here, loses its beauty, and becomes impassable, resist-
> less, awful. The earth no longer swells into soft eminences, or
> displays lovely proportions, but is riven and precipitous, scorning
> art and culture, hard of access, rugged and dark and lonely. It is
> among such scenes as these that the sublime dwells, and the
> human heart never knows the sublime unless it first in some
> measure shrinks from these very forms and objects that inspire it.

In all this, there is an obviously paradoxical element. Sublimity
on the one hand is the highest form of beauty but it is the beauty
of destruction, terror, the *mysterium tremendum* that transcends
nature and is, indeed, strange and extra-natural. It is, nevertheless, the supreme goal, the experience to be sought above all else
although it might mean much physical and spiritual risk and even
harm. In the course of time, Romantics often came to assume that
sublimity was un-nature or faulted nature and vice versa; indeed,
for many tourers the quest for the sublime came to mean

searching for the exceptional, the odd and bizarre, the un-natural. To do all this successfully meant not so much intellectual discipline as the sharpening and tensing of one's emotions and sensibilities: after all, only the Man of Sensibility could fully appreciate the sublime.

Like every other human ideal, the search for the sublime deteriorated over the years and became not much more than a somewhat self-indulgent curiosity for mere oddities and abnormalities. Time and again, we find the Tour books dwelling at great length on what they term the odd native folk customs of the Welsh. Marriage customs, for instance:

> The ceremonies of the Cambrian peasants, in the unpolished parts of the country are no less singular than those of their wooing . . . The friends and relations of both parties not only testify the usual demonstrations of joy during the daytime but keep it up the whole night; the men visitors putting to bed the bridegroom, and the females the bride; after which the whole company remain in the chamber, drinking jocund healths to the newly-married couple and their posterity, singing songs, dancing, and giving into every other festivity sometimes for two or three days together.

Even more frequently do we find delighted and even learned discourses on the supposedly unique Welsh custom of courting in bed – titbits well calculated to titillate jaded English palates of the early nineteenth as well as those of the late twentieth century. J. T. Barber dwells on the matter thus:

> Our companion . . . denied the existence of the custom; that maids in many instances admitted male bed-fellows, he did not doubt, but that the procedure was sanctioned by tolerated custom he considered a gross misrepresentation. Yet in Anglesea and some parts of North Wales, where the original simplicity of manners and high sense of chastity of the natives is retained, he admitted *something of the kind* might appear. In those thinly inhabited districts, a peasant often has several miles to walk after the hours of labour to visit his mistress; those who have reciprocally entertained the *belle-passion* will easily imagine, that before the lovers grow tired of each other's company the night will be far enough advanced, nor is it surprising that a tender-hearted damsel should be disinclined to turn her lover out over bogs and mountains until the dawn of day. The fact is, that under such circumstances she admits a *consors lecti* but not in *nudatum corpus*.

But these scenes and 'customs' were not the only fruitful sources of the romantic *mysterium*. Romantics also looked backwards, and amongst relics of the past saw ruined castles and abbeys, fallen bastions suggestive of violent battles between legendary princes and kings. William Sotheby, one of the earlier tourers is so overcome by all the ruins he saw that he wrote his tour completely in verse. This is Caerffili Castle:

> ... The mellow tints
> That time's slow pencil lays from year to year
> Upon the ancient towers, spread o'er the wreck,
> A grateful gloom, and the thick clouds that sweep
> Along the darken'd battlements, extend
> The melancholy grandeur of the scene.

Or again, looking at the ruins of Ewenni Priory, he gives us a piece worthy of M. G. Lewis or Mrs Radclyffe at their gothic best, – including the supernatural, which is an indispensable part of their works:

> ... while in the murky cells
> Of old Ewenny, superstition's slave
> Starts at the thunder of his lonely tread
> Echoed along the vaults, and horrid shapes
> Flash on his wildered eye; mournful I seek
> The desert spot in village records marked
> Where oft the fairies, in fantastic dance,
> Circled the moonlight green.

Eventually, Sotheby comes to north Wales and the inevitable Aberglaslyn Pass. Here he really lets go the reins:

> Fled are the fairy views of hill and dale;
> Sublimely throned on the steep mountain brow
> Stern Nature frowns, her desolating rage
> Driving the whirlwind, or swoln flood or blast
> Of fiery air imprisoned, from their base
> Has wildly hurled the uplifted rocks around
> The gloomy pass, where Aberglaslyn's arch
> Yawns o'er the torrent. The disjointed crags
> O'er the steep precipices in fragments vast
> Impending, to the astonished mind recall
> The fabled horrors by demoniac force
> Of Lapland's wizards wrought.

Here again we have something of Freeman's sublime, together

with the suggestion of some elemental, mythopoeic force; it is all to be felt in this Pass. But although his body was actually walking through it, Sotheby's mind and imagination were fast bound in Lapland or some other similar Shangri-la. What he does here is to transpose Aberglaslyn into something or somewhere else; he does not really see the view in front of his nose. Note again the typical stock romantic clichés: 'desolating rage', 'sublimely throned', 'grateful gloom' and the like.

Without extending this article to book-length I cannot quote further instances of the Romantic tourer's *descriptio Cambriae* in English, nor can I reproduce here any of the ample illustrative material that shows precisely the same Romantic preoccupation. Batty, Gastineau, Pugh, Roscoe, Freeman, to name only a few, all print engravings of Welsh views that are in complete accord with the Romantic interpretations of the prose (and poetry) texts that accompany them. Mountains appear far higher and steeper than they actually are, ravines are darker, waterfalls and cascading brooks and rivers more precipitous and gloomier. The sketchers shared the same general aesthetic views as the tourer himself. Human figures, when they appear at all, are grotesque and one is almost persuaded that the Welsh were a race of troglodytes, mis-shapen, ugly, almost neanderthal and certainly caradoc-evansy. The polite English reader was left in no doubt at all that here, less than a hundred or two hundred miles away from his villa gates, there existed a region as wild as Lapland, and a strange people, speaking a mysterious language, having outlandish customs, superstitious, illiterate, bardic, but yet living among ruins that suggested former prowess and glories both of sword and book. Could they be living in some sort of state of nature where the writ of polite society did not run or were they merely fallen into depravity? Certainly, it all seemed to suggest that the romantic philosophers, whether German, French or just plain English, could be right after all. In any case, it all made fascinating reading during the long boredom of the closed season and, with the French wars going on interminably and making the Grand Tour a very dicey affair indeed, one could do worse than savour the wildernesses of Scotland, the Lake District and Wales.

As I have already mentioned, it was the railway more than any other single factor that brought the age of the Welsh Tour to an end. From the late 1840s onwards, Wales, within quite a short period, ceased to be remote and mysterious. Small seaside villages like Rhyl, Colwyn, Llandudno, Aberystwyth, came within reach of the Lancashire and Midlands day-tripper. These villages themselves became small towns and after the publication of the 1847 Blue Books on the state of education in Wales, Welsh people did all they could to become Sassenachs, of sorts. The number of tourists increased, especially from the 1860s on; the resorts became more and more crowded, less and less Welsh. No longer could the Romantic afflatus be felt on Welsh coasts; it was driven away by the philistines of Liverpool, Brum, the Welsh industrial centres, and hid itself in the inland glens and valleys. The new travel literature of the tripper was short-winded, factual and business-like; it offered little to the imagination – like Gradgrind's school it was a heap of facts often liberally mixed with more dubious factoids. Still, the disappearance of the Tour book left a vacuum and it was this, very largely, that seems to have prompted the fiction writers to take up Wales more earnestly than it had been considered before.

There have been eighteenth-century novels and plays that made use of Wales as a background or as *terra incognita* where anything might happen. Such, for instance, were Mrs Aubin's *Life of Madame de Beaumont* (1728) or *Powis Castle or Anecdotes of an Ancient Family* (1788) or Mrs Bennet's *Anna, or Memoirs of a Welch Heiress* (1796), and many others we could mention. Generally, these writings make no effort to delineate Welsh characters (or Welch ones for that matter); even the 'Powis Castle' mentioned above bears no relation to the mansion near Welshpool; if I remember rightly it is placed somewhere in the south of England. These authors obviously knew hardly anything at all about Wales beyond the mere name; it was just a far-off and unfamiliar place like the Wild West or the Central African jungles of later novelists. They are very tedious to read.

During the last quarter of the nineteenth century, there was a fairly rapid growth of middle-class leisure, particularly leisure for women who could afford maids and cooks to do their domestic chores. From about the end of the 1850s a few novels of some Welsh interest begin to appear but it is not until the last decade of the century that stories about Wales begin to multiply significantly – many of them in magazines. All this fiction (which can, I suppose, be termed anglo-Welsh) is the work of writers who were either of non-Welsh origin but who lived or had lived in Wales or writers who were descended from Welsh stock but who had become anglicized. Many, possibly the majority, were women. Allen Raine (Mrs Puddicombe Beynon) was a descendant of the well-known Welsh divine and poet Dafydd Dafis, Castellhywel, but her own upbringing and most of her adult life had been English. She either had no direct knowledge of Welsh life or she has overlaid it in her novels with such a thick layer of romantic mush that it hardly makes any difference. Other women writers – Gwendolen Pryce, Bertha Thomas, Marie Trevelyan, Edith Nepean, Hilda Vaughan and many more followed her lead; or rather, they all followed the only lead really available to them which was that of the Romantic tourist. For indeed, the fact is that in most of the English novels and stories written about Wales and Welsh-speaking characters from, say, 1890 until 1950 or so, we are continually meeting the 'customs', oddities and primitivenesses we have seen so amply offered us in the Tour books. Practically the only new addition to these is the 'Wales is a singing nation' line of Richard Llewellyn; Welsh choral singing and male voice choirs did not exist in 1800.

It would require far more space than I have here to show how the anglo-Welsh novel and story of 1890–1950, by taking over the functions of the former Tour book, took over also its usual themes and romanticism and perpetuated them in the form of fiction thereby creating an impression on the untutored reader that these still persist and are real. In the writings of the women I have mentioned and others, one meets again the village poet-shaman (or 'bard'), the peasantry that still contrive to live in a state of nature, the superstitions, the odd religions, the ubiquitous 'bundling' or courting in bed (*The Black Venus* by Rhys Davies is an absurd novel on this theme), the strange language (Welsh), the ever present beetling mountains and sinister ravines. In the dialogue parts of these narratives there are efforts at rendering in English something of the supposed aura of the Welsh which the characters are understood to be talking; that it is so utterly weird to a real Welsh-speaker must be accounted for by the fact that Welsh, romantically speaking, is descended from the Jaspian or some such auncientry. This, for example:

> 'Oh stop you,' said Betti, 'I am not like the beast that perisheth. On Sundays,' and she waved a knife in the air, 'I am thinking a lot for

the good of my soul, about my chapel, of my hymns and the 'Pwnc' that we are learning, 'tis the twenty-fifth of Hebrews next Sunday and there's long it is.'

(Allen Raine, *On the Wings of the Wind*)

Hebrews, incidentally, has only thirteen chapters. No matter; here's another:

'Oysters we are not,' he opened. 'Tongues have been given us to discuss matters . . . but a black beetle our chapel is not. Nay, but a viper she can be in defence of her young, yea, and she can have the teeth of a scorpion . . . A man of jealousy is the Reverend I have mentioned.'

(Rhys Davies, *The Black Venus*)

One would have to quote the whole body of Caradoc Evans's writings; he seems to have enjoyed inventing a vast number of these things.

Here again are a few sons of the soil in the manner of Pratt, or Manby or Evans or Barber:

Their dimmed and larchy faces, the antique cut of their garments, the slow dramatic voices and timely gestures, as much as their conversation, were for Chris windows upon new terrain. Their talk was a folk art . . . Their feet had walked a primitive earth, the god-fearing Jacob Williams more than any of them.

(Gwyn Jones, *The Flower Beneath the Scythe*)

Or see him posed, leaning on his pitchfork, in a winter-bound wood, looking like an untidy Faun, or some higher deity in sylvan disguise; his garb all run to fringe as usual; his face – well, if unclean, it was certainly not common, but it had never had fair play nor good treatment.

(Bertha Thomas, *Picture Tales from the Welsh Hills*)

Sitting by his winter fires with the rushes of the river tapping at his window, Tom's short life with Martha was the past, present and future in the hands of the Lord. For Tom the Faith knew it all, from Genesis to Revelation and back return journey, and every Sunday at dawn he would stand up to his neck in the river to atone for the sins of the village.

(Alexander Cordell, *The Hosts of Rebecca*)

For some reason, the novels of Hilda Vaughan are particularly loaded with these grotesqueries, possibly because she views the 'natives' around her manor through the eyes of a High-Anglican Tory of the North-West-Frontier imperial type. Scenes such as:

> Cupfuls of tea were emptied into saucers and blown upon with mournful whistling sounds, slice after slice of bread and butter, slab after slab of flat apple tart, bite after bite of spoon cakes [*sic*] disappeared, not without noise, but without mirth or speech.
>
> (*The Invader*)

Further quotation would be tedious. The reader who comes to these writings for the first time will imagine he is in another Cold-Comfort-Farm world and that the whole thing is one huge leg-pull. Sadly, after reading a few first pages, he will realize that these authors are in deadly earnest and that, to them, this is what Wales means. It is, of course, nothing of the sort; it is the Wales and the Welsh caricatures of the Tour books; the last trickle of the late eighteenth- and early nineteenth-century Romantic Movement and almost the only available literature on the subject to the non-Welsh reader for the best part of the last century.

I said 'almost'. The serious student could have read the massive Land Commission Reports of 1896 where much of the real life of rural Wales throughout the century is described objectively. In the end, it is a matter of living roots; the literature I have all too briefly touched on here has none in any really Welsh community and has, therefore, no real identity. To anyone who knows Welsh cultural history much of the contents of the Tour books is, at best, irrelevant; the one outstanding exception being the work of Thomas Pennant.

By 1850, most of the Welsh people could read their own language and the Welsh periodicals – monthlies, bi-weeklies, quarterlies – between 1800 and 1850 must be counted in scores. Owing to the work of Gruffydd Jones's circulating schools and the later efforts of Thomas Charles and the Sunday school movement, literacy in Welsh was fairly general before the middle of the century; that is, before the spread of the National and British elementary schools from the late 1840s onwards. These schools, largely because of the recommendations of the 1847 Blue Books, pursued the insane policy of teaching monoglot Welsh children through the medium of English with the predictable result of a steady decline in literacy of any sort. Indeed, had it not been for the Sunday schools of the Nonconformist denominations, the Welsh press, the local and regional eisteddfodau and similar institutions,

Wales by 1890 would have been almost completely illiterate. It is a measure of the rootlessness of so many anglo-Welsh writers before 1950 that these are precisely the institutions they attack and hold up to ridicule.

From the mid-1850s, too, political interest grew rapidly and by 1868 the traditional power of the anglicized Tory squirearchy had been heroically and successfully contested. Men and women lost their homes in 1868 for opposing the political wishes of their land-lords – particularly in Cardiganshire, the county of Allen Raine's idiot 'bards' and Caradoc Evans's grotesqueries.

But all this is far too wide a matter to be entered on here. Nowadays, the anglo-Welsh story and novel of rural and Welsh Wales are very different from the material discussed here. Significantly, this change has been pioneered by Wyn Griffith, Glyn Jones, and Emyr Humphreys; three writers whose first language is Welsh.

Scotland and Wales – Notes on Nationalist Prehistory

TOM NAIRN

From Planet 34, November 1976

I

People talk of the betrayal by the Tudors, of the decline of the Welsh nobility; of the disappearance of the bardic profession; of the beginnings of the middle class and wealthy merchants who saw nothing in Welsh culture; of the wrong done to the Welsh language; of the anglicizing of education . . . All these are secondary causes. There was a deeper cause: the thing that destroyed the civilization of Wales and ruined Welsh culture, that brought about the dire plight of Wales today, was – *nationalism* . . .

It is fifty years since Saunders Lewis electrified the audience at Plaid Cymru's first Summer School with these words. He was of course warning it against the perils of a merely political, power-hungry nationalism – against a development in any way like what he imagined the course of modern English history to have been. And the warning was accompanied by his plea for a distinctively Welsh development: for a spiritual and cultural nationalism founded on native tradition and looking back to the Middle Ages.

It is about fifty years, too, since Scottish nationalism first assumed an embryo yet vaguely recognizable shape with John MacCormick's National Party of Scotland, in 1928. This broad and already moderate political movement was only one ancestor of today's SNP; but it had begun to lead the way out of what one pioneer, Lewis Spence, saw as the giddy confusion of the cultural nationalists in Scotland. On that side, he wrote, the movement in favour of a national rebirth has attracted 'many of the greatest cranks in Christendom . . . a maelstrom bubbling with the cross-currents of rival and frequently fantastic theories, schemes and notions, riotous with tumultuous personality and convulsive with petulant individual predilection . . . There is no chart, no plan, nothing approaching a serious, practical Scotsman-like policy in either art or politics'. Within a short time the serious and Scotsman-like trend was to emerge triumphant, expelling the culture-heads and littérateurs to a Celtic outer darkness.

Although not many would now swallow Lewis's medievalism, or denounce the Scottish literary renaissance quite so sharply, the two images are still quite familiar. They reflect, respectively, a nationalism in which cultural issues have been predominant, and one in which culture has occupied a very secondary place. It would be exaggerated to say that Welsh nationalism was culturist in outlook while Scottish nationalism was philistine. But few would fail to recognize some truth in the contrast.

This contrast is linked to many others, and to a great deal of mutual misunderstanding. Few Scots easily understand or sympathize with the anguishing dilemmas of the language problem here; on the other hand, Welshmen are often puzzled by the very existence of a nationalist movement without a language of its own. The Scot perceives a colossal fuss being made about nothing; the Welsh nationalist is intrigued by a country where there seems nothing to make a fuss about. Welsh nationalism has always been strikingly internationalist in outlook, finding a natural affinity in many movements and personalities on continental Europe. Scottish nationalism has tended to be somewhat solitary, with only its Gaelic fringe seeking actively for such contacts. Although sometimes voicing the proper sentiments about repressed nationalities and minorities, the SNP mainstream shows distinctly greater enthusiasm for bourgeois Scandinavia than for the Bretons or the Basques.

And so on. We still do not understand each other very well. After fifty years, we ought to understand one another better. It has become practically and politically important to do so, as well as culturally desirable. The pre-history of Welsh and Scottish nationalism is over, and we are now launched into the irreversible process of the history of these movements – a history in which Wales and Scotland will have many more common interests and struggles than when they were tame provinces of empire.

However, it is not so easy. Although it is high time we advanced beyond the base-line of sonorous sermons about solidarity and common foes, it is actually difficult to work out a line of march. The trouble is that we still lack reliable charts.

A mere point-by-point comparison between two national movements – or between two nations – will not reveal or explain very much. Anyone can see that Wales and Scotland are remarkably different countries: but in itself, such observation will remain superficial and a matter for anecdotes rather than analysis. To get farther we have to have some kind of theory that embraces both of them, a theory which deals with places like Wales and Scotland and situates them in an intelligible historical context. Only then, surely, will we be able to determine more realistically where we stand, and what we can do together or hope to learn from one another.

II

The small-state concept . . . seems not only a matter of expediency but of divine plan, and on *this* account makes everything soluble. It constitutes, in fact, nothing but the political application of the most basic organizing and balancing device of nature . . . social blessings are concomitants of social size – small size. (Leopold Kohr, *The Breakdown of Nations* (1957), pp.97–8)

We do not yet have a theoretical framework which will let us do this properly. But this is not all. The trouble is that a phoney theory has arisen, a framework which to some extent actively misleads us in the quest. Were we merely in the normal condition of being in the dark, this would be bad enough. As it is, a lurid light falls across the landscape, and conveys a grossly over-simplified technicolor image.

The theory I have in mind may be called for purposes of argument that of 'cultural colonialism'. Its key notions are those of cultural identity and cultural oppression. The identity it focuses on is that of the smaller, peripheral communities and regions of western Europe; the oppression lies in the way they have been treated by the politically dominant nationalities, the 'core areas'. Metropolitan domination has of course assumed economic form. It has extracted what it needed from these regions, in labour power and other resources; and such development as it has fostered there has been typically lopsided and transitory. However, the theory characteristically emphasizes cultural robbery rather than economic. Large-scale, over-centralized capitalism has eroded or destroyed old community identity. It is through a battle for the recovery of their culture that these regions are reviving today – a struggle primarily against 'alienation', and the brontosaural bureaucracy epitomized by the Swansea Licensing Centre.

In *The Centralist Enemy* John Osmond has summed up many elements of the view as follows: 'The road of the Corporate State leads to a dead end . . . The only rational alternative is a view of life that gives precedence to the concept of community. This requires a new philosophy: one that will put community interests first, even at the expense of economic interests . . . The first requirement of a community is that it be given a human scale in which people can reasonably seek a sense of purpose, responsibility and identity'. Naturally, communities can fight for this philosophy best when they have a strong ethnic and linguistic basis. So these particular vehicles of nationality are seen as especially significant.

I am well aware of the powerful Welsh stake in this new European *Weltanschauung*. Twenty years ago Leopold Kohr produced an advance philosophical benediction of it, in the shape of *The Breakdown of Nations*. More recently, as well as John Osmond, Ned Thomas's *Planet*, Patricia Mayo, and a number of others, have played a part in formulating it. It fits many aspects of Welsh experience rather well, obviously. And as an ideology it probably appeals particularly to the strong cultural dimension of the Welsh national movement.

The taproot of this new smallness-and-beauty world-view may lie in Vienna, like so many others. However, the stirrings of the last decade have produced many new versions of it. Apart from Wales, it is probably most influential now in regions like Occitania and Brittany. Outside Europe it has a certain importance in Canada, in the more anarchist form given it by George Woodcock and his school. From North America also have come two recent *tours de force* on the subject, Michael Zwerin's breathless travelogue of neo-nationalism, *A Case for the Balkanization of Practically Everyone*, and Michael Hechter's imposing study of *Internal Colonialism*.

The latter is particularly important. It represents a definitive academic anointment of the thesis, complete with Ph.D.-worthy tables of figures, prodigious variety of arcane references, and a style of argumentation tortuous to the point of incomprehensibility. Underneath the armour, though, the idea is the same. British capitalist development produced a set of 'internal colonies' in its Celtic fringe, for basically the same reasons as it created external colonization all over the globe. It is the contradictory nature of capitalist growth to do so. After external de-colonization the liberation movements of the interior colonies have begun. 'The most recent crystallisation of Celtic nationalism may ultimately be understood as a trenchant critique of the principle of bureaucratic centralism', he writes. Alas (he continuous in characteristic vein) 'bureaucratic administration seldom seems to enable less advantaged groups to achieve resources equal to those of dominant groups', and the under-advantaged finally tumble to this and demand something better.

Their demand has to be couched in cultural terms. This is why Hechter takes such a kindly view of Wales, and such a chilly one of Scotland. Unable throughout his argument to cope with the fundamental error of locating Scotland in the 'Celtic fringe' at all, he ends by chastizing us for our addiction to GNP and input-output tables. Still recovering from the shock of being told they were really colonized Celts, most SNP-ers would be even more disconcerted to learn that their party's 'lack of a strong appeal to the separate cultural identity of Scotland' means that the SNP 'tacitly admits the cultural indistinguishability of Scotland from England', and is therefore a form of nationalism 'available for cooptation with appropriate ceremony and rewards' by Mother England.

Something is wrong here. It is not merely that the author fails to realize that there might be another sort of 'cultural identity' altogether, one having little to do with literature or emblems, which Scottish nationalists fail to appeal to only because they feel so secure in it. Nor is it the absurd confusion about the Celtic and the non-Celtic in Scottish history. There is also something more deeply amiss on the plane of theory.

This theory is wrong because it lumps too many different things together. Both in analysing the causes and in considering the effects of new nationalism in Europe, it is too superficial. It may be effective ideology, but it rests on rather poor history. Both the causes and the results and the probable future of these movements are more various than it allows for. In spite of Professor Hechter's massive attempt at legitimation, the theory remains too abstract, and too neat.

The acid test of this and similar generalizations is the comparison between Wales and Scotland. Although parts of the same geographical island and ruled by the same state, they are possibly the most different of the emerging countries, above all in a deeper historical sense. As I said, we need a theoretical framework to put them together and they in turn should be the main proving ground of such a theory.

III

In most respects Wales and Scotland are very different countries. Scotland is, to use nineteenth-century terminology, a 'historic nation' . . . Wales on the other hand was a typical 'non-historic nation . . .' Eric Hobsbawm, *The Attitude of Popular Classes towards National Movements for Independence* (1966).

The new political romanticism perceives Wales and Corsica, Scotland and Galicia, Friesland and the Basque Country as so many detachments of the same army, fighting broadly the same battle. No doubt they do have certain things in common. But the only way of being sure what these are is to take full account, at the same time, of the remarkable differences among these territories and situations.

There is one such difference which we ought to concentrate on. More than any other, I think it may help us to grasp the differential location of Scotland and Wales within the larger process. There are at least two contrasting sorts of problem at work. One might define these, in an admittedly crude way, as the problem of relative underdevelopment and the problem of relative over-development.

'Under-development' in this context is of course relative to the general conditions of the 'metropolitan' area of Western Europe. It does not imply any wider identification with Third World under-development (an analogy that has frequently been taken much too literally). Here, it refers to those predominantly agrarian regions – usually of peasants or small cultivators – which were exploited as sources of manpower and food or raw materials during the first century and a half of the Industrial Revolution. They were also typically exploited in a political sense, as the basis for political conservatism in the core areas. And nowadays they have usually become zones of summer holiday development or tourism; Corsica, Occitania, Brittany, Galicia, the Highland region of Scotland, Friesland – these are some among many examples of this situation.

In all these cases uneven development has simply thrust back regions and peoples. It has induced depopulation, cultural impoverishment, a psychology of powerlessness and dependency, and fostered particularly fragmentary or distorted kinds of economic growth. The 'regional policies' of the big states and the Common Market were intended to counteract this pattern, but were probably too little and far too late to do so.

But there are also a number of regions whose key problem has been determined in a wholly different fashion. They occupy a different location altogether in the general history of the economic development process. These are the areas whose problem is that they develop more rapidly and successfully than the territory surrounding them. They have never been 'relatively overdeveloped' in relation to the European core-areas of industrialization, of course – the Ruhr, the English Midlands, and so on. But they have been so in relation to the larger states dominating them politically. They became dynamic, middle-class enclaves in a more backward country – capitalist societies struggling to be free, as it were.

Naturally, there are fewer stories of this kind than of the other. Yet there are considerably more of them than one would think, and their importance is greater than most writers on nationalism have realized. Western Europe contains four such zones: Catalonia and the Basque Country in southern Europe, and Protestant Ulster and Scotland in northern Europe.

Three of these are notorious problems of European history. In Spain the Industrial Revolution took place mainly in the periphery of the state, and in countries with strongly marked separate identities. As a consequence, strong bourgeois societies developed around great urban centres like Bilbao and Barcelona, and constituted a permanent threat to the backward and parasitic state centred on Madrid (a state whose social supports lay, incidentally, in underdeveloped provinces like those just referred to, such as Andalusia, Estremadura, and others). The Civil War was fought partly to solve this problem – or rather, as far as the Spanish Conservatives were concerned, to liquidate it. But as we know, it is still there, rendered more acute by forty years of re-action.

In Ireland the Industrial Revolution also occurred mainly in an ethnic periphery, creating the large Protestant 'city-state' of Belfast. Here, too, uneven development worked to separate the successful middle-class enclave from the more backward land-mass around it. When that southern region managed to constitute its own political state, the relatively overdeveloped north refused assimilation, and of course it continues to reject it today. It does so, in spite of the archaic religious dimension of the conflict, essentially as a more advanced ('civilized' is the ideology for this) social formation fearful of being dragged down and preyed upon.

The fourth case, Scotland, has only recently entered the category. Although an old industrial society like Catalonia, with its own cities and native capitalist class, it previously developed at approximately the same rate and with the same cadences as the larger society it was linked to, industrial England. Only with the dramatic decline of the latter, and the sudden differential impetus given to the Scottish middle class by North Sea oil production, has a crisis of uneven development arisen. Although recent, this fissure is growing extremely rapidly, and creating a political situation basically similar to the others. Even more clearly, the outlook of the previously rather quiescent Scottish bourgeoisie is one of restive impatience with English 'backwardness', London muddle, economic incompetence, state parasitism, and so forth.

Obviously, in any categorization of this kind there are bound to be many qualifications and exceptions. But let us ignore these for the moment, for the sake of the argument. The two types of nationalist dilemma in Western Europe are, respectively: under-developed or pillaged regions that have finally begun to react against this treatment; and quite highly-developed epicentres of industrialization, middle-class cultures that are for one reason or another out of phase with the ruling nation-state, and want separate development to get ahead faster.

Not only are there more of the former than of the latter. They are also much more visible intellectually. In the usual theoretical perspectives they have had a high profile. This is mainly for an interesting reason, very relevant to the comparison between Wales and Scotland. In the general history of nationalism material underdevelopment has always had ideological and cultural overdevelopment as its companion. Faced with the culture of deprivation and enforced ruralism, rebels have always had to compensate with forms of militant idealism. They want to redeem lands devoid of the real powers of redemption – lands without the institutions of self-defence and change, countries by definition robbed of a normally constituted civil society, and so of the normal motor of development. So they have to lay correspondingly extreme emphasis on the ideal society the national movement want to will into existence, often in a very romantic and dream-like fashion.

The intellectual dominance of ideas reflecting this sort of nationalism is not peculiar to present-day Western Europe, of course. Quite the opposite: their salience in the theory of neo-nationalism is due to the world climate already fostered by extra-European national and anti-colonial movements. Those are the mountain-ranges whose influence leads us to look for and find the same shapes in our native hills. If the shapes are not there, we may even be led to invent them (like Professor Hechter).

So far I have made this typology purely in developmental terms. However, there is another important set of co-ordinates we should consider, since they are again very pertinent to the Scotland–Wales contrast. This is the notorious scheme of 'historic' versus 'non-historic' countries.

The notoriety derives from the original misuse: Hegel and Friedrich Engels employed the distinction mainly to discredit the smaller and more backward peoples whom they found a nuisance on the map of Europe. The Slavs, in particular, regularly had this poison served up to them. 'The ruins of peoples', snorted Engels, 'still found here and there and which are no longer capable of a national existence, and are absorbed by the larger nations, or maintain themselves as ethnographic monuments without political significance.' With the exception of Southern Ireland, the ethnographic monuments of Western Europe were not noticeable enough to be worth dismissing.

However – as is usually the case with such thinkers – the basic concept is stronger than its polemical misuse. All it means is that among the great scatter of territories and peoples who had not managed to form their own modern state, some had previous experience of existence as a state and others (the great majority) had not. This state history is very important, although certainly not all-important as they imagined. The inheritance it leaves behind, both institutionally and psychologically, is an enormous asset to any later political movement even if the institutions are destroyed, the recollection of such a past remains prominent in national consciousness. In the nineteenth century the story of the re-emergence of the two nationalities which had been awarded the 'historic nation' accolade, Poland and Hungary, demonstrates this very well.

Among the reviving nationalities of Western Europe at present, two seem clearly to be 'historic nations' in this sense: Scotland and Catalonia. These were states whose independent existence ended at about the same moment, in the early eighteenth century, and then suffered different forms of assimilation by a larger unit. Of course the destruction of the Old Catalan state was much more total; but on the other hand it was dramatically revived by the experience of the short-lived Catalan Republic in the 1930s – an experience which has now itself become something like the 'historic nation' to which the contemporary independence movement looks back.

The other two industrially developed areas I mentioned, Euzkadi and Ulster, were not historic entities in the Hegelian sense. They are nineteenth- and twentieth-century creations. Yet as they now are they do have at least certain aspects of this character. They have both been semi-independent states in living memory: the Basques at the same time as the Catalans, under the liberal Republic of the 1930s, and Northern Ireland from 1922 until 1972. And in quite different ways this recent state existence will remain the crucial factor in the eventual transition to self-rule.

So, of the four relatively developed countries, it would perhaps be fair to say that the Scots have retained an astonishing amount of the structure of their 'historic nationality', the Catalans recovered it; the Basques acquired it; and the Ulster Protestants had it thrust upon them. Although the political parabolas of these state histories are wildly divergent, what they have in common is some relation to industrialization and bourgeois development: it is the more 'middle-class' societies which kept or got some kind of statehood. To them that had was it given (and will be given again).

The other, more numerous underdeveloped countries in

Western Europe are 'non-historic' ones whose contemporary efforts to stop being ethnographic monuments mainly take the cultural form mentioned above: the idealist nationalism of compensation against their history of forced transformation into 'ruins of peoples'.

IV

> Recently Professor Brinley Thomas has been showing that it was the Industrial Revolution which kept the Welsh language alive in the second half of the last century. Were it not for the coal-mining valleys and the industrial undertakings of the South the drift of people from rural Wales would have been the death of Welsh . . .
> (Saunders Lewis, *The Fate of the Language* (1962).)

Returning now to the Wales–Scotland comparison, it is clear where Scotland is located according to the co-ordinates we have traced out. It is one of the most evolved societies among the buried nationalities, in the sense of industrial and social-class development; and it is easily the most intact of the historic nations. A constellation of national institutions was left in existence by the peculiar contract of 1707, and is mostly still there. The separate legal system and courts, with the substantial middle class which serves them, the educational system, the Church of Scotland, the administrative apparatus slowly built up through a whole series of devolutionary concessions over the last century – these famous bulwarks are little diminished. They are surrounded by an interminable and growing list of associations, societies, museums, institutes, clubs, foundations, all as 'Scottish' as their titles, and all concerned with this or that national interest.

So the survival of Scotland's 'identity' has never been primarily a question of literature or of a cultivated self-consciousness. The culture it rests on is a deeper, more articulated social structure, and one not necessarily visible on superficial acquaintance. It is like a set of rock formations, which may be almost underwater reefs from many points of view. It is certainly not to be met with while strolling down Princes Street (or even at the annual conferences of the SNP). Indeed, any displays one is likely to encounter on Princes Street – in the shape of tartan performances in the gardens, pipe bands or 'Highland' restaurants – are guaranteed to be 99 per cent unrelated to these realities.

105

So Scotland might be depicted as high up on the right-hand corner of the graph, with a high developmental and 'historic-nation' quotient. Where does Wales fit in? I believe that its position could be symbolically depicted as dead centre.

Wales does not belong neatly to either of the two first categories I outlined. This is perhaps its peculiarity in the wider European context: perhaps its peculiar importance as well. Historically Wales shares many of the features of forced under-development: depopulation, cultural oppression, fragmentary and distorted development, and so on. These features are strongly evident in the Welsh national movement too, in so far as it has been a battle for the defence and revival of rural-based community and traditional identity – an identity evoked overwhelmingly by literary and musical culture, and having as its mainspring the language question. But of course in another key respect Wales is more akin to the relatively over-developed group: like them, it is a great secondary centre of the European Industrial Revolution.

This ambiguous, midway location is explained by the nature of Welsh industrialization. It was unlike the sort of economic development normally inflicted on backward provinces in being massive, and in transforming (eventually) the conditions of life of most of the population. Speaking of the Heads of the Valleys, the Plaid Cymru Economic Plan states: 'Somewhere on Blackrock, between Gilwern and Brynmawr, there should be a notice: "Welcome to the birthplace of the modern world" – the birthplace of modern industry. Here the early ironmasters established industry on a scale never before seen throughout the world. South Wales became the centre of the iron and steel industry and the techniques developed were copied in every developing country. . . For once, Wales led the world.' Nothing remotely comparable could be said of any of the other European countries whose nationalisms superficially resemble that of Wales.

However, this industrialization was like that of such periphery regions in being overwhelmingly guided from outside: it was not the work of a native entrepreneurial bourgeoisie accumulating capital for itself (as in Scotland or the Basque Country) but much more like an invasion from outside. Previously without the main motor of effective separate development, an urban middle class, Wales now acquired an English or at least highly Anglicized bourgeoisie. This combination, an industrialization at once enormous and decentred, was probably unique to Wales.

If we turn now to the other broad distinction made earlier, that between so-called historic and non-historic nationalities, the position of Wales is again less clear-cut than might appear at first glance. Although not an example of 'historic' nationhood in the sense of Poland, Scotland or Catalonia, it is not a straightforward case of the 'non-historic' either.

The non-historic features of the Welsh past are very well known: 'a territory inhabited by an agrarian population united by . . . a primitive social and economic structure and by the fact of not speaking English', as Eric Hobsbawm has put it, without much urban development until the Industrial Revolution, and without an indigenous aristocracy or bourgeoisie. None the less, even in the form which it assumed, the south Wales Industrial Revolution could not help altering the meaning of these conditions. We saw before how ethnic-linguistic nationalism has been usually a compensatory reaction to retardation. But what is striking about the Welsh reaction in this comparative view is its size and success.

None of these other European regions knew an institutionalized culture movement comparable to the Welsh one of the nineteenth century – a movement which, on the foundation of eighteenth-century Welsh Nonconformity, extended from the renewed Eisteddfod to the University Colleges of Wales, from the Welsh National Library to the great museums of Cardiff. Although still in the narrower sense 'cultural' – concerned primarily with *Kultur* – here is a movement which from the beginning passed beyond simple poetic protest or the dreams of small intellectual coteries. It created something like the cultural form, the tracery of a nation where no state had existed. It became a substantial force in the new civil society of nineteenth- and twentieth-century Wales, even without political, legal, and other institutions.

The movement was in reaction against the Anglicizing capitalist invasion of the south – yet also to some extent based upon it. It sought to defend the language and traditional life – yet also to adapt the nation to a more modern existence. As Saunders Lewis recognized in his famous 1962 broadcast, the Industrial Revolution which so threatened Welsh language and life also gave it a new chance of life – indeed, the only chance of surviving permanently and avoiding the fate of Cornish, Irish and Scottish Gaelic. By becoming the language of the industrial Valleys, Welsh had come part of the way towards the condition of Catalan, in Western Europe, or Czech or Slovene among the smaller ex-Hapsburg countries of Eastern Europe.

To say that the Welsh situation is unusually central, or suspended between the standard alternatives of European neo-nationalism, is of course to say that it is unusually divided. It is not necessary here to comment on the strong antagonisms and dilemmas built into the national movement by this history: Welsh versus Anglo-Welsh, Adfer versus bilingualism, ethnic traditionalists versus south-eastern modernizers, and so on. All that should be stressed is that this internal conflict has a wider comparative significance. It reflects, within Wales and Welsh nationalism, certain deeper dilemmas of choice which can be seen operating everywhere else. In the Welsh knot the usual forces of uneven development have been tied together unusually closely and graphically.

V

Q. Do you believe that a 'sense of Welsh nationhood' is more consistent with one particular attitude of life and affairs than any other?

A. If I catch the drift of the question, I would say that I do feel that the Welsh National spirit has had to bank itself up in the Welsh Language for want of being able to express itself politically . . .

John Cooper Powys, Answer to Wales Questionnaire, 1939,
Obstinate Cymric (1947).

What happens to Scotland on the road to self-government has some significance for other countries. But less than might appear superficially. It would be principally through a general demonstration-effect, by which the constitution of any new state in the west of Europe will encourage the rest. The paradox of Scotland's strong 'historic-nation' status is that it makes the country less relevant and weaker as an example, above all in relation to the more typical countries where cultural nationalism prevails.

What happens to Wales is likely to be far more influential in the long run. This is the point of the Welsh centrality in the nationalist spectrum which I have tried to analyse. All Western Europe's deprived and reawakened peoples want and need stronger economic development, for example. Given the condition they start from, such development is bound to be in large measure from outside, whether by multinationals or by investment and aid from other countries. Wales had already gone through this, in the most violent and chaotic fashion: such de-centred, invasive industrialization created the whole problem of modern nationalism in Wales. Hence, how the Welsh national movement – or a future Welsh political state – copes with the question is directly relevant in all these places.

If Welsh nationalism can arrive at a viable political integration of its contending elements, then many others can hope to. If the ideal, 'cultural' nation can be reconciled with the industrial one here, then the formula may eventually be copiable elsewhere. Nationalism has always been a struggle to connect romantically conceived tradition and culture with the need for modern social and economic development. In modern Welsh history these two things are thrust together with special intensity, imposing a duty of political leadership on the nationalist movement.

The romantic theory of cultural colonialism described earlier sees all the resurgent nationalities as essentially the same (and all are of course also 'unique' in the same way). The less idealist account I have tried to begin here perceives them as different, even opposed, and certainly classifiable in a number of interesting ways. A materialist theory focuses primarily upon their real location in the modern process of socio-economic development – it sees them as real places, in this sense, no less real and diverse than the bigger nation-states they are still attached to. But I am conscious of having done little more than suggest the starting-point of a theory of this kind. There are many things we have not looked at at all here.

For example, the question of the causation of the wave of new nationalist movements in Western Europe. It seems very unlikely that these have arisen out of a general protest against impersonal centralism, or against the synthetic culture of bureaucracy and multinational business. Presumably there are deep economic changes behind the new climate. But why are they especially operative in three of the old states – the United Kingdom, Spain and France – and unimportant or non-existent in others? Why should the new forms of inter-dependence promoted by multi-nationals have undermined these ex-imperial nations but – e.g. – left the Netherlands largely unaffected? Why should Italy, a country marked by gross and longstanding uneven development, have been untroubled by separatism in the recent past?

These are all questions that seem to call for much more discriminating and realistic answers than the ones nationalists are at present tending to give. The same might be said of attempts to prospect a nationalist future. The results, as well as the causes, of a new nationalist success are not easy to see. There will be a new map of Europe. But it is not likely to resemble the diagrams of a subdivided, small-nation continent which became fashionable a few years ago.

Returning – in conclusion – to the Scotland–Wales direct comparison, what further inferences can be drawn from the argument so far? I have chosen to emphasize our differences, and to plead for a more cautious, sceptical approach to inter-nationalist relations. The aim of this is to reinforce such relations – on the assumption that realism ought to balance ideology, and will preserve what is positive in the latter by doing so.

Like other movements, these ones have the strengths of their weaknesses (or vice versa). The great Welsh cultural movement, with which Welsh nationalism is so closely associated, may have led to a certain over-emphasis upon these factors. There is a great deal both in Welsh history and in current ideology that underwrites this emphasis. Looking back again to that address of fifty years ago, one cannot help being struck by the extreme prudence – even fear – with which political authority is regarded. 'The Welsh civilizing concept is the only worthwhile argument for self-government,' said Lewis; '. . . that being so, we must have self-government. Not independence. Not even unconditional freedom. But just as much freedom as may be necessary to establish and safeguard civilization in Wales.' A political state not one hundred-and-one per cent sanctified by cultural needs and values is, frankly, the work of the Devil of Materialism. Cultural nationality and power-hungry nationalism are conceived as real antitheses.

Unless I am greatly mistaken, this underlying attitude is still quite strongly felt in Wales. It must be the only country where one regularly hears nationalists denouncing nationalism. Since Saunders

Lewis's antithesis is not a real one, and no state institutions can ever exist purely and solely to cultivate cultural traditions in that sense, I suppose this is a kind of weakness. I suppose therefore that the Welsh national movement ought to give the Devil his due more than it has done in times past, and try to adopt a mildly more Machiavellian attitude to the state and the other non-cultural institutions of power. But it is hardly for me to make recommendations about that.

As far as the Scots are concerned, I feel on stronger ground. The weakness of the Scottish national movement is the contrary of the Welsh one: it is the consistent, canny philistinism of the movement from its earliest days, and the chronic divorce between what Lewis Spence called the 'practical, Scotsman-like' policy and the somewhat erratic flight of the intelligentsia. The Scottish movement benefits from the existence of a powerful middle class; but one of the traits of that class is a powerful distrust of culture in any spectacular form. Along with the seriousness and practicality, there is of course a dreadful conceit buried in this outlook. One might describe it as the unjustified conceit of a once 'historic nation' which deep down still feels itself to be such. Nor should one forget that, while in Wales Calvinism figures as a creed of prolonged popular opposition to the high and mighty, in Scotland it has been mainly a creed *of* the high and mighty. The Welsh may be too apprehensive about state power; the Scots are not apprehensive enough. Authority appears to them naturally dressed in a Minister's gown and a halo.

With the imminence of self-government, this Scotsman-like weakness has become a more tangible threat. Never having imagined an ideal nation with the visionary enthusiasm found in so many other nationalist movements, they are at a loss. There is a sudden, rather belated rush to invent actual things to do. The SNP has produced a philosophy, or something like a philosophy, bearing some distinct resemblances to the radical ideology of other European nationalist movements (I refer to the newly published volume, *The Radical Approach: Papers on an Independent Scotland*). In deference to the new mood, one or two intellectuals were seen openly circulating at the recent party conference in Motherwell.

Satire apart, Scottish nationalism desperately needs to counter this malformation, by integrating politics and culture more deliberately than in the past. We need new institutions to do this – new means of forging links between practical politics and cultural ideas, between the institutions of power and the imagination of a new nation. I have myself been involved in recent months in the formation of such a body, an International Institute specifically concerned with the problem. It is intended as a centre to foster just that interaction between the political and cultural movements which has been lacking in the past.

The title 'International' is itself a recognition that we cannot accomplish such a task by ourselves, or with our own resources. We are compelled to look outwards to tackle it seriously. To study the culture of a nation inwardly demands, in today's circumstances, that one look at it comparatively. A realistic international perspective is not only ethically desirable, but intellectually – and, increasingly, practically – necessary. A cultural nationalism that fails to make this effort will end up drowned in its own mythology.

Given the evident complementarity of Welsh and Scottish problems, Wales is one of the places to which we look with the keenest sense of useful difference. Countries so different can never become 'like each other' in a merely imitative sense. This need not matter. What matters is to learn to change, inevitably in one's own way, through the constant stimulus of contact and studied comparison. This is, for us, the new internationalism which ought to arise out of Europe's new wave of national movements.

Crow-stepped Gables

ROBIN GWYNDAF

From Planet 34, November 1976

As far as we can ascertain it was Rhisiart Clwch (or Sir Richard Clough), a wealthy Denbigh-born man, who first introduced crow-stepped gables into Wales when he built Plas Clough, near Denbigh, in the parish of Henllan. This was in 1567, the same year as he married the celebrated Katheryn of Berain. One of his descendants still lives in the house today.

Sir Richard Clough was also probably the first, it seems, to build houses in Wales with walls of load-bearing bricks. Plas Clough itself was one of two such houses which he designed. The other one was the strange house of Bachegraig, in the parish of Tremeirchion, Vale of Clwyd, built in 1567, with many windows in the roof, rising from floor to floor in the shape of a pyramid. (Four tiers of dormer windows in a steep-pitched Flemish roof, similar to the windows at Bachegraig, may be seen today in the old Myddleton Arms, now incorporated in The Castle Hotel in St Peter's Square, Rhuthun.)

Sometime after June 1567 the poet Wiliam Cynwal composed a *cywydd* 'to send the hawk to call Richard Clough and Katheryn of Berain home from Antwerp':

> (The bird is told to beg them to return home quickly to inspect the noble building – the court which is a mirror to the country. The mansion is strong like a mighty rock, its walls like those of Troy and its tower rising into a fine summit. It is a protection to Christendom and is comparable with [the house of] Calais. It is a castle to welcome a host of people at a cost which is as much as that

of [the famous feast said to have been held by Arthur at] Caerleon. Its stone floor is excellent and its parlours full of mead. It is a remarkable mansion – the St Paul's of Gwynedd. Indeed, there never was, and never will be, a house so spacious and beautiful.)

> ... Troea mur, grym tramawr graig,
> Trum iach agr, tŵr Machegraig;
> Cwlas i Gred, Calais gron,
> Castell llu fel cost Lleon;
> Pur lawr main, parlyrau medd,
> Plas hynod, Powls i Wynedd.
> Yn wir ni bu, cu rhag haint,
> Wiwdeg gwmwd, dŷ cymaint ...

Unfortunately, Bachegraig was completely demolished by John Salusbury Piozzi, the heir of Mrs Hester Lynch Piozzi (Dr Johnson's Mrs Thrale) soon after the latter's death in 1821. However, the old gate-house still exists today, part of which was converted into the present farmhouse at Bachegraig. This Renaissance-type gate-house was probably the first of its kind to be built in Wales, and here we see another aspect of Sir Richard Clough's architectural innovations.

In his capacity as factor to Sir Thomas Gresham in Antwerp, Richard Clough was one of the key men responsible for strengthening the financial position of the English government during the first decade of Queen Elizabeth's reign. Elizabethan architecture, as we well know, was greatly influenced by the Low Countries, especially Flanders. Because Richard Clough was stationed in Antwerp, the entrepôt of Europe at that time, he was, naturally, in an ideal position to be fully acquainted with Flemish building techniques. For example, not only was he one of the first to suggest a Royal Exchange for London, but also most of the materials for building it were imported from Antwerp under his personal supervision.

Both Plas Clough and Bachegraig show clear Flemish influence in design and detail, and the tradition that they were built with the help of Flemish craftsmen using imported materials is probably well founded. Simwnt Fychan, another contemporary poet, says in his *cywydd* that Richard Clough designed and built a court:

(a beautiful building which will benefit the island. He made at Bachegraig (as if it was situated in Berwick-upon-Tweed or Boulogne) a fort, white-washed with lime. It contains hewn stones

– stones from Antwerp – according to his own desire. Stones, marble-stones and timber have been placed where they are best suited. It is a fine mansion.)

> Adeilodd, cyfleodd lys, –
> Adail wen a dâl ynys.
> Gwnâi, fal Berwig neu Fwlen,
> Gaer galch ym Machegraig wen.
> Main nadd, fal y mynnodd 'fô,
> Main o Anwarp maen' yno,
> Main o gwŷdd, man y gwedda
> Marbwl ystôns, mawrblas da.

Crow-stepped gable houses were fairly common in Flanders. A glance, for example, at the Hotel van Lyere or 'The English House' (which, after 1558, accommodated the British merchants in Antwerp) will at once bring out the resemblance. Richard Clough himself could have resided at this house for some time.

The two Flemish-styled houses were so unusual in the Vale of Clwyd and built in so short a time that they made a great impression on the minds of the local inhabitants. Consequently, many legends became connected with them, especially Bachegraig.

No wonder that these houses were so strange! Was not the Devil himself the chief architect? Indeed, in one of the houses, namely Bachegraig, it is said that His Grace always reserved a room for his own free use! It is also said that the bricks were baked in the Devil's own infernal pits and that he supplied a daily quota to the builders by placing them along the side of a near-by brook which is still called by the present family at Bachegraig today Nant y Cythraul (the Devil's brook).

But perhaps the most colourful legend is that which relates how Sir Richard spent many hours every night in a secret, windowless room at the top of the roof at Bachegraig to study the stars, or, more often than not, to hold conferences with the Devil. One evening, according to the story, Sir Richard's wife, Katheryn, became suspicious. She crept quietly upstairs and peeped through the keyhole. There she saw her husband in deep conversation with His Majesty. She instantly opened the door, but the Devil seized Sir Richard in his arms and dashed through the wall with his prey, causing bricks and mortar to fly!

At Bachegraig Richard Clough also built large warehouses, and tradition says that out of regard to his native land he had intended to introduce trade into the country and use these buildings for that purpose. Tradition also tells us that, to foster such commerce, he had formed a scheme for cutting a canal from Rhuddlan to Bachegraig, or of making the River Clwyd navigable. But he died in 1570 *yn rhy gynnar* ('too early') when he was only about forty years of age, before this scheme could be implemented.

Over a hundred of Richard Clough's letters are known to have survived, preserved in the Public Record Office. These letters clearly reflect his sincerity of purpose, his devotion to his work and loyalty to his fellow men. Sir William Cecil, the Secretary of State at that time, admired his skill. Humphrey Lhuyd, the geographer, referred to him as *vir integerrimus* ('a very honest man'). When he died, he was greatly mourned by the poets. And, in 1662, Thomas Fuller referred to him as one of the 'worthies' of his day and age.

He was a man of vision. So too were many of his long line of descendants, such as: Arthur Hugh Clough, the poet, Anne Jemima Clough, first principal of Newnham College, Cambridge, and, in our own days, Sir Clough Williams-Ellis, the grand old man of architecture.

In the field of architecture the Renaissance was the 'Age of Display' – the age of the 'great rebuilding'. Many of the landed gentry now had more money, and one way of displaying this new wealth was to alter their existing homes and build new ones on a scale unknown before. Furthermore, all this coincided with important developments in building techniques.

Plas Clough and Bachegraig may be regarded as the first two houses in Wales which clearly reflect the Renaissance. It was an age with the emphasis on splendour and ornament. This, it seems, is why the stepped gables were included in Plas Clough. It was a purely ornamental Renaissance feature, which also reminds us perhaps of gentry pretension, so characteristic of the period. It had little or no connection with the few examples of medieval, Graeco-Romano military-type stepped gables to be seen today in south Wales, for example at Plastŷ'r Esgob, Tŷ Ddewi (St David's). Nor did it have, it seems, much in common with the stepped gable houses to be seen in Scotland, East Anglia and other parts of the eastern coastline. In the Scottish and English instances the use of stepped gables was probably the result of importing clay tiles from the Low Countries. There stepped gables were built mainly for practical reasons. A plank was placed on the steps of the gable ends across the roof for the purpose of laying and repairing the tiles.

By adopting the north German Gothic type of stepped gables prevalent in Flanders Sir Richard Clough began a completely new architectural fashion in Wales, which was followed by other gentry, such as Robert Wynne, who built Plas Mawr, Conwy, in 1576. He, too, apparently had lived for some time in the Low Countries. The fashion was popular until the eighteenth century, but it was mainly confined to the counties of Denbigh and Flint, with a few examples in Merioneth, Caernarfonshire and Anglesey. These crow-stepped gable houses in north Wales, therefore, are unique in Britain.

We should also note the significance of the fact that the greatest number of stepped gables are located in Clwyd, because from the literary and architectural point of view, at least, the Vale of Clwyd and its surrounding districts was the cradle of the Renaissance in Wales.

Note

For further information relating to crow-stepped gable houses, see Peter Smith, *Houses of the Welsh Countryside* (1975), pp. 270–1, 518–19. For further information relating to Sir Richard Clough and his connection with these houses, see the third part of my study in *Transactions of the Denbighshire Historical Society*, Vol. 22 (1973); pp. 48–86. An exhibition of photographs of these houses was mounted in 1975 for the North Wales Arts Association.

Catalunya – Back in the Running

MIQUEL STRUBELL I TRUETA

From Planet 39, August 1977

The Catalan parties scored a most impressive victory in the Spanish parliamentary elections of 15 June. Joan Reventós of the Catalan Socialist Party held talks on autonomy with the king and the Spanish prime minister within days of the election result, and the government in Madrid has since announced interim autonomous powers pending full constitutional measures. Taradellas, Catalunya's exiled president, has flown in from France, providing the constitutional link with the Generalitat, the Catalan Parliament of the 1930s. The restoration of the Statute of Autonomy of 1932 and of the Generalitat is the number one priority of all the Catalan parties and it is in everyone's interests that Catalunya's institutions should be speedily restored, so that Catalans may say 'Viva España' and Spaniards 'Visca Catalunya' as happened in the Spanish Cortes on 9 September 1932, when the first statute was passed.

Forty-seven seats in Congress were at stake in the election in Catalunya. First place went to the Catalan Socialist Party, an independent party which formed an election pact with the Spanish Socialist Workers' Party led by Felipe González, and which undoubtedly owed many votes to the latter's TV appearance at peak hours. Second was the Pacte Democràtic with eleven seats. This is a nationalist grouping of liberals, social democrats, and a smaller group of socialists. The Pacte was disappointed by the results in the province of Barcelona, where it polled 16 per cent of the votes instead of an expected 25 per cent; but it came top of the

118

poll in Girona and Lleida. Third came the Madrid-inspired Democratic Centre Union, whose views on autonomy are rather dubious, with nine seats, and one seat behind them the Catalan Communists, who were very pleased at coming second in Barcelona. Two seats were won by the Christian Democratic Party of Catalunya whose Spanish counterparts failed utterly in the rest of Spain. One seat went to Esquerra de Catalunya, the party that won overwhelmingly in the 1930s, and to which Macià and Companys belonged; and one seat also to the Popular Alliance, the ultra-Conservative Madrid-based party led by Manuel Fraga Iribarna, formerly Spanish ambassador in London. This party, which is estimated to have spent some £13 million on election propaganda, failed dismally throughout Spain, and its array of former Franco ministers could only muster 17 seats out of a total of 350 in Congress.

All in all, then, the Madrid parties won only 10 seats out of the 47 in Catalunya, and the Catalan parties are agreed on their immediate aims, as we have seen. All this augurs well for the re-establishment of flourishing Catalan institutions and culture.

Catalan culture, though regarded by most people as one of Europe's 'minority' cultures, not only enjoys a far more healthy status, and looks forward to a more promising future, than many other cultures – Breton and Scottish Gaelic for instance – but its language is more widely spoken than a number of important European national languages: Danish, Finnish, Norwegian, Slovak and Albanian. Though there are no official census figures regarding the total number of Catalan speakers, most estimates put the figure somewhere between six and seven million. At the same time, Catalan culture is widely expected to be at the start of a tremendous upsurge in the next few years. In this article we shall be looking at the present state of the Catalan language and culture, and comment on some of the factors that both threaten and encourage its development.

Historically speaking, Catalan is a Romance language that evolved in the mountain valleys of the eastern Pyrenees following the collapse of the Roman Empire, at the same time as Occitan, French, Castilian, Portuguese and the other members of this linguistic family. Though dating the emergence of Catalan as a fully fledged language is a hazardous business, because of the lack of written evidence, we may quote Joan Gili:

> The earliest documents entirely written in Catalan date from the
> second half of the eleventh century. In somewhat earlier Latin doc-
> uments, however, Catalan words and phrases appear in the text in
> increasing numbers.

The development of Catalan, and its geographical extension,
run parallel with political events from this time on. Catalunya
became independent from the Franks under Count Berenguer
Ramon I (1018–35), who made Barcelona his capital. At this time
the Moors controlled the greater part of the Iberian peninsula, and
the Christians, whose strongholds were in the mountains that run
east–west across the north of Spain, gradually fought their way
southwards, reclaiming land from the Moors. In 1137 Catalunya
united with Aragon to form the Kingdom of Aragon. Aragon
proper is a landlocked region, with a harsh climate; its capital
was and is at Saragossa. This uniting of forces led to a great expansion both southwards in Spain and eastwards across the
Mediterranean. The Catalan language followed in the wake of this
expansion, both to the Kingdom of Valencia (of which all but some
inland areas was colonized by settlers from Lleida, or Lérida) and
to the Balearic Islands. Aragonese spread south only weakly, and
was eventually replaced by Castilian from the west: today it is
spoken in only a handful of valleys in the Pyrenees. The expansion
in the thirteenth century gave rise to what are today termed 'Els
Països Catalans' – the Catalan lands – and at this point we may as
well define as clearly as we can the area in which Catalan is
spoken today.

The Catalan-speaking area comprises an area of about 22,000
square miles, and has a population of a little over nine and a half
million people (1974). This is not to say, of course, that all the
inhabitants speak Catalan, but we will look at this question later
on. The area consists of the whole of Catalunya proper (12,000
sq.m.), most of Valencia (6,000 sq.m.), the Balearic Islands (2,000
sq.m.), Rosselló in France (1,000 sq.m.), Andorra (180 sq.m.) and a
strip of land about ten to fifteen miles wide, and about a hundred
miles long, running down the border between Catalunya and
Aragon, in Aragon (1,000 sq.m.). There is also a linguistic enclave
in Alghero (Sardinia), a small town which reminds us that the
Catalan-Aragonese empire in the fourteenth and fifteenth centuries extended across the Mediterranean, including the Kingdom
of Naples, Sicily, and the Duchies of Athens and Neopatria in

Greece, as well as Sardinia. The case of Rosselló (or Roussillon) in southern France is worth mentioning in more detail. It was part of Catalunya throughout the Middle Ages, and France's attempts to annex it – based on the somewhat dubious argument that France had a claim to all land north of the line running from peak to peak across the Pyrenees – finally succeeded in the Treaty of the Pyrenees (1659), which was followed by uprisings and rebellions in Rosselló at least until the French Revolution (1789). Following the annexation, Rosselló was subjected to an intense campaign to wipe out its links, including the language, with the rest of Catalunya. Even its church was 'de-catalanized' (a process paralleled by Franco after the 1936–9 Civil War), and many monasteries were closed down, including Sant Miquel de Cuixà, most of whose unique early Romanesque cloisters later 'emigrated' to New York, where they can be admired. Despite this campaign, however, Catalan is still well rooted in Rosselló (or 'Catalunya-Nord', as many Catalans call it). However, it clearly occupies a culturally inferior position, or a diglossic one, with respect to French.

Let us now take a closer look at the number of Catalan-speakers. As regards Rosselló, there are no census data, though two general practitioners – Dr Català and Dr Carrère – noted down the language used in all the families they visited on their rounds over a period of years, and found that the overall proportion of Catalan-speaking families was about 50 per cent – two-thirds in rural areas, and one-third in urban ones. Taking the population as 305,000 (1975 official estimate), this gives a total of 152,000 Catalan-speakers, roughly. In the three main Catalan-speaking areas of Spain (Catalunya, Valencia and the Balearic Islands), we must deal in estimates since again we have no census data. However, a number of studies can be used to obtain a fair idea. It seems fairly safe to conclude that the number of Catalan-speakers lies somewhere in the region of six to seven million. What is more, nearly all this number actually use Catalan on a daily basis; since Catalan had been kept out of schools until comparatively recently, the situation is quite different from, say, that of Gaelic in Éire where only a small proportion of those who know the language actually use it.

Other studies which look at the proportion of Catalan-speakers tend to be limited to geographical areas – e.g. Barcelona city – or to more restricted sub-samples, e.g. schoolchildren. Badia i Margarit found that 63 per cent of a sample of 223 Barcelona householders visited personally by his research students normally spoke Catalan. The sample, though randomly chosen, is obviously very small; nevertheless we can be fairly confident that the true figure lies within 6 per cent of his result.

Another study looked at the language of schoolchildren in Barcelona and gave Catalan as the language, or one of the languages, used in the homes of 45 per cent of the sample. A further 17 per cent stated that they were 'oral bilinguals', though Castilian was the language at home. We may now look at the Castilian-speakers in a little more detail.

The most striking point is that nearly all of them are either first- or second-generation immigrants from the rest of Spain, at least as far as Catalunya proper is concerned. Until the post-Civil War immigration flood began, the proportion of Catalan-speakers must have been extremely high. Today, the only long-established Catalan families that do not use Catalan as the family language (leaving to one side mixed marriages of course) are to be found in the upper-middle class élite who apparently regard Castilian as a 'superior' language. Most Catalan-speakers treat them as cultural heretics, and their importance is small in Catalunya. Nevertheless, in Valencia Catalan is being spoken less and less in middle-class homes, and the same applies in Rosselló: the signs of diglossia are much clearer in these areas than in Catalunya proper. Other Castilian-speakers who are unlikely to become culturally integrated are civil servants in government posts appointed from Madrid, and their families. But the main bulk of Castilian-speakers are first-generation immigrants who provide unskilled manpower in Catalan industry. Many studies have shown that they do tend to be absorbed culturally within a couple of generations. We can cite, for example, the work of a sociologist (Maluquer), an anthropologist (Esteva Fabregat) and of several sociolinguists such as Francesc Vallverdú and Rafael Ninyoles. It seems safe to say that the number of people who can speak Catalan is increasing steadily. This is surprising when compared with most other minority cultures in Europe, and yet the evidence is quite clear. For example, the FOESSA study mentioned previously asked housewives what the first language they learned was, and what language they spoke with their husbands. In both Catalunya and Valencia the trend was for the second percentage to be higher than the first: 52 per cent and 61 per cent in Catalunya, 47 per cent and 53 per cent in the Valencian case. In the Balearic Islands there is little immigration and both figures were therefore virtually the same, and very high – 84 per cent.

The reason why immigrants are learning Catalan is, basically, that Catalan enjoys high status in Catalunya. It is the language of the well-off and the boss, and is therefore one of the aims of the social climber. The massive working-class immigration has pushed Catalans up the social ladder, and enhanced the social status of their language and culture (through no special merits of its own, needless to say!). A large number of studies have looked at motivational aspects of this question, and all agree that a large majority of immigrants want their children to grow up speaking Catalan. It is worth pointing out that the only way to do this until quite recently was to pick it up in the playground or the street, as Catalan was banned from schools, mass media and public events by the Franco regime until just a few years ago.

All the same, the other side of the coin is not so encouraging. Since the Civil War immigration has been on such a huge scale that Catalunya has at times been incapable even of housing all new arrivals, and shanty towns mushroomed up round Barcelona. Though these have fortunately disappeared, the hundreds of thousands of non-Catalan workers now live in what used to be quiet little towns in the Barcelona hinterland. Today, these cities – Terrassa, Sabadell, Badalona, L'Hospitalet – are packed with Castilian-speakers, leaving Catalans in a clear minority. One study showed that in these cities only 29.2 per cent of the primary schoolchildren speak Catalan at home. This puts Catalan in a critical spot: there are cultural ghettoes where it is not the everyday language of most of the people. Thus many second-generation immigrants are not getting the opportunity of learning the language. This can be understood by Welshmen when they realize that Welsh began to decline, in the south, soon after the opening up of coal-mines and steelworks led to the inflow of workers from England; and eventually Welsh virtually ceased to exist there as a living community language. There are many differences – especially in the sense that Catalans are very conscious of the problem, and that their language enjoys considerable prestige – but nevertheless dire warnings have been voiced. The link between the country and the language that has allowed people to state quite correctly that 'everyone born in Catalunya speaks Catalan' for a thousand years, is in danger of being broken, and this could have consequences which many other cultures have suffered. Let us end this section, though, on an optimistic note provided by Professor Glanville Price, who has looked at the plight of many west European minority cultures: 'Catalan is the most striking exception to the gloomy tale of one-way-only assimilation.'

To complete the background of Catalunya's culture we must consider her recent past. Catalunya lost all her autonomous rights – which had survived the formation of the Kingdom of Spain when Ferdinand and Isabella married in 1469 and subsequently inherited their respective kingdoms (Aragon and Castile) – as recently as 1714, when Philip V invaded Catalunya and imposed upon it the centralist 'Ley de Nueva Planta', closing down and abolishing all her institutions and traditional rights (legal, university, self-government and cultural), and imposing direct rule from Madrid. Following a cultural revival – 'La renaixença' – in the mid-nineteenth century, Catalan nationalism erupted at the beginning of this century, and led to the Catalan 'Estatut d'Autonomia' which restored the Catalan government ('La Generalitat') and paved the way for a prolific effort to provide Catalunya with all the trappings, cultural and otherwise, of a modern nation. However, the Republic was not forgiven for 'yielding' to Catalan pressure, and the Spanish Civil War, with General Franco becoming leader of the Nationalist Army, led to the abolition yet again of Catalunya's autonomy and her institutions. In addition, a virulent campaign to wipe out the language was undertaken. Catalans (and Basques too) were told in no uncertain terms to 'speak the language of the Empire' (*sic*) and were treated very much as rebellious colonies of Castile. Catalan was banned from schools when Irish Gaelic was being taught throughout the Republic of Eire, and the first *ysgol gymraeg* was being opened in Wales; it was not allowed in any official dealings whatever (even telegrams). It was not permitted in any public events, in newspapers (in pre-war days all newspapers in Catalunya were in Catalan except for 12 of Barcelona's 19 daily papers). Catalan literature skidded to a censored halt (1933 figure: 740. In the seven years after the end of the Civil War in 1939, only 12 books were allowed to be published, of which 11 were reprints).

But two movements in the sixties began to reverse the tide. One was the Second Vatican Council and its recommendation that Mass be said in the language of the people. This was quickly taken up by the Catalan clergy, and especially by the monastery at Montserrat, which has for centuries been a spiritual and cultural centre for Catalans. The second was the 'Nova Cancó Catalana', a movement of folk singers in Catalunya – including many from Mallorca and Valencia – which, in spite of insistent harassment by the authorities managed to gather momentum thanks to its massive grass-roots support, especially among the young. Names such as Raimon, Joan Manuel Serrat, Mar del Mar Bonet, Lluís Llach and Ovidi Montllor have played an invaluable part in bringing about the reawakening of Catalan feeling which is such a feature of Catalunya today. They have also helped to counter the centralist theory that Valencian, Mallorcan and Catalan are different 'dialects', for any of them can sing quite happily anywhere in the Catalan lands, without language problems.

Attention has been fixed on the election of 15 June, and its results. But as well as the political activity one should note that cultural activity behind the scenes is quite overwhelming in scale. One organization, 'Omnium Cultural', has 19,000 members, and is working hard, without a peseta from the Madrid government, to train teachers of Catalan (so far, 1,100 have passed through their hands), to organize and run Catalan classes in schools (this year 227,000 children are being catered for by Omnium), to sell Catalan books (to date, their library-on-wheels service has sold 335,900 books), and to subsidize research. The 'Institut d'Estudis Catalans', a highly respected centre for cultural and scientific research founded in 1907, which had to live through a semi-clandestine period after Franco invaded Catalunya, is in full academic swing. Catalan is once more back in the universities, both as a subject and as a medium of instruction. No field of human thought has been left uncovered in recent Catalan literature. Catalan culture is bounding back into all aspects of this little nation's life. To crown the effort, a gigantic 'Congrés de Cultura Catalana', constituting a broadly based analysis of all aspects of Catalunya, including her language, literature, ecology, educational system, and nearly twenty other similar fields, has brought together thousands of experts and enthusiasts. They are trying to make up for lost time, having experienced almost forty years of right-wing centralist dictatorship. The whole project is estimated to cost about 300 million pesetas – over £2.5 million.

The will to overcome the problems is there. The Catalan people are economically well-off. Catalan culture is returning to its rightful place in Europe, though the threat of another senseless period of centralist rule and domination gives the whole task a sense of urgency that outsiders might not understand. Let us hope that Catalunya – indeed, Spain as well – receives active support from all over Europe, in this massive uphill task of cultural recovery.

The Other Aneurin Bevan

ROBERT GRIFFITHS

From Planet 41, January 1978

Few people today would presume to write an essay on the late Aneurin Bevan, cowed – as they should be – by the knowledge that it could only wither in the shadow of Michael Foot's masterful biography! Yet, as Foot himself would probably concede, there is one field of issues which entirely escapes the expansive grasp of those two volumes.

Foot wrote the first volume of his predecessor's biography in the early 1960s and completed volume two by early 1973. Devolution had not then assumed the significance it presently commands, whilst the Welsh-language controversies of this and the last decade would appear – even now – to dwell only on the periphery of Michael Foot's political consciousness. More realistically, no prime minister had yet passed the slippery Devolution ball to Michael with instructions to jink through a pack of hostile Labour MPs with it. Were Foot to retell the second half of Bevan's life it is inconceivable that he would again ignore his subject's views on the Welsh language and Home Rule.

Aneurin's father, David Bevan, was a Welsh-speaking native of Tredegar in Gwent, an *eisteddfodwr*, chapel-goer and a member of the Cymmrodorion. Every Sunday night he and his family would gather around the organ to sing hymns and Welsh folk-songs. Phoebe Bevan (née Prothero) was descended from Anglo-Welsh border stock but it was she who urged David Bevan to pass on Welsh – a language she did not share with him – to their children. Although six of the ten offspring were given thoroughly Welsh christian names, their father declined to bless them also with his mother-tongue. However, the fact that Aneurin, like his brothers and sisters, was thus disinherited did not prevent him from forever harbouring an abiding affection for the Welsh language. Even as the most controversial MP of his time, clashing with Attlee and Churchill on issues of enormous international gravity, he did not forget the old language of his native valleys. For example, during the Welsh Day debate of 12 December 1953 he declared:

> Although those of us who have been brought up in Monmouth and in Glamorgan are not Welsh-speaking, Welsh-writing Welshmen, nevertheless we are all aware of the fact that there exists in Wales, and especially in the rural areas, a culture which is unique in the world. And we are not prepared to see it die.

His editorial in *Tribune* on 'The Claims of Wales' (republished in the Spring 1947 issue of the prestigious magazine *Wales*) eulogized Welsh culture and appreciated the essential place in it of the language:

> People from other parts of the country (*sic*) are surprised when they visit Wales to find how many Welsh people still speak Welsh, and how strong and even passionate, is the love of the Welsh for their country, their culture and their unique institutions.
> In all this there is nothing to deplore. On the contrary, it is very much to the good that distinctive cultures, values and institutions should flourish, so as to counteract the appalling tendency of the times towards standardisation, regimentation and universal greyness. Furthermore, a wholesome patriotism should be cherished when it is the only custodian of these precious verisimilitudes, and multi-coloured flowerings of human experience. A passionate dedication to, and jealousy of, national cultures have inspired some of the noblest achievements of mankind, and we should lose touch with much that helps now to adorn our world if the super-state were allowed to obliterate all the differences which people have from each other.

None the less, it would be wrong to give the impression that Bevan was unstinting and unambivalent in his support for Welsh. He regarded the all-Welsh National Eisteddfod rule as a malicious act of bigotry. He stretched his understandable empathy with 'Anglo-Welsh' culture to the point of paranoia about the Welsh language. As he told his fellow MPs on 28 October 1946:

The culture and cultural institutions of Wales do not belong entirely to North Wales or Mid Wales. There exists in the English-speaking populations of Monmouthshire, Glamorganshire and some parts of Carmarthenshire, a culture as rich and profound as that which comes from the Welsh-speaking people of North Wales. There has been too great a tendency to identify Welsh culture with Welsh speaking . . . what some of us are afraid of is that, if this psychosis is developed too far, we shall see in some of the English-speaking parts of Wales a vast majority tyrannised over by a few Welsh-speaking people in Cardiganshire . . . the whole of the Civil Service of Wales would be eventually provided from those small pockets of Welsh-speaking, Welsh-writing zealots and the vast majority of Welshmen would be denied participation in the Government of their country.

The temptation to introduce the current Member for Pontypool at this point is irresistible – but we should note that, although Leo Abse preaches a similar message today, he has never waxed eloquent about the Welsh language or pristine Welsh culture in the way that Bevan could. Not that Abse denies his Welsh connections in the way that, for example, Roy Jenkins does. Indeed, in his diagnostic book *Private Member*, Abse can barely contain his contempt for the way in which Jenkins (under his mother's influence) has spurned his background, just as Bevan could not resist poking fun at Jenkins's flight from his Welsh and working-class origins. More than once in his anti-devolution outpourings Abse has invoked Bevan's outlooks, notably the latter's aversion to such House of Commons institutions as the Welsh Parliamentary Labour group and the annual Welsh Day debate. It is true that Bevan looked down on these manifestations of clubby Welsh provincialism with a mixture of scorn and embarrassment. Yet here again there was a touch of schizophrenia about his behaviour: in December 1944 he allowed himself to be nominated – and then elected – chairman of the Welsh Parliamentary Party, an all-party sham of even less worth than the Welsh Labour Group.

His editorial in *Tribune* explained why he considered the Welsh Day innovation to be a piece of nonsense. Problems in agriculture, coal, steel and the other industries should, Bevan argued, be solved on a United Kingdom level; it was futile to cram them into an artificial Welsh context for one day a year. He reasoned:

In so far as Wales is different from England, it is the difference and not the similarity, which requires special recognition and a special constitutional medium of expression. Wales is different, not in the fact that she possesses coal and steel, docks and harbours, factories and an intricate web of economic activities. These are part of the common life of the United Kingdom. She is different in that she has a language of her own, an art and a culture, and an educational system and an excitement for things of the mind and the spirit, which are wholly different from English ways. It is in the commonality of this difference that Wales has a claim for special recognition and where she should seek new forms of national life.

A special constitutional medium of expression, new forms of national life . . . what was Bevan suggesting? It is doubtful if he ever knew himself, but some remarks in a Welsh Day speech are interesting. Before launching his diatribe against what was the first Welsh Day in Parliament, he said:

Wales has a special place, a special individuality, a special culture and special claims and I do not think that this is the place where any of them can properly be considered. There may be an argument – I think there is an argument – for considerable devolution of government.

Could he have been thinking of a Welsh Grand Committee, along the lines of the Scottish one already in existence? – unlikely, as such a body would still meet in the House of Commons and, anyway, would hardly qualify as a measure of 'devolution'. Almost certainly Bevan was not expressing some veiled desire for a Welsh Parliament: he detested the nationalism which demanded a degree of separate statehood for Wales, and would never have countenanced the devolving of economic or industrial powers to an elected – or nominated – Welsh authority.

Bevan had an opportunity to register his opposition to Welsh Home Rule on 4 March 1955 when S. O. Davies presented his Government of Wales Bill for its Second Reading in the Commons. Such staunchly anti-devolution Welsh Labour MPs as George Thomas, Jim Callaghan, Jim Griffiths, Ness Edwards and Iorrie Thomas stayed until 4 o'clock on that Friday afternoon to help defeat the Bill. Only five Welsh Labour MPs played no part in the parliamentary proceedings, Bevan being one of them. The previous night he had participated in a momentous Commons division on defence policy; on Sunday 6 March he was ill at home with influenza.

Undoubtedly the well-organized opponents of S. O.'s Bill pleaded with Nye to grace the 'No' lobby with his stature and authority. Perhaps he was too ill on 4 March to do so, or he had engagements which he judged to be of greater importance. Or he could not bring himself to strike an irrevocable, possibly lethal, blow against Home Rule for the land of his birth. At no time did Bevan publicly express his views on this, the most definite and detailed proposal for a Welsh Parliament in his lifetime.

The Tory Under-Secretary of State for Welsh Affairs, Lord Mancroft, told a Conservative meeting in Cardiff on the evening of the Bill's defeat that Wales had been spared a parliament of its own – and so had escaped the terrible prospect of 'Mr Aneurin Bevan as the first Governor-General of the Principality'.

In preparation for the 1959 general election the Labour Party's National Executive set up a subcommittee under Jim Griffiths to formulate policies for Wales. Much to Griffiths's sorrow and exasperation, his pet scheme of a Secretary of State for Wales at the head of a Welsh Office was blocked by Bevan. After one meeting of the committee Griffiths and Bevan left the room together, still arguing; as they walked along the corridor Bevan turned to Griffiths and asked: 'How much do you really want this thing?' His compatriot and fellow miners' MP stopped and answered, 'With all my heart and soul.' Bevan simply replied 'Oh, alright then, have it.'

At the committee's next meeting Bevan announced his Damascean conversion to Griffiths's proposals and Labour's 1959 Manifesto duly contained the commitment to a Welsh Secretary of State and a Welsh Office. Bevan's Welsh heart had triumphed over his British head. Yet whatever else this episode reveals about him, it clearly indicates his lack of enthusiasm for administrative devolution.

Hence we return to the question: what strain of devolution would Bevan have advocated or, at least, tolerated? The only remaining model would seem to be one of an elected all-Welsh body discussing, administering and probably legislating upon peculiarly or characteristically Welsh issues like the language, education, local government and the arts. But here again, above all, Bevan was a man who, Michael Foot claims, grasped the realities of political and economic power. If so, it is difficult to imagine how Bevan the Marxist – according to Foot – could accept the disentanglement of such matters as culture and education from the mesh of those realities. Whatever he wrote for *Tribune* in a flush of patriotism, he would have been the first to savage any scheme which devolved matters of the heart and the spirit to Wales, but retained matters of the purse and political muscle in England. Such a notion would, to use Bevan's favourite adjective, be 'frivolous'.

The lines of enquiry would appear, therefore, to be exhausted. How intriguing that this political giant, so definite in the minutiae of health and housing or on the principles of socialism and capitalism, should flounder in the affairs of his small native country. His Welshness – so readily perceived by friends and enemies alike – was a phenomenon with which Bevan himself never fully came to terms. Later in the 1960s his long-time Monmouthshire friend and comrade Archie Lush came very close to joining Plaid Cymru, so deep was his disillusionment with the post-Bevan Labour Party. What on earth would Nye have made of that?

The Heroic View of Life in Early Welsh Verse

A. O. H. JARMAN

From Planet 44, August 1978

The earliest reference to verse composed in the Welsh language is found in the *De Excidio et Conquestu Britanniae* of Gildas, written not later than *c.* 547 AD. This work contains an uncompromising denunciation of the evil way of life of five British kings of the period, the most notable of whom, in the extent both of his power and of his wickedness, was Maelgwn Gwynedd, king of north-west Wales. In particular Gildas reproves Maelgwn for his readiness to accept the praises addressed to him by the bards of the royal court, twenty-four in number according to later saga, who are described as a 'rascally crew yelling forth, like Bacchanalian revellers, full of lies and foaming phlegm, so as to besmear everyone near them'. These bards were, no doubt, continuing an ancient and traditional custom but Gildas condemns them for rendering to an earthly monarch praise which should be reserved for God alone. Neither their names nor a single line of their verse have survived. There can, however, be no doubt that the language in which they composed was Welsh, albeit in a very early form. It is clear that the theme of their verse was panegyric and this continued to dominate the Welsh poetic tradition for over a thousand years. Many centuries were to elapse before panegyric again attracted to itself censure in terms similar to those used by Gildas, and in the Middle Ages it was established practice for Welsh princes and nobles to receive the praise of their bards both for their prowess on the field of battle and for their worthiness as pillars of a stable society. In due course the scope of the poets' eulogies was extended so as to include bishops, abbots and other functionaries of the Church, and by the end of the medieval period the praise in verse of the established order was given a sanction expressed in moral, theological and philosophic terms.

Poets composing in Welsh are first mentioned by name in the *Historia Brittonum* of Nennius, a collection of historico-legendary material put together during the first half of the ninth century but using earlier sources. It includes a list of five early poets, of whom two, Taliesin and Aneirin, were considered in the Middle Ages to be the authors of the poems contained in two thirteenth-century manuscripts, known as the 'Books' of Taliesin and Aneirin. The Nennian list also mentions Talhaearn 'Father of the Muse', and there can be no doubt that in the ninth century he was regarded as the earliest Welsh poet. He may perhaps have flourished during the third quarter of the sixth century but no poems ascribed to him have been preserved. In later Welsh tradition he was displaced by Taliesin, who came to be known invariably as the 'Chief of Poets'. Taliesin was in all probability slightly earlier than Aneirin but both must nevertheless have been contemporaries who sang towards the end of the sixth century. In considering the poems attributed to them it must always be remembered that the geographical context of their work is to be found, not in Wales, but in northern Britain, more particularly in southern Scotland and northern England. During the two centuries following the end of the Roman occupation there were large areas of Welsh-speaking territory throughout western and northern Britain, and in the North, in particular, three separate kingdoms maintained a vigorous independence, two until the seventh century, and the third for very much longer. These were Rheged, Gododdin and Strathclyde, with their capitals respectively Carlisle, Edinburgh and Dumbarton. It was within this region that the medieval Welsh bardic tradition had its fountain-head. Taliesin was the poet of Rheged and Aneirin of Gododdin. After these two kingdoms had been absorbed by the advancing Anglo-Saxon power their cultural traditions were transferred to Wales, possibly via Strathclyde, at a date difficult to determine. Taliesin is principally remembered as the poet of Urien, king of Rheged, but one poem ascribed to him is a eulogy of Cynan Garwyn, king of Powys in north-east Wales. If the ascription is correct Taliesin could have commenced his career in Wales and then migrated northwards to become the court poet of Rheged. This would give the poem to Cynan a dating of *c*. 580, making it the earliest existing poem in the Welsh language. On the other hand the poem entitled *Y Gododdin*, attributed to Aneirin, deals with an entirely northern situation and there is no evidence to suggest that its reputed author ever set foot in Wales.

In 1932, in the first volume of their comprehensive work *The Growth of Literature*, H. M. and N. K. Chadwick included a full discussion of the poems ascribed to Taliesin and Aneirin in the chapter on 'Heroic Poetry'. In the same year C. M. Bowra in his *Heroic Poetry* chose to ignore the poems on the ground that 'heroic poetry is essentially narrative'. It is true that only a few brief passages of narrative occur in early Welsh verse. This is largely celebration poetry consisting of eulogy and elegy, and much of it is lyrical in tone. As early as 1912, however, in his pioneer volume *The Heroic Age*, H. M. Chadwick had published a short note on 'The Heroic Poetry of the Celtic Peoples' in which he anticipated many of his later conclusions in this field. Here he claimed that the early Welsh poems 'plainly show all the marks of Stage I' of the scheme which he had constructed to illustrate the development of heroic poetry. This stage he described as that of 'the court-poems of the Heroic Age itself'. In Stage II he placed 'epic and narrative poems based on these'. A consideration of the subject-matter of the Welsh poems led him to conclude either that they must be accepted as genuine products of the period to which they refer, or that they are 'exceedingly clever imitations of such works, composed at a time when the latter were still in existence'. This was a bold claim for Chadwick to make at a time when the prevailing view among Welsh philologists was that in the sixth century Welsh had not evolved out of the parent Brittonic and that to suggest a date of *c*. 600 for the poems attributed to Taliesin and Aneirin was absurd. The researches of later Welsh scholars have pushed the evolution of the essential features of Welsh back to the early sixth or the fifth century, thereby buttressing Chadwick's argument. The controversy, however, continues. The problem, indeed, is not only to what extent the poems, in the form in which they have been preserved, reflect the stage of development reached by the Welsh language in the late sixth century, but also how much textual alteration and corruption has occurred during lengthy periods of both oral and scribal transmission. We must also ask whether the poems could have been composed by later poets who were able to reproduce and describe in their work the historical background and milieu, the atmosphere, and to a considerable extent the language of the sixth century. This seems improbable, whether considered from the standpoint either of feasibility or of motivation. In my opinion the view of the Chadwicks that the early Welsh texts, however much alteration they may have undergone, both contain and reflect an essential nucleus of early poetic composition cannot lightly be dismissed. It is in this poetry that we find the full expression of the ideals and concepts of what is usually regarded as the Welsh or 'British' heroic age. These concepts are its prevailing mode of thought and for the literary historian their expression in verse constitutes one of the main interests of the literature of the period.

Two distinct concepts of the hero are found in Welsh literature. Firstly there is the hero of saga based on myth or folk-tale. He is normally the son of an other-world father and an earthly mother. In his early years he is a wonder-child, as when Pryderi in the *Mabinogi*, at the age of four, bargains with the grooms to let him take the horses to water. As a grown man, too, he usually displays superhuman powers. An early poem says that when Cai son of Cynyr struck his adversary no physician might heal the wound; in battle his death was unattainable 'unless God should accomplish it'. His Irish counterpart was Cú Chulainn, whose powers were even more remarkable. This was the quintessential hero of Celtic saga who, in terms of heroic combat, was invincible. As Marie-Louise Sjoestedt has observed, Cú Chulainn was finally overthrown by the use of a non-heroic force, consisting of magic and sorcery. The fate of Achilles, struck from behind, and Roland, betrayed by Ganelon, may be compared. Similarly in the *Mabinogi* Pryderi was slain not only 'by dint of strength and valour' but also by 'magic and enchantment'. In contrast with these heroes of saga, there are the very different heroes celebrated in early Welsh verse. They are not invincible on the battlefield, they wield no superhuman powers, and they belong to a fully-attested historical setting. They nevertheless represent a concept of the hero which, even in the sixth century, was rooted in ancient tradition.

References by classical authors to early Celtic peoples, including assessments of their temperament and descriptions of their material habits, achieve a basic unanimity of view. In the fourth century BC Aristotle mentioned the reckless bravery of Celtic warriors in battle but attributed much of this to ignorance or madness, or simply to high-spiritedness, 'as when the Celts take up arms to attack the waves'. Later writers such as Athenaeus, Diodorus Siculus and Strabo, whose descriptions of the Celts depended on a lost chapter of the *History* of Posidonius (135–51 BC), are agreed about their love of war, their quarrelsomeness, their readiness to boast of their own valour and that of their ancestors, their predilection for single combat and their custom of preserving the severed heads of their vanquished enemies as trophies. Athenaeus in particular quotes a passage which refers to the presence of bards at the assemblies of the Celts. They are described as 'poets who deliver eulogies in song' and their function is further defined as the pronouncement of 'praises before the whole assembly and before each of the chieftains in turn as they listen'.

We do not have evidence of this sort for the British Celts in pre-Christian or Roman times, but the denunciation by Gildas in the sixth century of Maelgwn Gwynedd for his willingness to listen to the praises of his bards shows that at that time the tradition of eulogy was well established in Wales. For Gildas these praises were merely vain flattery. The poem addressed by Taliesin to Cynan Garwyn would no doubt have differed little, if at all, in the sentiments it contained from the bardic effusions so roundly condemned by Gildas, or indeed from the 'eulogies in song' which are first referred to by Posidonius. Its content is fawning adulation of a warrior-king expressed in the simplest terms. The king of Powys is extolled for his victorious campaigns against his fellow-countrymen in Gwent, Anglesey, Dyfed and Brycheiniog. Dire threats are uttered against Cornwall and the 'wretched rulers' of other territories are commanded to 'tremble before Cynan'. The king is also praised for the gifts he has given to the poet, namely horses, mantles, bracelets, brooches and a yellow-hilted sword. Thus the dual character of Welsh panegyric verse for many centuries is well illustrated in this very early poem. The king's prowess on the field of battle is matched by his generosity to those who attend his court. The same two themes are dominant in the eleven other poems which scholars now ascribe to Taliesin. Most of these are eulogies of Urien Rheged, who fell as the result of treachery while besieging the English at Lindisfarne. Taliesin testifies that in his court Urien was as bountiful as Cynan. His bravery and fierceness as a warrior are also singled out for mention. On hill and in dale he smites and subdues his foes, and one poem contains a graphic description of bloodstained men, the defeated enemy, with hands crossed and pallid cheeks laying down their arms before him at the ford, while the reddened waves of the River Eden wash the tails of the warriors' horses. 'Lone weary men', presumably Urien's champion fighters, watch the proceedings. The poem ends with the assertion that 'battle will be the lot of him who is Urien's man'.

Here we have the true milieu of heroic poetry. The portrayal is stark and unromanticized. The Urien poems differ from the poem to Cynan Garwyn in one important respect. Cynan is depicted as an aggressor whose sole interest is personal aggrandizement. Urien could, no doubt, be as aggressive as Cynan but the purpose of his actions is primarily defensive. On all sides his kingdom is surrounded by enemies. When he attacks them he does so to protect his people so that they may dwell undisturbed on their homesteads. The poems refer to him as his subjects' 'far-flung refuge', his 'land's anchor', and as a magnanimous dispenser of wealth. He thus accepts responsibility, not only for leading his people in war, but also for their well-being when victory has secured the peace. Taliesin's poems to Urien stress his courage, his fierceness, his dominating personality. They do not, however, contain a statement of the heroic ideal in its pure, undiluted and unadulterated form. For this we must turn to the *Gododdin* of Aneirin.

The name *Gododdin* carries three meanings: (1) the tribe or people so called; (2) the territory inhabited by them; and (3) the poem which celebrated their heroes. Containing 1,257 lines arranged in 103 rhymed stanzas the *Gododdin* is formally an elegy. It laments the fall at the battle of Catraeth, or Catterick in Yorkshire, of the war-band of the Gododdin, three hundred strong, which the tribal chieftain Mynyddog Mwynfawr had sent to attack the advancing Angles of Deira and Bernicia. Historical sources tell us nothing of the battle. It could have been one of many unrecorded skirmishes which must have occurred in the conflict between Angle and Briton and may probably be dated c.600 AD. We gather from the *Gododdin* that for a year Mynyddog had maintained, and no doubt trained, a picked troop of mail-clad horsemen before sending them forth on a hazardous expedition which he must have deemed to be of supreme strategic importance and the success of which he may have regarded as vital for the survival of his kingdom. In the event it was a disaster. The warriors of the Gododdin were annihilated by a numerically superior enemy; only one escaped. The poem, however, does not treat the battle in strategic or political terms. Nothing could be further from the minds of the warriors than calculated planning. Their values are purely heroic. The period of preparation at Mynyddog's court is described as a 'mead-feast' or a 'wine-feast', participation in which bound the warriors in a relationship of absolute fidelity to their chieftain. When, at his command, they have gone forth to battle and fought without flinching until struck down by the foe, they are said to have 'paid their mead'. Their readiness to do this was for each of them a matter of personal honour, and it was the determination never in any circumstances to deviate from honour's stern demands that constituted the essence of the heroic ideal. At some moment during their expedition the war-band must have realized that their campaign could only end in defeat. Flight, however, was unthinkable. Even if worldly wisdom and common sense counselled it, the charge of cowardice which would ensue would have been unbearable. The war-band fought on until the end. By so doing they achieved the immortal fame to which their steadfastness entitled them. In the words of the *Gododdin*:

> Although they were slain, they slew,
> And until the end of the world they shall be praised.

In this matter, the poet was deemed to be the final arbiter. Another of Aneirin's stanzas closes with the line:

> The poets of the world shall be the judges of the man of stout heart.

Much of the poem is, of course, pure elegy. The youthfulness of the warriors, their short lives and their kinsmen's sorrow after them are continually emphasized. The poet declares that 'their ardour shortened their lives' and that 'before their hair turned grey death came to them'. There is also panegyric in the conventional or Taliesinic sense. One gathers that, like the heroes of the Iliad, each member of the war-band was a minor chieftain in his own right, and the munificence and even opulence of their courts are praised. They dispense mead to their guests, gifts to the minstrels, and the liberality of one is compared to the flowing sea. In battle, however, their ferocity knew no bounds. With expected hyperbole the poem states that before one warrior 'armies groaned' and that 'five fifties fell before the blades' of another. About eighty of the warriors are named and eulogized individually in this way. The poet also took especial pride in the war-band as a whole. For him it was a splendid sight to see them setting forth for Catraeth, riding 'on rough-haired steeds, swan-coloured horses, tightly harnessed':

> A host of horsemen in brown armour,with shields,
> Spear-shafts held aloft with sharp points,
> And shining mail-shirts and swords.

The exultation in these lines does not, however, express the prevailing tone of the poem. Unlike the armies of Urien, Mynyddog's war-band did not go forth to battle with a fair prospect of victory in sight. As a body it was doomed to destruction. The poet was fully aware of this as he composed each line of his poem. It is an indication of his quality as a poet that he was so often able to set this awareness aside momentarily in order to give expression to his admiration for the achievements, the high morale and the resplendent appearance of the war-band. However, in one line he declares that at Mynyddog's hall the warriors 'drank yellow sweet, ensnaring mead'. It ensnared them because it was the symbol of a bond which led to ineluctable disaster. This was a bond of the warriors' own choosing. For them renown, achieved at whatever cost, was the supreme good. It was for this, rather than for any tribal, national or political gain, that they fought. Nai son of Nwython 'slew a great host in order to win reputation', and Cydywal son of Sywno 'sold his life for the mention of honour'. Heedless of their own survival, they pledged their personal allegiance to Mynyddog and 'paid for their mead-feast with their lives'. For this the poet promises them 'praise without limit, without end'.

Such is the concept of ideal heroic behaviour as formulated and expressed by the poet of the *Gododdin*. Whether the men of the war-band really felt and acted in this way, we cannot tell. Situations like that at Catraeth have occurred time and again in the history of human conflict. Men have often been required to choose between the demands of discretion and those of valour, and have usually done so with less single-mindedness than the warriors of the *Gododdin*. It is therefore noteworthy that early Welsh literature contains a counter-statement to the *Gododdin*'s assertion of the validity of the heroic ideal. This is found in the verse-cycle associated with the name of Llywarch Hen. Llywarch was possibly a northern sixth-century figure, a cousin of Urien Rheged, who seems to have become the central character in a saga which depicts him as having migrated to Powys in Wales, where he was faced with the task of defending his borders against the English enemy. The scene is set in the late sixth century, but the earliest acceptable date for the composition of the poems is the ninth. Moreover, their unknown author manifests a profound interest in various problems posed by the heroic ideal. He not only seeks an answer to such questions as why are some men reluctant to go to war and what is the motivation of cowardice, but also asks the more fundamental question: what is the justification for the pursuit of renown?

Llywarch is portrayed as an uncompromising upholder of the martial values. He has brought up all twenty-four of his sons as trained warriors, and twenty-three of them have fallen in battle. The sole survivor, Gwên, has been living a life of ease at Urien's court while his father, alone, continued to resist the enemy. Hearing of Llywarch's plight, however, Gwên returns to Powys. In a dialogue between father and son Llywarch urges Gwên 'not to lose the honour of a man', and Gwên replies that he is ready to endure the hardship of battle and promises that, wherever he chances to be 'spears will be shattered'. He qualifies these assurances, however, with reference to the possibility of retreat if the pressure of battle becomes too great, and in one line he utters the words: 'I do not say that I shall not flee.' This leads to a charge of cowardice and the dialogue ends on a bitter note, with Llywarch boasting of his early prowess while Gwên points out that though he has survived, his witness is dead. This poem is followed by Llywarch's elegy to his son. In the sequel Gwên had not fled but had stood his ground fighting until he fell. Now Llywarch claims for himself the credit for his son's bravery. 'Because he was my son', he says, 'he did not flee.'

Parallels to this dialogue are found in other poems of the Llywarch Hen cycle. One of these deals specifically with the theme of cowardice. Cynddilig, another son of Llywarch, cites the frozen lake, the falling snow, the strong biting wind and the short day as excuses for not going to war. Llywarch replies with an outright attack on cowardice but nevertheless resigns himself to an acceptance of his son's failing, telling him that he will not be called upon to serve in the hour of need although he is neither a cleric nor an old man. He then adds the exclamation: 'Alas, Cynddilig, that thou wert not born a woman!' Had that been the case, Llywarch would have been spared the shame of avowing kinship with a self-acknowledged coward.

Thus, in a cycle of verse which retains much of the heroic ethos, we find a poet examining problems which would not even have occurred to his precursor who composed the *Gododdin*. The severe standards of the heroic age are being replaced by a much more complex view of life. This is very clearly shown in a poem entitled 'The Old Man's Lament', in which Llywarch is depicted as a forlorn wanderer, rejected by all, bereft of family and kingdom. Of his twenty-four sons he says: 'Through my tongue they have been slain'. He has now concluded that it was his own immoderate boasting, his incessant exhortations to his sons to emulate his martial exploits, that have led to their destruction. He then adds the general statement that 'too much renown is evil', although 'a little (renown) is good'. Admittedly, he has not been favoured by fortune. Unlike Urien, he has no sons to sustain him. Unlike the warriors of the Gododdin, he has survived his battles. But the final verdict on the heroic ideal is that it is compounded of presumption and arrogance. Its essence is pride and its end is ruin.

Need the Language Divide Us?

J. R. JONES

From Planet 49/50, January 1980. The original lecture in Welsh was delivered in 1967.

The Language difference splits Wales in two. And the split is deepening and the prejudices and hatreds which are a consequence of it are worsening.

Mr Aneirin Talfan Davies called from the stage of the National Eisteddfod in Aberafan for a 'dialogue' between the two sides, and his appeal was published shortly afterwards in *Barn*. He and others of the same persuasion have, then, given their answer to our question – 'need the language divide us?' – and that answer is 'no', a dialogue *is* possible between Welsh and English.

May I begin there then – by giving my reason for doubting that answer? 'Dialogue', says Mr Davies, is one of today's favourite words. We hear, for example, of the dialogue 'between the Church and the denominations' so that they may come better to understand one another. They may indeed; and this dialogue, and others similar to it, are quite possible. But he goes on to say: 'Do we not need a dialogue like this between those Welshmen who do and those who do not speak Welsh?' – But now we have moved onto different ground. The churches and denominations in Wales are divided on a number of matters and issues, and the dialogue about these questions will be conducted *in a language*, either English or Welsh or possibly both. But the Welsh are split by a difference of language itself – so that what is needed here is a dialogue somehow *between the two languages*. And here the whole idea of a dialogue falls apart. A dialogue must be *in* a language, and for the

143

dialogue to be a genuine exchange between the two languages, those taking part on both sides must speak both languages. Where Welsh-speakers and non-Welsh-speakers are concerned, then, there can be no dialogue *between* the two languages. It would be a dialogue *in* the English language *about* the Welsh language and culture. Welsh would indeed be the subject of the dialogue, but since it would have no part as the *language* of the dialogue, the dialogue would be distorted to the disadvantage of Welsh from the very start.

Ultimately, then, this was a call to unite Wales by means of the English language – not of course by ousting Welsh to replace it with English, but by building across the split a sort of English bridge – a bridge which non-Welsh-speaking Welshmen could understand – between themselves and what remains of Welsh-speaking Wales.

Now what I would like to call for is a different sort of coming together – for a link which would unite, not by means of English, but of Welsh, and which would unite not over the top of the rift but beneath it.

Because, if it is not made clear from the start that the uniting must be done *through the medium of Welsh*, an undertone of hidden prejudice in favour of English will run through all your arguments. It will be as though you see the greatest significance in the Anglicized sector – 'the overwhelming majority of the nation', as A.T.D. put it – with Welsh-speaking Wales no more than a thin residual streak running through it. This undertone can be detected beneath the surface of more than one of Mr Davies's arguments. He refers to 'that part of the nation which knows no Welsh – the people on whom the Eisteddfod, as in Aberafan this year, must depend so much; the people who have worked so assiduously – in English – for the last two years'. And he asks: 'Who would deny them the greatest praise for this lesson in practical tolerance?' *Tolerance?* Yes, that was the word. But what was it that they tolerated? The context gives the unmistakable answer – they tolerated *the Welsh language!* – they tolerated the fact that they were giving their time, their money, and their labour for an eisteddfod held in *Welsh!*

The newspapers made such of Mr Davies's comparison of the 'Welsh rule' in the Eisteddfod with the Maginot Line, and of the way he pointed out the 'negativeness' of retreating behind the ramparts in Wales. The truth is, of course, that those who call for the fortification of those areas where Welsh is still strong call for retreat not for its own sake, but so as to concentrate the remaining resources. And retreating for this purpose, as part of a purposeful strategy, is positive retreat – it arises from a disciplined desire to stem the disappearance of our separate identity. And the truth is that the really hopeless, negative retreat is contained in Mr Davies's own reasoning, the retreat which lies in admitting that the only hope of a purposeful strategy is the positive tolerance and sanction of the 'British' Welsh. The real meaning of his appeal to the Welsh-speaking Welsh in Aberafan was –'do all you can to avoid losing the goodwill of the other half of the nation; your fate as Welsh-speaking Welshmen is in their hands.'

I should like to ask this: whence came all these voices of late advocating conciliation and dialogue? To build walls and gather into strongholds, they say, is to give up, to flee, to go into hiding. But what 'giving up' or 'retreating' could possibly be more fatal than this submitting to 'Britishness', admitting that Anglicization has already, finally, succeeded in Wales, and that Welsh will in the future only exist through the 'practical tolerance' of those already Anglicized?

No – a way must be found of healing the rift which is more positively favourable to the continuance of Welsh than the negative and submissive craving for 'dialogue' and 'tolerance'. The burden of this appeal to the Anglicized Welsh is: 'try and tolerate Welsh; would it not be a catastrophe if we were to lose such a colourful supplement to our culture as this beautiful old language?' I would maintain that the battle is already lost if we cannot change the whole emphasis and character of the appeal. We must be able to call on the increasing number who have to explain – 'I am Welsh but I don't speak it, see,' to undergo a sort of mental transformation with regard to Welsh and come to feel respect for it and pride in it, although they themselves cannot speak it, and to do this because they have seen a new significance in Welsh – in the way in which it is *inwardly connected* with that which makes it possible for them to know they are Welsh – although they do not speak the language. This means that we will have to start thinking in terms of a new approach or slogan – not 'unity through dialogue (in English), over the rift', but 'unify through Welsh, from beneath the rift'.

But a difficult question arises immediately: how on earth can you get people who no longer speak a language to try and come to an understanding with those who have kept the language *through the medium of that language itself?* Is not the difference between knowing a language and not knowing it the most irredeemable split there is? 'Language', says Lady Megan Phillips, 'divides.'

To answer this question – and before we can proceed further – I must refer briefly to some of the foundation of my argument in *Prydeindod.* One of my premises in the book is that communities, as far as their structure is concerned, are defined in terms of the least number of bonds sufficient for their formation and continuance. And on this basis, I suggested a definition of two types of national community – or if you will, two levels in the structure of a full nation. To bond people into a nation in the full sense, it seems to me that at least *three* structural bonds are necessary: (1) a definite territory; (2) a language peculiar to that territory; and (3) that the sovereign authority over the lives of the territory's inhabitants is in the hands of the community itself. A full nation, then, has three bonds, it is a trivalent community. But within this community or (diachronically) on the route to it, there is a simpler, more primitive form of national community, a population which has occupied its own territory throughout the ages and which has always spoken its own language in that terrritory, but – for historical reasons – is not now organized as a separate state but rather has been taken under the authority and government of another state. I shall call this community a People. A People is a bivalent community. The basis of its formational structure is the interpenetrative marriage of language and land.

In the same book I drew a distinction which will be a key to the argument of this address. It is a distinction between two levels in the structure of a People (or a nation) not dissimilar to the distinction made in the structure of a body between its anatomy on one level, and on the other level its physiology, the biological processes which go on within its anatomy all the time. I have called this second level the functional level – the level in which a People or a nation live their lives from day to day and from experience to experience, just as the blood circulates through the body or food is digested in the intestines. Since I intend to use this term frequently from now on, I should like you to grasp the technical meaning I am giving it. The other I shall call the structural level. This corresponds to the anatomy of the body. The separate identity of a

146

People or nation is at this level: the bonds which *originally brought the community into existence* as a people or nation are structural. I had this in mind when I said that the 'basis of the structure of a People' is the interpenetration of the bond of separate language and the bond of separate territory. On the other hand, the bonds of economic and cultural intercourse in the life of a People work on the functional level. Briefly, if we called these the 'bonds of their life', then the structural bonds, in contrast, would be the 'bonds of their *existence*' – the bonds which *form* their separate identity.

We have seen that it was implied in the argument of *Prydeindod* that Wales could not really be considered a nation, in the full sense of the word at least, and I have been criticized for that suggestion. But since there is no independent Welsh state and we are forced to concede that we do not, as we stand, satisfy the definition of a nation, the important, structural, point is that we are a People and as such have the potential to become a trivalent nation, that is a People with their sovereign authority over their lives arising from their original bivalent structure, that is of the interpenetration of their territory and the particular language of that territory.

With respect to the step from bivalent to trivalent, one important note of caution must be struck, that it is not sufficient just to add the bond of 'self-government' to the bond of the interpenetration of our land and language, to satisfy merely formally the definition of a nation: because an *outside power* could give us that. The British government, for instance, could give it as part of the process of breaking up its empire and allowing the 'sub-nations' independence. No: however our independence comes, we shall not be ready for it until the *will to be a nation* awakes in the Welsh People itself. The fulfilment of the definition of a nation is a nominal step only. The only thing which can form us into a nation, make us ripe for nationhood, is the will to demand sovereign rule over our own lives. For independence to be allowed us constitutionally as a matter of 'democratic justice' would not necessarily make us fit to receive it. The only thing which will make the majority of our people ready to carry the burden of responsibility which is freedom is the will to demand sovereignty, not as 'justice', but because our will to demand it is internally linked to the fact that we *exist* as a separate People. Because, look at Wales now! How could receiving the outward form of a nation (as defined) make this mixture of servile Anglophiles and

147

'Britishized' parasites worthy of being a nation? We must first undergo the purification of wanting and *demanding* to be a nation before we shall be ready.

But what is important to us at the moment is that the basis of our potential to be a nation – the only place from which the will can spring – is our structure as a separate *People*, a structure which has been formed through the ages by the interpenetration of our territory and the proper language of that territory, the Welsh language. If ever we became independent on any other basis, that is, if gaining the title of 'nation' depended on removing the Welsh language from the basis of our structure, leaving it as no more than the sub-language of a scattered minority or as a sort of esoteric cultural luxury possessed by a fortunate few, then we would not have gained independence for the Welsh nation at all; we would have created another community which would not be a constitution of the original Welsh structure but a continuation of the weakening and decay of that structure. And we are not seeking a means to our *disintegration*, provincial independence for an Anglicized Wales where Welsh-speakers will continue to be at the mercy of the 'practical toleration' of the rest!

But now, having laid the foundations, my argument upon those foundations will be this: that it is on the functional level – in the comings and goings of everyday life – that the Welsh are split by the language difference. And of course bridging the split at this level is impossible. You could seem to build a bridge, of course, but it would not achieve its real aim. Because, as I said, it would have to be an 'English bridge' – the 'dialogue' would have to be in English, and so loaded from the start against any hope of restoring precedence to Welsh.

But building a bridge by *means of the Welsh language itself* is possible on the other level – the structural level, that is, not bridging by speaking the language – although it would be hoped that the language would be restored as well – but bridging by bringing the bulk of the people of Wales to see it in the light of its structural significance. And what is that? That Welsh is the *only* language making the Welsh a *separate People*, even those Welsh who do not speak it, and who have, even, turned to hate it on the other level. In a word, it is at the structural level that 'unity is possible *from beneath* the rift'.

For what would you appeal, calling for this unity? For all who consider themselves to belong to the community called 'Wales', to be filled with a basic respect for the Welsh language, and with a noble and stubborn pride in its long history and its beauty, and because it is, on the structural level – however few remain able to speak it – the only language giving us a separate identity. I do not know exactly what could be expected from English-speaking Welshmen after such a change of heart in their attitude to the language. But it is difficult to believe that, unlike Welsh-speakers with ideas similar to those of Mr Talfan Davies, they would not fight to keep the Welsh Rule in the National Eisteddfod, and they would do so because it would be obvious to them that it must be kept. And if they devoted themselves to work for the Eisteddfod or any other Welsh institution, it would be an insult to congratulate them on their 'practical tolerance'.

The historian Lewis Namier maintains that nationality can be understood and the communities 'People' and 'nation' defined only in a territorial sense – and not in terms of language. A nation, he says, is composed of the inhabitants of one territory under one sovereign state. And so *Britain* is a nation. But he refers to Wales as well, saying that the idea that *language* can make a nation or a People must be rejected or else Wales would be split into *two* communities from top to bottom. He would have us suppose then that if the Welsh have a separate identity at all, it must be understood in terms of territory – a matter of being brought up within the borders of that part of Britain known as 'Wales'. But how can this be? If 'Wales' is part of Britain, and *all* the population of one State's territory constitute *one* nation, then Britain is a nation and Wales is not a nation at all – or a People either. The truth is that if the territory of a People is taken out of its interpenetration with their proper language by allowing that language to die then the territory will be sucked into the main territory of the State to which they are subject. And sooner or later the consequence of that will be the blotting out of the ethnic or national difference of the inhabitants of the assimilated territory. As Sorokin says: 'The total loss of a language by a group means the loss of its identity and nationality.' I say this in an attempt to press home my message – that the interpenetration of the territory of the Welsh *with the proper language of that territory*, the Welsh language, plays a vital part, not only in the formation of our Welsh identity, but also in its continuance. In other words I reject the opinion of the *Western Mail* on the significance of Welsh (in a leading article about the Act giving equal validity to Welsh): 'A language represents the consciousness of a nation and is a safeguard of its individual identity. If we let that die then perhaps a part of us would die too.' True enough, *but there is no 'perhaps' about it.*

But it was to say something else that I mentioned Namier. By maintaining that Wales would be split in two by the addition of the bond of language to that of territory in the structure of a People, he reveals one of his hidden preconceptions, that the connection of the structure of a People with their language comes to an end the moment they lose their language, and therefore begins to end as soon as the language begins to weaken. The basis of my message is that this view is mistaken. It is a shallow view, based on a failure to differentiate between the everyday life of a People on the one hand, and their structure on the other – between the functional level and the structural level. I maintain that neither a People's connection with their language nor their attachment to it come to an end when they cease to be able to speak the language. Because their structural connection with it remains, and is visible in the fact that they *exist* as a separate People. That language, along with their land, has been *built into their structure* as a separate People.

In a radio discussion on the programme *Disgwyl Cwmni* this January, Mr Alwyn Rees observed that until recently religion had kept the Welsh language alive, *by giving it a task to perform*, the task of saving souls. And to save Welsh in the second half of the twentieth century, he said, we must again 'find it a job to do'. Now saving souls was a job on the functional level – the level of everyday life. It had nothing to do with the separate structure of the Welsh. The English language in England was given exactly the same job in the eighteenth century. It is a measure of the state of crisis we have reached now that no task on the functional level can be found for the language that English is not already performing, and indeed performing better for the fact of being first in the field. In a word, in public life on the functional level, English has taken over all the important tasks. Is it not then a mistake to search for a functional task for Welsh, because by doing that you would be involving it in a contest too obvious and unfair with the more dynamic language already at the task? Push Welsh too much in the functional sphere, and you invite the complaint that there is no profit in it – no profit and no use.

By trying to use it through, for example, teaching it in the 'English' secondary schools – a subject lacking dignity taught by unsympathetic teachers – you allow people to crow that the language has no use, and that this experiment, as it were, proves that to be so!

Is this not the truth? You can look at the whole range of public life today in Wales at the functional level without finding a single special and unique task which Welsh could perform. They are all performed already by English. So what is the point? The condemnation is, in a way, just. Note, though, *that it is a condemnation on the functional level.* The conclusion to be drawn is that we must start looking for the *special* task of the Welsh language in a completely different direction – a direction in which we do not often look when enquiring about the usefulness of a language. My message is that there is such a definite and inalienable task for the Welsh language in the second half of the twentieth century – a task which nothing else in the world could perform – the structural task of being the *only means of saving the separate identity of the Welsh People.*

You see that I continue to talk about saving. The task of Welsh in the days of the religious revivals was that of saving the souls of the Welsh *as individuals.* Its only possible special task now is the structural one of saving the separate identity of the Welsh *as a People.* And I wonder if anything less than a revival could waken us to this task – not a religious revival, but a national revival?

And this is the question I should like to raise next – what will waken us to the task? How can those Welshmen who speak no Welsh be given the motivation to take pride in it again as the language which gives them their separate identity?

It follows from my confession as to its worthlessness on the functional level that there is no motivation on that level which could be strong enough to overpower the prejudices created by the 'split'. For example, there is no point trying to prove that Welsh can be a material advantage, or that being able to speak both languages is an educational advantage, or that it is just as easy to pass on culture – even technical and scientific culture – in Welsh as it is in English. Not that there is not a measure of truth in each of these claims. The point is that no one of them alone, nor all of them together, can create sufficient motivation to withstand all the anti-Welsh pressures working at the functional level – pressures which turn an ever-increasing number away from the language and make the old one unreasonably hostile towards it. That is why I maintain that the 'functional split' can never be repaired except by going down to the structural level, aiming to invite the Welsh people *beneath* the split. By beginning to restore the respect for Welsh in this way, on the structural level alone to begin with, we can hope to win people over to reclaim it functionally later, that is to learn it anew, or at least to make absolutely sure that their children learn it. To come again to love it, not in the hope of profit – whether material or educational – but because a People who are aware of the dignity of their separate identity cannot help but be possessed of an immense respect for that language *which brought about their separate existence.*

There is therefore a condition which must be fulfilled, that the Anglicized bulk of the Welsh population must find a new awareness, on a wide and revolutionary scale, of their separate identity as Welshmen. And that being the condition, do we not immediately come up against a mountain of difficulties?

Do we not come particularly against the problem of the mental conditioning of the Welsh population which I tried to analyse in *Prydeindod*? By *Prydeindod*, 'Britishness', I mean (as some failed to understand) the ideology – that is, a belief with the power to persuade unconsciously and against the will – which traps the Anglicized Welsh, and Welsh-speakers too, into considering themselves to be British and not Welsh, as far as nationality is concerned. This belief has for generations planted in the minds of the majority of people in Wales something which has sometimes been likened to schizophrenia, an uncertainty or ambiguity as to their national identity, as to who exactly, or which People, they are. This means we have to work with a situation where ambiguity of identity is rife. And the battle to restore the awareness of their separate identity in the minds of the Welsh population will be more and more a battle against this ambiguity. It is my belief that if this awareness could be restored on any significant level, then pride in the Welsh language, and respect for it, would increase even in those who could not speak it – because they would now be rediscovering, as it were, its significance as the language of their separate identity. But to *make* them aware of their separate identity to start with, you have to combat the whole seduction of the idea of belonging not to Wales but to Britain.

And as though to reinforce this obstacle there is another phenomenon supported by the whole tendency of modern civilization, the extreme poverty of our awareness of the past.

One of the mistakes which had contributed most to our conditioning to restrict the language and its significance to the functional level is our idea that language is nothing more than a means or technique of communication. This idea arises from ignoring the dimension of the past in a language – the way in which it becomes, after being spoken over the generations by the inhabitants of the same region, a vessel to collect and store their past, and through that a means to form them into a People. This misapprehension causes language to be confined to the present. And that is a certain way to turn Welsh in Wales into a bone of contention and a means to split, when a language should integrate. Because in the present, after removing the other dimension, Welsh to an increasing number of Welshmen is a language they do not speak – a technique of communication which they do not possess, a privilege to those who speak it, a deprivation to those who don't. That is the unpleasant truth, if you limit yourself to the present. Because in the present alone, language is a technique of communication and nothing else, and either one can speak it or one cannot. And it is exactly there that language cuts cruelly through the bowels of the nation.

But by understanding language in the light of the past and by restoring to it its past – the dimension of its attachment to the existence of the People who own it – it becomes possible even for those who do not know it 'functionally', that is, as a technique of communication, to come to see it as the language of their separate identity – the language which built for them *the only structure they have* as a separate People. They will respect it when they see that without it they are not a People at all. The slogan which I should like to see plastered over the walls and bridges of Wales is – 'Remember Cornwall'.

But then, there is another obstacle, this time more from the direction of those who speak Welsh. It is difficult to make people with reasonably deep roots strongly and visibly aware of their separate identity because they instinctively take it for granted and allow it to slip from sight into the back of their mind. It is generally true that making *structural* considerations a matter of conscious importance is a painfully difficult task. There is a very strong temptation on the functional level, the everyday level, to look at the question of structure – *who one is*, to which nation or People one belongs – in the same way as the ground underfoot, which one takes for granted. On the functional level, the important thing is living itself, to ensure and safeguard one's livelihood. And for the sake of livelihood and 'getting on in the world', a host of voices *in Welsh-speaking Wales* tell us that 'the language is worthless: it is nothing more than dead weight around our feet'.

Indeed, looking at the situation as a whole, those who are fighting to restore respect for the Welsh language face a threefold obstruction. On one side, there is the wall of indifference of the Welsh-speakers who take their Welshness for granted without any real pride or respect in it. On the other side there is the enmity and mockery of some Anglicized Welsh. And from behind, filling the background, there is the duplicity of a government ready with promises but reluctant and evasive when it comes to fulfilling those promises. In this confused and seemingly immovable situation, it is only to be expected that an aware minority – Welshmen who clearly see our structural crisis – will become increasingly defiant and restive – ready to go to the borders of illegality and unconstitutional action. I am thinking of course of the Welsh Language Society. Some people fail to understand why the society is so impatient and unyielding in its dealings with the Welsh Office. May I say a word on its behalf?

The Welsh language today – in the age of the mass media – is fighting for its very life on the cultural front – fighting the flood of foreign cultural influences with which its foundations are awash. We cannot *legislate* these influences away, we can only fight them with cultural weapons. The Welsh language is in the middle of that battle today, and its chance of winning is obviously in the balance. But in the cruel battle – for no less than its hope of continued existence – it fights under a terrible disadvantage: an old disadvantage but one which now has a new sting because it has come to the fore just at the time the language is fighting for its existence. That disadvantage is its lack of 'official status'. Constitutionally, to be exact, *Welsh does not exist*. It must, because of that, enter the battle with the forces threatening its existence as a language without prestige, and so without dignity or respect. And this disadvantage, the lack of a secure foothold in people's respect and administration, is a cruel disadvantage to a language fighting for its life. I said that we cannot legislate against cultural influences – only fight them. But we can legislate to remove this legal disadvantage. And what the language society asks of those who govern us is that they do legislate, and that they do it quickly and that the legislation does *more* than recognize the existence of a second-rate minority language, that it *creates the conditions* for the restoration of Welsh to precedence in its own land. The truth is that the language, after the long feebleness of centuries of being ignored and humiliated, is now in danger, because of the weight of the odds against it, of losing its battle with the forces trying to destroy it. And failing to remove the disadvantage, or just pretending to remove it, *under the present circumstances*, is just the same as taking part in its destruction. Everyone who tries to postpone the removal of the disadvantage or who pushes for a half-hearted, toothless measure, is himself a destroyer. These words are too strong, you say. I say that administrations who live only in their own day and age cannot hope *to sin against the centuries* and remain unrebuked.

But is there not an obstacle deeper than any of those I have named, that my own argument is circular? My argument is this: that a condition of restoring respect for Welsh is that there should be a definite increase in awareness by the Welsh of their separate identity. But is it not true that we have nothing now which makes our separateness except the living language? So – no language, no real separate identity: but without an awareness of our separate identity, we have no motive for respecting the language and restoring its precedence. Have we not here a vicious circle? Indeed, to generalize, are we not really discussing a hopeless situation, if only we could face the truth?

If that is the case, this address is a call to do the impossible. And is that such an empty and irresponsible idea – 'doing the impossible'? No: it has always been – in civilization's crises – a challenge innately connected with the greatness of man's spirit. The sense of this greatness has today become weak and uncertain – the greatness which is in man's *spirit*, in his will to do the impossible because it *must* be done to save the civilization of a small part of the world from destruction. Man's inner greatness has shrunk to nothing before the external greatness – greatness in size – of his technical inventions and products. And a new outlook commensurate with that has taken possession in the world of politics and government – the world in which the fate of a People is moulded – the view that politics is no more than the *art of the possible:* the art of organizing powers of a particular sort, of vision – but the powers at the call of the wizard in the techniques of forecasting and in determining different strata of the population's patterns of voting behaviour. To fit the 'impersonal' tensions of society to the needs of a reasonably 'practical' and minimal policy so as to avoid any enthusiasm and extremism which could take the 'last word' out of the hands of the prime minister – that is the modern, 'Technological', Wilsonian idea of the essentials of political action. And this is shallow – shallow in the same way that the attitude of our scientific-technological civilization is shallow throughout – trivializing the spirit of man and drowning culture in banality and superficial cleverness.

'The art of the possible' – that slogan crystallizes perfectly the attitude of the 'social engineer'. This lot have all become too cynical and pseudo-scientific to be at all aware of the possibilities of the spirit – the power which is hidden in the will of a People to snatch salvation from the jaws of despondency. Because *no* revival, *no* return to the roots, *no* attempt to rescue a whole civilization from obliteration, is *impossible* in the world of *man*. It is those who worship statistics and generalizations – the carriers of the various strains of social pseudo-science – who say otherwise. To them, every crisis is beset by a thousand and one different considerations, a thousand and one reasons to be sensible and cautious. But the fate of the Welsh turns on one question, and that question is not how to ensure that the Anglicized Welsh tolerate the Welsh langauge, but, rather, who or what is going to arouse in us an awareness of our separate identity?

Do not be fooled: the call to regain the lost faith in the greatness of man's spirit is a call back to a more human life. And that is the call which comes to us in Wales now, because the crisis which faces us is not one of a temporary disarray in the order of our society – such as in England – but a crisis of the *end of our civilization*. The only thing of use in a situation such as this is a generation of young people sworn to *do the impossible*. And my appeal is, mainly, to the young. As Fichte said in the address I included in *Prydeindod*, if they too yield to the persuasion of the 'art of the possible' and fall back on the old pattern of compromise, 'how can the redeeming generation ever be born?' Today, in the time of the present generation, the gestation has come to an end, the fateful hour is upon us.

And that is why we must beg those of the older generation

whose attitude is more conservative and compromising to stand aside. In the words of Fichte: 'You are not asked to help, but for this once, do not, for God's sake interfere; do not get in the way as you usually do with your wise words of caution and your many objections. For this is a matter which has not a thousand aspects, but only one; and this is something which you do not understand. If your wisdom were able to open the vision doors this nation would not now be in this sorry state, because it has up to now arranged its life by your advice. You have been false lights. But this will not be held against you. Only learn at this late hour how to know yourselves and be silent.'

There is in the book of the prophet Jeremiah a symbolic example of this faith which enables a man to do what is to all appearances impossible, a story which stands out against the gloomy background of the book like a torch of hope.

'The king of Babylon's army besieged Jerusalem', and all the suburbs of that city, including Anathoth, where Jeremiah was brought up, had been overrun by the oppressor. Furthermore, 'Jeremiah the prophet was shut up in the court of the prison' because he had prophesied the unpalatable truth that Jerusalem would fall into the hands of the enemy.

> And the word of the lord came to Jeremiah, saying: Behold, Hanameel, the son of Shallum, thine uncle, shall come unto thee, saying: buy the field that is in Anathoth; for the right to redemption is thine to buy it. So Hanameel mine uncle's son came to me in the court of the prison according to the word of the Lord and said unto me: Buy my field, I pray thee, that is in Anathoth which is in the country of Benjamin, for the right of inheritance is thine and the redemption is thine; buy it for thyself.
> And I bought the field . . .

Note that this was a case of redemption to begin with – Jeremiah buying back his own land, his family's land, the proper land of his People – and that not before, but after it had fallen into the hands of the enemy. We see here the greatness of the will to keep a heritage from destruction in the face of circumstances which seemed hopeless. We have here a vision of the possibilities of man's spirit which are at the opposite pole to the talk of politics as the art of the possible. And this, I believe, is the symbolic significance of the buying of the land: it is an act of setting the prophetic union of will and hope against the safe, anti-heroic, unradical attitude which sees politics as just a sort of game – a sort of exercise in cunning which ensures that it never sets its aim higher than the least amount of improvement, or renewal, or liberty, that is technically possible.

Note too that not only is the land in Anathoth, which Jeremiah is invited to buy back, in the hands of the enemy; Jeremiah himself is in prison and there in bonds conducts the purchase.

So it is with us in Wales: not only had the heritage of the Welsh language been overrun by the enemy, but those who fight for the language suffer every sort of curse and disadvantage. They are accused and reviled on all sides – as dangerous, irresponsible romantics, traitors and supporters of narrow-mindedness and dis-unity, bitter fascists, parochial, fugitives to the past and enemies of progress, and – above all – as anti-Christian, enemies of the Christian emphasis on the similarity and brotherhood of all men. We are indeed bound and rejected in more than one kind of prison.

And yet – in bonds – Jeremiah carefully and ceremonially, so that everyone would understand the significance of his action, went about buying back the land of lost hope.

> And I bought the field of Hanameel, my uncle's son that was in Anathoth, and weighed him the money, even seventeen shekels of silver. And I subscribed the evidence and sealed it and took wit-nesses and weighed him the money in the balances.
>
> So I took the evidence of the purchase . . . and I gave it unto Baruch the son of Neriah in the sight of Hanameel and in the pres-ence of witnesses and before all the Jews that sat in the courts of the prison and I charged Baruch before them, saying: Take these evi-dences, this evidence of the purchase, both which is sealed and this evidence which is open; and put them in an earthenware vessel, that they may continue . . .

– in the face of the black prospects and the forecasts of the end – THAT THEY MAY CONTINUE!

> For houses and fields and vineyards shall be possessed again in the land.

> *Translated from the Welsh by John Phillips.*

158

The Night of the Fire

EMYR HUMPHREYS

From Planet 49/50, January 1980

I

In the small hours of Tuesday the eighth of September in the year 1936 three men wearing hats and raincoats sat in a car parked in a farm lane a few miles from Pwllheli. Two were smoking cigarettes and all three were staring anxiously towards the south-west. There was a stiff wind blowing and a threat of rain. To pass the time they were discussing a short story the bespectacled non-smoker was trying to finish. The title was appropriate enough. *Dros y Bryniau Tywyll Niwlog* – 'Over the Gloomy Hills of Darkness' (that is the opening line from one of the better-known hymns of William Williams Pantycelyn). The short-story writer had also cut a finger. It had been carefully bandaged by a doctor friend earlier in the evening and he was playing with it as he peered through the wind-screen like a man waiting for a signal. At last the signal came. A red glow in the night sky that grew even as they watched. The man at the wheel finished his cigarette.

'We shan't need to put on the lights. The fire will see us all the way to Pwllheli.'

The car drew up outside the police station at half past two in the morning. The three men asked the yawning constable on duty whether they could speak to the Superintendent. He showed some reluctance to comply with their request until one of the men told him that Penyberth was on fire. Penyberth was the name of the fifteenth-century farmhouse which had been demolished recently to make way for the first buildings of a bombing range in the course of construction for the use of the Air Force. When an Inspector of Police finally appeared, they handed him a letter and asked him to read it. In the subsequent trial this Welsh declaration appeared as Exhibit Number Seven with a translation attached to it.

September 7, 1936

To the Chief Constable at Caernarfon.

Sir,

We, the undersigned, acknowledge our responsibility for the damage inflicted this night, September 7, on the buildings at the Bombing Camp at Penyberth.

From the moment the intention of creating this Bombing Centre in Llŷn was made public, we along with a host of other figures prominent in all aspects of Welsh public life did everything we could to persuade the English government to refrain from establishing in this most conspicuously Welsh homeland an alien institution that would inevitably damage and ultimately destroy its venerable culture and way of life. However, in spite of all our appeals, in spite of humble petitions and protest meetings, in spite of lengthy arguments and letters from hundreds of organisations both religious and secular, and in spite of a petition signed by thousands of electors in Llŷn itself, the English government refused so much as to receive a deputation from Wales to discuss the matter. All this effort conducted in a diligently peaceful manner within the law failed to gain for Wales even a show of common courtesy from the English Government.

Therefore, in order to compel attention to this immoral attack on the well-founded natural rights of the Welsh nation, we have been obliged to resort to this act as the only method left to us by a government that has treated our nation with insulting contempt.

We remain yours in the bonds of Wales,

Saunders Lewis
Lecturer in the University of Wales,
9, St Peter's Road,
Newton,
Mumbles, Swansea.

Lewis E. Valentine
Minister of the Gospel,
'Croeso', St Andrews Place,
Llandudno.

D. J. Williams
Schoolmaster,
49 High St.,
Fishguard.

When he had finished reading the letter, the Inspector showed that he was deeply disturbed. He asked the three men whether they fully realized the gravity of the situation in which they had placed themselves. They had made a most serious and damaging admission. Like the vast majority of his fellow countrymen at that time, Inspector William Moses Hughes was a sober chapel-going Nonconformist and he was here confronted with three men representing the two things in life for which he had the most profound respect, religion and education. Furthermore the three men were not only confessing to a criminal act. They were also making a political proclamation deliberately calculated to disturb the calm surface of Welsh life, challenging the authority it was his duty and his office to uphold. As he went through the motions laid down by long experience in the service of the law his mind must have been agitated by a sequence of uncomfortable and disturbing questions. The three men were locked in cells overnight. A friendly policeman in attendance was able to complete a quotation from a much loved sonnet by Robert Williams Parry, a close friend of the three. A quiet joke was also made about the old proverb that said 'three tries for a Welshman'. Mr Williams, the short-story writer, had had some trouble with his box of matches. The Inspector followed the Fire Brigade to the scene of the fire.

II

There is a simple sense in which History can be interpreted as the continuing interplay between premeditated acts and a surge of uncontrollable events. The year 1936 is now, of course, part of what is described in curricula as Modern History. These are the events, we say, with the modest confidence of would-be historians, which gave the world in which we continue to live its particular shape and flavour. We like to think the passage of time opens up the perspective whereby we can discern the patterns of the past with that academic detachment necessary to handle calmly all the mercurial elements involved, so that they mean something and do not vanish like ghostly fool's fire into the mists of irretrievable time.

161

The letter handed to the Inspector of Police indicates that these three men (of whom two are still alive; the short-story writer D. J. Williams died on 4 January 1970, in his eighty-fifth year) at that point of time saw the course of history as a tidal wave that threatened their nation with a destruction as final as that famous edict put out by Haman the Agagite in the name of King Ahasuarus decreed for the Jews.

Not all Welshmen in 1936 were equally worried about their national existence. During the long campaign against the establishment of a bombing school in Llŷn many appeals were made from various bodies for the support of the most influential and celebrated Welshman of that time. The boyhood home of David Lloyd George was no more than ten miles from the proposed site. Throughout his career the former prime minister and war leader had at all times been aggressively Welsh. Even now, with one home in Surrey and another in Cricieth, he compelled all those who came in contact with him, or as some biographers would have it, all who came under his spell, to accept his Welshness and to appreciate with equal force terms of endearment or chastisement in his native tongue. All his life Welsh remained the language of his emotions. The annual renewal of the life-long love affair with the land of his fathers took place in suitable druidical surroundings every Thursday afternoon of National Eisteddfod week. There could be no doubting the sincerity of his affection. But in this marriage, passionate as it was, the devotion tended to be one-sided: Wales, over and over again, proved more faithful to her wedded hero than he to the indulgent and doting wife of his bosom. At last in the midsummer of 1936, when two thousand bodies representing over half a million Welsh people had made their objections known, the great man spoke. He did so in characteristic fashion. In July the minister of the Calvinistic Methodist church in Cricieth wrote a personal appeal to Mr Lloyd George. Busy as Lloyd George was with plans to re-establish himself as a dominating figure on the world's stage – there were plans afoot for a prestigious visit to Adolf Hitler, and a visit to America to study the New Deal and to confer with President Roosevelt, and possibly a holiday in the West Indies with his second family – he did not neglect to reply, in Welsh, to the minister's letter. His reply arrived on 29 July and on the same day a lucid English translation appeared in all the English-language newspapers circulating in north Wales. (In the case of *The Times*, for example, the letter appeared only in the Welsh editions.) He claimed to have given the problem of the bombing school his close attention. He was in full sympathy with the view expressed by his fellow Welshmen. Nevertheless he felt it was most urgent to link the question of bombing with the larger issue of disarmament. Bombing from the air should be outlawed by international agreement, and but for the intervention of the British government this vital step would have been taken already at the Disarmament Conference. Now as long as aerial bombardment was countenanced by the great powers, it would be inconsistent not to train personnel to reach a level of proficiency in the art and even more inconsistent to expect this to be done in some other part of the country that the air force was created to defend. He himself was disturbed day and night by the noise of military aircraft over his house in Surrey: but he would never be so selfish as to join any movement among his neighbours to remove the nuisance to plague fellow citizens in another part of the realm. If bombing had to be, then there had to be a bombing school somewhere. But of course his answer as always was to get at the root of the problem and work for the abolition of aerial bombardment by solemn international agreement.

When set side by side these two letters, both carefully considered before they were written, throw much light on the characters of the men who composed them in the year 1936: and even more perhaps on the nature of the society which produced and to some extent moulded them. It is not merely that teachers and preachers usually do have greater freedom to demonstrate their tender conscience than politicians. Over this sensitive issue we are witnessing exceptional men operating within the limits of a strictly Welsh context. It is as if Merlin with all his arts and quasi-supernatural skills were being confronted and challenged by Gildas, that grim sixth-century Savonarola, and asked to state without the aid of eloquence, in monosyllabic and unequivocal terms, to which kingdom of this world, to which language, to which culture, and to which society, he was prepared to give his first allegiance. Although he may not have been aware of it at that moment in the summer of 1936 the former prime minister, and prototype of a twentieth-century dictator, was being faced with a conflict of interest that externalized an even more profound conflict within his own nature. And this conflict was made more acute because he shared it with the majority of his fellow country-men of his time, and because something of its presence could be traced back in the history of his people for at least a thousand years.

If it had been possible, there is no doubt that his answer to the question of first allegiance would have been 'both'. After all, for most of his career that had been his answer. But self-deception and equivocation are no easier for people with two faces than for people with one. To be two-faced is not merely a defect of charac-ter. If you are two men, you are obliged to have at least two faces. Throughout the successful phase of his public life, David Lloyd George had in fact been obliged to be two men. In Wales he was always the great Welsh nationalist (with a small 'n') who more than anyone else had taught his fellow countrymen to lift up their traditionally downcast eyes and to face the world, to challenge it and to conquer it. In Wales he was always the Welsh champion armed like a medieval knight with the breastplate of Nonconformity, as ready as Peredur or Geraint or Galath to enter the list and take on all-comers. But in England he was what Mr A. J. P. Taylor has described as 'the greatest ruler of England since Oliver Cromwell'.

As ruler of England Ll. G. was in control of British imperial policy at a time when it still seemed capable of laying down a new world order. By that strange sleight of hand which seems to be history's continuing legacy to the ambitious Welshman, he was able to use his own fierce private and personal version of national pride as a channel for the abiding patriotism of the English. In 1918 he stood as the chief architect of victory and the architect-elect of a new Europe and a new world. At this point it is fair to say that his attempt to confront the surge of uncontrollable events with premeditated action was on a scale permitted to few men in history. But individuals remain individuals. There is, mercifully, no order of magnitude that allows the great, whatsoever the degree of their megalomania, to reproduce themselves as often as their photographs and images. By the same token, ordinary mortals have no right to expect even the most potent men of destiny to exert that strain of superhuman force that is alone capable of diverting a tidal wave. The best we can do is to record respectfully and accurately the degree of effort made by both the mighty and the weak to alleviate the damage.

One of the signatories to the letter handed to the Inspector of Police in the early hours of 8 September 1936, had already had occasion to make this assessment of the nature of the achievement of the great man; or to put it more precisely, to criticize the great man's basic assessment of his own achievement. In June 1930 an enthusiastic public meeting was held in Caernarfon to celebrate the fortieth anniversary of D. Lloyd George's election to the Parliament at Westminster as Liberal member for the Caernarfon Boroughs. His words were reported in indirect speech in the Welsh-language weekly press:

> . . . and he was sometimes reproved for not giving all his time to Welsh questions and leaving other matters to other people. This was a question that did not affect his career alone, but affected also the great number of young Welshmen who were liable to be called to a wider sphere of service. Were they to resist such a call or was it their duty to answer it? There was also something much deeper involved. In this world no man may foresee any more than a river, the course his career may take him. The speaker would not wish to claim for himself anything more than the status of one of the smaller tributaries sprung from the hills of Wales (*laughter*) . . .
>
> Then in conclusion, Mr Lloyd George referred to the Severn and how on his way back to Wales to celebrate this anniversary he had observed the winding course of this river. It began as a little brook secluded in the safety of the mountains and then flowed down the side of Plynlimmon to water the valleys of Cardiganshire and having gained strength there turned eastwards to pass through the sweet meadows of Montgomery and then crossing the border to fertilize with prodigal generosity the broad acres of England. Then we see the river turn westwards, back to Wales – the old land of its birth – (applause) before losing itself in the sea. Who would accuse the Severn of turning its back on Wales? The river, Mr Lloyd George said, like everything and everyone else, was in the hand of God. Thus it is that Welshmen must serve their generation as Providence directs them. As for himself, whenever his time came in due season, he hoped to find his last resting place in the bosom of Wales so that on the day of the great awakening his eyes would open to look upon her ancient hills (*loud applause*).

The following month, in the July 1930 issue of *Y Ddraig Goch*, the nationalist paper which he edited, Saunders Lewis published his comments on the Caernarfon speech under the title 'Mr Lloyd George's Confession of Faith'. It is worth reproducing in extended quotation because it demonstrates the polarization of attitude between two generations that had taken place by that date. Lewis was in his thirties. Lloyd George was in his seventies.

> The great statesman used the occasion to review his career and towards the end gave us a glimpse of his philosophy of life . . . It is our duty to scrutinise his message and as far as we can to ignore the rhetoric and the loud applause . . . I discern two frightening elements in Mr Lloyd George's confession of faith. The first is the light it throws on his character as a politician and leader. The second and more disturbing is the philosophy he cherishes and now offers freely as a rule of living to the young Welshman of today. About the first element I shall say no more than to invite his electors and fervent followers to consider whether they wish to continue to follow a leader who, on such an occasion and carefully measuring his words, announces that he is not and has never been responsible for his actions: a leader who insists on comparing himself to the river Severn, at the mercy of every wind that blows, twisting and turning, without will, without character, without design, driven on only by the whim or circumstance and his own irresistible instincts and desires . . .
>
> Let us turn to the philosophy Mr Lloyd George offered as a guide to our young people in Wales and what he teaches about the place and the purpose of Wales in the world and in contemporary life. These are the key sentences.
> 1. 'No man can foresee, any more than a river, the course his career may take him!'
> 2. 'Who would accuse the Severn of turning its back on Wales?'
> 3. 'It is in the hand of God, as we all are.'
> 4. 'Thus it is that Welshmen must serve their generation as Providence directs them.'
>
> The reader will forgive me for repeating platitudes that are in fact old and simple truths well known to everyone, but denied by Mr Lloyd George and forgotten by the audience at Caernarfon that greeted his words with 'Loud applause'.
>
> A man is a responsible being. To this end he enjoys the freedom to choose. He can choose the hard road in life or he can choose the easy way. He can choose and he has the obligation to choose. The man who refuses to make a choice and looks upon himself as a river is lost because he has abdicated his humanity. The river Severn 'loses itself in the sea': but a river can offer no example for the life of a man, and a man is not 'in the hand of God' in the same way as a river. It is true that the Severn begins as a small stream in

the mountains of Wales and having gained strength, that it crosses the border to water the fruitful English fields: and it is true (as far as we know) that she remembers nothing of the land of her origin. But, to quote the words of Gruffudd Robert of Milan, an experienced exile, 'The man who denies his father or his mother or his country or his language is never a reliable or a virtuous companion'. 'Who would accuse the Severn of turning its back on Wales?' No one in his right mind. And although Mr Lloyd George only makes the modest claim of being 'no more than a little tributary' we can not allow him this defence nor this frightening denial of his responsibility as a human being and a Welshman. We summon him before the bar of history and reason as every man 'who gained his strength in the mountains of Wales' shall be summoned, and we declare that his excuse is insufficient and feeble, and that he has a responsibility that he cannot throw away and that the Welshman who follows the course of the river Severn in his own life also degrades his own humanity.

Every Welshman must choose. Every man who takes up politics and a political career must choose, must plan, must use foresight. 'In this world no man may foresee any more than a river the course his career may take him', says Mr Lloyd George. This is simply untrue: a person can foresee a great deal more than a river. He can foresee that difficulties and temptations will beset him. Of course what Mr Lloyd George is really saying is: 'if I could have foreseen in 1890 that one day I would have the chance to become prime minister of England, I would not have gone about preaching Welsh nationalism. If I could have foreseen that my own past would one day be thrown in my face, I would not have begun a crusade in Meirionydd against T. E. Ellis because he broke his vow and accepted office in the English government. All my life I have been obliged to eat my words and break my promises – a man can foresee no more than a river.' That is the true meaning of Mr Lloyd George's words. But he does not have the right to transform the story of his own career and the fickleness of his own character into a general example to be followed by the youth of Wales.

We have not come to the end of the sorry articles of faith of 'the most famous Welshman in the world'. We would protest emphatically too against his belief that it is natural for every brilliant young Welshman to turn to England to seek 'a wider sphere of service' and that 'Providence' leads every gifted Welshman into the service of England as effortlessly as the river Severn flows over to the English plain. Let us set aside the comic blasphemy that equates the ambition and lust for power of a man with 'Providence' and 'the Hand of God'. Apart from that, we take leave to doubt the inevitability of the movement from the service of the smaller country to that of the larger. Let us compare Mr Lloyd George's position today with that of Thomas Masaryk. They both set out as leaders of small oppressed nations. The same temptation offered itself to them both, that is, deserting the small country to serve the great empire of the larger. One accepted the offer: the other rejected it. We may ask who is the influence for the good and the inspiration of the best European spirit in 1930? David Lloyd George or Thomas Masaryk? There are too many happy examples in history of the influence of great men in small countries enriching the life of mankind for us to accept uncritically the snobbish servile notion that the size and material strength of a country automatically elevates it into 'a wider sphere of service'. We believe it is through Wales that a Welsh statesman can most effectively serve Europe and humanity. And more than that: through the service of Wales that statesman's character will be best formed and his life best fulfilled and enriched. Through England and the service of England, Mr Lloyd George obtained two things that would never have been his had he dedicated himself to the service of Wales: great material wealth and comfort, and the enjoyment of world-wide fame. The effect of these gifts has been to transform him into a hard-faced cynic. Underneath his doctrine of the nature of the relationship between Wales and England we can discern his cold contempt for his own country.

'I hope', he said at the end of his speech, 'to be allowed to rest in the bosom of Wales.' We would prefer men ready to live and work for Wales than a sentimental cynic who wants to return to be buried in her bosom. The evil effect that Mr Lloyd George has had in Wales and continues to have, is to treat her like a bondslave feeding her with lies and rhetoric. His confession of faith at Caernarfon deserves nothing but outright condemnation. There is something terrible in the thought that this is the harvest of forty years' intense political life.

III

Six years later, David Lloyd George was pursuing his political career as intensely as ever. On the night of the fire at Penyberth, 8 September, 1936, he was at Berchtesgaden, still basking in the afterglow of two cordial meetings with the German Chancellor, Adolf Hitler. We know from contemporary accounts that both men were much drawn to each other. More than a year before, Hitler had invited 'the man who won the war' to visit him. The newly appointed German Ambassador to the Court of St James, Joachim von Ribbentrop, had renewed the invitation in pressing terms, and by September 1936, Lloyd George could resist the temptation no longer. Many of his more promising schemes to return to power had proved abortive. There was no place for him in the National government in London. His section of the Liberal Party was an ineffective and demoralized rump. The bright promise of the Council of Action had faded. In such a situation, the political dividends to be gained from a visit to Hitler seemed well worth collecting. It would outflank, embarrass and possibly madden Stanley Baldwin. This was a delight in itself. He knew that Baldwin was toying with the notion of meeting the Führer. Furthermore it would capture the headlines all over the world and he would appear once again in his favourite role of conciliator and international peacemaker, and by implication, still fully capable of being the arbiter of the fate of nations. His power base might have shrunk, but his charisma could be shown to be undimmed. If it were true that Adolf Hitler admired him so much, it was not beyond the bounds of possibility that he would take his advice. While spellbinders were not obliged to fall under each other's spells, face to face, they could, as would not be the case with more ordinary politicians, talk as equals. A meeting of exceptional personalities would take place: and this would augur nothing but good for Europe and for the world. With the garrulity of an energetic 73-year-old, Lloyd George enlarged on these themes to his entourage of willing listeners.

According to the published diaries of the ubiquitous Thomas Jones, Hitler himself appeared to consider the visit a historic event. Both Jones and Conwell-Evans record that Hitler could not take his eyes off the Welsh Wizard. Both noted too, the striking similarity in the magnetic power of two pairs of piercing blue eyes. There were statesman-like exchanges. Hitler declared once again that there was nothing closer to his heart than an agreement with Britain and France. The civilization of Europe had to be protected from the Bolshevik menace. Lloyd George expressed a cautious sympathy with this view but said he was more immediately concerned with the conflict that had just broken out in Spain between 'two sets of extremists'. Thomas Jones records his own irritation at the whirring of A. J. Sylvester's cine camera as the assiduous factotum crept around the cavernous drawing-room taking moving pictures of the historic encounter. Nevertheless, in retrospect, the noise of the camera was the most significant sound being made. The ghostly images can still be seen. Neither of the two pagan heroes was camera-shy. They were both acutely aware of the importance of the new media in the sacred process of moulding the primeval will of the masses. In this sense the meeting at Berchtesgaden was the encounter between the old elected monarch of manipulation and his more fearsome heir apparent, – the genial Welsh Wizard on a semi-official visit to Grendel's lair.

Lloyd George regretfully declined an invitation to attend the forthcoming Nürnberg rally. This did not mean his enthusiasm for the constructive aspects of the New Germany were in any way dimmed. Were they not in fact the energetic realization of all the splendid plans he had drawn up himself for the conquest of unemployment in Britain: those new motorways – so essential to a modern industrial nation; the work and welfare schemes; the great building projects; the new popular art; the agricultural settlements, the labour camps? He approved wholeheartedly of all the glossy symbols of a new and energetic national socialist society. But the rally he could not attend. The discarded god of one tribe could not easily find an appropriate role at the organized ceremonial of the god of another. But Thomas Jones attended one session and saw forty-two thousand polished spades flash in the sun on the shoulders of the brown ranks of the *Appell des Reichsarbeitsdienstes*.

As the evening wore on, Lloyd George showed signs of relapsing into a mood of peevish despondency. He had seen the Führer twice and now the rest of his three-week visit to Germany could so easily develop into a boring anticlimax. He was daunted at the prospect of endless visits to factories. Thomas Jones recognized the danger signals. He ordered Pommard 1928 and egged on Lloyd George to tell some of his stories of the great Welsh preachers for the delectation of Lord Dawson of Penn. Over the years Ll. G. had collected a large quantity of material about men like John Elias, Christmas Evans, Mathews Ewenni, and John Jones Talysarn. It was his intention to write a book about them. The emphasis of the book would have been on the power of their performance and their ability to arouse vast congregations, to seize the imagination and emotions of the masses, to mould an entire nation in the image of a chosen people marching fearlessly in the direction of salvation. It is not recorded which selection he gave from his repertoire on the evening of the 7 September 1936. His preference was always for the Old Testament. As he said he preferred majesty to meekness. He was extremely fond of relating John Elias's sermon on Belshazzar's Feast and the writing on the Wall. He described how carefully John Elias set the scene. He would visit the chapel before the service and direct that the candles should be arranged so that his hand, as he stood in the pulpit, would cast a long shadow on the wall. Lloyd George revelled in describing the alarm and terror spreading among the congregation when at the climactic moment the message was actually seen appearing on the wall. Whatever the choice of anecdotes the result was pleasant. Thomas Jones writes that they were all in hilarious mood as they made their way to bed.

On 4 October, the Reverend Lewis Valentine was the annual guest preacher at Salem Chapel, Porth, in the Rhondda Valley. The chapel was full and there was a higher proportion of men attending the service than was usual in the Rhondda. They sat mostly in the gallery. They all knew that the guest preacher, with his two companions in fire-raising, would be before the Court of Assize in Caernarfon the following week. They wanted to show some sympathy and solidarity even though many of them could hardly be classified as Christian believers, let alone members of the Baptist Church. Lewis Valentine took his text from the sixth chapter of the gospel according to St John.

> From that time many of his disciples went back and walked no more with him. Then said Jesus unto the twelve, 'Will ye also go away?' Simon Peter answered him, 'Lord, to whom shall we go? Thou hast the words of eternal life.'

An eye-witness describes the sermon as deeply affecting; not merely the content, but even more the calm spirit in which the message was delivered. The presiding minister referred to Mr Valentine as a prophet and the following morning a large crowd escorted him to the train.

IV

At Caernarfon the Court House stands, appropriately enough, in the shadow of the medieval castle. There, because of a persistent rumour that students intended to hoist the Red Dragon on the flagpost of the Eagle Tower the night before the trial, the entrance to the tower steps had been boarded up with planks. The court room was gloomy and dominated by the judge's bench. Above his chair a large oil painting caught what little natural light entered the room. It depicted Edward I presenting the first English Prince of Wales to the Welsh nobles, a baby on his shield. Admission to the trial was by ticket and the courthouse was surrounded by heavy police reinforcements. The crowds in the streets and in the square had been gathering since early morning. In the five weeks since the fire at Penyberth, after an initial period of local hostility, popular support had been growing for the three men. The court-room was packed tight long before the trumpets sounded to announce the approach of the judge's procession.

Before the trial began the traditional words had to be read out:

> ... His Majesty's Justice of Assize do strictly charge and command all persons to keep silence while His Majesty's Commission of Assize is produced and read, upon pain of imprisonment.

The Associate opened a great parchment roll and read out in a loud voice:

> Edward the Eighth, by the grace of God, of Great Britain, Ireland and the British Dominions beyond the seas, King and Emperor, Defender of the Faith, to the Honourable Mr Justice Lewis, Knight ...

The judge picked up the black cap on the bench in front of him and bowed his head each time the commission referred to him by name. The commission concluded with the words: 'doing therein as to justice doth appertain, according to the laws and customs of England'.

In the case of the King v. John Saunders Lewis, Lewis Edward Valentine and David John Williams, the charges were arson and malicious damage to property. The 'Particulars of Offence' stated that they had

> on the eighth day of September 1936, at Penrhos in the County of Caernarfon, maliciously set fire to certain buildings belonging to His Majesty the King.

In 1937 a full account of the trial and of the circumstances sur-rounding it was published in Welsh by Dafydd Jenkins under the title *Tân yn Llŷn* (Fire in Llŷn) recently republished. Among the illustrations in the book is a photograph of the three men on their way to the trial. They all wear hats and carry attaché cases rather like old-fashioned ministers on their way to a weekend preaching engagement. They are smiling and confident. By the time the book was published they were all three so well known to the Welsh reading public there was no need for Mr Jenkins to say very much about them.

We can see from the photographs that D. J. Williams was the eldest. He was in his fifty-first year. In the second volume of his lively autobiography he tells us that he left home at the age of sixteen to work in the coal-mines of Glamorgan. Home was a hill farm in Carmarthenshire, where, he says,

> were stowed my notions about religion, about education, about my country, about language and about life before these abstract terms conveyed anything to my understanding. It was an atmosphere and a tradition that came down from generation to generation . . . I believe I was the first ever, of all my line, to leave the land . . My family's inheritance of land has grown smaller with the centuries, until by my time it has almost vanished. But this does not worry me, because I am aware that I have been allowed somehow to keep something that is dearer in my sight than land or possessions – the consciousness of the ancient values of my ancestors bound with a feeling of responsibility for their continuance.

The story of his life is evidence of the sincerity and the truthfulness of these words, although they were written with the wisdom of hindsight when D. J. Williams was approaching old age. From his autobiography we learn that once in his early twenties he was filled with a sudden desire to emigrate to the United States of America. He had an uncle who ministered to Welsh churches in Kansas and Colorado. This uncle wrote and published in America Welsh temperance novels in which teetotallers always triumphed. In the depth of the coal-mine at Blaen Dulais, D. J. lowered his mandrel to ask himself a question: 'How long do I have to stay down here punching out my soul in this black hole of hell?' Like so many others underground, the young man dreamed of buying land in the Far West where land was still cheap and building up a ranch that would be a bit of old Wales in the shadow of the Rocky Mountains. In those far-off days, he tells us, he did not stop to think of the tribal rights of the Indian tribes that were in fact not so unlike his own sense of inheritance. But the American uncle, like a recurring character in so many Welsh plays of the period, came home, so to speak, in time for Act Two. He directed his eager nephew's attention to the alternative nineteenth-century Welsh dream – education. Instead of going to America, Davy John, after many epic trials, most amusingly described, found his way to Aberystwyth and Oxford. But everything that ever happened to him seems to have strengthened that resolute Welsh patriotism so deeply rooted in his native soil.

It seems an ironic parable that his old home today should be buried under the lines of Germanic spruces planted by the Forestry Commission, as neatly mute on the hillside as the crosses of the War Graves Commission.

Llanddulas, the village on the north Wales coast where Lewis Valentine was brought up, has also suffered in the name of progress. What is left of it clings to the side of a motorway that facilitates the annual invasion of the area. What was once a village of outstanding beauty has become as unsightly as the Jersey shore. Valentine's father worked in the quarry and like Lloyd George's Uncle Lloyd, preached on Sunday in the small chapels of the Baptists, in that part of the world. He writes of his father, 'he was the most amiable Puritan I ever encountered. My recollection of his sermons is poor, but his prayers I shall never forget. They preserved me from many excesses in the course of my life.'

In the photograph of the three on their way to the trial, Valentine walks in the middle. He is a tall handsome figure and the idle reader is tempted to speculate about the excesses that could have tempted him. As a theological student he joined the RAMC during the First World War. He arrived in France in time for the first Battle of the Somme. He was one of the thousands who looked up at the leaning Virgin of Albert. In his diary he wrote:

> Formerly with her arms outstretched she offered her Holy Son to heaven, now she looks like a mad woman ready to hurl her child to the ground as a sacrifice to the blind rage of destruction.

After the war he took a good degree in Hebrew and for a while considered an academic career. He also followed the honours course in Welsh and was elected president of the Students' Council at Bangor. It was in this capacity that he organized protests against the use of the Black and Tans in Ireland. To the embarrassment of the prime minister, Mr Lloyd George, in 1920, university students in his constituency paid silent tribute to the body of Terence Mac Swiney, the Lord Mayor of Cork, as it passed through Bangor. This demonstration, organized by Valentine, was condemned by local Liberals as little short of treason. It is not altogether surprising that, when a Welsh political party was at last formed in the course of the National Eisteddfod at Pwllheli in 1925, Lewis Valentine, at the age of 31, should have been elected its first president.

There were in fact only six men present at this inconspicuous inaugural and David John Williams was not one of them. His train from the south was late. He was met on the platform by Saunders Lewis whose first words to him were, 'the thing has been started'. By 'thing' he obviously meant that a new political party had been established by the union of the two or three spontaneous movements that had already come into being among the workers and students in the north and the academics in the south. But the reverberations went much deeper. The 'thing' was nothing less than an attempt to hold up and even reverse what the majority of Welshmen were coming to accept as an inevitable historical process: even that redoubtable nationalist with a small 'n', David Lloyd George.

The third accused, John Saunders Lewis, was born in Wallasey, Cheshire, in 1893. His father was a Welsh Calvinistic minister. And so for that matter was his grandfather, Dr Owen Thomas of Liverpool as he was known throughout Wales. And his great-grandfather, William Roberts, Amlwch, the friend and companion of John Elias and John Jones, Talysarn, was among the galaxy of great preachers that Lloyd George so much admired. Merseyside at the turn of the century was to Welsh minds no more than a convenient extension of north Wales. (The exact opposite one might say, to the present-day situation.) More than a hundred thousand Welsh speaking souls earned their living in and around Liverpool. A high proportion of them were virtually monoglot Welsh. A recurring theme in the memoirs of nineteenth-century north Walians was the experience of arriving in the metropolis and being unable to ask the way. (A variant on the same theme was the parallel arrival in Philadelphia or New York. Before the 1880s very few Welsh emigrants would have acquired English before leaving home.)

175

Lewis was educated at home and in chapel entirely in Welsh until at the age of eight he was sent to Liscard High School and from that moment we can only assume that like any other immigrant, he was made conscious of the dualism of belonging to two worlds. Home and chapel were Welsh, school was English. Under such circumstances a boy is obliged to shine or go under. It is quite clear that the young Lewis, small and frail as he was, shone.

He attended Liverpool University, reading English and French. On the morning of 4 August, 1914, crossing the Mersey by ferry boat he opened his morning paper and learnt that war had been declared. He volunteered that day for military service. He was commissioned and served with the South Wales Borderers throughout the war in France and in Greece. He was wounded but he survived. The great war had a grim appetite for poets: Apollinaire, Wilfred Owen, Péguy, Edward Thomas, Alain Fournier, Hedd Wyn, Jean Pierre Caloch, Isaac Rosenberg. But some escaped. Men like Ungaretti, Robert Graves, Bert Brecht, David Jones, and Saunders Lewis. War seems to have disturbed him rather less than most writers. In all his work, plays, poetry, novels, literary criticism, there is hardly any mention of his personal war experience, unlike the work of his friend David Jones for example.

Nevertheless the war changed his life. During the grim Battle of Loos he read Maurice Barrès for the first time and was given a new vision of the nature of the relationship of the artist to the society to which he belonged. Then came the Easter Rising in Dublin. This seems to have affected him no less than it did the Irish poets. And in the same fateful year, home on convalescent leave, he wanders into a bookshop in Swansea and picks up a biography of Emrys ap Iwan, that lonely voice in nineteenth-century Wales, a European Welshman who lived in France and Germany and Switzerland and urged his fellow countrymen to look to Europe and not be mesmerized by the cultures of England and America. This was the deepest resistance of all. The language barrier could be more formidable in the end than the bullet or the barricade. From this time forward he took the path that led inevitably to the trial at Caernarfon.

V

'How say you, John Saunders Lewis, are you guilty or not guilty?'

Lewis answers in Welsh. 'Yr wyf yn ddieuog.'

The judge leans forward. His name too is Lewis. Sir Wilfred Hubert Poyer Lewis, grandson of a former bishop of Llandaff, educated at Eton and Oxford and a captain in the Glamorgan Yeomanry during the war. Captain Lewis faces Captain Lewis. Not so much two sides of the same coin as two aspects of Welsh life now placed in positions of open conflict.

'Is John Saunders Lewis the person who is described in the indictment as a lecturer?'

He gives sarcastic emphasis to the last word. Lewis in the dock continues to speak in Welsh.

'Ie, darlithydd wyf i, yn Llenyddiaeth Cymru, yng Ngholeg y Brifysgol, Abertawe.' ('Yes. I am a lecturer in Welsh literature at the University College, Swansea.')

The judge is irritated. Not only is it inconceivable that an educated man anywhere in the British Isles should claim not to be able to speak English. There is also the alarming possibility that some obscure disrespect is intended, perhaps to a judge only recently knighted and on his first circuit as a member of the King's Bench Division of the High Court. Breathing deeply he prepares to assert the dignity of the law and the authority of the Crown.

'Listen to me. Do you tell me that you cannot speak or understand English?'

The defendant continues to speak Welsh.

'Mi fedraf Saesneg, ond Cymraeg yw fy mamiaith.' ('I can speak English [lit. I can manage English] but Welsh is my mother tongue'.)

The judge adopts the style of a barrister cross-examining an unreliable witness.

'Do you mean to tell me that you cannot understand or speak English?'

There is a moment's pause while Lewis considers his reply.

He speaks again, in measured tones, in Welsh.

'Yr wyf yn gofyn yn ostyngedig i'm Harglwydd ganiatáu imi ateb yn Gymraeg, am mai hi yw fy mamiaith. Gofynaf i'r cyfieithydd gyfieithu hyn.' ('I ask humbly that your Lordship permits me to answer in Welsh since that is my mother tongue. I ask the translator to translate this.')

'Do you understand and speak English?'

At last Lewis speaks English.

'I can understand and speak English, but Welsh is my mother tongue.'

The judge remains acutely dissatisfied.

'Do you understand and speak English? Answer me. Yes or No.'

'Yes, my Lord.'

'Very well then. You will plead to the indictment in English.'

The indictment is read again in English and the accused is asked whether he pleads guilty or not guilty. Lewis replies in Welsh.

'Yr wyf i yn ddieuog.'

The judge leans forward menacingly.

'I will give you one more chance. Do you speak and understand English?'

VI

Sir Wilfred Lewis was ready to administer the law of England with all the confidence of a man called to the bar by the Inner Temple in 1908. Every law book he had ever read began by extolling the supreme virtues of the Common Law and the English Judicial System. What was left of the law of Wales had been abolished by the Act of Union exactly four hundred years ago in 1536 along with most of the trappings of independent existence. The twentieth section of that Act declared:

> Also be it enacted that all justices, sheriffs, coroners, escheators . . . and all the other officers and ministers of the law, shall proclaim and keep the sessions, courts, hundreds, leets, sheriff's court and all other courts in the English tongue: and all oaths of officers, juries, and inquests . . . be given and done in the English tongue; and also that from henceforth no person or persons that use the Welsh speech and language shall have or enjoy any manner of office or fees within this realm.

The Act of Union offered the learned judge no compromise. King Henry VIII could express a profuse and 'singular zeal, love and favour towards his subjects of this Dominion of Wales'. His dynasty owed the throne to the singular zeal, love, favour and sacrifice of the people from whom they sprang and to whom his father had appeared as the *Mab Darogan*, the national saviour whose coming had been so vividly prophesied by the bards and poets. But Henry VIII was always a demanding lover. Too often his tender embrace could end in a kiss of death: 'his said country or dominion of Wales, shall be, stand and continue for ever from henceforth incorporated united and annexed to and with this his Realm of England.'

Mr Justice Lewis must have been aware that the trial would develop into a political occasion. The three men had deliberately set fire to the sheds and materials in order to draw public attention to their cause. They had presented themselves at the police station with a letter already written, carefully setting out their motives for committing the offence. The three had appeared twice before the magistrates before being sent to trial at the Caernarfon Assizes. But they had not given evidence or called witnesses. Although the Crown solicitor had pointed out that the maximum penalty for the crimes of which the three were accused was penal servitude for life, the magistrates had allowed bail on condition that they would not make propaganda in relation to the case. On submission by his solicitor, it was agreed that Mr Valentine should be allowed to keep his preaching engagements.

It is doubtful that Mr Justice Lewis would have been aware of the warmth of the reception the preacher received in the chapels he visited up and down Wales. But he would have known that the defendants had engaged W. H. Thompson, a company of solicitors well known for their expertise in political cases. And he would also have been aware that the protesters against the bombing site in Llŷn had made much use of the fact that the Air Ministry had abandoned similar projects on Holy Island, Lindisfarne, and Abbottsbury, Chesil Bank, in deference to local sentiment. Their claim was that Llŷn with its historical and religious traditions and its living language and unique culture, was entitled to at least the same degree of consideration as bird sanctuaries in England. His summing up at the end of the trial showed that Mr Justice Lewis had been prepared for this: 'Let me say this. It may be that you and I and everybody in this court – I do not know – it may be that we all think it is a pity that the aerodrome was placed at Penrhos – we may all think that – I do not know – but that fact does not in law justify the act of burning it down . . .'

What seems to have taken him by surprise was the demand of three educated men to be tried in their mother tongue and not the official language of the court. This simple fact reveals a great deal

179

about the strange course of Welsh history after the Act of Union. It is true that the old aristocracy, who throughout the Middle Ages had been the chief defenders of Welsh culture and national identity, for the most part had responded with alacrity to the Tudor policy of merging Wales into the centralized English state. A new middle class emerged to exploit the new system. A breed of lawyers appeared and multiplied. The profit motive and the new law walked hand in hand. But even in the legal system there were men prepared to speak up for the old language as they might have done out of charity for a ragged beggar-maid pleading for entry at the gates of justice. In 1575 we find a judge of the Great Sessions writing to Walsingham urging the appointment of at least one judge able to understand Welsh,

> since now a judge must needs use an Interpreter, and therefore the Evidence is told according to the mynde of the Interpreter, whereby the Evidence is expounded contrary to that which is saide by the examynate, and so the Judge gyveth a wrong charge.

The Great Sessions absorbed the bulk of the more considerable business formerly conducted in the old Marcher courts and also relieved the work of the Court of the Lord President and Council for Wales and the Marches. The four English shires that came under this jurisdiction much resented their position under the Lord President. It seemed to lump them in with the Welsh and deny them the full privilege of being Englishmen of the first quality. The Marches that were of mixed population and had for so long belonged neither to Wales nor England were now overwhelmingly eager to be in every respect completely English. During the Commonwealth, the Council declined in importance and after the Revolution of 1688 it was abolished. But the Court of Great Sessions continued in active operation until 1830.

At that time, again after much agitation in English legal circles in London, a bill for the more effectual administration of justice in England and Wales proposed the extension of the jurisdiction of the Superior Courts of England to Chester and Wales. In the Commons, Sir John Owen, MP for Pembrokeshire, John Jones, MP for Carmarthen, Rice Trevor, MP for Carmarthenshire and later the second Lord Dynevor, and one or two others, opposed the bill vigorously. They urged that the bill would entail great additional expense on Welsh suitors. The lower classes were almost entirely

Welsh-speaking and the complete incorporation into the English system would put them at a grave disadvantage. They were only voices crying in the wilderness. The bill became law. In 1830 the majority of Welsh members were country gentlemen who rarely took part in debate. They sat in mute and comfortable agreement on the government side. For some years the Act inflicted much hardship on Welsh suitors. Writers of the time complained of the want of sympathy shown by English judges going on the new Welsh circuits. They made no attempt to conceal their assumption that Welshmen were beings inferior to Englishmen, and the Welsh language an incumbrance of the ignorant. It was not until the new Welsh Liberals entered the House of Commons in 1868 that matters showed any improvement. This, we are told, was due to the arrival of a new generation of Welshmen in the ranks of the legal profession imbued with the new spirit of pride in their language and nationality. However deep this new spirit may have been, and there certainly was a great political assertion of nationhood, it had little effect on the law courts or on conservative legal custom and practice. Lloyd George, the politician, for example, was a far more fervent devotee of his native language than Lloyd George, the Porthmadog solicitor. The educated Welshman of the great Liberal era was only too anxious to display his English education and his brilliant command of the English language. His aim in life was to excel in all the courts of the English and to climb as high as he could to attain the commanding heights of the Imperial English System. It was a miraculous change to look down instead of being looked down upon. The word 'British' had come into common usage, Matthew Arnold had decreed that the Empire needed the vital spark of Celtic imagination to extend the power of the Empire and complete its superiority in every sphere over all the nations of the earth. So be it. Platoons of bright young Welshmen lined up to offer their services. The language was left at home to remain a suitable vehicle of religious devotion (hence the cant phrase so widely in use 'the language of heaven'), for nostalgic songs, for eisteddfodau and for the cloistered delights of Welsh childhood, and for watered-down praise poetry. It was not wanted for the sterner pursuits of building and maintaining the great Empire in the world. And since English Common Law was one of the more obvious benefits bestowed by the Imperial System to unruly lesser breeds scattered about the globe, it was patently

181

clear that English was the only possible language for the proper dispensation of the law wherever a court should find itself in session. There is very little evidence that the Liberal Welsh nationalists with a small 'n' ever contested this proposition except to defend the rights of interpretation for their less fortunate fellow countrymen who had not enjoyed the manifold blessings of an English education.

VII

The effect of Mr Valentine's speech in his own defence was completely spoiled by the mechanics of translation and to a lesser extent by frequent interruptions from the judge who insisted that much of the substance of the speech was irrelevant to the case in hand. The interpreter rendered each sentence as it was delivered.

'My denomination takes the point of view I do on the matter of the bombing school and so do all the Nonconformist denominations in Wales today. Let me quote the declaration made by the Archdruid of Wales from the presidential chair of the Union of Welsh Congregationalists at Bangor this summer.'

The judge interrupted.

'I am not going to allow you to quote what any Archdruid or anyone else has said.'

Valentine stretched an arm towards the bench.

'I plead with you, my lord, in my difficulty.'

'I see no difficulty. You describe yourself as a minister of the Gospel and are presumably a man of intelligence. You will address the jury solely on the matters which are relevant to the charge.'

In spite of its dignified and impressive content, most people in the crowded court room appeared relieved when Valentine's address at last came to an end. The ventilation was bad. The High Sheriff, Mr Ronald Armstrong Jones, father of the distinguished photographer, could be seen leaning back in his chair, stifling yawns and staring fixedly at the ceiling. During the fractured progress of speech and translation the sound of singing rose and fell in the streets outside. There were hymns and repeated renderings of 'Hen Wlad fy Nhadau': also the undergraduates had a series of new verses about the burning of the bombing school. Porth Neigwl, the bay where the bombing markers would be placed, was for some reason called Hell's Mouth in English. The lampoonists were able to make great play with all the infernal implications. A powerful myth was being sent on its way, even as the trial was in progress. Friendly policemen beguiled the singers away from the court by subtle appeals. An inspector said, 'Now then, lads, now then good friends, don't disturb the court. Saunders Lewis is speaking and he's speaking marvellously too.'

The tactics of the defence had been worked out with a certain skill. There were several issues at stake. While they were all related it was important that the progress of the trial should reveal the intrinsic importance of each one in turn. The question of the inferior and disenfranchised position of the national language came first. The natural eloquence of the Reverend Lewis Valentine was as it were sacrificed for this cause. His difficulty demonstrated a fundamental point. Language, these men were saying, was central and fundamental to human dignity. All forms of behaviour, positive or negative actions, even questions of guilt and innocence, were defined by the language used to express the experience. Something of the value of the experience was inherent in the value of the language. If the language was treated with contempt, so were the people to whom the language belonged. They were on trial for wilful and malicious damage: the nature of the proceedings would be made to show just how much wilful and malicious damage had been and was being inflicted on their native language; and by the same token, how the native culture was still being eroded by an alien system of law and authority.

When he had made his formal protest about the way in which Mr Valentine's statement had been ruined by piecemeal translation, Saunders Lewis proceeded to address the jury in English. Of the three defendants it had been agreed that he was the one best capable of expressing their case with the necessary clarity and vigour in the English language. His style of delivery was cool and measured. He admitted the facts, explained the background of constitutional opposition to the bombing school, and outlined the cultural and religious traditions of Llŷn.

> It is impossible for one who had blood in his veins not to care passionately when he sees this terrible vandal bombing range in this very home of Welsh culture. On the desk before me is an anthology of the works of the Welsh poets of Llŷn, *Cynfeirdd Llŷn, 1500–1800* (*Early Poets of Llŷn 1500–1800*) by Myrddin Fardd. On page 176 of this book there is a poem, a *cywydd*, written in Penyberth farmhouse

in the middle of the sixteenth century. That house was one of the most historic in Llŷn. It was a resting-place for the Welsh pilgrims to the Isle of Saints, Ynys Enlli, in the Middle Ages. It had associations with Owen Glyndŵr. It belonged to the story of Welsh literature. It was a thing of hallowed and secular majesty. It was taken down and utterly destroyed a week before we burnt on its fields the timbers of the vandals who destroyed it. And I claim that, if the moral law counts for anything, the people who ought to be in this dock are the people responsible for the destruction of Penyberth farmhouse

At this point, the spectators could no longer restrain themselves from applauding. The judge ordered everyone to be quiet, and the officers of the court to remove anyone who dared to break out into further cheering. One or two learned genealogists present at the trial were much taken with the hidden irony that the judge himself, Sir Wilfred Lewis, belonged to just such a family of Welsh *uchelwyr* as had lived in Penyberth for so many centuries. And now the judge had been so thoroughly Anglicized that he was hardly aware of the true nature of the culture the three men were claiming to defend. Even had he wanted to, he lacked the ability and the means to relate all the spiritual values that were being described to any moral law that his mind could usefully connect with the law of England it was his duty to administer. In a sense of course this made his task much simpler, and the private thoughts of genealogists were not available to him. But it was clear that he very much resented being looked upon, by so large an assembly, on his first circuit as a High Court Judge, as some latter-day manifestation of Pontius Pilate. And he resented too the disturbing possibility that the jury were paying more respectful attention to the defendant than they were to him, in spite of all the traditional courtesies he had extended to the twelve good men and true. His interruptions were the more forceful because they were needed to concentrate attention on the proper seat of appointed authority. The defendant Lewis was coming to the end of his statement. It seemed perilously close in tone and argument to a judicial summing up

You, gentlemen of the jury, are our judges in this matter . . . We ask you to have no fear at all. The terminology of the law calls this bombing range 'the property of the King'. That means the English government. It means these bureaucrats in the Air Ministry to whom Wales is a region on the map, who know nothing at all of the culture and language they are seeking to destroy.

But there is another aspect to this trial that gives it special importance. We have said from the beginning, and it was the point we emphasized in our letter to the Chief Constable of Caernarfonshire, that our action was a protest against the ruthless refusal of the English state even to discuss the rights of the Welsh nation in Llŷn. Now, everywhere in Europe today we see governments asserting that they are above the moral law of God, that they recognize no other law but the will of the government, and that they recognize no other power but the power of the state. These governments claim absolute powers; they deny the rights of persons and of moral persons. They deny that they can be challenged by any code of morals, and they demand the absolute obedience of men. Now that is Atheism. It is the denial of God, of God's law. It is the repudiation of the entire Christian tradition of Europe, and it is the beginning of the reign of chaos.

The English government's behaviour in the matter of the Llŷn bombing range is exactly the behaviour of this new Anti-Christ throughout Europe. And in this assize-court in Caernarfon today we, the accused in this dock, are challenging Anti-Christ. We deny the absolute power of the State-God. Here in Wales, a land that has no tradition except Christian tradition, a land that has never in all its history been pagan or atheist, we stand for the preservation of that Christian tradition and for the supremacy of the moral law over the power of materialist bureaucracy. So that whether you find us guilty or not guilty is of importance today to the future of Christian civilization and Christian liberty and Christian justice in Europe.

If you find us guilty the world will understand that here also in Wales an English government may destroy the moral person of a nation.

At this point the Judge interrupted.
'That is absolutely untrue.'
Lewis ignored the interruption.

You declare that the government may shatter the spiritual basis of that nation's life, may refuse to consider or give heed to any appeal even from the united religious leaders of the whole country, and then may use the law to punish with imprisonment the men who put those monstrous claims of Anti-Christ to the test. If you find us guilty . . .'

The Judge broke in again.'That is untrue. Will you stop? I am not going to allow you to make statements which are not only untrue but almost blasphemous.'

'If you find us guilty . . .'

'You are not to say that again!'

> I wasn't going to. If you find us guilty, you proclaim that the will of the government may not be challenged by any person whatsoever, and that there is no appeal possible to morality as Christians have always understood it. If you find us guilty you proclaim the effective end of Christian principles governing the life of Wales.
>
> On the other hand, if you find us not guilty you declare your conviction as judges in this matter that the moral law is supreme; you declare that the moral law is binding on governments just as it is on private citizens. You declare that 'necessity of state' gives no right to set morality aside, and you declare that justice, not material force, must rule in the affairs of nations.
>
> We hold with unshakeable conviction that the burning of the monstrous bombing range in Llŷn was an act forced on us for the defence of Welsh civilization, for the defence of Christian principles, for the maintenance of the Law of God in Wales. Nothing else was possible for us. It was the government itself that created the situation in which we were placed, so that we had to choose either the way of cowards and slink out of the defence of Christian tradition and morality, or we had to act as we have acted, and trust to a jury of our countrymen to declare that the Law of God is superior to every other law, and that by that law our act is just.
>
> We ask you to be fearless. We ask you to bring in a verdict that will restore Christian principles in the realm of law, and open a new period in the history of nations and governments. We ask you to say that we are Not Guilty.
>
> Thank you, my Lord.

The defendant finished with a courteous bow in the direction of the bench as if he had borrowed the authority of the court for the duration of his speech and was now handing it back to its legal owner.

VIII

The judge's summing up, when it came, was complex and repetitive: as if he had become a little uncertain of the jury's capacity for following a legal argument in English. Even as he spoke the centuries seemed to be rolling back and the men who listened to him identified with their ancestors: as if they had just received from a beneficent monarchy the bewildering gift of English citizenship and a more experienced adherent of the Crown was guiding their uncertain steps in the complexities of English Common Law.

> I am here to do to the best of my ability the duty which I have sworn to do, namely to administer the law of England. You when you went into the jury box took an oath to administer the law of England and it is your duty to accept from me what the law of England is.

Their reaction seemed to waver between appreciation and resentment as they struggled to forget the stirring call of the defendant and concentrate like well-behaved pupils on their first morning in a new school.

'This case has lasted some time. It is really as simple a case as ever it became the lot of the jury to have to consider.'

The frowns on the faces of the jurymen as they struggled to follow Sir Wilfred's increasingly complicated exposition suggested they found the case anything but simple. The testimony of a night-watchman had to be disposed of. He had claimed that he had been set upon by two or even three unknown assailants. They had held him down while the fire was started. All three defendants had testified that the night-watchman was lying. The man was a one-armed veteran of the Battle of Ypres and the London press had given great prominence to his story. The judge went over it all in great detail. He was not prepared to say whether the night-watchman's evidence was true or false. He was not even prepared to tell the jury whether or not they should take any notice of it. At one point he seemed to be saying that it was irrelevant: nevertheless he had just gone over it in considerable detail and this seemed to imply that it was a central issue. He also dwelt on the individual characters of the three defendants for some time before suggesting that those considerations too were not for them to consider.

> Members of the jury, let me only say this one other word. You have heard from the lips of two of the accused a suggestion that the whole of Wales approves of this act. You may know, I know, that there are many many patriotic Welshmen – real patriotic Welshmen – who would shudder at the thought of such an act of violence as this. I only mention that because the accused have suggested to you that this act which they have done is an act which has

received the approbation of the whole of Wales. Whether it has or whether it has not, you may know better than I; but whether it has or has not the approbation of the whole of Wales has got nothing whatever to do with this court; and if you are satisfied that this was done it is your duty, unpleasant though it may be, to find a verdict of guilty.

Now members of the jury, will you be good enough – I have no doubt you would like to retire – to consider your verdict in this case, and to let me know whether or not you find the prisoners guilty of both or one or other of the two charges, or whether you find them not guilty on both? Will you now retire and consider your verdict?

The jury took three-quarters of an hour to consider it. They returned to the court and stood in their places while the clerk asked them:

'Members of the jury, are you agreed upon your verdict?'

The foreman of the jury, by name Harlech Jones, replied,

'We are. We have failed to agree.'

The judge intervened.

'Is there any chance of you agreeing?'

Harlech Jones answered.

'I am afraid, my lord, there is no chance.'

'Very well, then the case will go over to the next Assizes.'

For a moment there was silence. The news reached the crowd outside and they reacted immediately as if a great victory had been won. They began to sing 'Hen wlad fy nhadau' so loudly that the proceedings in the court room were thrown into confusion. The formalities of bail were gone through, but the defendants remained in the dock as if they had still not realized that they were free to leave. Once outside the three men were hoisted on the shoulders of young supporters and carried through the town. The police appealed to Saunders Lewis to help restore order and he did so. He spoke from the steps of the Welsh Nationalist Party's offices and within minutes the crowd had dispersed.

The judge had directed the jury to ignore the defendants' motives, but it was clear from the verdict that they were unable to do this. It has been recorded that five wished to return a clear verdict of 'not guilty' and seven were in favour of 'guilty'. In present-day terms, the verdict was as accurate a reflection of Welsh public feeling as an opinion poll. Certainly this was the view taken by the office of the Attorney General and the government in London. It became clear to them that a verdict of 'guilty' would be difficult to obtain in any Welsh court. No Welsh jury would be capable of distinguishing between the defendants' motives and the offence committed. On 7 December, the Crown made application before the Lord Chief Justice for the trial to be moved from Caernarfon to the Central Court in London. The Law of England and the spirit of the Act of Union were not to be lightly set aside. Welsh national sentiment could well be glowing, as the American magazine *Time* put it, with a refulgence not seen for four hundred years; it was less than dust in the balance of the well-tried scales of English justice.

But the glow was bright enough to awaken an ageing giant dozing fitfully in the Jamaican sun. When Lloyd George heard the news of the transfer of the trial to the Old Bailey by a writ of *certiorari*, he was moved to write angry protests to his daughter Megan in telegrams and letters.

> I think it is an unutterable piece of insolence, but very characteristic of this government. They crumple up when tackled by Mussolini and Hitler, but they take it out on the smallest country in the realm which they are misgoverning . . . In the worst days of Irish coercion, trials were never taken out of Ireland into the English courts . . . This is the first government that has chosen to try Wales at the Old Bailey. I wish I were there, and I certainly wish I were 40 years younger. I should be prepared to risk a protest which would be a defiance. If I were Saunders Lewis I would not surrender at the Old Bailey: I would insist on their arresting me, and I am not sure that I would not make it difficult for them to do that . . . It makes my blood boil

Lloyd George bore no resentment against Saunders Lewis for the fierce attack printed against him in *Y Ddraig Goch* in the summer of 1930. An inability to bear a grudge was indeed one of the most attractive aspects of his character. In the mean time he had had occasion to collaborate with Saunders Lewis on the Advisory Committee of the University of Wales on Broadcasting. It was this collaboration that secured some measure of recognition from the BBC of Welsh nationhood and led to the creation of a BBC Welsh region. And we know from his brother William's memoirs that the great man had formed a high opinion of Lewis's character and capacities.

But in the case Rex v. Lewis, Valentine and Williams, Lloyd George could do nothing: any more than he could prevent Stanley

Baldwin from forcing the Rex in question to abdicate in order to marry Mrs Simpson. Guided by the government, the Law of England took its inexorable course. At the Old Bailey on 19 January 1937 the three were found guilty and sentenced to be kept in prison for nine calendar months.

It was a comparatively light sentence and commentators at the time saw in it a measure of political sagacity: too much should not be done to exacerbate and inflame Welsh feeling. Whatever this new phenomenon of Welsh Nationalism with a capital 'N' might be, there was no sense in going to extremes and helping it to 'catch on'. The Imperial government was saddled with enough problems in Ireland and India and even in darkest Africa; it would be too provoking if the ghost of ancient national sentiments across Offa's Dyke suddenly took on the too solid aspect of flesh and blood.

At the end of their sentences, Lewis, Valentine and Williams were given a tumultuous homecoming. More than twelve thousand people filled the old Pavilion in Caernarfon – where Lloyd George had held so many memorable meetings – at the Welcome Meeting organized by J. E. Jones, the indefatigable secretary of the Welsh Nationalist Party. It must have seemed to them then that there was a rich political harvest to be gathered. Were they not the inevitable successors to the kingdom of Lloyd George? But the new-found zeal and enthusiasm quietly melted away. Although Williams and Valentine returned to their old posts, Lewis had been dismissed from his by the Council of the University College of Swansea. There was not enough power in the new head of Nationalist steam to reverse this decision. It only needed a couple of committees to rule the motion out of order for the new leader to be left out in the wilderness like a sacrificial goat. In the valleys of the south, the quick sympathy of the Welsh workers, employed and unemployed, was being rallied to the support of Republican Spain. It became the overwhelming issue of the day. The Left Book Club made rapid headway in the colleges. Side by side with Pacifism, Utopian Internationalism, and a heady variety of idealism difficult to imagine today, there was also a growing sense of fatalistic foreboding. The threat of another world war was a black cloud growing on the horizon.

It was not a good time for reflection. Events were moving so quickly they collided against each other as if the increase in the world's output of machines was taking a hand in history, and

190

speeding up the process. Each new machine increased by a thou-
sandfold the capacity to destroy and forget.

All that could be recorded was that three men had been willing
to act as though a Welsh nation existed in the modern world and
needed saving: and that when they so acted, a large section of
their fellow countrymen, including Lloyd George himself, for so
long the hero of the people and the wizard of British politics,
rallied to their support. Politically, at the time they gained very
little. But their moral victory was great. They had reaffirmed the
existence on the plane of reality of a nation that was on the verge
of becoming an unsubstantial and sentimental shadow. And it
was the language that made them do it.

Romani Chib – The Romani Language Movement

GRATTAN PUXON

From Planet 49/50, January 1980

As Mahatma Gandhi said at the height of the Indian language struggle back in 1916, 'Our language is the reflection of ourselves'. Without this mirror to its identity, a nation is seriously handicapped in endeavours to maintain a separate existence and culture, though some who have lost their own tongue have overcome even this mutilation. None the less, language flows in the body of a nation like blood in the individual human being. And we may note, therefore, in respect of the Romani people, that whatever hardships and sufferings history has inflicted upon Roma, it has left them with their language very much alive.

The present Romani language movement is in a very real sense a continuation of that broad language struggle outlined so eloquently by Gandhi in the holy city of Banaras over sixty years ago. In what is perhaps its final phase, it has moved from the Indian subcontinent to Europe, following the thousand-year-old migration of Roma from their North Indian homeland. And it is not surprising that, as in India, many of us involved in the language movement are engaged in efforts both to create an accepted literary language and, in the political arena, to gain realization of our language rights.

The attempts to suppress Romanes as a living language date from an early period after the arrival of Roma in Europe. Prejudice manifested itself in equal measure against the black appearance of Gypsies and their so-called cant. Between the fourteenth and fifteenth centuries harsh legislation to outlaw 'Gipsy gibberish' on pain of death and banishment was enacted and enforced to varying degrees in Spain, France, England and the German states. In the eighteenth century the speaking of Romanes was prohibited in Hungary, where *cigani* were to be known henceforth as *New Magyars*. Yet parallel with this official suppression came an awakening in some quarters of an academic interest in the language. It was brought about by the discovery that Romanes belonged to the linguistic family of North-Indian and Iranian languages. The 'discovery' was rather like that which Columbus accomplished in America. The *natives*, or at least some of them, and indeed Arab writers from Hamsa to Ebu el-Fadil (died 1311) long knew of the connection with India. During the opening years of the fifteenth century Roma in Italy had told an enquirer that their people came from the land of the Indus river, while in Germany they continue to call themselves *Sinti*. But it is still pedantically recorded that for western European scholars the classification of Romanes as an Indian language began with Stefan Vali, an Austrian minister, in 1760. Some years later Jacob Rudiger made known the fact in print. Over the following hundred years a number of scholars and writers made studies of Romanes and published works on the language and history of Roma. Notable among them were Grellman, with *Die Zigeuner* in 1787, George Borrow, *The Zincali*, 1841, and Pott, who in 1844 published his *Die Zigeuner in Europa und Asien*, which linked the Roma in Europe with the *Jat* (called by the Arabs *Zott*) peasants of the Punjab. Later in the same century Alexander Paspati at Constantinople collected much original language material from among settled and nomadic Roma in the Ottoman Empire.

By this time the Gypsy Lore Society had been founded in Britain, reflecting a widening degree of attention to the language and folklore of Roma, if not to their predicament as outcasts on the fringes of industrialized society. While Borrow was instrumental in creating a romantic image of the wandering Gypsies, John Sampson devoted twenty-five studious years to compiling what remains one of the finest books on the Romani language. His *The Dialect of the Gypsies of Wales* provides both a description of the inflected language and a summary of almost all that was known of Romanes at the time. Up until then, while a minor Gypsy-studies industry had been created and the term Gypsiologist coined to label its devotees, Roma themselves had little opportunity to contribute to serious language work. Everywhere lacking education and formal language training, they were invariable relegated to the role of *informants* by the linguists and dilettantes who sought them out in their camps and settlements. Indeed the Gypsiologists did the Romani people a considerable disservice by repeating through scores of books and articles the myth that Roma was a rapidly dwindling race, and that their language, inevitably, was dying with them. This bias is still evident among those who lack contact with their fast-growing urban communities in south-east Europe.

It remains a matter of argument whether Roma brought to Europe two, or more, distinct dialects of a single parent language. This in turn would have been similar to one of those spoken in north India about the tenth century, that is, just before the process of modernization of the vernaculars started. But it is indisputable that during more than six hundred years' sojourn in Europe the language has become further differentiated. This differentiation, the outcome partly of geographical separation, adds greatly to the difficulties faced by those who wish to encourage the emergence of a single (or perhaps two or more) literary forms of Romanes as a means of cultural communication between, as far as possible, all Roma. Most likely, as has occurred with other languages, one of the existing major dialects, such as that of the Arlia, will become dominant in the literary field. At present they have the advantage of numbers and, within Yugoslavia, of socio-political circumstances.

Down the centuries Roma have, of course, been extremely protective of and even secretive about their language. If they had not been it would not have survived. But more than any other single event, what enabled Roma to begin to develop a literary form was the Russian Revolution. Soviet policy towards the minority languages, coupled with universal education, within a decade produced among Roma the first members of new-style cadres. His *political* career I have charted elsewhere, but the contribution of Nikolai Pankov (born Petrograd 1895) to the language movement was also crucial. Among his earlier literary efforts were translations into Romanes of Pushkin's *Cigani* and Lermontov's *Mtsiri*. Later he collaborated with A. P. Barranikov, professor of Indian languages at Leningrad University, on the first Romanes-Russian dictionary, published in 1938. A larger dictionary which Pankov compiled alone, and worked on up until his death in 1959, has remained unpublished. A milestone in the political and language movement was the circulation in 1926 of a broadsheet explaining to nomadic Roma how to petition for free land. At the same period Romani wall-newspapers appeared, and soon after a regular journal. The first-ever broadcast in Romanes was made over Radio Moscow and in 1928 Pankov and Nina Dudarova produced a Romani primer entitled *Nevo Drom* (New Road) containing essays on various current topics. The book's ninety-six pages set a standard for written Romanes using the cyrillic alphabet. In July 1930 a section for publication in the Romani language was set up at a state publishing house and thereafter literature was printed and distributed on a scale never matched in any other country since. It included collections of songs, stories and legends edited by Aleksander Germano, and a series of essays by the same author. Numerous children's books were produced for use in the twenty-five elementary schools, and one junior secondary school, by then teaching through Romanes. However, the only book to appear in the Soviet Union since the war has been a small collection of poems (1970) by the Moravian-born writer Djordjis Cantea, one of the ten Roma who are today members of the Soviet Writers' Union.

A further important development was the establishing of the Moscow Romani Theatre. Its premier production, in 1931, was a political review of one-act sketches by Mikhail Gezliudski, now living in retirement near Rostov. Interestingly enough, during the Spanish Civil War, the theatre was the first in Russia to stage García Lorca's *Blood Wedding*. A second translation into Romanes has recently been produced by a new Romani theatre group in Yugoslavia. Lastly, it may be recorded that Romanes first reached the cinema in the Soviet film *The Last Tent* screened in 1936.

Two short-lived Romani newspapers came into existence elsewhere during the 1930s. These were the *Glasul Romilor* in Bucharest and *Romano Lil*, organ of the Roma Association in Belgrade. Literary activity in the immediate post-war years was at a low ebb, though the horrors perpetrated by the Third Reich gave rise to a wealth of both sad and satiric popular songs. Exceptional were the publication of a multi-dialect dictionary by Rade Uhlik in Sarajevo in 1948, and a book of verse by the poetess Papusza in Poland. The establishment of the journal *Études Tsiganes* in Paris in 1955, though run by *Tsiganologues*, has ever since provided a limited outlet for Roma writers. A bi-monthly newspaper in Bulgaria, *Nevo Drom*, included poems in Romanes during its early years, but has since changed its name to *Nov Pat* and is now printed only in Bulgarian.

A lone figure at this time who had a great contribution to make to the language movement was Dr Jan Kochanowski, a Latvian-born Rom trained as a linguist at the Sorbonne. During the 1960s Kochanowski spent four years studying in India. His twin volumes on the language and history of the Romani people marked a breakthrough in academic circles, and helped to arouse the interest of India in Roma in Europe. Around the same time, in Canada, the author Ronald Lee, though handicapped by lack of formal language training, wrote a treatise on Romani grammar. His unpublished work formed the basis for a Romani language course put together in collaboration with Dr Donald Kenrick, in London. A focal point for these various language workers was provided by the formation of the Language Commission at the First World Romani Congress in 1971.

The commission was able to review in broad terms the situation of the Romani language and its chances of survival and growth. Regarding numbers, as noted, Romanes was in a comparatively strong position when compared with such more or less successful revivals as Welsh, Irish, Danish, Macedonian and Hebrew. The fact that the estimated ten million Roma were scattered across Europe and America, with large outposts in the Middle East and distant Australia, was not a unique handicap. However, those committed to the language struggle were up against two formidable barriers, one purely linguistic, the other political. It had to be recognized that the Romani language exists in competition with, and has been penetrated to varying degrees by, at least thirty other languages. As we have seen, much groundwork had been carried out in the Soviet Union including the training of Romani teachers at a special pedagogical institute. At the time of the London congress, nothing comparable was being done, though now Romanes is being used in a few schools in Sweden and its introduction is under discussion at top level in Yugoslavia. For a short period attention was given to the question of its use in schools in Czechoslovakia. A training course for teachers was prepared but the plan abandoned in 1973.

The Language Commission, during the second congress in Geneva, was able to help overcome some of the technical difficulties. It recommended the adoption of a standard alphabet and gave guidance concerning the use of international terms and new borrowings from Punjabi and Hindi. The compilation of a comprehensive standard dictionary was planned. There have been indications since that the tide is just beginning to turn in our favour in the language struggle. The Romani movement as a whole has become much stronger and possesses a greater number of institutions and publications than even a few years ago. Among the more recent are *Roma*, the journal of the Indian Institute for Romani Studies, and *Rom-Som*, put out by the *Ciganyszovetseg* in Budapest. The biggest, *Krlo E Romengo*, published in Belgrade, unexpectedly ceased but is to be replaced shortly by a newspaper produced and printed at Nis, which will have an international distribution. More important, there are scores of young writers, particularly in Eastern Europe, producing verse, plays, translations and occasional prose. Little of their creative writing is getting published but the pressure for it to have outlets builds up monthly. Most promising is the situation in Yugoslavia where a volume of poems by Rajko Djuric has appeared and last year a biography of President Tito, translated by Prof. Saip Jusuf. A small book of children's songs has been issued in Hungary and, in East Germany, a collection of folktales is at the printers. An excellent grammar has been prepared by Prof. Jusuf, covering the dialects of the Arlia and Dzambasa, but its publication in Skopje has been delayed for almost five years. In the United States, Dr Ian Hancock, of the University of Texas, has written several papers on the problems to be faced in creating a standard literary form of Romanes. Taken together, these efforts, within a reasonable period of time, should prove sufficient to surmount the linguistic obstacles.

But the decisive battle is for a place for Romanes in the state schools. At present Romani children everywhere are learning everybody's language but their own. Their mother-tongue remains a largely unwritten language spoken only in the ghetto, bidonville or temporary camp. Through the schooling system – which in this respect is not an education – Romanes is forcibly replaced by the language of the majority, often enough of a people which has fewer speakers than Roma. The five examples quoted above are cases in point. The absence of their own language in schools robs Romani children of the right to assemble in their formative years the essential elements of their cultural heritage, as other children do. Moreover, the obligation to learn, and then study through the *gadjo* language places on them a crushing handicap. How often I have fretted to see the youngest of my brothers-in-law spread their school books in a corner and grapple with Macedonian and its cyrillic script. According to UNESCO research, such a system places upon children a disadvantage equivalent to three years' schooling. It shows up clearly in the records of school achievement. These indicate that less than half complete elementary school and not more than three per cent take up secondary education. The record is only worse in those countries, among them France, the Federal Republic of Germany and parts of Romania, where the majority of the children of nomadic groups hardly attend school at all.

Of course Roma need to be literate in the language of the country in which they live. But surely this does not necessitate the *outsider* language, inevitably the carrier of alien cultural patterns and values, being forced upon them to the exclusion of their own. Obviously the language situation varies considerably from one place to another. Where big concentrations exist, as in the towns and cities of south-east Europe, Romanes should be the teaching medium at least in the primary grades. Elsewhere it ought to have a place in the curriculum alongside the *gadjo* language. The use of Romanes in secondary and higher education, intimately linked with the question of just what volume of literature can be produced in the next few years, is an issue to be tackled later. To summarize one may say that whatever the outcome, most Roma will continue to be bilingual. The Romani language movement fights for the opportunity to be literate in two languages instead of, at best, being semi-literate in one. The current educational system, based on the assumption that assimilation is both possible and desirable, has proved a chronic failure, dumping most Roma still illiterate among the unskilled and the unemployed. At the same time by weakening Romanes, it raises artificial language barriers between Roma already separated by geo-political frontiers and thus works against internal integration and cultural unification. Yet one frequently hears the argument that this brutal and divisive process is imposed for their benefit. The only tangible political result is that the Romani language, a living link with India, has through its suppression become the symbol of national liberation.

Come In Planet –
Your Time Is Up

NED THOMAS

From Planet 49/50, January 1980.

The decision to cease publishing *Planet* was a voluntary one. No financial crisis precipitated it, no Arts Council engineered it. Indeed now, when the magazine cannot possibly be thought to seek favour, is the time to say clearly that in a moderately controversial nine years we were never subjected to any kind of editorial pressure from our funding body.

Neither was the decision a response to the referendum on Devolution. It was taken well before 1 March, 1979, though with one eye on that day. Had a Welsh Assembly materialized, a different kind of magazine would have been necessary. But if the Devolution proposals were defeated, we argued, would there be a place in the atmosphere that prevailed for the kind of militant reformist pleading that *Planet* represented?

The editorial of *Planet* 1 (August 1970) was entitled 'The George Thomas Era' and was commented on as reflecting a new verve in the Welsh critique of Britain and the left-nationalist critique of the Labour Party, against whose provincial establishment its barbs were chiefly aimed. But what strikes one most on re-reading that editorial now is the unspoken but buoyant assumption that the British State could be reformed, both constitutionally and in respect of Welsh-language rights, by a little pleading and prodding and reasoning. There is something rather plaintive now about that assumption.

What could not be foreseen at the time was the pace of acceleration in the British economic landslide, with all which that has meant in terms of loss of political confidence and cultural shock to Britain. This has provided the controlling context within which the reformist phase of Welsh politics has played itself out. The unconvinced and unconvincing reformism of the Labour Party in Wales has to be set in that context. Nationalists and a few real devolutionists were convinced enough in *their* reformism, but were overtaken by that very same landslide on 1 March.

Devolution Day is only a convenient symbolic marker. Throughout Welsh institutional life (which is, of course, a compartment of British institutional life) there has been a long-standing accommodation between British and Welsh interests based, as often as not, on the person of the *Cymro Da*, the 'good Welshman' (usually a Welsh-speaker), who argued the case for Wales within British institutions, and the case for necessary caution and compromise within Wales. Such people may still do good work as individuals, but as a public phenomenon their credibility is gone.

Their plight and dilemma extends in some measure to large sections of the Welsh professional class. In a period of nominal reformism at Westminster and rising nationalism at home, their route was clearly plotted. *Planet* in a sense formulated some of the terms on which a new and more equitable accommodation between Welsh and British interests might be established. Our readership divided almost equally, so far as an editor is able to judge, between Welsh-speaking intelligentsia, their Anglo-Welsh equivalent (an undefined though not negligible group) and liberal or left-leaning English people within Wales. These groups are closer to each other today than they were ten years ago, for which *Planet* may, perhaps, claim a little of the credit.

But if the terms of a new accommodation are not on any Westminster agenda – and no reformist agenda now exists – then these groups will have to commit themselves one way or the other. If the commitment is towards Wales then it implies a closing of ranks between north and south, English- and Welsh-speaking, socialist and nationalist. Our own divisions were too easily overlooked while the arguments were directed elsewhere. Now they have to be worked out thoroughly, and a period when worsening conditions throw us together may not be a bad time to do this.

What is now needed is an English-language publication belonging to a much more popular level of Welsh life than *Planet*, which will help to build solidarity and understanding at that more popular level. As I write, news comes that *Rebecca*, which seemed set to become our successor as a recipient of grant-aid, has been turned down at the highest level in the Arts Council. This rejection raises questions for all those engaged in cultural effort in Wales, whatever they think of the particular *Rebecca* scheme. If this is the first sign that culture is to be interpreted more narrowly in future, then Raymond Williams's introduction to the recent volume *The Arts in Wales* will read like their epitaph. If the arts are to be defined in Wales as in London, then many schemes on the Welsh-language side will be in peril. On the other hand, if a distinction is to be made on grounds of language, and more 'popular' projects funded only in Welsh, then this is to compound the cultural deprivation of the most culturally deprived. One cannot believe that this is really the intention of the Arts Council, whose distinctiveness and reputation outside Wales rests largely on the wider involvement it has with the life of Wales.

When, after nine years of editing, one comes to think of the letters unreplied to, the manuscripts lying in the drawer or even lost, the books unreviewed, the promises unredeemed, and the many other sins of omission and commission, they are all compounded by the thought that after this last issue they can never be put right, at least within the covers of *Planet*, where this general apology must suffice. The thanks, too, must necessarily be general, to authors, artists, designers, printers, advertisers, subscribers, readers, supporters of all kinds and our initial backers, whom (remarkably) we have been able to reimburse. Sara Erskine and John Tripp I shall mention by name and leave it at that, on the principle that for those thanks which cannot adequately be expressed one had best not seek words.

As I Was Saying...

NED THOMAS

From Planet 51, June/July 1985. Five years after its demise in 1980, Planet was re-launched with this leading article. The long miners' strike of 1984–5 had recently come to an end.

The Spanish poet and mystic, Fray Luis de Leon, returned to his lectern at the University of Salamanca after years of imprisonment by the Inquisition with the words *como deciamos ayer* – 'as we were saying yesterday'. De Valera said something rather similar on his release from imprisonment by the British. The problems of the Editor of *Planet*, a magazine that now comes back into existence five and a half years after it discontinued publication with its fiftieth number, are rather different. Can one in any sense continue what one was saying then? Is Wales the same place? Are we the people that we were?

Fundamental and precipitous changes in the British economy are producing deep conflicts and new political divisions. Wales as a disadvantaged area within the UK is drawn into this new British politics, and the political agenda of the seventies in Wales – devolution and language rights – which took up a great deal of space in the earlier *Planet* seems to be relegated. But the pattern is more complicated than that. The miners' strike which seemed pre-eminently a British issue, turned out to have some distinctive features in Wales. These were cultural features operating in what appeared to be a straight economic confrontation, just as the earlier 'culturalist' campaign for a Welsh-language television channel led to the hardware of studios and transmitters and the economic reality of jobs. The whole is an object lesson in Raymond Williams's view of base and superstructure, which sees them as indivisible and interdependent, not primary and secondary. The sense that we need now is a sense of dialectic. The language activism of the seventies and the miners' strike of the last year both revealed strengths in Wales and defined the limits of those strengths. The atmosphere of popular front conceals some unresolved questions but at least Welsh people are turning to each other and talking to each other more than before, and *Planet* hopes to be part of that process.

Planet is a cultural magazine within an understanding of culture broad enough to encompass this dialectic. It will not tell anyone how to vote or recite the strictly party political arguments. These have ample coverage. But the tensions produced in Wales by the Falklands War or youth unemployment – these are our culture, they are what writers write out of as surely as the late Dr Kate Roberts wrote out of the pain and loss of the First World War.

In the seventies *Planet* was associated with putting the case for greater rights for the Welsh language. That struggle is by no means won but it is not for lack of being articulated. We cannot fail to touch on language issues from time to time, but that is not our *raison d'être*. Language solidarity is, however, built into the base of our enterprise. As well as *Planet* we are going to publish an annual volume in Welsh which will consist of material about other societies or translated from other languages. We invite *Planet* readers and subscribers to support that volume also.

Planet takes the whole of Wales, geographically and linguistically, as its subject and hopes to project its various communities to each other and to the world outside. Certain types of community stand out in our mythology, notably those of the Welsh-speaking *cefn gwlad* and the south Wales valleys, but both are minorities now and unless we are content to say that outside of these, Wales does not exist, we must speak to each other from a wider variety of situations. This number gives some attention to Gwent, where *Planet* is being relaunched. Our next number does the same for the Rhyl area of the northern coastal strip where the National Eisteddfod is being held in August.

Is *Planet* a literary magazine? Such clear definitions in the field of writing are now an anachronism, but we are interested in the kind of sustained argument or inward response to the time, or making of personal experience into common experience that writing still does best. We invite those who are doing research that has a bearing on Wales to get in touch with us, and in particular we invite women – who have been under-represented in the literary world – to approach us with contributions or ideas.

This magazine is substantially funded by the Arts Council and will live by the continued support of that body and of its readers. We have decided not to take advertising which might involve us under the new VAT regulations in effort that is not commensurate with the extra income obtained. But we are willing to carry notices of particular interest to writers where these are not commercially inspired. We shall, of course, be reviewing books.

Finally, though *Planet* comes back into existence after a number of other attempts to found magazines for Wales have failed, and although we cannot do or attempt to do what *Arcade* or *Rebecca* did, if we have an audience it is because these other attempts were made, made valiantly and with immense personal commitment; Wales is on the agenda because a succession of people have decided to keep it there. And we hope to do our continuing bit.

THE BURNING TREE

Ned Thomas

It was May
it was morning
it was 1985

it was a winding track
it was in third gear
it was a four-wheel drive

it was where the gate opens
        where the field slopes
        where the river flows
it is there, over on the other side
the burning tree grows/glows

it is half flame, it is half foliage
it is gold, it is green
it is varied, it is vivid
it is verdant, it is seldom seen

it is the renaissance, it is the resistance
it is the poet's leaves, it is the people's lives
it is farm, it is furnace, it is the moment's vision
it is the tree's flamboyance, it is a present brilliance
it is tree rooted, it is tradition

it stands where we stand, our hands upturning
it is a tower of leaves breathing
it is our tree of life burning

The Craft of the Short Story

SAUNDERS LEWIS INTERVIEWS KATE ROBERTS

From Planet 51, June/July 1985

My agreeable task, Kate Roberts, is to try to persuade some writers of the short story to talk about their work. It is appropriate that you should be the first to sit before the microphone since it is with the short story that you have won your place and made your name in literature, though you are also, we know, a novelist. I remember your first stories appearing in the magazines three or four years after the Great War, a war which – as we can now see – decided the course of people's lives in our generation. I remember my growing conviction that an author of importance had appeared; and in 1924, with your stories 'Y Weddw' ('The Widow') and 'Henaint' ('Old Age'), we all realized that the Welsh short story had taken a definite step forward in terms of artistic creativity. The short story now had a new function: it was to be the expression of a vision.

But now, before I go any further, there is one question that naturally enough occurs to me: how did you come to choose the short story as a form for your writing? It was not at that time very popular in Welsh. It didn't count in the same way as an awdl *or a lyric poem, although the occasional volume, such as Gwynn Jones's* Brethyn Cartref *and Dic Tryfan's stories had appeared, and John Morris-Jones had opened the columns of* Y Beirniad *to the stories of Dewi Williams and others. What made you choose the form? Why the short story?*

I don't really know why the short story and not the novel, unless it be that experience produces oblique illumination rather than lighting up the whole life. It is difficult to say after a quarter of a century. A single idea crosses the mind, and one sees in it the

206

makings of a story, and perhaps thinks that there is not enough time to make a novel out of the idea. But also the short story was popular in English and in English translations from various languages; on top of that, Gwenda Gruffydd had given me a taste for Maupassant in Welsh. Someone like Katherine Mansfield attracted attention because she had brought a new style of writing to the short story, a style which made people forget O'Henry and his like who wrote stories for the sake of their striking endings. I admired the Welsh stories you mentioned but there were not enough of them, and when one is young, there are never enough books to be had.

That hints at yet another chapter in the history of the influence of English literature on Welsh. But then could there not be Welsh roots to your work? Glasynys, who wrote many short stories, came from the same part of the country as yourself. I have edited a selection of his stories, and he says that there was a tradition of story-telling in his youth, and that he heard his mother telling fairy-stories and folk-tales by the fire.

Yes, there was a tradition of story-telling in my area, but if story-telling around the open hearth went on in his time, then it was in the large farms on the edge of the parish and in Rhostryfan. But I never heard of that way of spending an evening from my parents, although they spoke of wedding feasts. In Rhosgadfan, the life is that of the smallholder, and the farms are carved out of the moorland. It is only since the coming of the buses that they have taken down the 'red gate' which stopped the sheep coming down from the mountain. Compared with Rhostryfan and the bottom of the parish, the village is not old. Nevertheless, there is a tradition of story-telling, of quarrymen going to each others' houses in the winter evenings, arriving without having been invited. On these occasions stories would always be told, but they would be humorous, of the anecdotal type, and of how workmates got their come-uppance.

Well, was there some skill in the way these stories were told?

Yes, the ability to tell these humorous stories was important. I remember there was criticism at home when someone had laughed at his own story, or told pretentiously a story which then ended flatly.

The way people listened to such a story-teller would really

have been enough to make him stop half-way through, had he had sense enough to notice. Anyway, the tradition you mentioned could have influenced the local quarrymen indirectly, since many of them came from Llŷn, where there was a tradition of story-telling, I believe. But if you will permit me to say so, I cannot see that tradition was important in this connection, it would only have been a short tradition whatever, and everything must be started by someone. (If Adam had written stories, he would have had neither tradition nor influence behind him.) And I do not believe that the influence of foreign authors counted for much either. Reading short stories from other languages did not make me want to imitate their style, or to borrow anything from them at all; it simply showed me that there was the raw material of litera-ture in the life of my own area. I felt this particularly after read-ing authors who did not use the clever ending to their stories. It in fact made me decide on a style completely opposite to their own. Reading, though, always stimulates me to write.

Yes, well it is obvious that we cannot connect your craft with the medieval story-telling tradition, although I do not think that Glasynys imagined hearing his stories. It is clear, though, that the tradition has not continued into our own time. In this respect there is a remarkable differ-ence between Wales and Ireland. But now, what exactly was it that first moved you to start writing?

The death of my youngest brother in the 1914-18 war; I was unable to understand what was happening and had to write to prevent myself from suffocating. (Politically it drove me to the Nationalist Party.) I am an exceptionally thin-skinned woman, everything wounds me deeply and the hurt remains for a long time. Life itself hurts me. The encounter with Death removes the scales from a person's eyes, gives him a shock and, as in a flash of lightning, throws new light on a character, or on society, or indeed on life as a whole.

Yes, that comes very close to a definition of the type of short story which you often write. It is not only Death which removes the scales from our eyes in many stories, but any event which produces, in that flash of lightning, a new view of a character or of life. For instance, here you describe an old man reaching his seventieth year and going to work as usual on the morning of his birthday, but his wife looks at him:

This was the first time it had struck Betty: today, she saw and heard everything as if it were new. It came into her head that her husband, having reached the age of seventy, would have to leave the quarry and live on his pension, and that all that he had done on this and every other morning for so many years would come to an end. Betty looked long at her husband; she had not thought so much about him since the days before they were married.

And at the end of the story:

She thought to herself, 'Soon he'll be lying in that old graveyard over there, with his hands folded for all time.'

There it is – in a flash, a new view of a character and of the whole of man's life on this earth.

Can I interrupt you just to say one thing? In Caernarfonshire there is a particular meaning to the Welsh phrase 'to be with one's hands folded', namely to be idle. In fact it is almost synonymous with 'lazy'. You see that I was unable to stop myself completely from trying for a clever ending, by playing on the ambivalence of that idiom within the story.

No, I wouldn't call that 'clever'. It is completely fair, and it deepens the moment with its vision that all the meanings fit in that context. Idleness is a sort of death, and death is rest for the body. Would you, Kate Roberts, venture to define what is the essence of the short story for you?

A difficult question. I sometimes think that there are as many types of short story as there are of author. I like Princess Bibesco's definition, 'the shooting-star of literature', and a 'shooting-star' is a fair description of what I have tried to write – a single experience, or a single flash of light on one thing, or a series of closely related events in a short story, the emphasis is on one more than the others. There should be a 'ninth wave', although the other waves ought also to receive attention. Some will have it that the parable of the Prodigal Son is a short story, one of the world's greatest stories. On the face of it, it seems more like the synopsis of a novel; but I believe that it *is* a short story, reaching its climax when the father forgives his son. (Some might say that the great moment comes when the son decides to go home.) Looking at it in terms of the craft of the short story, perhaps there is no need for the story of the eldest son – he is material for another story.

All right, we'll approach it from another angle: how do you perceive that something is material for a story and come to grips with it?

Again, it is difficult to say. It is difficult, indeed virtually impossible for a builder to say how he places brick upon brick to build a house, only that he starts with the foundation and goes on to the walls and then the roof. But he cannot tell you how he does that. The foundation, which is out of sight, must be strong, though. And in my opinion, that which is *out* of sight – the experience – is the more important. Occasionally, though not very often, I remember something that happened to someone, and see sufficient significance in it for me to write a short story. It was like that with 'Henaint' ('Old Age'), 'Y Taliad Olaf' ('Final Payment'), and 'Y Llythyr' ('The Letter'). But of course I forged them in my own self and placed my own emphases where I thought they should be; for example, in the case of 'Y Taliad Olaf' I happened to hear that an old woman, a close relative of mine, had been unable to finish paying off a debt while she was farming the smallholding, and had only been able to do so when she got the money from selling up her stock; and it affected me so much, hurt me if you like, to realize that the effort to pay one's way is so heart-breakingly long, that I decided to make it the subject of a story. But I do not think that the person to whom this happened looked at it in that way at all. Of course it is not often that one and the same person can live through something and look in from the outside on that living experience as well.

Yes, unless of course time passes between something happening and thinking back to it afterwards. You are not like that though. You look at the lives of others, rather than at your own life, in your stories.

At all events, looking over my stories today, I think my method was to see with my imagination the experience of the people among whom I was raised, experiences that derived most often from the fight against poverty. I describe the events leading up to the experience (I suppose that is why there is so much looking back in the stories), building up the story with the things which I think are necessary to arrive at the climax. Sometimes a remark made by someone will be enough to provide the subject of a story, or perhaps hearing that someone very ill has come home from hospital with no hope of recovery, or seeing a bare tree in front of a lonely house in autumn, or seeing hens sheltering from the wind.

I want to emphasize that the very slightest thing is enough to give me an idea, and the result is that my stories seem thin. Several reviewers have referred to this thinness, to the absence of great emotions in the stories, and the lack of reference to great events such as war. An English reviewer once said of me: 'Her sadness is like a long, low sigh across the water.' Well, there is something greater behind a sigh after all. The only thing I can say is that the *effects* of the great emotions are there. My stories are like small waves on the surface of a lake, but there is a disturbance in the depths. Phoebe Williams would not have had to wrap her quilt around her head if something important had not happened to take the shop from her.

This is interesting to me because it throws light on the way many poets and story-tellers work. Let me try to put it as I see it. The first stimulus, the thing which sets off the work, comes from something, some word or event, which forces itself on the mind and holds fast. Then, in thinking over it, meditating upon it, a whole host of experiences, memories of all sorts, take hold of it and become fused with it. In fact this is the way the poet thinks, not reasoning anything new into the event or working out a logic of consequences or causes, but dipping into and choosing from the store of past memories and emotions which this new experience awakens and helps to connect with each other. It is a sort of fishing. You are a fisherman, whipping with your rod the dark lake of experience and memory and life. In what sort of lake have you fished? Or to put that image aside, can you tell us from where you took your experiences, your material as a story-teller?

From the society in which I was brought up, a poor society at a poor time in its history; because of that I was not attracted to write stories about sex, or about conflict between people of differing character, or about the soul's spiritual quest – it was always the fight against poverty. Note, however, that the characters have not plumbed the lowest reaches of poverty, they are fighting against it, fearing it. Indeed they are proud, they like things such as glass plates when those are in fashion, and Fanny Roland fingering cloth for its quality is a symbol of the entire society. Richard Hughes Williams's stories about people who are so poor as to have to go to the workhouse strike me as odd. Many critics have

211

said that there is no effort in my stories. The effort is there, but perhaps the emphasis is more on the serenity which was attained in the end. And if I may say so without being accused of blasphemy, I believe that this serenity is almost as spiritual an experience as Williams Pantycelyn's in the verse:

> Mi orffwysa f'enaid bellach
> Ar yr annherfynol stôr,
> Ac mi ganaf yn y dymestl
> Ar y graig sydd yn y môr.

Some critics have suggested that this is a reflection of my character. But the exact opposite is true. As I said, I am a thin-skinned woman, easily hurt, and I am a great rebel by instinct. My hackles rise immediately against everything I see as injustice, whether inflicted by individuals, by society, or by the state. Indeed I sometimes wish I could have a great stage on Plynlymon, where I could stand and denounce every injustice, such as the injustice I personally felt that the government was taking the children of Welsh farmers who spoke no English to fight the battles of the empire, and then sending a letter to say that those children had been killed, in a language the parents did not understand. But some instinct told me that a story was not a stage from which to shout, and I have had to discipline myself exceptionally strictly, both as an individual who has to go on living, and as an author trying to write, so as not to become embittered towards everyone and everything.

The same review says: 'I cannot find in her work a single line that expresses even a hint of ferocity.' Another one says there are in my stories no feelings of anger, hatred, pride, self-pity, or bitterness. That those feelings are absent is not something to be praised of course, because they could be given to particular characters; what I am trying to say is that the absence of those feelings from my stories does not reflect on my own character. On the contrary, these very feelings within me gave rise to many of the stories. It was a hard battle though, like fighting with the devil himself, to keep my feelings in check, and bring my characters to that same plane of serenity.

I must thank you very much for what you have just said; I know that everyone will find it a great help in entering the world of your stories, since you named two things which make the stories themselves masterpieces, namely the special quality of the society depicted in them, its poverty and its everlasting daily fight against that poverty; and your own particular quality as a woman whom everything hurts, whom life itself hurts. It takes a rare maturity of mind to say something so penetrating and so simple. I know too that you would not expect my sympathy or pity for anything you have said. Rather, I must congratulate you. You have been lucky in your society, lucky in the material you had for literature. People who are weighed down by circumstances, whom life hurts and disappoints, these are your characters, Eve's exiled children. And reading about them, I compare them not with anything in contemporary English or foreign literature, but with the characters of the early Greek poets, Hesiod, or Homer himself. There is a primitive atmosphere, Greek and classical, about them. They wear themselves out fighting valiantly with rock and earth, knowing there is no rest until death releases them. Take that last sentence I mentioned before, the old woman looking at her old husband and saying, 'Soon he'll be lying in that old graveyard, his hands folded for all time.' Hector could have said that – indeed he said something in a similar vein to his own wife when he left her for the last time. These Greek touches, the timeless, fashionless classicism, that to me is the power and fascination of your stories.

Can I interrupt once again to say that there is another side to this question of poverty. What if I had been born into a well-off society? I do not mean well-off in the sense of worldly possessions exactly, but an educated, literate society, a society which had existed for centuries in the world of books and high culture? Would I not be a better author because of that? I tend to think that two-thirds of the literary career of authors born into that sort of world has happened before they are born. Perhaps there is not the time this evening to discuss the advantages and disadvantages of the two types of society.

No indeed. And had you been born into another sort of society, you would not be Kate Roberts, and we would not be here talking this evening. It is a very good thing that none of us is able to choose his parents, even if only for the sake of the short story. However, let us now turn for the remainder of our time to lighter things. You have already explained how your stories grow. That implies that the technique of the story, how it should be developed and ordered, is not important to you. But what about language and style, remembering that you are one of John Morris-Jones's old pupils?

213

That is quite true. I am afraid I have not given much consideration to the technique of the story, and just thought of beginnings, middles and endings. My early stories show traces of efforts to find an unexpected or surprising ending, but I gave up trying to be clever after your article in *Y Faner*. On the other hand, I have given considerable thought to words and sentences, trying to find the right word to express what I was trying to say, and not just using words for their own sake, although I was tempted to do so at first. But the big thing with me is experience, seeing by feeling, and trying to express what I feel in a word; trying to be accurate, and because of that often having to leave out stylistic ornamentation. To me, there is no point in a sentence unless it is an accurate expression of experience. That, to me, is the meaning of the saying that the style is the man.

Can you give an example of that?

Well, there is that sentence about the quarryman who is ill in 'Henaint'; his hands are said to be 'clean'. That was a word about which I thought for a long time, and it is so simple that one could pass over it as an example of completely bare and worthless style. But to say that about a quarryman, whose fingers are seamed by ingrained slate-dust and water, shows the seriousness of his illness. One Englishwoman saw what I meant, and one Welsh labourer.

You had an important advantage – a formal education in Welsh – a very rare thing for authors before our generation.

Although I had more opportunity to learn Welsh than many – that is, I was taught Welsh in the elementary school and the County School, and at college – we studied mostly language, and I cannot say that we learnt anything about the worth of literature as literature in the whole course of my education. Just think now, that neither at school nor at college did I encounter any critical discussion of Daniel Owen. The nearest thing I heard to literary criticism of Daniel Owen was at home. Something like this: 'I don't like *Gwen Tomos* – it's too sad, and there's no need for it to be. Why send her to America to die? The story should've finished when they got the money and married.' But although I did not have the benefit of literary criticism, I learnt one very important thing at college, I was shown the glory of the Welsh language, and that was a great help to my style. Reading the *Mabinogi* in the original with its clear, bare style, the short sentences full of meaning, has been a great help to me, subconsciously perhaps. I consider myself to have been wonderfully fortunate, to have had monoglot parents with all the richness of the Welsh of Llŷn and Eifionydd on their lips, and then to have learnt the science of language thoroughly at college. And I was fortunate in another thing as well, although this is perhaps not the place to discuss it.

It is certainly, that is our purpose in being here.

Well, it is that I was brought up in an original kind of family. We were never afraid, particularly my mother, to criticize and measure up people's characters. Her instinct for knowing someone's character surprised me on countless occasions, and nine times out of ten time would prove her right. Of course it was in the home, not outside it that the knife would do its work: judgement would be passed amongst ourselves only. But you need something like that to write stories. A good story-teller is not made by shutting his eyes to people's weaknesses.

And what about your plans? Are you pondering and preparing any new stories for us?

I never cease to ponder stories, and if it was possible to invent a machine which could record one's thoughts as well as one's words, I am sure I would have in no time as many stories as you could read. My fear now is that I shall stand apart from life just looking at it, instead of living myself. I cannot explain it properly. It is as though I were moving in a vacuum watching life pass by. There are plenty of things about which to write so long as there is life. You see, when I began to write, it was not that I had an idea for a story, it was an idea about life, and because of that, the vision has to continue. When an author gets an idea for a story, that is it until another idea comes along. But if one has a vision of life, another story will press itself on one before the first is finished. It is very possible that I may write short stories again, but I feel now that I should like to write a short novel. I do not believe I could write a long novel, it would be too much bother to write the filling-in bits.

What about new movements and tendencies in literature, do they affect you?

215

I don't know. I feel at present that the old way of writing in Welsh has not yet been fully explored, although it is obviously finished so far as English is concerned, from the experiments which are continually being tried. I fear I am too old-fashioned to chase after these new fashions, but there is one English author whose style could, I think, be imitated in Welsh, that is Miss Virginia Woolf. I agree completely with her that it is not necessary to write down every single thing that the characters do or that happens to them. More important are the impressions on the author's mind, and here the Welsh language is particularly suitable for expressing the appropriate visual forms and images; it has been the language of a great poetry down the centuries, and the everyday speech of ordinary people is full of visual imagery, so I believe a novel of this type could be written in Welsh. But anyway, there is plenty of material for novels in that same life which I use in the short stories – there is a life to represent that could not, really, be used up in a whole lifetime, even though it is often a grey, featureless life. But one must carry on looking and thinking and working. I fear that I suffer from the weakness of my nation, namely laziness, so I don't know when the novel will see the light of day. The wish is there, but it needs a genius to make that wish come true, and I am not a genius.

'It was not that I had an idea for a story, it was an idea about life when I began to write' – that is what you said just now. You could not have given a better explanation of the secret of your stories. The ordinary events of daily life turn into symbols as they open out for us a vision of man's life on earth.

Translated from the Welsh by John Phillips and Ned Thomas.

Welsh in the Valleys of Gwent

SIAN RHIANNON WILLIAMS

From Planet 51, June/July 1985

Monmouthshire has acted the part of a buffer state, and has received the main stock of foreign immigration . . . A continuous stream of immigration into any county which keeps a foreign born population to the rate of 15–25 per cent must, in a long series of years, materially alter the racial and social characteristics of such a county.

Such was the conclusion arrived at by J. E. Southall, a Herefordshire-born printer from Newport, trying desperately to explain the 'painful array' of 'poor miserable percentages' displayed by the 1901 language census in Monmouthshire. As a member of the original Cymdeithas yr Iaith Gymraeg (1885) and probably one of the first examples of a *dysgwr* who consciously set out to learn the language, Southall was poignantly aware of the destructive effect on the Welsh language of such factors as the growing influence of English education and the English press, and the increasing popularity of new forms of entertainment. But while these and other contributory factors were central to its decline, the all-pervading influence was the continuing movement of population, both in and out of the county, which steadily eroded the base on which the Welsh-language culture of Monmouthshire's industrial valleys stood. In recognizing the relationship between migration and the relative strength and weakness of the Welsh language in local communities, Southall touched upon one aspect which has not ceased to be directly relevant to its survival.

It is a well-known argument that the massive displacement of the Welsh-speaking population of rural Wales to the new industrial centres of the south-east during the nineteenth century ensured that Welsh did not suffer the fate of other Celtic languages. It has already been shown, however, that Professor Brinley Thomas's original hypothesis (recently reiterated) needs to be modified, and a closer examination of smaller individual areas will probably show that further modification is required. That is not to say that the Industrial Revolution did not revitalize the Welsh language and culture: it did. There was, for the first time in the history of Wales, a populous, Welsh-speaking, industrial society which could afford to support a flourishing Welsh-language press, and innumerable Welsh social and religious institutions. Monmouthshire was therefore able to make a valuable contribution to the cultural life of the nation for a considerable portion of the century. But the language was not conclusively 'saved' by this development. There are several reasons for the decline which followed, which must be viewed in the historical context of the growth in the influence of central government, of the expansion of the British Empire, and of the nature of class structure and social philosophy in Victorian Wales. But central among them is the fact that population movement to and from the industrial areas was not always beneficial to the Welsh language. The nature of the economy of south Wales was such that this new Welsh society, suddenly at the heart of national cultural life, would not receive the regular inflow of life-blood necessary to sustain its language.

During the first half of the nineteenth century the population of Monmouthshire was growing at a faster rate than that of any other county in England and Wales. The centre of balance moved from the old established market towns of Monmouth and Usk to the rugged valleys of the west, as thousands of workers flocked to the furnaces and mines. Sir Thomas Phillips described this population in 1849 as one 'congregated together in large numbers, which has grown with the rapidity of which there is scarcely another example, not by the gradual increase of births over deaths, but by migration from other districts.' The 'other districts' were in the early years mainly Breconshire, Glamorganshire, Cardigan, Pembrokeshire and Carmarthenshire. There is no doubt that during the period of dynamic growth the majority of the immigrants hailed from Welsh-speaking areas of Wales, and were more than likely to be

Welsh-speaking. In relation to the period before the advent of the linguistic census (first taken in 1891) assumptions have to be made on the basis of data noting the county of birth of the population, available in printed form after 1851. One estimate made in 1840, however, described as 'Welsh' 61 per cent of the population of Blaenafon, and 51 per cent of that of the parish of Trefethin (including Pont-y-pŵl). Moving westwards, the Welsh migrants would constitute a higher percentage of the population. Dr Gwyn Davies's study of the parish of Bedwellte reveals that in 1851, 79 per cent of the heads of household were natives of Wales and Monmouthshire. A survey of the 1851 Census Enumerator's Schedules in the district of Twyncarno in my native town of Rhymni, which was until 1974 situated in the extreme north-western corner of Monmouthshire, shows that over 75 per cent of the heads of households were born in Welsh-speaking rural Wales, while the vast majority of the remaining 25 per cent were drawn from the surrounding parishes of Glamorgan and western Monmouthshire, also overwhelmingly Welsh in speech at that time. Due to the nature of in-migration, this locality was thoroughly Welsh, and it is not surprising therefore to find that it remained the last stronghold of the Welsh language in the old county.

> Os bydd y Gymraeg farw yn Sir Fynwy,
> ar lethrau Twyncarno y digwydd.

> (If the Welsh language should die in Monmouthshire it is on the slopes of Twyncarno that its demise will occur.)

Ben Davies's prophecy of 1934 has not yet come true. Twyncarno, now in Mid Glamorgan, still has its native Welsh-speakers who naturally use Welsh in their everyday conversation.

The survival of the language is in large part related to the early migration patterns. The eastern valleys attracted a larger portion of workers and their families from nearby England, especially from Gloucestershire, Herefordshire and Somerset, and were therefore more susceptible to Anglicization that the more westerly parishes of Bedwellte, Mynyddislwyn and Aberystruth. The way in which newcomers tended to congregate together meant that the linguistic situation also differed within the industrial towns. The Briery Hill area of Ebbw Vale was more Anglicized than Beaufort, while Sirhywi and Nantybwch remained more Welsh than other parts of Tredegar.

Even though migrant groups were often spatially segregated,

there was considerable if not universal social interaction. In the early years of the century Welsh was the dominant language. One factor which testifies to the densely Welsh nature of the society was the way in which English immigrants learnt Welsh with ease and became thoroughly assimilated. The history of the Nonconformist chapels reveals many examples of English immigrants such as Richard Wornell and Peter Skyman, both prominent members of Bethesda Welsh Baptist Chapel, Beaufort, who became fluent in Welsh. The chapels with their Welsh or bilingual Sunday schools provided the ideal channel for assimilation. It should not be assumed, however, that it was only those of religious persuasion who became thoroughly Welsh. A character by the name of John Treasure, well known for his efforts at bardic composition in the public houses of Rhymni, was said to have felt that the only way in which he could become truly accepted socially was to master the mysteries of *cynghanedd*.

The workplace also gave immigrants the opportunity to learn the language, where this happened often by necessity rather than choice. The Lefel Glai (Brickyard) (1837–95) of the works at Rhymni was, according to D. T. Williams in *My People's Ways* (1978) 'opened, managed, worked, run and closed in the Welsh language . . . Irishmen and migrants from Gloustershire, Herefordshire, and Somerset . . . needed to have a working knowledge of Welsh in order to have a workmanlike approach to the job.'

It has been suggested that English migrants were often more careful of the Welsh language than the natives. When for example parents of Mynyddislwyn schoolchildren were balloted in 1898, the strong feeling in favour of teaching the language in the Board Schools 'was said to exist more strongly among many of those of English descent than among the Welsh themselves'. But although the successful assimilation of English-speakers was general in the case of people who had moved to industrial Monmouthshire before 1851, it was not universal, and was not to continue. Moreover even though Welsh was most certainly the main language for a considerable though declining portion of it, this Welsh-speaking society was never a homogeneous one. In some areas, the majority of immigrants were not assimilated, and while many did learn Welsh, large numbers of the Welsh were also learning English. The attitudes which emphasized the value of English as the language of commercial progress and social enlightenment led to the decline of the Welsh language from mid-century onwards. This process was accelerated in many areas by local economic and industrial factors which caused significant population movements. The assimilation of English immigrants could only occur while the inflow from other parts of Wales reinforced the Welsh population.

It would be incorrect to view this process as one of gradual and inevitable decline. The variation in the relative strength of the two languages differed greatly in localities within a few miles of each other, and even within towns and villages. A sudden influx of English workmen to a certain area sometimes meant that local social institutions became Anglicized almost overnight, while a change in economic fortune could possibly reverse the process. It is unwise to generalize in the dating of linguistic change in Monmouthshire, but it certainly seems as though the 1860s and 1870s were key decades. Social dislocation followed the upheaval when iron manufacture was replaced by steelmaking and the mining of coal for export. The flood of immigration increased but it was now mainly from England:

> Englishmen, English capital and enterprise, English customs, are rushing in upon us like mighty irresistible torrents, carrying away before them our ancient language, social habits, and even our religious customs.

In the face of this seemingly irresistible power the Reverend Thomas Rees, author of the above quotation and minister of Carmel Congregational Chapel, Beaufort, led the movement to establish English chapels. One cannot doubt the integrity of the patriotic Welshmen of the period who believed that the Welsh nation was naturally religious in character and that the incoming English, who had not the same advantages as themselves, constituted a threat to Welsh nationhood. Ironically, however, their well-meaning religious fervour did the Welsh language no good. The Welsh chapels, the main centres of Welsh culture in the Monmouthshire valleys by the second half of the century, allowed and even encouraged the cream of their congregations to establish English 'causes'. Many of these chapels were started by almost monoglot Welshmen and remained small, failing to appeal to the mass of the English immigrants. The effect of this policy, as the

Reverend David Hughes of Farteg stated in a Congregationalist Convention in 1867, was not to evangelize the English but rather to Anglicize the Welsh. During this period when English education was having an effect on the language of the Sunday schools, the Welsh chapels could not afford to be weakened, particularly since there was an increasing tendency to limit the use to the religious sphere.

This 'mission' to the English was all the more detrimental to the language during these years because while the English were pouring into Monmouthshire many of the Welsh were moving out as the older-established iron towns declined. The new developments in the pioneering pits of the Rhondda Valleys, for example, attracted Monmouthshire ironworkers as well as the main portion of new migrants from rural Wales. After mid-century it seems that new industrial developments in Monmouthshire (the Rhymni Valley excepted) attracted labour from the south-west of England rather than Wales, while many Welsh-speakers from the most westerly valleys of Monmouthshire chose to move to Glamorgan rather than to other parts of Monmouthshire.

While the people suffered *economic* hardship during periods of industrial depression, local *cultural* life sustained by the Welsh language often received a mortal blow when these same people were forced to move. The first major experience of depression during the early 1840s had a detrimental effect on Welsh social life as Welsh miners and ironworkers emigrated to America and the north of England. During the 1860s the effect of large-scale emigration was even more devastating to Monmouthshire's Welsh communities; this time, unlike the earlier period, it adversely affected chapels and other Welsh institutions which never recovered their former strength. Where economic recovery did take place, it seems that on the whole it was English rather than Welsh workmen who replaced those who had left. This certainly was the experience of Blaenau (Blaina) between 1867 and 1874.

It was often the skilled workmen and those younger people who had a considerable social contribution to make who ventured to emigrate. In a farewell poem to a colleague from the Sirhywi Literary Society, the poet and satirist Myfyr Wyn described America as a wide open grave in which so many of his fellow countrymen were buried alive. In his *Atgofion am Sirhywi a'r Cylch* he contrasted the lively Welsh cultural life of the village during his youth with the bleak situation of the 1890s. There were no new-comers to replace the Welsh 'characters' who had left, and the younger generation, having lost the Welsh language, was unable to sustain the cultural traditions.

In certain localities, however, economic stagnation proved to be advantageous to the language since it followed that in these areas large-scale in-migration did not occur during the latter part of the century. It has been suggested that the lively Welsh culture which flourished in Rhymni for almost half a century after the closure of the ironworks in 1890 was due to the fact that the town did not experience an influx of population. Nearby Abertyswg, built around the newly sunk Maclaren collieries, was more Anglicized than Rhymni due to considerable in-migration at the turn of the century. Between 1901 and 1911 Monmouthshire as a whole was once again attracting population, now mainly from England. In the Sirhywi Valley, new colliery villages like Markham and Oakdale were almost totally populated by English-speakers. In the eastern valleys, this influx finally drowned the Welsh language once and for all. It continued only as the language of a small and declining minority in a few Welsh chapels that soon became bilingual.

In some areas, population growth due to developments in the mining industry created a new Welsh-speaking community, so that a few places experienced re-Cymricization as the linguistic decline was arrested for a time. The poet Islwyn's home village of Cwmfelinfach near Ynys-ddu is one example, for when Nine Mile Point colliery was sunk in 1904 many workmen were drawn from the quarries of Caernarfonshire. Babell Calvinistic Methodist Chapel increased its membership as a result and a new Welsh Baptist chapel, Noddfa, was opened in 1911. Welsh cultural life in other villages was also revitalized by migration: New Tredegar, Aberbargoed and Trethomas near Bedwas are particular examples. But this new vitality was to be short-lived, and those who came to Monmouthshire in the early twentieth century were soon to be dispersed by the industrial and economic depression of the 1920s and 1930s. Rhymni excepted, the Welsh cultural life of western Monmouthshire since then has only occasionally been revived by small-scale in-migration of Welsh families attracted to developing industries. It is unlikely that the National Eisteddfod would have been held in Ebbw Vale in 1958 had there not been a new generation of Welsh-speaking families and individuals attracted to the town by the expansion of the steelworks during the previous twenty years. And although a few dedicated native Welsh-speakers and non-Welsh-speaking parents have led the movement to establish Welsh-medium primary schools in Monmouthshire since 1955, migrants from other areas have also played a large part. More recent developments at Cwmbrân and Llanwern have also been significant in this respect.

Monmouthshire's past experience makes it difficult to be confident about the long-term future of today's Welsh-speaking communities in rural Wales and even of the survival of the language itself, considering present trends in population movement in Wales. The historical context has of course changed, for the language now has official financial support, it is not excluded from the education system, and it is not solely the language of religion. Consequently social attitudes towards its value and future are different. Nevertheless such changes are not sufficient to ensure its long-term survival. The demise of the language in industrial Monmouthshire has been intricately linked to economic and industrial factors. Today, as ever, migration is a key factor.

The last census showed that the percentage of the population of Dyfed born outside Wales was 17.3 per cent. It was even higher in particular areas within the county: Ceredigion District — 22.0 per cent, Preseli — 21.5 per cent. Efforts are being made to assimilate the younger generation of immigrants, but these cannot succeed while so many young people from Welsh-speaking families have to move away to find work. Nor does the fact that many of the more academically qualified of these are moving to Cardiff and Bangor, and therefore staying within Wales, guarantee the future of the language. Even though many English immigrants are not antagonistic towards the local culture of rural Wales and support Welsh-medium education, many native Welsh-speakers like the Gwentians of the nineteenth century would still rather have their children concentrate on English. Given also the continuing tendency to change the language of local cultural activities to English in order to accommodate newcomers, it is frightening to contemplate the effect that even small-scale localized immigration can have in transforming the linguistic situation.

Some would say that the hope for Welsh now lies once again in the populous areas of south-east Wales. But statistics since 1971 show an increase in the emigration of young people from these bleak areas of economic decline. As this trend continues, the likelihood of the pupils of the Welsh-medium schools of Rhydfelen and Cwm Rhymni being able to remain in their home towns becomes more remote.

The communities of both the Welsh heartland and the industrial valleys are under threat and their future, like that of the Welsh language, is directly related to economic planning. Although the long-term effect of the Industrial Revolution was to create a linguistic divide in Wales, the movement of population to the industrial areas also forged links between the north and west on the one hand and the south-east on the other. If Wales is to withstand the present threat, those links must be reforged.

Europe Begins Beyond the Pyrenees

NED THOMAS

From Planet 54, December 1985/January 1986

The entry of the peoples of the Iberian peninsula into the EEC at the end of this year allows us at one and the same time to assess the progress of, and reassess our own relation to, some of those European territorial minorities which received considerable attention in the first series of *Planet* during the seventies.

The world drama of the superpowers, the sufferings of the local victims of their struggles – Nicaragua, El Salvador, Afghanistan, Poland; the natural disasters compounded by wars that have brought famine to several peoples of the Sahel and the Horn of Africa, all these have driven the less spectacular developments in Spain to the inside pages of our newspapers, and its 'minorities' to a slot of their own in television series which often manage to make them seem something apart from real everyday politics. The reason why they nevertheless have a claim on our attention is that they are not only themselves undergoing interesting changes that may have some relevance to Wales, but they are helping to change the shape of that Western Europe to which, willingly or unwillingly, we belong.

The conventional wisdom is that the Spanish state is slowly but surely democratizing itself; elected governments, with considerable help from the king, have ridden out two attempted army coups, and a socialist government is managing to combine some redistribution of wealth and power with a degree of modernization of industry in preparation for the competitive conditions of the Common Market.

Certainly nobody who knew Spain in the Franco years and returns there now can fail to recognize a freer and more lively atmosphere. The autonomous governments at Vitoria and Barcelona are proof that this democratization has also had a spatial dimension. Using their new political powers and economic strength the Basques and Catalans have been able to move ahead quickly in certain spheres. The Basques, for example, tired of waiting for central funding to set up a TV channel in Euskera, the national language, set up one on their own, going from scratch to forty hours a week within a year.

Nevertheless there are very real limits to Spanish democracy where the non-Spanish peoples of the state are concerned. The new Spanish constitution does not permit parties that have independence in their programme to contest elections legally (Herri Batasuna in the Basque Country gets round this by not being a party but rather an electoral slate, a list of candidates put up by an alliance of groups). It follows that Spanish democracy does not include the right to self-determination. Yet both Euskadi and Catalunya vote overwhelmingly for parties that, were they allowed to, would seek independence. It is said that the right to self-determination cannot be conceded by the Madrid government without risking army intervention, and this is no doubt true; but it allows Basques and Catalans to argue with some reason that Felipe Gonzalez, the Socialist prime minister, is in this respect the heir of Franco and the generals. The right-wing monarchist, Calvo Sotelo, said at the beginning of the Civil War 'antes España roja que España rota' (Spain would be better red than pulled to pieces) and this view still grapples together the unlikely forces of the army and the Socialist government. It is widely held that in the wake of the second attempted coup, the army was given, in return for an undertaking of loyalty to the Crown, a free hand in the specially designated ZEN (Zona Emergencia Norte) which corresponds almost exactly with the territory claimed by the Basques (the area of the autonomous regional government of Euskadi plus Navarre). Here, wide emergency powers are available to the various security forces, and are used to such an extent that repression in the last three years in the Basque Country is held to be worse than at any time since Franco. A glance at the Amnesty International Report for 1983, for example, confirms this. Virtually every substantiated case of torture in Spain occurred in the Basque Country and was carried out by the forces of law and order.

Recently the Basque National Party (PNV) in the Vitoria Parliament joined with the left-nationalist Euskadiko Ezkerra (EE) and the extra-parliamentary Herri Batasuna to demand that law and order in Euskadi be handed over to the newly established Basque police force and the Spanish security forces withdrawn. This more than anything else would transform the situation. It would strengthen Spain's claim to be a democracy immensely and force ETA to rethink its activities.

But while the Basque question testifies to the old antagonisms within a nation-state, the entry of Spain into the EEC cuts across nation-state divisions. The Basques and Catalans are trans-frontier peoples and the lowering of the political and economic barriers at the Franco-Spanish border will help to create zones that neither belong to one nation-state nor are nation-states in their own right. In time one can expect institutional trans-frontier arrangements to arise of the kind that already exist on a limited scale between France, Germany and Switzerland around Basel. There are many obstacles on the way to a full European regionalism – the weakness of the European Parliament, the absence of any truly European parties or a European press, and most of all the continuing great-nation chauvinism within the EEC's Council of Ministers, but is it more utopian to think in this direction than in the direction of the mini-nation-state which Plaid Cymru is now rediscovering its commitment to? More statues? More parades?

Rising national feeling in many of the European minorities during the seventies led to a possibly uncritical identification with situations that have turned out to be as remarkable for their differences. Tom Nairn was one of the earliest to point out the historical differences that marked off Catalunya and Scotland on the one hand from Brittany or Wales on the other. *Planet* in the seventies undoubtedly contributed to the uncritical discovery of other peoples who seemed to share more of our experience than they in fact did. However, certain similarities stand.

Just as the experience of colonialism created a certain limited solidarity between third-world countries that turned out to be as different in wealth and power as Nigeria and Chad, or Trinidad and Dominica, so similar experiences, particularly in respect of language, offer a limited basis for solidarity and co-operative action between European territorial minorities.

Secondly the European context is an important reminder that in Wales too we are dealing with *territorial* claims. This is easily overlooked in Britain where Welsh problems are too easily confused with those of immigrant ethnic minorities. There are, of course, overlapping areas, but also differences. It was confusion on this issue which led to the confrontation between Gwynedd County Council and the Commission for Racial Equality. It is interesting that the territorial principle is reasserting itself inside the ecology and anti-nuclear movements. The care of the earth, however much elevated to a general principle, has to relate in concrete terms to some particular patch.

'Not where you come from but where you're going to' used to be the slogan addressed to immigrant Spanish workers on the posters of the Basque Left. Unfashionable though it is to say this in the atmosphere of harsh 'realism' cultivated by the present British government, one of the best reasons for continuing to perceive ourselves among the European minorities is that it offers a long-term hope and an embryonic programme of collaborative action to transcend the nation-state which has created our minority status.

Foot-sore on the Frontier

NIGEL JENKINS

From Planet 54, December 1985/January 1986

> A frontier has been described as a line which you can draw where
> you like so long as you have force enough, the problem being to
> ensure respect for your line when you have drawn it. The moderns
> use concrete, guns, and barbed wire, the ancients constructed a
> bank and ditch or a wall . . .
>
> Sir Cyril Fox, *Offa's Dyke: A Field Study of the Western Frontier Works
> of Mercia in the Seventh and Eighth Centuries* AD.

To walk the Dyke, north to south, from sea to sea, in the year of
its twelve-hundredth anniversary — that was the plan. But the
feet had other ideas, and after tramping only the first third of it I
found myself sent bootless home and blister-beaten back,
resigned to the modified project of tackling it in sections as soon
as skin and smarting meat had stuck themselves together again;
not that I wasn't tempted, as I stumbled into Oswestry, by the
thought of hijacking Gwyn Alf's helicopter for the remaining
two-thirds . . .

It is of course dodgy history to pin such an anniversary on the
year 785; the Dyke was up to twenty years in the making, and we
don't know for sure which years of Offa's reign (757–96) they
were. A nineteenth-century declaration in stone near Knighton
that it was built in 757 is even dodgier history; the Mercian king
would have been too preoccupied in his wars against the Welsh
to have started work on the Dyke before the more settled 780s.
Modern convention has plumped for 785 as 'the year', and this

seems to be tolerated by the experts, including the late Sir Cyril Fox who was *the* Dyke authority.

This unnoticed birthday coincides with a lesser, the thirtieth anniversary of the designation of the Offa's Dyke long-distance footpath, although it wasn't until 1971 that it was formally opened as a walkable proposition throughout its 176 miles. Now between eight and nine thousand dykers a year stump the whole way between Chepstow and Prestatyn, and many more enjoy medium-range excursions along popular stretches such as the Wye Valley and the Clwydian or Black Mountain ranges.

'The Marches' are aptly plural, for you keep acquaintance on this walk with three 'marks' that cross and shadow and cross each other the border's length: the modern boundary, the line of the path, and the Dyke itself, the most potent symbol of what is one of the oldest frontiers in Europe. Conflict has been fundamental to this belt of land from pre-human times, and signs of struggle between the forces that have contended for it are everywhere to be seen, from hills and valleys squeezed, gouged and smoothed into shape by the clash of 'Welsh' and 'English' icefields, to the castles of the Normans who lorded it here a mere eight or nine hundred years ago.

The political frontier has fallen neatly into place along an obvious geological rift between English lowland plain and hard Welsh highland. It was on these hills, formidable enough to scrape by as mountains, that the first Celts in these islands built their 'Iron Age' forts, the huge ramparted refuges of Ffridd Faldwyn, Foel Fenlli, Penycloddiau. On even the hottest day there's a breeze on such heights that chills the sweat – our earliest homes in this land the last places, now, that we'd want to settle for more than a few minutes.

These forts were eventually overrun by the Romans whose comparatively brief occupation, with a network of new roads, towns and fortifications, rendered this territory unmistakably a frontier zone, although it would be a good three hundred years after Roman withdrawal (AD 410) before the defining process solidified physically in the great earthwork behind which the latest invaders boxed us away as 'Welisc', foreigners.

It happened gradually, nevertheless, and there was more than one dyke involved. What both isolated and created Wales, and set the scene for Mercian expansion, were two fateful British defeats in the late sixth and early seventh centuries which drove wedges between 'the Welsh' and their fellow Britons in the West Country and Cumbria. Then a civil war in Mercia thrust Offa to the throne as the most powerful Anglo-Saxon yet, the first to style himself King of the English, and a European power with whom both the Pope and Charlemagne were obliged to deal on equal terms. Doubtless he would have been imbued by the saga literature of the time with a strong sense of destiny. The seventh-century poem *Widsith* refers to a namesake ancestor in Sleswig who gained by arms 'the greatest of kingdoms whilst yet a boy' and struck out with his sword a boundary between two peoples; here was a tradition worthy of emulation.

But there were urgent practical reasons for the Mercian dyke-building programme. From the time of Penda (623–54) these pushy frontiersmen, grabbing and trying to farm what land they could hold, had thrown up localized defences in the form of short dykes, sixteen of which are traceable today in the central march; they were to regulate passage along the ridgeways and to block off from Welsh attack the precarious valley settlements. Then, further to the north, came the 38-mile Wat's Dyke, running from Holywell to Oswestry, believed to be the first effort of the Mercian state to define precisely its limits of conquest – limits which Offa was to push even further west.

Of the dozens of Dyke and border books, Sir Cyril Fox's yard-by-yard study, based on field surveys made between 1926 and 1931, remains the central account. Like a walk of the Dyke, the going is tough and sometimes a chore, but the views, the detailed insights are worth all the sweat. In some of his conclusions he is understandably tentative, certain questions posed by the Dyke being beyond the archaeological resources of his day. Many exciting reappraisals can be expected from the Extra-Mural Department of Manchester University who are currently undertaking a complete re-survey of all dykes associated with the West Mercian frontier – using new methods such as the 'land systems' approach which examines the earthwork within the context of geology, relief and drainage, rather than viewing it as an isolated archaeological monument. They hope to solve such problems as why there are only short sections of the Dyke in the Herefordshire plain, and why there was no Dyke built for a thirty-mile stretch north of Redbrook in the Wye Valley.

The Dyke is its own most numinous document. Its guiding

principle was not that it should bristle with soldiers and weaponry throughout but that it should be Mercia's eye on Wales. Accordingly, we find that wherever possible it occupies west-facing slopes and hardly ever risks turning its back on Wales. Yet if, through the *beirdd*, the news from Powys is bad and from Pengwern disastrous, it must not be assumed that imperial Mercia had it all its own way. The presence of English place-names west of the frontier (Buttington, Forden, Evenjobb, Cascob), the unexpected deviations away from its alignment – on Long Mountain, for instance, or Rushock Hill – are evidence that the course of the Dyke was negotiated rather than imposed, Offa accommodating to some extent the territorial claims of Powys in particular, the most powerful of the three border kingdoms with which he had to contend.

You need to follow the Dyke on foot through the sometimes bewildering confusion of broken country over which it travels in order to appreciate the skill of its navigator and the vast ambition of the project. There had been nothing like it in these islands since Hadrian's Wall, and the Mercians were plotting it with none of the precision instruments available to the Romans; laying it out in the field, with the aid of marker posts and hand signals, seems to have been the basic method. If Offa was himself its guiding intelligence, the actual construction work was carried out by a number of gangs under the command of the local magnate through whose land the Dyke in that section passed. Thousands of serfs from a forty-mile radius must have been pulled in to work on each section, and kept at it for years; some may have been Welsh slaves, captives from the wars.

Work began perhaps in the Kerry Hill region where Fox detects signs of experimentation: 'We seem in this zone to be at the birth of a work of genius; to be studying the great earthwork in the limited area where it was evolved, and where by the greatest good luck its condition is sufficiently perfect to permit an exact analysis of its original structure. Here the engineer learned his job: elsewhere he cast off the defects – the mere boundary bank thrown up from a succession of spoil holes – which dim his achievement.'

Local human resources and geological conditions account for many 'inconsistencies' in structure and design. The basic model is a bank, averaging 6 foot in height, with a ditch on the west side, the whole having a median width of 60 feet. There are humbler stretches appearing as little more than hedgebanks, and these may have been supplemented by timber palisades; but there are many lengths that rear above 20 feet — at Lippet's Grove in the Wye Valley, one of its proudest sections, the Dyke had a scarp of 31 feet. Here, perhaps, Offa used the miners of the Forest of Dean whose particular skills were to be in great demand in the Middle Ages for the ditching of castles. Sometimes on this walk there's the excitement of coming across the point where two gangs, working towards each other and using slightly different methods, have at last met up, as between Middle Knuck and Hergan where there's a most unusual right-angled join.

Soldiers would have been stationed only at certain points to control trade and traffic between the two peoples, and patrols would have ridden out from garrisons such as Knighton (Chnichten – town of the horseman) to look out for Welsh trouble. There were laws to govern the Dyke including a jury system of six Welsh and six English to settle disputes, many of them to do with cattle raiding, a major industry for hundreds of years of this Wild West terrain. But many of these differences continued to be settled in traditional bloody border style, as the famous anti-Welsh jingle recalls:

> Taffy was a Welshman, Taffy was a thief;
> Taffy came to my house and stole a leg of beef.
> I went to Taffy's house, Taffy was in bed;
> I picked up a chopper and chopped off his head.

Of the 149 miles of Offa's original frontier, 81 are traceable on the ground. It is seen at its best in limestone country (between Dee and Vyrnwy; the lower Wye Valley) where erosion and silting have had least effect; where it's made of sandy soils it has often sprawled and lost definition, or been washed away in floods. Human activity has also reduced the earthwork: it has been ransacked for building and road construction, ploughed over and quarried through, built upon and conifer-obliterated; in the grounds of Chirk Castle it disappears beneath the waters of an artificial lake. The most contentious eroder is the human foot: there are archaeologists who want walkers banned from the Dyke, to whom the Offa's Dyke Association reply that little harm is done as long as walkers stick to the parapet of the Dyke rather than scrambling up and down its sides.

Few of those controversial feet seem to be Welsh. I was the only (aspiring) long-distance Welshman that I, or any of the other Dykers I met, had seen the hide of, although there were plenty of local evening strollers and joggers. The long-distance majority are English; the Dyke is also quite big with the Dutch who have, plainly, a national interest in such things.

The path itself, which coincides with just a third of the Dyke, is about 180 miles long: most people walk it from south to north – in about a fortnight if it's mainly for the exercise, or three weeks if any investigation of the *meaning* of the area is to be made. There are a fair number of masochistic Chepstow-to-Prestatyn streakers who have little apparent interest in their surroundings: 'Llangollen?' queried one, 'You don't want to go down there, mate, it's off the route.' And there was the young TA type who was running it in military gear, his head plugged in to a walkman – no skylarks for him. The walking record must go to the Swansea-based sculptor Philip Chatfield who does it ritually once a year in four days, Llangollen first stop, walking for as long as it's light and sleeping wherever he drops at nightfall . . . although Phil, to be fair, is one flash o' blue who *does* know his border. A different kind of challenge was being met by an American couple walking the path with their ten-month-old baby.

I chose to walk it from north to south, not because I'd therefore be 'walking down hill', as a sage in the pub had it, but because, being a south Walian, there'd be the carrot of 'walking home'. Two slight disadvantages are that none of the travel guidebooks covers the path in a north-south direction, and you have to face the toughest stretch of the walk, the Clwydians, in your first couple of days. The path is now well signposted, and there are not likely to be the navigational problems that were common in the early seventies. Good maps are nevertheless a must, both to get a sense of context and to cope with those few places where cantan-kerous farmers have fiddled with the signs to confuse walkers. It is sufficiently well-trodden these days to be frequently visible, the very grass, in lusher pastures, brushed in a south-north direction; pioneers of the path used to run a high-summer gauntlet of nettles, brambles and thistles in some places, but there are fewer such troubles now.

Borders, frontiers, shadow lines of one kind or another are a familiar and sometimes painful condition of Welsh life. But a walk down the Dyke concentrates the mind on what has made us one, a nation, in spite of our notorious internal dissensions; it invites us to recognize, in Waldo Williams's words, that we have 'un gwraidd dan y canghennau', one root beneath our many branchings. It reminds us too that less than a century after Offa had thrown up his vast earthwork – an engineering project to dwarf all others in eighth-century Europe – his almighty kingdom of Mercia had been annihilated by a combination of West Saxon and Danish invaders; we compatriots, however, are still here, if only just, twelve hundred years later.

Big Road Blues

JOHN BARNIE

From Planet 58, August/September 1986

Coming face to face with a culture you have known only at a distance can be a discouraging experience. Like going back to where you once belonged, the territory is there but the maps you carry are all wrong. Some things are better left to imagination or memory. The thought occurred to me as we flew in a long arc from Boston via Toronto to Memphis, Tennessee. After twenty years of collecting blues on record and reading all I could on Southern Black culture, I was to spend five months in the Mid and Deep South. How well would my imagined world hold up against the real one?

At Nashville we changed planes. It was the beginning of August and I had my first intimation of Southern heat as we filed out of the aircraft. There was a twelve-inch gap between the fuselage and the hydraulic tunnel leading to the airport. As we stepped past it, warm air shimmering off the tarmac was like the heat-glare from a furnace, sucking the breath away. But in the air-conditioned transit lounge the intense sunlight and thunderheads punched up into the blue outside seemed unreal, divorced from that second of muggy unbreatheable heat.

When we reached Memphis it was sundown and as we set off in an airport minibus, the city cooled like an oven. 'Where to?' asked the driver. I asked for a hotel downtown and he laughed. 'Ain't nothing there.' But he took us all the same to a Ramada Inn and left us with our luggage on the deserted sidewalk. Traffic lights blinked from red to green and back to red again, but at this dead time of the day there was no traffic to control. Downtown seemed to consist of two parallel streets of shops and office build-ings that dissolved into slums and vacant lots. From the sealed window of our ninth-storey bedroom I looked down on the street: a few Blacks talked quietly in a group, and an elderly drunk stum-bled by, whistling a tune whose off-key notes echoed off the empty buildings. The last sunlight glowed on concrete and brick.

After existing for two weeks in the windowless basement of a dormitory, we found a flat in mid-town, rented furniture from the Acme Furniture Company and began to take bearings. The first thing was to learn to cope with the heat. The Center for Southern Folklore where I worked was thirty minutes' walk from the apart-ment, yet even in the comparative cool of early morning, my shirt was soaked through with sweat when we arrived. It stuck icily to my skin for hours in the air-conditioned building. At home we discovered that air-conditioning was too expensive and did the best we could with what passed for a draught between the open windows. After a cold shower and a change of clothes it was pos-sible to feel cool for a few minutes, but sweat soon began to ooze from the pores and you were covered again by a smear of grease.

The ice-making machine communal to the apartment block became indispensable, disgorging chips of ice into a basin where you could plunge in a jug or bucket. So too did Joe's Liquor Store on the corner which had a fine display of Bourbon whiskey – two walls lined from floor to ceiling with shelves of half-pints, pints and fifths, a liquid library where I browsed most days, undecided between Old Crow ('Generation after generation, men of fame and discriminating taste have enjoyed and preferred this smoothest and mellowest of Bourbons') and J. W. Dant ('The unusual and distinctive taste of this unique charcoal perfected whiskey is the result of an old and famous formula, matured and mellowed by natural agents and time in charred barrels'). Or should it be Rebel Yell ('Fourteen years before the great victory at Chicamauga, W. L. Weller founded our distillery and produced his first barrel of Bourbon. The whiskey in this bottle is made from the same Southern sour mash recipe that made his Bourbon famous'). And what about Evan Williams, 'Kentucky's first distiller'? How had he found his way to Bardstown, Nelson County, in 1783, to set up in that un-Welsh activity, distilling strong liquor? In Bardstown did he sweat out *englynion* in the

Kentucky heat too? At any rate his descendants distilled a good straight Bourbon whiskey, 'every ounce charcoal filtered', for which I was grateful.

At work I began sifting through hours of reel to reel tape of Delta blues, recorded in the 1960s by one of the Center for Southern Folklore directors, Bill Ferris. The aim was to edit sufficient material for a documentary LP, but the slow process of listening, listening again and note-taking, was not so different from listening to the blues on record at home. What I wanted was to go down into the Delta itself, the triangle of fertile bottomland between the Yazoo and Mississippi Rivers, with Memphis on its base line and Vicksburg at its apex.

Earlier this century the Delta had one of the highest densities of Black settlement in the South and had produced a rich blues style which extends in unbroken tradition from the turn of the century to the present day. I had listened to the Delta blues from my early teenage years and in one sense I knew it better than any other music. 'Yet and still' as they say in the Delta, blues is the music of a different people and a different culture from my own. Listening to it on record was therefore an act of the imagination in complex ways as I gradually built up a social, historical and human context for a music I could only know as an outsider. To journey into the Delta would be to put my imagined world and all it meant to me to a test.

Highway 61 is a road that features in many blues. It runs from New Orleans through the Delta and Memphis to Chicago and was one of the great routes out of the South for Blacks. It was the road we took to the Delta, descending a bluff from the hamlet of Walls into the flattest land I have seen. The highway ran for miles with military precision through featureless fields, or rather giant plots of crops, one 'field' ending where another crop began. It was no longer all cotton, for the time had gone when cotton dominated Delta economy, but there was more of it than I had expected, straggling hip-high bushes with the cotton bolls mostly hidden by leaves. Later in the fall the leaves would be shrivelled to a burnt brown and the bobbed white bolls could be seen for miles like a falling, timeless snow, while on the horizon giant red harvesters moved humped over the fields, sucking out the cotton and shooting it into high-sided wire mesh trailers.

Sometimes an acrid smell lingered over the cotton where the

crop had been sprayed from the air with defoliant. Leaves were a nuisance to the harvesters. Side by side with the cotton were acres of soya beans, the new cash crop of the Delta. Presumably the defoliants drifted onto them as well.

Now and again a hamlet loomed up, perched at a crossroads, its name prefigured for several miles on the communal water tower that hovered on stilts above the countryside. Most were collections of clapboard shacks, some painted white, but others unpainted and weathered to grey. Many were shotgun houses – each room set one behind the other so you could shoot from the front porch through every room to the back (according to the popular derivation of the name). Like most things in Mississippi they had the air of being temporary, with rubbish of all sorts often accumulating in front yards – gutted cars, oil drums, cans, rusting, junked and abandoned. Larger towns like Clarksdale had suburbs with more substantial brick bungalows with neat lawns, where the Whites lived, but the outskirts were always the same – one-storey clapboard buildings, many of them short order cafés, streets cluttered with billboards and poles, criss-crossed with wires. No one was staying, the streets seemed to say, everyone was about to move on . . .

I found I liked this. In Europe, two thousand years and more of history can seem oppressive at times, every inch of land tied by its names, buildings, ruins, to tradition, everything dragging you back. Temporariness can have its advantages, freeing you into the this-ness of living now. Freeing you too, in the case of the Delta, into recognition of the transient nature of our lives. In the heat and humidity, under the blinding blue sky, it was easy to believe this flatland would revert to wilderness in a generation, if left to itself. Anything abandoned – an old shack in a sea of cotton – was overwhelmed by creeper choking the chimney stack, by heat and rot buckling the shingles and crumbling the boards.

This somehow went with an undertone of violence. Earlier this century the Delta had been one of the most violent places on earth. Since the late sixties, lynchings had come to an end, yet an air of violence remained as if it were implicit, a given condition of the land. ILLEGAL TO SHOOT FROM HIGHWAY said a large sign on Highway 61, but the sign was pitted from shotgun pellets. At Stovall, where Alan Lomax had encountered Muddy Waters in 1940 and made the first recordings of him for the Library of

Congress, a Black man was examining a shotgun outside the isolated post office. The White by his side, eager to make a sale, encouraged him to take aim and fire alongside the open country road. 'Whenever I hear a truck pull up at night, if I don't know the sound of the engine, I reach for my shotgun,' a Black told me in Panola County. Shotguns were in evidence racked across the rear windows of some pick-up trucks belonging to Whites – good ole boys or rednecks, depending where you stood.

Dead things littered Highway 61, run over and left to rot in the heat. Some were large, deer or dogs with legs stuck stiffly at angles from the bloated belly. Smashed black heaps, a few feathers ruffled by passing traffic, were the remains of black vultures that fed on the roadside carnage. Many were pulped flat on the hard shoulder, run down by someone deliberately going out of his way. With ugly heads, ungainly on the ground, black vultures soared with the grace of eagles high in the Mississippi sky.

All down Highway 61, God and death were companions. 'Jesus Is Lord' said the destination board of a bus outside a brick church in Port Gibson. 'A family that prays together, stays together,' advertised a billboard. It was juxtaposed with an advert for life insurance. A few yards down the highway, the red and beige guts of a deer spilled and shone on the tarmac.

Back at the Center, I listened through headphones to the voices of older bluesmen as they described a Delta that was the same and savagely different. The region had been cleared of dense primeval forest in the mid-nineteenth century to create one of the richest cotton growing areas of the New South. The labour-intensive crop meant an influx of slaves on a massive scale from the east coast states, and to be 'sold south' to work in the harsher conditions of Mississippi plantations was a threat used against recalcitrant slaves in the Old South. Black lives were cheap and remained so well into the present century, finding echoes in the cynical sayings of levee camp bosses recalled by older men: 'If you kill a nigger, I'll hire another one. If you kill a mule, I'll buy another one.' 'Burn out, burn up (said to men dropping with fatigue from carrying logs all day); fall out, fall dead.'

During Reconstruction, ex-slaves who stayed in the Delta were drawn into a system of debt peonage, 'cropping on shares' as tenants on the old plantations. The system tied Black families to the land as surely as slavery, for the tenant farmer was obliged to

241

the landlord for most of his essential supplies, often including mule and plough. These were drawn from the 'commissary' or plantation store, and their cost set against the sale price of the farmer's cotton in the fall. Anything left over was 'profit' for the farmer. In practice, the tenant rarely made a profit and ended the year in debt to the landlord. Even in a good year the landlord who fixed the price of goods in the commissary, often sold the cotton for the farmer, and kept account of mounting commissary debts, could ensure that his tenants came out in debt to him. Poverty, a ruthless police force and a corrupt judiciary made escape difficult in the early years of this century for a Black farmer with a large family. The system lingered on well into the fifties. Older informants on the tapes I listened to had bitter memories of cropping on shares, and the blues I had listened to for years celebrated the struggle of the spirit to survive such conditions.

One late afternoon in September, we drove with friends from Memphis, headed for Tate County just north of the Delta. We were going to the annual barbecue given by Othar Turner on his small farm near Senatobia. The barbecue was a big event in the locality. Several days before, Othar Turner had slaughtered a goat and a pig, and as we entered the yard we were met with the smell of meat being barbecued over hickory charcoal. The yard was beginning to fill up with an assortment of cars, station waggons and pick-up trucks, as people wandered in from surrounding farms and hamlets. Tate was a 'dry' county, but canned beer and pints of Bourbon whiskey had been ferried across the county line for the occasion, and could be bought from the shack from the older women who had congregated there to chat. In the yard a daughter sold barbecue goat or pigmeat sandwiches, dripping with juices.

As the yard darkened in the evening gloom, someone gave a preliminary roll on a drum and the shrill notes of a cane fife pierced the air over the hubbub of conversation. The party was beginning to take shape. Othar Turner was the leader of one of the last fife and drum bands that were once common in northern Mississippi and parts of western Tennessee. How such bands originated is uncertain, though their roots may lie in early White military bands, whose instruments and rigid march rhythms where wrenched by Blacks into their own idiom and for their own purposes. Turner's band consisted of two snare drums and a bass drum slung by shoulder straps and played at a slant across one hip. Turner himself played cane fife. The band moved Indian file in a rough circle, the fife reaching out high and clear over the syncopated, polyrhythmic beat of the drums. As the drink passed round, some of the men began to dance, singly, or holding each other by hand or arm in lines of two or three, feet shuffling with and against the beat of the drums, free hands balancing cans or pints of whiskey.

Sometimes the tunes had words, an isolated blues verse sung several times, or a version of 'Sitting on Top of the World', a song recorded by the Mississippi Sheiks, a popular string band in the twenties; or it might be 'My Babe', a fifties hit by the Chicago blues harp (harmonica) player Little Walter, transfigured, brought back into the fold of an earlier downhome music where the urban 'My Babe' had its roots.

I came back from the shack with a pint of whiskey to be approached by a group of men who wanted to explain that 'Dusty' had meant no insult. Dusty had driven down from Chicago for the barbecue and had suggested to my wife that if she drove back with him to St Louis they could have a real good time. Friends and relations had put him straight, and now he strolled over and shook hands with a smile. Since many men carried weapons of some kind, I was glad my honour had come to no harm.

As we left around midnight, nosing our car onto the dirt road, a sheriff's sedan drew up outside Othar Turner's shack, and a White constable stepped out. In a dry county I assumed there was going to be trouble, but he had just stopped by to enjoy himself a while and be paid off with a few drinks.

Black music began to take on new connotations as the months passed. Performances of the kind I had listened to on record were only a part of it. At a party like Othar's, few stood around listening to the music, it was there to be danced to, talked over, while people milled around drinking and laughing, shouting encouragement to the singer. At times someone from the crowd would seize the microphone and sing a stanza or two. The blues was good-time music as well as 'blues', and I came to understand more clearly how it was formed out of the land that stretched flat and vibrant behind juke joint or shack into the dark. 'Tout à fait comme en Afrique,' remarked a French scholar of Afro-American literature at Othar Turner's band. But it was not just like in Africa.

243

Yet and still, good-time blues is the lighter side of the Delta's dark coin. 'Do you know what "on the killin' floor" means?' asked 'Black Eagle' in the Arkansas flatlands that extend to the west of the Delta. We nodded. 'Well, I'm on the killin' floor now.' I looked around the sixty-year-old harp-player's shack. His wife sat on a lumpy-looking sofa; there was a chest of drawers against one wall; a piece of frayed carpet on the bare boards; a large black and white TV set where the adverts flickered silently. Skip James had recorded 'Hard Time Killin' Floor Blues' in 1931. For Black Eagle, who had played with some of the greatest Delta bluesmen, but had never recorded himself, time had changed little.

In a world of poverty 'Black love is Black wealth', wrote Nikki Giovanni in a poem that vehemently denies White assumptions that poverty means endless suffering. Her childhood had been a happy one, despite the poverty. At a birthday party for his teenage daughter in his shack near Coldwater, Tate County, farmer and blues singer R. L. Burnside beat out a shattering electrified downhome blues with his band of lead and bass guitars and drums. Apart from four-foot-high amplifiers, his living room was as bare as Black Eagle's had been. Unlike such a party at home, though, a dozen or more children from toddlers to adolescents milled around the drinking, dancing, laughing adults. When the band took a break, an eight-year-old grabbed his father's guitar, while a younger brother took over the drums. Between them they played a fast blues-boogie with a seriousness and precision that pleased everyone. Later, a little girl squatted and peed on the floor but nobody seemed to mind. She was led away by the hand and the mess mopped up.

'Come and see my children,' said a man I'd been drinking with. On a big brass bed in the next room ten or twelve children lay huddled and sprawled asleep. 'This one of ems mine,' he said proudly, picking a child out of the pile like a puppy, 'And this one, and this one.' I admired them, and we went back to the party and the noise and the drink.

Several months in the South, I came to realize, had not so much changed my imagined world as enlarged it. Disembodied voices on a thousand recordings, black and white photographs of singers, posed or caught in the moment, words on the page, were given depth of colour and movement, were rounded out by sight and sound and the feel of a landscape and community. What I had imagined was real, but lacked that final sense of the contingency of things, the quotidian events that formed a bluesman's life and his songs.

Earlier in the evening we had stopped to eat barbecue at a café and to stock up on whiskey and beer before crossing the county line. Turning off the highway, down narrower and narrower dirt roads we finally bumped across what seemed to be a field to R. L. Burnside's isolated shack. A large pollen-dust moon had lighted our way, dirt roads glimmering whitely as we passed the humped immobile trunks of trees shrouded in kudzu vines that had strangled and killed them.

Returning to Memphis, the moon had gone down, and we drove along dark roads empty of traffic. On the highway we passed through a hamlet and straight through a crossroads. From nowhere a sheriff's car overtook us and flagged us down. A tall Black constable strolled over.

'Is there anything wrong, officer?'

'I didn't see all four wheels stop at the crossroads back yonder.'

'I'm really sorry,' said our White woman driver, 'we didn't notice.'

He leaned one elbow on the car door and peered inside.

'Where you folks headed for?'

'Memphis.'

'Memphis, huh.'

He considered giving us a ticket.

'Alright. I guess this time I'll let you slide on by.'

Waldsterben

ROBERT MINHINNICK

From Planet 59, October/November 1986

I didn't understand what the white crosses in the forest meant. Perhaps they were advertising hoardings or we might have been passing a war cemetery. It wasn't long before I was given the answer. The crosses were indeed memorials to the dead, but not to soldiers or the citizens of the prosperous Dutch towns we had been driving through. It was trees that were being commemorated. Not individuals, but whole plantations of oak, beech and the varieties of pine that in a country without any remaining natural woodland constitute a vital recreational and scientific resource.

Talking to naturalists and environmental campaigners in the Dutch town of Boxtel, it soon became clear that many of the trees of Holland are threatened by the slow poisons of general air pollution and acid rain. So urgently do these people view the problem that they have organized a series of nationwide 'forest alarms', in which suitably qualified tree-watchers take parties of people into the forest to show them the surprising richness of Holland's woodlands, and how much of these are being affected by pollution. Last year ten thousand people made such an excursion on one day. They included the Dutch Minister for the Environment. Very gently the questions were put to him that are on the lips of ordinary people throughout Europe. Why are the leaves of beech trees yellowing as early as July? Why do such trees, early in their growth cycle, have such inadequate foliage? Why are fir trees losing their needles and putting out 'distress' shoots in their myriads? Why are these pines dead when a few years ago they were healthy trees? Answers that put the blame on wind damage, root fungus, old age and past droughts were considered and discounted. Scientific caution and governmental blather could no longer blur the truth that acid rain and air pollution are now disastrous phenomena of destruction in European forests. Dutch trees, like Scandinavian freshwater – the Norwegian lake at Bukketjenn is as acid as vinegar – are seriously endangered.

It seems that a greater crisis looms in Germany's Black Forest. In Britain there are no places like Freudenstadt, a town of twenty thousand people and wholly dependent for its livelihood on the tourist attractions of the forest and the timber its trees provide. Here, as in many parts of the country, the word 'Waldsterben' (forest death) is on everyone's lips. Images of dead trees and demands for government action take the forms of stickers on car and shop windows. Certainly there was a sense of current emergency and imminent crisis amongst the foresters who escorted us around this enormous area. These men had lived in the forest all their lives and were intimately acquainted with its every aspect. They were under no illusions as to the cause of death of the German trees. The killer is acid rain, generated by power stations and factory chimneys built without pollution controls, and the other forms of air pollution. (One of the staple trees of these German forests is the silver fir. This tree is almost never found in Britain, but until the nineteenth century it was common in northwest England. What killed it off were the smokestacks of the Industrial Revolution.) Here in Freudenstadt was worse evidence of tree damage: thin, yellowing beech, firs with dramatic needle loss, stands of skeleton pines. Repeatedly we were asked what the British government is doing about our power station emissions of sulphur dioxide and nitrous oxides. In fact, British pollution rarely reaches Germany, going north instead to acidify Scandinavia, but our refusal to reduce our sulphur dioxide emissions by 30 per cent, as directed by the EEC, is a constant source of amazement and irritation in Europe. And even this figure would be inadequate. Many environmentalists feel that a 75 per cent reduction is necessary. All we were able to say was that the CEGB is spending hundreds of thousands of pounds of public money making videos which claim that the UK is not an exporter of air pollution. The replies were suitably acidic.

After Freudenstadt we travelled to the Czech border. From the castle tower in Hohenburg we looked out on fir and beech-filled slopes stretching into the east. We were eager to be down inside the aquarium light of the forest, with its granite crags and pillars of moss. Beside us some American soldiers also scanned the trees. Automatic rifles bumped along their thighs, binoculars glinted against green and dying Czechoslovakia. For while we are playing our border games both sides are losing the acid war. In the Erzgebirge, Czech tourists wandered bewilderedly amongst what remains of vast forests, blighted by unchecked air pollution and industrial *machismo* — Czech bank notes are emblazoned with images of factory chimneys billowing smoke. Here, immediately south of the East German border, *Waldsterben* was already taking place. The death throes of a forest are the ominous sway of trunks above withered roots, the crashing of its ruined timbers. There is nothing like the Erzgebirge to be seen in Britain but that gives no grounds for complacency.

Since this journey I've looked at trees more intently. It is difficult now to enter a wood without my first thought concerning itself with the health of the trees. This type of curiosity can be a curse. It's as if I'm treating a woodland like a doctor's waiting room, eyeing the patients and wondering what's wrong with them. But I'm also now determined to enjoy the trees while I can. Ironically this has meant several recent trips to the unnamed pine plantation at the heavy end of Margam steelworks. This must be one of the unlikeliest places in Wales for a still flourishing, if stunted, woodland, wedged as it is between the sea, the smoking moraine of the Port Talbot Borough Council rubbish dump (creeping at more than glacial pace towards the trees) and the huge coal pyramids around the coke ovens. These trees provide a habitat for a dazzling flora. Indeed you can be knee-deep in orchids and helleborines while listening to the Big Brother voices on the works tannoy barking out warnings. This isolated and permanently threatened coppice is a fragment of the old Margam estate, and undoubtedly one of the most positive activities of the coal aristocracy was the planting of unusual, even astonishing species in unlikely places. I grew up in a village surrounded by such a coal-created pseudo-manorial estate. Tulip trees, their leaves like cats' faces, the octopus branches of monkey-puzzles, and the wellingtonia's red and streaming bark were all familiar sights.

The salt-defying evergreen oaks, digging into the clifftops at Dunraven, are a similar legacy. Planted by the privileged, such trees are among the last reminders of those families which grew fat on the wealth of industrial south Wales.

Today we don't seem to be planting many tulip trees. Slow-growing oak is not an economic proposition and beech takes too much room. Instead we have the proletarian spruce. I, for one, would not mind if a sudden almighty deluge of acid rain wiped out all the Forestry Commission's Welsh plantations of this species. The anonymous battalions of sitka that stain so many hillsides might look attractive from a distance to someone interested only in scenery. But in reality they create stifling and sterile environments. The air in these forests is silent and dust-filled, the ground one enormous orange pincushion of spruce needles. The only wildlife likely to be encountered is that unprepossessing Welsh mammal, the feral sheep. Unshorn and shifty, its thorny fleece usually gives it the look of an enormous hedgehog. This is not an animal you would coax over to your picnic. Moreover, these dense plantations have left countless hillsides, stream sources and historic sites virtually inaccessible. On a recent attempt to reach Llyn Fach, north of the Rhondda, a walk that should have taken under an hour became a literally bloody expedition through the dagger-like conifers. A million Christmas thistles are turning the mountain black behind Treherbert. Thus that small but magnificent lake, a glacial scoop beneath the stunning cliffs of Craig y Llyn, is now almost unapproachable. Anyone who does reach it will know that the silence of the forest that encloses it, and the height of the mountain on its northern shore, make Llyn Fach a strangely eerie place. In short, it's an excellent spot for those maverick ewes to hide out. And so tightly are the trees packed together, not even the chainsaw man can tell the wood from the *picea sitchensis*.

This brings me to the puzzling question of what most trees mean to most people — apart, that is, from the forgotten facts that they provide us with a bearable climate, keep the soil in the ground, provide oxygen. Telegraph poles with leaves is too harsh a definition. What do we really think of when the flashcard with 'tree' on it is presented to us? Those self-seeded sycamores in abandoned city gardens might be one answer. The pollarded monstrosities above bus shelters – like the arboreal equivalents of toy poodles – might be another. Perhaps in Gwent some might dream of beech, in Gwynedd, birch. For me on the Glamorgan coast it is currently the tiny wayfaring tree with its bloody saucers of seeds. What is clear is that a sense of identification with woodland, a feeling that forests confer spiritual healing or regeneration, that what they have to offer is integral to the quality of our lives, are long dead in this country. In Freudenstadt I watched stately German matrons walk slowly down forest rides to benches where they would sit for hours, knitting, talking, thinking. For trees are naturally and essentially part of the lives of many German people. Even the Dutch, crowded in a country that makes use of every available square yard of ground, have a regard and a need for trees. But those of us who don't give a damn for oak or spruce (a magnificent tree in its proper environment) will still notice the corrosive intrusion of acid rain. Around Cologne Cathedral I saw the saints' stone faces washed smooth and indistinct as Victorian pennies. Buildings show the acid effects; so do metals. Fresh water is the first indicator, and anyone who doubts that acidification is a problem in Wales should visit the upper reaches of the Afon Tywi. Meanwhile in mid-August the beeches at Tintern are already yellowing. Who will say now that this is not another sign of the new and poisoned autumn we are creating for ourselves?

The Last Great Victorian?

R. GERALLT JONES

From Planet 64, August/September 1987

T. H. Parry-Williams, whose centenary falls this year, has been described as the first Welsh poet to display some of the character-istics of Modernism. This claim is generally made on the strength of his early Eisteddfod poem, 'Y Ddinas', which casts a naïvely critical eye on life in an industrial city. Looking back at the whole body of his work, I feel there is a much stronger case for thinking of him as the last, and much the most complex, of the great Victorians born too late and thrown unawares into the modern world. He was born in 1887 and was just ten years old when the Queen presided over her sumptuous Jubilee Durbar in Hyde Park, when representatives of all parts of the Empire on which the sun never set gathered to do her homage. But those ten years had measured out the parameters of Parry-Williams's poetic sensibil-ity. For no other Welsh writer has been as completely dominated as he was by the experiences of early childhood and by the way in which he was torn away from the magic and the stability of those years conclusively and traumatically at the age of eleven.

Towards the end of the Writers of Wales volume on T. H. Parry-Williams, published in 1978, I said this of him:

> Parry-Williams . . . in a very particular and specific way, was unique. The world of his work . . . will never occur again in the Welsh language. For he, in his generation, was able to combine the confident deployment of a rugged colloquial speech that belonged to a monolingual and highly literature society with the whole massive impact of modern science on the human consciousness. In

his own person, searching, highly intelligent, but utterly rooted in his childhood land, the two worlds met. He, within himself, was the microcosm of the complex interaction of opposites he saw in the world around him.

My main purpose here is to elucidate and substantiate this comment, with the one qualification that I now see in his natural cast of thought more affinity with the determined but often undirected mental quest of the Victorian natural scientist than with the more tentative and specific probing of the Modernist. And yet there *was* a tentativeness about him, a deep uncertainty, a bleak view of a universe hostile to human hopes and fears. Consumed with curiosity, possessed of formidable intellectual equipment, he was deeply fearful of the answers he might uncover to the cosmic questions he sometimes found himself impelled to ask.

His birthplace was the village of Rhyd-ddu, at the foot of Snowdon, an unremarkable place, by the poet's own admission. But he was born to a family blessed with remarkable creative gifts. One of his cousins was Robert Williams Parry, certainly one of the finest Welsh poets of the century, and another was Thomas Parry, one of the leading scholars of his time and principal of University College, Aberystwyth. His own early achievements, both as a scholar and as a poet, are legendary – his progress from Aberystwyth through Oxford and Freiburg to the Sorbonne, and his hitherto unheard-of winning of both crown and chair at the same Eisteddfod on two separate occasions. But outstanding talent within a family of outstanding talents is not, after all, unique. The particularity of Parry-Williams's position in Welsh literature arises, for me, from the juxtaposition of powerful and conflicting influences.

In the first place, unremarkable as it was, Rhyd-ddu, for the young Parry-Williams, was a microcosm of a loving, ordered and peaceable, if often mysterious, universe. The fact that he was torn away from this place at the age of eleven, when he went to the County School in Porthmadog, and had to go into lodgings in that town, no doubt deepened and clarified his image of the place that for ever afterwards represented truth and beauty for him. It is this place that is lovingly recreated time and again in the volumes of poems and essays which appeared regularly once the ice had been broken with his first collection of essays in 1928. It is certainly a comment on his own ambivalence that a man who had gained such eminence in youth and who had grown to be a major figure in Welsh literature nevertheless waited until he was forty-one before publishing his first volume of creative work. It is equally significant that he very carefully limited his metrical output to two forms not representative of the great body of Welsh verse, the sonnet and the rhyming couplet, and often used the essay form to meditate on topics which he also encapsulated later in verse form. It is all part of the whole wide-ranging investigation, the search for meaning, but it is also a kind of denial of ultimate seriousness, almost a coyness. Although a proven exponent of the Welsh strict metres, those majestic rhythms that have carried major themes of life and death over the centuries, he turns his back on them entirely, and chooses untrodden paths.

All this, of course, both in terms of theme and method, calls another poet very much to mind. And there is a sense in which Parry-Williams's obsession with the innocence of his childhood place is Wordsworthian. Passages from *The Prelude* do come to mind as we read his essays in particular. The sense of a living environment that encompasses and ennobles the individual is common to both, and it is no coincidence, of course, that in both cases it is a remote and forbidding mountain landscape that comes to life before our eyes. What is quite different is Parry-Williams's constant insistence on applying principles of scientific examination and analysis to external phenomena, in so far as these methods will prove useful to him. For Wordsworth, the mysterious essence which breathes life into all creation, 'the presence which is not to be put by', is total, all-embracing. For Parry-Williams, that which is mysterious is the sticking-point. It is what remains after the ceaselessly enquiring mind has done its best; it begins where the poet's powerful sanity fails him.

As his restless mind contemplates the universe and sees in it, time and again, a fractured and strange reality, he needs a touchstone somewhere, a starting-point, a still centre. For Parry-Williams, as for most of his agnostic generation of Welsh writers, this touchstone could not be found in any ordered religious belief or in any political dogma. It could only be found in the integrated reality that was Rhyd-ddu and its environs, shaped and perfected in the poet's imagination.

As one reads his detailed and loving account of individual path and rock and lakeside land, in poem and essay alike, one has the compelling feeling that here was a total imaginative world. In his sense of oneness with these remembered surroundings was a complete universe, a self-sufficient cosmos wherein lay all the secrets of life, ready to be probed and examined, but destined ultimately to rise above all such examinations, triumphantly inexplicable.

In one outstanding essay, 'Oerddwr', he expresses both the marvellous clarity that sometimes shoots through man's customary muddied thoughts, and also the fact that this clarity only takes the mind a step further into the mists of incomprehension. Oerddwr was a mountain farm, his mother's family home, and he describes his feelings as he climbs towards it:

> . . . all kinds of serene thoughts and clear imaginings hatched themselves out in my head. Oh, you might say, the effect of the more rapid and stronger circulation of the blood after the effort of climbing the steep hillside. But I must believe that there was something in the fact that Oerddwr lay at the end of the climb, for I never experienced quite the same thing while climbing to other places. Fast-flowing blood or not, it was worth experiencing the crystal clarity of those mental processes . . . to see and to realize anything, however simple, with total clarity and absolute positiveness with the brain is an experience that no one should belittle – it is such a rare thing in life and in the history of the brain . . .

He goes on to stress the strangeness of Oerddwr; a sense of otherness actually breathes through the solid earth upon which the farm was built. It was a place one came to at the end of a journey:

> Arriving at Oerddwr from anywhere was always to reach journey's end. No one called, or calls, there; one arrives.

But, like Eliot's Magi, all he found at journey's end was a further series of questions. Nothing was clear-cut, nothing was straightforward. Even those moments of clear-sightedness he had experienced on the way up had disappeared by the time he arrived.

And so the scientific method, the Victorian scientist's pressing need to examine, analyse and classify willy-nilly all the diverse phenomena of the external world – the wind, earthworms, mountain landscapes, neighbours, parents, motor-bikes — is constantly being applied to a mirage. Two and two, as he says himself, are for ever adding up to five.

In 'Dieithrwch' (Strangeness) – an essay of major importance in his work – he muses on the effect of separation on his consciousness. The microcosmos of which he felt himself to be an integral part was, after all, alienated from him, for he had been torn away from it and was never again destined to feel a part of it or of any other environment. The theme of alienation runs through all his essays like an insistent ground bass underlying the variety of themes and harmonies. In another essay he refers directly to the initial separation in one of his deceptively simplistic comments:

> It was forever afterwards a locality to visit, although I would always be 'going home' when I went there, even after my parents died. There was there for me no 'abiding city' . . . And I knew that as soon as I was forced to go away to school for the first time.

Those fourteen miles from Rhyd-ddu to Porthmadog stretched out endlessly and forced him to seek rest and reassurance in a world of his own creation.

The fact that he did not find it is a comment both upon the unwavering honesty with which he pursued his investigations, and also upon the nature of his own personality which, for all its desire for safety and stability, was in essence a restless, questing spirit, always setting off on spiritual journeys, never giving up the hope that one day the Grail would be discovered. Had he not also been afraid of the journeys he wished to undertake, it would not have been improbable to think of him as one of the compulsive breed of explorers who tramped Africa during the nineteenth century – Burton in search of the source of the Nile, maiden ladies in long skirts leading their native bearers along the banks of the Congo. He did in fact undertake two forays into the great world, once to South and Central America in 1925 and once to North America in 1935, and saw strange and wondrous things. But they were no stranger than the eclipse of the sun he witnessed once at Oerddwr.

I have referred in the main to his essays in this brief glimpse of the work of a man who represents better than anyone else, in my view, the dilemma of alienation that has overtaken the whole of Welsh Wales during my lifetime. This has been quite deliberate. In his sonnets, undoubtedly his finest artistic achievements, the ordered beauty of the sonnet form, its inevitable rhythms and its ultimate finality, enable him to conceal the ultimate uncertainties of modern man. It is in the more unstructured musings of the essays that we sometimes catch him unawares, a greatly gifted man, longing to make sense of the universe, but caught in the 'widening gyre' of Yeats's fractured civilization and often staring bleakly into the dark.

How Green Was *My Valley?*

IAN BELL

From Planet 73, February/March 1989

When I first came to live in Wales in 1976, I knew what to expect. Miners in mufflers would shout themselves hoarse at rugby matches. Amid green fields of daffodils, chapels would swell with the sound of choirs. Women would appear to me as either dark-eyed temptresses called Megan or homely smiling figures called Mam. Times might be hard, mun, but we be strong people, duw. Dai and Ianto would say that to me often, their faces still black from the pit. I was ready for all this because, like nearly everybody else, I had read or seen or somehow just absorbed *How Green Was My Valley*. It took me some time to dispel my disappointment at Wales's failure to live up to its advance publicity.

I exaggerate, of course, but there can be no doubting that for fifty years now Richard Llewellyn's novel has been a key text in the imagining of Wales. It has been continuously in print since 1939, and still keeps a following in a way that comparable middle-brow writers of the time like Howard Spring or A. J. Cronin would envy. Whereas powerful and important Welsh novels by Lewis Jones and Gwyn Thomas only stay in circulation through the ministration of the Welsh Arts Council, *How Green Was My Valley* stays in private hands and thrives. Whatever you think of it, that novel is the most pervasive and influential fabrication of Wales and the Welsh ever invented. Along with the leek and the daffodil, it is the portable symbol of all things Welsh, and both in print and on film it carries images and definitions of Wales all round the world. Like it or not, the book has become a Welsh icon, a prism through which Wales is invariably seen.

Why is it so popular? First of all, it is unquestionably a 'good read'. I went back to it when I started thinking about this piece, and was all ready to pour condescension over it. But I had forgotten just what an easy book it is to read. It is clear, emphatic and bold, unsubtle perhaps, but powerful. The characters are simply drawn, stylized in presentation, and easy to remember. The plot is episodic and melodramatic, the emotions heightened and stark. It has the illusion of sexual frankness in its passion and intensity, but is inexplicit and unembarrassing. Perhaps most importantly, it is located in a simplified environment, with identifiable institutions and rituals. The valley is a self-contained community, a complete miniature world of its own. The dramas it displays take place in the house, the chapel, the pit, the pub, the school, or, at moments of the greatest intensity, on the mountain. This pastoral enclave is conveyed in a language that is lexically limited, by repetition and the use of a simple vocabulary, and syntactically stylized. The inversions and the distortions of the style serve to make the register sound at once strange and authentic. The book's 'voice', the narrative presence of Huw Morgan, helps us find our place in the book, in a world where moral values are reassuringly definite and issues are capable of sudden and effective resolution. This is a book where you always know exactly where you stand.

This voice is very important in the novel for it is a consistent tone which holds it all together. The mood is one of loss, of regret, 'of so much that was good that has gone'. And here is where the problems begin. For although this looks like a fantasy of the past, of a place and time that never really were, the book does attach itself to history, and gives its events a historical and geographical location. Huw Morgan is not asking us to think of never-never land, after all, but of Wales in the nineteenth and early twentieth century. The intense nostalgia the book sustains is a yearning for a world we are asked to believe actually existed. The parable about the despoiling of a coherent way of life is a way of attaching the book to the lived experience of south Wales, and inevitably the story has a point and a purpose. It becomes an interpretation which flatters the bourgeois sensitivities of a comfortable reading public.

Huw Morgan's fantasy is of a past which was almost literally a golden age:

> But in those days money was easily earnt and plenty of it. And not in pieces of paper either. Solid gold sovereigns like my grandfather wore on his watch-chain. Little round pieces, yellow as summer daffodils, and wrinkled round the edges like shillings, with a head cut off in front, and a dragon and a man with a pole on the back. And they rang when he hit them on something solid. It must be a fine feeling to put your hand in your pocket and shake together ten or fifteen of them, not that it will ever happen to anybody again, in my time, anyway.

The splendour and plenty of the past is contrasted with the poverty and decay of the present. Like that other astonishing bestseller of the time, *Gone With the Wind*, this book is an exercise in selective recollection, carried on by a kind of *ante-bellum* reverence for things past. Llewellyn/Morgan presents us with a version of the land of his fathers in which the good old days have gone, never to return. The valley of his youth and innocence has been despoiled by industrialization, and all it entails, and Morgan has to leave.

As it stands, such a narrative pattern could carry many meanings. It could provide an opportunity for a critique of industrial capitalism, for an exploration of the rootlessness and despair of modern life. To an extent, Llewellyn does attempt this, but the terms of his critique are odd ones, profoundly fatalistic and racist. Although he is prepared to dramatize the contradictions in his organic community, he also seeks to smooth them over in a rather unsubtle way. At one point, the young Huw Morgan is outraged by the barbarous and hypocritical public humiliation of a young girl — a 'fallen woman' — in church. Morgan cries out against this cruel severity, but is later brought to his senses by a piece of pious doublethink from Mr Gruffydd, the intelligent cleric:

> You must realise, Huw . . . that the men of the Valleys have built their houses and brought up their families without help from others, without a word from the Government. Their lives have been ordered from birth by the Bible. From it they took their instructions. They had no other guidance, and no other law. If it has produced hypocrites and pharisees, the fault is in the human race. We are not all angels. Our fathers upheld good conduct and

rightful dealing by strictness, and it is in Man Adam to be slippery, and many are as slimy as the adder. The wonder is to me that the men of the Valley are as they are, not barbarians all. I was sorry for Meillyn Lewis, too. But the session of the deacons was helpful as a preventative. It was cruel, but it is more cruel to allow misconduct to flourish without check.

The community, in this version, is beyond the laws, self-regulating and fundamentalist. To be sure, Mr Gruffydd holds out some possibilities of progress – 'I must make alterations slowly'– but it is very gradualist, and he makes no effort to confront or assail the narrow-minded patriarchal institutions he inhabits.

Llewellyn seems to venerate these institutions rather than deplore them. Through the figure of Huw's father, Gwilym Morgan, he shows the possibilities of toughness and endurance, but there seems to be no irony in Gwilym's inability to adapt to change. It is clear in the book that virtually all change is to be seen as a kind of deterioration, and Gwilym voices the extreme fatalism of fundamentalist faith:

'Bad thoughts and greediness, Huw,' my father said, 'want all, take all, and give nothing. The world was made on a different notion. You will have everything from the ground if you ask the right way. But you will have nothing if not . . . All things are given by God, and to God you must look for what you will have. God gave us time to get His work done, and patience to support us while it is being done. There is your rod and staff. No matter what others may say to you, my son, look to God in your troubles. And I am afraid what is starting down by there, now this moment, is going to give you plenty of troubles in times to come.'

What is starting down by there is industrial unrest, which Gwilym casually attributes to greed on both sides. The unrest is thus motivated in the book, not by a desire to improve things or confront injustice, but by a misguided failure to accept things as they are, to be patient and trust in God. The original sin of greed has entered the happy valley and is corrupting it slowly.

The story that runs through the whole book is of a community breaking down. Gwilym's sons are dispersed over the world, and the valley can no longer be self-regulating. Gradually, the laws of man replace the laws of God. In some popular forms, this moment of institutional achievement is seen as being indicative of civilization, and is celebrated – I am thinking here of Westerns

like *My Darling Clementine* or *Fort Apache* — but in Llewellyn it is
seen as an index of just how far things have fallen:

> Before you are much older . . . you will have policemen here to
> stay. A magistrate next. Then perhaps a jail. And the counterparts
> of those things are hunger and want, and misery and idleness. The
> night is coming. Watch and pray.

The coming of the law is thus seen as a symbol of things
having got out of hand –'Wickedness was creeping into the
Valley without halt or check' – and this is presented as an
inevitable result of original sin.

If that was all it was, then the book would be a straightforward fundamentalist parable about the need to accept God's
ways. Huw's struggles to control his own sexuality, and his
sense that maturity is a process of loss, would be a dramatization
of basic Christian ideas about sin and self-control. However, the
book goes further than this and combines its Old Testament
fervour with a very disconcerting racial ideology. The happy
Valley of Wales has been polluted, it seems, not just by original
sin, but more forcefully by 'foreigners'. The integrity of the
Valley is frighteningly associated with its racial purity, and any
influence from outside is seen as a threat to be combated at all
costs.

Once again, Llewellyn gives xenophobia the full authority of
the narrative, by dramatizing the effects of having immigrants
around. A local child is ravished and murdered, and the community acts to find and punish the culprit. Their emotions are
stirred up by Gruffydd:

> Beasts live among you . . . working with you shoulder to shoulder,
> who will kill your children and go their ways unpunished. They
> will make of your community a morass of corruption. Will you
> laugh if I talk to you of the Evil One? Will you smile if I mention
> the name of Satan? Then let me show you the body of a child, torn
> by murderous claws. Perhaps I shall see your heads flung back in
> guffaws. This little soul met her death not at the hands of a man,
> but at the talons of a beast. A beast. And beasts of that sort are the
> sons of Satan. Such beasts you shall exorcise, as He did with the
> Gadarene swine. Are we decided? Are we in one mind?

The preacher creates a powerful demonology, and directs the
crowd's feelings in an obvious direction. For the culprit is not to

be found in themselves, in the real people of the valley, but in 'the houses where the half-breed Welsh, Irish and English were living'. In fact, the valley conducts a kind of pogrom of its immigrants, cordoning off their territory and, with no authority other than a burning sense of their own righteousness, interrogating suspects. The language used by the narrator is chilling and very emphatic:

> Up to the rows of houses where the dross of the collieries lived. These people did the jobs that colliers would never do, and they were allowed to live and breed because the owners would not spend money on plant when their services were to be had so much the cheaper. For a pittance, they carried slag and muck, they acted as scavengers, and as they worked, so they lived. Even their children were put to work at eight or nine years of age so that more money could come into the house. They lived most of them, only to drink. Their houses were bestial sties, where even beasts would rebel if put there to live, for beasts have clean ways with them and they will show their disgust quick enough, but these people were long past such good feeling. They were a living disgust.

One by one, these sub-humans are subjected to hard questioning– 'some Irish, some Scotch, some English, and some inter-breed Welsh'. Eventually, the culprit cracks. He is Idris Atkinson, whose very name confirms the racialist stance of the narrative, with its suggestion of a Welsh mother tainted by contact with an English or Scottish father. This 'inter-breed' is not handed over to the authorities, but given to his victim's father and brothers, and they bear him off for a painful, lingering death.

The intensity of the racial anxiety is startling. Whatever else it does, the book seems to be defining a pure Welshness which has to be defended against outside influences which can only cheapen and despoil it. There is no sense of a widening world, or of any attempt to embrace cosmopolitanism, and the whole strategy of 'Welshness' within the book is fearful and defensive. The hostility to outside influences of all kinds seems to recur throughout the tale, and no effort is made to criticize it or make it ironic. In political terms, this makes the book much less aggressive and frightening to an English (or non-Welsh) bourgeois readership, for it does not suggest the possibilities of a solidarity of class or a communality of feeling between workers of different nations. The supporting principle of the values within the book is an imagined past of individual integrity and craftsmanship, and this legendary, remote site is used at key points in the narrative to reject socialist ideas:

> 'I am not in favour of anything put up by a load of old foreigners,' my father said. 'Owain Glyndŵr said all that there is to be said for this country hundreds of years ago. Wales for the Welsh. More of him and less of Mr Marx please.'

This isolationist view is at the time challenged by Gruffydd, but later, in Huw's vision, the differences between them are much less obvious than the nationalist, anti-cosmopolitan stance they share:

> A stranger was talking about capital and labour, with the names of Marx and Hegel thrown in as candied peel is put in a cake . . . It was a pain to me that men could be so blind, but it was greater pain to know that my brothers and Mr Gruffydd, and the brave ones of early days had all been forgotten in a craziness of thought that made more of the notions of foreigners than the principles of Our Fathers.

Huw's bizarre form of ancestor worship and reverence for the past leads him into strike-breaking. But since the strike is orchestrated by 'strangers among them, who seemed to be giving the orders', there is little sense of a conflict of loyalties.

What the book puts forward, under the seductive disguise of Celtic historical romance, is an odd combination of a code of unimpeachable personal integrity, alongside a defensive and threatened sense of national identity. No doubt this was a very potent ideological cocktail in 1939, when the idea of fighting to maintain the community, resisting foreign influence, and surrendering class loyalties in favour of national ones was prominent. Indeed, although the book flaunts Welshness in a theatrical way, it goes beyond that specific national identity and yields wider meanings about the value of 'home', and the need for a loyalty to the family above all else. The stealthy message of the book, strangely parallel to the more overt message of the contemporary German novels known as *Heimatdichtung*, is that the family, the region, and above all the race are the final repository of value. At the end, when Huw is leaving his creaking house (an image of craftsmanship and skill) before it is submerged by slag

263

(an image of 'laziness and bad workmanship'), he keeps alive his ancestors in his memory. He has to do this, for if the past is dead 'then I am dead, and we are dead, and all of sense a mockery'.

I think the book is a kind of mockery. It produces a caricature of a national identity and then shrouds it in value. As I look at it more closely, I see an agreeable romantic novel turn into a crypto-fascist defence of racial purity. It is frightening to think of this text as the emblem of Wales and Welshness in Britain and abroad, unchallenged and uncontested. Popular fiction goes further and reaches many more people than nearly any other form of writing, and if this is what it provides as a definition of Welshness then it is dangerous. The values it offers need not be the sustaining values of Wales today, which is not betraying itself if it avoids rigid gender stereotypes, expresses curiosity about other cultures, or feels a sense of solidarity with other groups. What Richard Llewellyn's novel does is infiltrate into a popular romance the disconcerting ideology of defensive and exclusive nationalism. Can someone now, after fifty years, produce another popular text which might challenge or contest his book? After all, just how green *was* my valley?

Serbs and Albanians in Kosova

JOHN HODGSON

From Planet 74, April/May 1989

Kosova is in the news, has been so intermittently down the centuries, but is one of Europe's least-known corners. Reports in *The Times* of ethnic tensions between Serbs and Albanians are still accompanied by a little sketch-map showing Yugoslavia's six republics and the two autonomous provinces within Serbia, of which Kosova is one. Kosova is a little lozenge, bottom left. It is the geographic heart of the Balkan peninsula, a high plateau from which rivers flow north to the Danube and the Black Sea, south to the Vardar and the Aegean, and west through Albania to the Adriatic. 'Kosova' is the Albanian name for the province; its Serbian name is 'Kosovo'. To use one form or another is almost to take sides, for matters are now that delicate. 'Kosova-o' says the sign on the side of a bus.

To travel to Kosova from Belgrade, you must leave the international express trains with their Interrail back-packers, and take a tortuous branch line, mostly built in Ottoman times by *La Compagnie des Chemins de Fer Orientaux*. It is a slow, six-hour journey, so slow that open doors flap safely in the wind. The buffet car staff brew Turkish coffee in little pots on open gas rings for guest-workers returning home on holiday from the Ruhr, and soldiers returning from military service. The villages of Serbia are lush and trim, the trunks of fruit trees neatly limewashed. As the train nears the Kosova border, a militiaman checks the passengers. A foreigner is a rare, suspicious being. The militiaman rifles through your bag, and stares fearfully at a computer software cassette. 'Side 1, side 2.' He reads 'side' as two syllables; SIDA in Serbian is AIDS. 'Are you ill?' He is also worried about other kinds of infection. 'What is recorded here? Poems? Albanian poems? What are they about?'

As the train gathers speed over the Plain of Kosova, the track-side villages begin to look different from those in Serbia. In time, one learns how to read the villages of Kosova. Most are composed of clusters of windowless walled yards. These are Albanian villages, with cypress shrouded minarets, round which rooks caw. There are also houses without walls, with rooting pigs; these belong to Serbs. A few villages with both walls and pigs belong to the very small minority of Catholic Albanians. A lot of Serbian houses have signs tacked to their gates: 'Ka za prodaju.' House for sale. Serbs complain that Albanians have been forcing them out of Kosova, though there are also people who say that just about anybody who can is emigrating, for the province is the poorest in Yugoslavia. The villages resemble Anatolia more than Europe: water buffaloes lumber down muddy lanes, tobacco and red peppers hang drying on house walls. For the visitor, it may be idyllic, especially as the country people are so punctilious in their courtesy, and embarrassingly ready with hospitality. But pastoral is in the eye of the beholder. 'There is nothing harder than working your land,' says a villager who knows.

Post-war development schemes have brought industry to Kosova, and environmental disaster. There are mines round Mitrovicë; the air stinks, and lead pollution is many times higher than in Manhattan. There are no birds, and villagers round the town tell you their cows will not give birth: calves have to be brought in from outside. The massive power stations of Obiliq exploit local brown-coal reserves, and an orange pall hangs over the capital of Kosova, called Priština in Serbian and Prishtinë in Albanian.

Prishtinë especially is a monument to cheated hopes; the city is a whole world's fair of skyscrapers of reflecting glass, dominated by the Potala-like hulk of the Grand Hotel and the preposterous copper-roofed rib roast of the 'Boro and Ramiz Palace of Youth'. The Bank of Kosova is a soaring monolith, but the story goes that it was built back to front, and certainly the main entrance is round the corner, on a muddy path where begging women have spread sheets of cardboard in which they squat all day, faces screened, keening over swaddled babies. Pye-dogs scratch in the rubbish strewn around the Kosova Academy of Sciences, and the streets are filled with crippled rubbish skips, sometimes mysteriously in flames. The university (which had, until recently, absorbed unemployed young people to the extent that its enrolment was the highest in Europe) boasts a campus that is part Gulf-state modernistic, and part composed of dilapidated barracks that look like what they in fact are — the surviving structures of a concentration camp built by the Italians during the war. There are 14-storey apartment blocks, but lifts rarely work, and the water pressure is adequate to supply the upper floors only for a few hours at night. At its edges, the city degenerates into harsh bidonville suburbs.

If Prishtinë is nevertheless an exhilarating city, this is because of the extreme youthfulness of its burgeoning population. Evening on the main street is the time of the 'korzo', or promenade, a ritual processional way of conversation, gossip, and assignation. Living conditions are cramped, parental pressures strong, and young people form and maintain their friendships outside; those students who can afford it eat out in the dozens of fragrant little kebab houses with their sensuous Albanian popular music, which resembles the soft chug of some Oriental reggae. Gypsy boys clean shoes by the pavements, calling out for custom by tapping their brushes to complicated rhythms beyond the reach of musicological understanding. There are pumpkin-seed and chick-pea sellers, and business is conducted in four languages – Albanian, Serbo-Croat, Turkish, and Romani.

According to the official incantation, Kosova is inhabited by 'Albanians, Serbs, Montenegrins, and others'. In the 1981 census, the Albanian population numbered just over one and a quarter million, or 77 per cent of the population of Kosova, but there are more of them now, due to an extremely high birth rate which arouses great concern among many Serbs, although it is a normal one for a society at such a level of economic development. The Serbs and Montenegrins together (and, with their similarity of language and culture, they feel themselves united for most purposes) numbered 240,000 or 15 per cent, but they are fewer now because of emigration. 'Others' include 13,000 Turks, generally prosperous, long-urbanized descendants of the old Ottoman middle classes, and Romani Gypsies, who are usually very poor and employed in such traditionally Gypsy trades as smithing, music, and porterage.

If this ethnic mixture has in recent years become increasingly unstable, the shifting demographic balance in the Albanians' favour has been an important factor. Also, improving standards of education among Albanians have raised Albanians' aspirations and enabled them to compete for scarce jobs with the once better-qualified Serbian population. An Albanian smarts under what he perceives as Serbian contempt: 'They want us to remain as simple peasants.' Meanwhile, Serbs are alarmed to find their economic position relatively declining, while they are increasingly surrounded by people whose language they do not understand, and whose culture they have traditionally held in scant respect. In 1981, Albanians demonstrated for republican status for Kosova; ever since then, the authorities have dealt out harsh prison sentences for 'nationalist' activities, which may mean singing the wrong song, or owning books printed in Tirana. And so mistrust deepens, and even such bridges of understanding as once existed crumble away. A Serbian doctor once acquired some skills on the two-stringed *çifteli*, an Albanian folk instrument, but he does not dare play it any more. A Catholic Albanian once used to patronize a Montenegrin restaurant, where he could buy a pork dinner, 'But now someone might break a bottle over my head.' A Serbian academic used to enjoy practising his broken Albanian in the local vegetable market; he uses it no longer. An Albanian some years ago acquired a diploma of bilingualism, a useful job qualification. 'But I seem to be forgetting my Serbian now.' An Albanian student of English says it is difficult to make friends with Serbs: 'It is like *A Passage to India*, where Aziz says to Fielding that "we can be friends when you have gone". ' In these circumstances, tensions increasingly encumber daily life: to enter an unfamiliar office and to say 'good morning' in one language or another is less a greeting than a challenge, like a territorial claim.

Each side in the dispute has its history, around which emotionally-charged mythologies accrue, turning such innocuous antiquarian pursuits as archaeology or the study of place-names into political battlegrounds.

According to the Serbs, Kosova was the centre of a mighty, if transient, Serbian empire in the fourteenth century, until the defeat of the Serbian forces by the Ottomans at the Battle of Kosovo in 1389. There are material survivals from this culture in such monasteries as Gracanica, with its lovely, Byzantium-inspired frescoes.

The eyes of some of the saints have been gouged away. Serbs say this is Albanian vandalism; Albanians counter that Serbian villagers scooped out the plaster themselves to prepare charms to cure eye disease. According to the Serbs, a mainly Christian and Slavic population lived in Kosova under Ottoman rule until the late seventeenth century, when Patriarch Čarnojević, under Ottoman pressure, led a mass exodus of Serbian families northwards, thus leaving room for an influx of Islamized Albanians from Albania in the eighteenth century. It is at least beyond dispute that the return of Kosova to Serbian rule in 1912 was followed by a major colonization campaign under the Yugoslav monarchy in the 1920s and 1930s, when Serbs and Montenegrins were given free land. Many Kosova villages have a cluster of houses from this period; Albanians call them 'shtëpitë e kraljit' (the king's houses).

The Albanians, on the other hand, claim themselves to be the indigenous population, and the descendants of the Illyrians who inhabited the western Balkans in antiquity. They too have their archaeological sites, such as the ruins of the ancient town of Ulpiana outside Prishtinë, after which a housing estate in the modern city has been symbolically named. The Albanians point to place-names in medieval Kosova as evidence of continuous Albanian settlement. But there are migrations in Albanian history too. A Serbian victory over the Turks in 1878 led to the expulsion of large numbers of Albanians from what is now southern Serbia, and their settlement in what was then Ottoman Kosova. Prishtinë and other towns of Kosova still have their 'mehalle e muhaxhireve', or migrants' quarters, where these immigrants originally lived. There was also a policy in pre-war Yugoslavia, and even until the early 1960s, of expelling ethnic Albanians to Turkey. A young Albanian tells the story: 'My grandfather was supposed to go. He took the family down to the station at Skopje, but no train came for a week. If a train had come, I would have grown up a Turk.' Surviving resentments against measures of this kind, which are still historically sensitive, do much to stoke Albanian discontent.

It is above all language which is the nub of misunderstanding. Officially, a meticulous policy of bilingualism has been applied in Kosova since 1945, and is even extended to trilingualism in the town of Prizren, which has a substantial Turkish community.

Signs are in two languages, official life is supposed to be conducted in both, mother-tongue education is guaranteed to tertiary level; but in practice life does not work out so equitably. Second-language knowledge is very unevenly distributed. Although both Serbian and Albanian children are taught each other's language at school, few learn much of either. Very few Serbs speak any Albanian, and these are mainly in rural areas with a long tradition of peaceful coexistence. Few Albanian women speak much Serbian; not only is illiteracy among Albanian women still very high, but traditional family values have bound Albanian women to the home. But Albanian men will learn Serbian, if nowhere else, when on military service. This imbalance means that, in practice, Serbian is spoken in mixed company, and in the endless official meetings that are so much a part of Yugoslav life, except in such exalted forums as can afford simultaneous translation equipment. An Albanian complains: 'If there are nine of us, and one Serb, we must speak Serbian for his sake.'

The Albanians have none the less been energetic in cultivating their language. In pre-war Yugoslavia, the Albanian language had no place in public life, and Albanians studied at such schools as existed in Serbian. Members of the older generation are therefore often unable to write their own language, or do so, with bizarre results, in the Cyrillic alphabet. Their vocabulary may be heavily laced with Serbian or Turkish words. For the younger generation, the movement to promote the use of their mother tongue was encouraged, but also made more complicated, by a decision in 1972 to use 'unified' literary Albanian, the language standard of Albania, to replace the northern Albanian Geg dialect in public life. Very few people speak the unified language informally; it is jokingly known as 'gjuha e asfaltueme', or asphalted language, but to aim at it is a mark of culture. A group of Prishtinë students decide to drop a coin in a swear-box whenever they use a Serbian or Turkish word. Language reform has however exacerbated educational problems in a newly literate society. Moreover, as Yugoslavia's relations with Albania have deteriorated as a result of the conflicts in Kosova, so Albanians in Yugoslavia have less and less contact with the main cultural centre of their recently adopted 'standard' tongue.

Yugoslavia has since 1945 changed tack a number of times in its policy towards its Albanian minority. Between 1968 and 1981, Tito held out the prospect of satisfying Albanian cultural demands within an expanding economy. A deteriorating economy has now made these ambitions seem more threatening, and Belgrade has responded with repression. As for the future, inexorable demographic trends suggest that however Yugoslavia solves the economic woes and ethnic conflicts of Kosova, the province cannot be Serbian in anything but name again. The Serbs are just too few. A local bus travels across the site of the Battle of Kosova, whose six-hundredth anniversary will be marked, no doubt somewhat tensely, in June this year. The radio blares Turkish arabesque music, the news is in Turkish. Village women hide their faces from strangers behind scarves. Europe seems a long way away; the tomb of Sultan Murat, who was killed on the day his armies won on the battlefield, lies just off the road. His empire has vanished, but his cultural conquest seems to have held.

In Praise of Simple Things: Welsh Artisan Painters

PETER LORD

From Planet 76, August/September 1989

At the end of a lecture given by my colleague Delyth Prys at the Newport Eisteddfod in which she mentioned my research on the painter Hugh Hughes, I was told about a picture signed 'H. Hughes' belonging to someone in Pen Llŷn. But its date, 1813, was very early for a picture by Hugh Hughes – the only other works that I had found from that period were a pair of miniatures. I was told that the Pen Llŷn portrait was about 18 x 12in. and painted on a piece of tinplate. So without allowing myself to be too optimistic, I went with a friend to visit the substantial farmhouse at Rhiw where the portrait was kept. The picture we found there was remarkable, and, not for the first time, caused me to reassess the way in which we understand visual art in Wales in the eighteenth and nineteenth centuries. It was difficult to fit the delightful portrait from 1813 of Hugh Griffith, Bodwrdda, and two of his children, complete with *doli-glwt*, into Welsh visual art history. What we were looking at was much more like a piece of American art history, the work of what would be called there a folk painter. It had many of the characteristic features of that kind of painting – the full-face or full-profile depiction of the figures, the doll-like quality of the children's faces, and the painted frame. At that time the picture was unique and seemed without context. It now has a companion, painted in 1812, the two miniatures have become five, and I know of two more, from engravings, which have yet to be recovered.

Art history, like any other history, is very much a matter of context and viewpoint – the work looks the way you want it to look. As I have remarked before in *Planet* and in *Barn*, the viewpoint from which Welsh visual art has been regarded has not been designed to endow it with significance for us, but, on the contrary, to demean it. The application of the Anglocentric version of high art critique to these works by Hughes would find them sadly wanting. In this particular case the problem has not arisen, because the works have simply been rendered invisible by that critique, which is why they have had to be discovered. It is significant that this has not been a difficult process – the pictures have been patiently sitting around for over a century and a half waiting to be considered with sympathy.

There are a few pictures of the same period as the early Hugh Hughes's which are familiar to antiquarians (and which have been published from time to time in dismal grey reproduction) which emphasize the vital role of available and appropriate critique in making work visible. Helen Ramage, Bedwyr Lewis Jones and others have drawn attention to works such as the several versions of 'Twm o'r Nant' in the magazine *Y Casglwr*, for instance, but the status of these pictures in their various copies and versions has, of necessity, been that of the curio, interesting primarily because of the importance of the sitter. The only attempt, to my knowledge, to write something more considered was Bedwyr Lewis Jones's short article on William Roos back in the 1960s. The significance of the discovery of early works by Hughes, as well as a number of pictures by Roos, is that it demonstrates that pictures like those of Twm o'r Nant are not to be considered as a job lot of isolated curios, but as part of a body of work with coherent characteristics. That is to say, we are dealing with a particular kind of artist (artists who sometimes knew each other), particular kinds of patrons, a particular social context, and in a somewhat less particular, but none the less discernible way, certain visual characteristics. This work testifies to continuous visual art activity by resident painters from the second half of the eighteenth century (and in all probability, much earlier) into the late nineteenth century. At this early stage of research we have half a dozen named artists about whom we know something, with *oeuvres* ranging from just a few works to well over a hundred, and a number of, as yet, unidentified pictures. Most importantly, we find in the activities of these painters close parallels with other indigenous art forms, and works which are thoroughly integrated with the community from which they sprang. That community's alleged inability to express itself visually has become part of the received wisdom of the nation. Given the adoption of an appropriate critique, we have here the material for the creation of a tradition which exposes that idea for the nonsense it is.

In the United States a change of critique of this kind in the 1920s and 1930s had highly significant implications both for the sense of identity of American people, and for the creation of new American art. A very few individuals, in particular Gertrude Vanderbilt Whitney at the turn of the century, became interested in the work of largely untrained painters in the rural north-eastern states, and sought to understand its significance for contemporary American culture. Through the interest of these pioneers the work of Edward Hicks, Noah North, Ammi Phillips and others became known and valued precisely because it was not academic or high art but something much closer to ordinary people, the farmers and small traders in the towns and countryside from Maine, through Massachusetts to Pennsylvania. These people seemed to be distinctly American, involved in the development of their own communities from within, and not concerned, as were the urban intelligentsia of Boston and New York, with following European fashions. Therefore, the art of these painters could be construed as truly American art and the notion of an indigenous tradition with non-academic roots became an inspiration to a generation of painters and sculptors in the mid-twentieth century. It was not the only inspiration by any means, but to David Smith for instance, being American was fundamental to making his art: 'Beneath the whole art concept, every pass in the act, every stroke, should be our own identity,' he said.

For all that, the American term 'folk painter' is not a good one in my view because it confuses an already contentious area of definitions and counter definitions. Whatever folk art, and/or craft is, I don't believe it should include the painters of this tradition primarily because their form was derived from high art – that is, the portrait (in particular) or still life or landscape, painted to be framed and hung on a wall. This form was not a part of folk art if we take that to have been, in general, an art which repeated and developed forms which arose from the elaboration and decoration of the material necessities of its own peasant existence. Secondly,

274

the American painters, and our painters too, were on the whole (but not exclusively) professionals and specialists, so that the producer/consumer relationship was radically different to that found in folk art where that significant distinction is not usually to be made. There are wider definitions of folk art than this, of course, especially those which see it as a continuing phenomenon, but my view is that modern manifestations of material culture which are prevalent outside the circles of the intelligentsia differ from folk art in their purpose and means of production, and should be described by different terminology – popular art, mass art, and so on.

The absence until well into the last century of an urban culture in Wales, and of a Welsh political culture, had major implications for poetry as it did for visual art. We accept, in general terms, the well-established picture of the export of intellectual life to London and the Anglicization of the upper echelons of the gentry gradually eroding the intellectual context and the patronage which had sustained the court poets and then the poets of the aristocracy. The resulting circumstances have not, however, been perceived by historians as a literary vacuum because of the different kind of tradition which developed in its place (or, perhaps, became more obvious in the absence of its high-art counterpart). The *bardd gwlad* (literally: country poet) has been recognized and valued, and a high-art critique of aesthetic quality has not been employed to the end of denying the significance of the tradition. The relationship between individual poets, and the spectrum of activity extending into a new, self-consciously Welsh intelligentsia in the nineteenth century, of which the *bardd gwlad* was a part, has been explored in detail. There are many points of contact between this spectrum of tradition and the work of painters in Wales in the same period. It is significant that a number of the poets themselves clearly were in no way inclined to operate the critique which has subsequently rendered so much visual art invisible in the culture. In 1844, Hugh Derfel Hughes was touring the country selling copies of his book of verse, *Blodeu'r Gân*. He spent Christmas in Newtown where he met William Roos, the painter, also travelling to sell his work. His description of Roos is couched in colourful and idiosyncratic Welsh which is difficult to convey in English:

William Roos, the painter, born a Welshman from Amlwch, Môn . . .

275

is a man of average height, rather fat and fleshy. His round smooth face is shaven and ruddy, with a peaceful and satisfied expression. His walk is laborious and slow and his general manner low and humble. His pictures are fine and deserving of praise. Coming from a family of most humble circumstance, Roos worked his way up through many disadvantages to the aforementioned skilfulness. He took a very lifelike portrait of me in Newtown in Montgomery in the Christmas holidays in 1844 . . .

In January 1845, Roos wrote to Hugh Derfel, who by this time had reached Llangollen on his way back home, in even more idiosyncratic Welsh:

> Beloved friend,
> Here I am at last, thinking of you – I must admit I have become idle since you left Newtown – I have read many times your verses on the 'Cyfamod Disigl' [literally 'Steadfast Covenant', Hugh Derfel's most celebrated poem]. I must admit that they have had much moralizing effect on me – had I listened to a hundred sermons, they would not have had so much effect on me. I am now painting the portrait of Mr Williams, the Baptist minister – it is a big portrait . . .

This is clearly a relationship perceived by the participants as being between equals, and is not unique. Roos was celebrated by an epitaph composed by Ellis Owen, Cefn y Meysydd, in 1850. This poet was also in contact with Roos's older contemporary Hugh Hughes, who by 1845 (the year in which he painted Ellis Owen's portrait) had returned to the travelling painter's life of his youth. The epitaph proved somewhat premature, as Roos survived for another twenty-eight years!

> He painted life so well that Death
> Envied his art; – withdrew his breath:
> Although with mortals here he lives
> His fame both Time and Death defies.

These relationships suggest, I think, the adoption of the term *arlunwyr gwlad* to describe our painters in this tradition. The term 'country poet' is not used as a translation of *bardd gwlad*, so I think that the most appropriate description in English for the artist cousins of the *bardd gwlad* is 'artisan painters', for reasons which will become apparent.

Hughes was discussed as an earlier date (1823) in a correspondence between Peter Bailey Williams, vicar of Llanrug, and Richard Jones,

Gwyndaf Eryri, winner of the chair at the Caernarfon Eisteddfod of 1821. These were slightly more elevated circles, as Williams was one of a network of Church of England ministers who interested themselves in antiquarian and literary matters and who established the Cymreigyddion societies and the new eisteddfodau with their gentry patronage. Nevertheless, the reference reinforces the links between literary and artistic activity:

> My income is but small; the Llanberis tythe is only £50, and less than that some years; so I can't do much – but this I do wish, to support to the full extent of my ability every young man, in every craft and office, who is likely to bring honour to his country. I am not of the opinion that skill and talent is wanting in the Welsh more than the English, but there is a want of education and instruction. Men who draw praise to their country (in my opinion) are Mr William Jones, the painter, of Beaumaris; and Mr Hugh Hughes from near Conwy, engraver and skilled painter; and the like.

The references to improvement, and to William Jones, are significant. Blake had remarked, a little earlier and certainly not in the spirit of the age, that 'improvement makes strait roads; but the crooked roads without improvement are roads of genius'. By the time Peter Bailey Williams was writing, Hugh Hughes had been greatly improved in London, generally to his detriment, and William Jones had exhibited *The House of Sleep – Iris Entering with a Message from Juno* at the Royal Academy. Yet Jones's tradesman background is typical of that from which much of the kind of painting considered in this article emerged. He was a contemporary of Hughes, born in Holywell but brought up in Beaumaris where his father had a house-painting and decorating business. These kinds of enterprises often provided the schools for the artisan painting tradition. The sons and apprentices learned the skills of preparing grounds and mixing colours (tube paints were not available until the 1830s) and then applied them to decorating houses, coach painting, coats of arms and lettering, pub and shop signs (John Gibson remarked that his first inspiration to be an artist came from staring up at such signs), and occasionally portraits and landscapes. It happens that Jones senior's business in Beaumaris prospered so well that Jones junior probably received an academic art education as well as his basic initiation into painting skills. Penry Williams's story in Merthyr is similar – the son of a house painter, taken up by the local gentry and improved in

277

London – but fortunately paintings from Williams's days as an artisan painter have survived (although they are not, needless to say, exhibited).

No work has yet been discovered signed by Robert Owen of Caernarfon, but we consider him as typical of the tradition because of his humble origins and training. Robert Owen, the house-painter and artist, subsequently became Eryron Gwyllt Walia, the poet, and then the Reverend Robert Owen, as a result of which his early career is recorded in his memoir:

> When he was about 15 (in 1818) Robert Owen was bound as an apprentice with Mr Robert Roberts to learn the art of painting [that is, painting and decorating]. He achieved a high excellence in his art – he made some splendid oil paintings. He was sent when a young boy by his master to work for a period at Glynllifon Park, the seat of Lord Newborough. There he worked the arms of the family on a set of chairs in such a skilful and beautiful manner that they were accounted a masterpiece by good critics.

Many of the hallmarks of this broad kind of artisan training are discernible in the work of John Walters of Denbigh. Because so little research has been done in this field, it is not possible to do more than speculate about the nature of Walters's business; he may have been permanently resident there, or he may have specialized in art painting like Hughes and Roos, making it necessary for him to travel. Fortunately for us, he was favoured with a commission from the somewhat eccentric Phillip Yorke of Erddig to paint the series of servant portraits still to be seen there. These pictures date from 1791 and 1793, with a second batch painted in 1830. They are square – like pub signs – and make use of archaic high-art features such as the inscription on the face of the picture, elucidating the subject. This device went out of fashion in aristocratic painting in the seventeenth century but is a prominent feature of later artisan work, to be seen (at great length!) on pictures like the superb *Homfray Coal Train* by Inigo Thomas, one of the Twm o'r Nant pictures (*Twm o'r Nant, the Cambrian Shakespeare, Aetat 71*), and on works by William Roos such as the several versions of Dic Aberdaron: *Richard Robt. Jones, commonly called Dic of Aberdaron, self taught linguist, painted at Caernarvon by Wm. Roos, May 1838. Died at St. Asaph, 1843.*

Roos's curious ability to predict the time and place of Dic's departure for the next world tells us much about the unpretentious and practical attitude of these painters to their work. As well as his own pictures, Roos regularly copied other artists, even from memory, and in a late moment of financial extremis was observed colouring photographs in Oswestry churchyard. It was these photographs, as Roos himself observed, which put an end to the painting tradition to which he belonged. He turned belatedly to landscape – 'the only thing in art photography can't do'. As yet, not a single one of these landscapes has been identified.

The failure to perceive the coherence of the stream of work from our artisan painters has resulted in many other tragic losses, such as Hugh Hughes's early self portrait and Roos's subject paintings for the 1858 Eisteddfod. Fortunately, as well as copying their own pictures, our artisan painters also engraved, so that some images have survived even though the originals are lost. The work of Ellis Owen Ellis, Ellis Bryngoch, has suffered particularly badly and is known to us almost exclusively in prints and reproductions. Its loss is especially regrettable because, like Roos's eisteddfod pictures, his work widened the subject range of our artisan tradition. Because American society, particularly in the north-east, was not subject to the economic and social stresses which have destabilized our own, and because hegemonistic attitudes were thrown off, the survival rate of their paintings has been much greater than ours. Pictures such as Hicks's celebrated *Penn's Treaty with the Indians* have survived whereas Roos's *Death of Glyndŵr* and Ellis Bryngoch's *Battle of Rhuddlan Marsh* and *Fall of Llywelyn* have disappeared. Judging by the single, poor-quality halftone which survives of *Oriel y Beirdd* (The Gallery of the Bards) which Ellis Bryngoch produced in about 1855, these losses can, without exaggeration, be counted as disasters. Our lost pictures are directly comparable with the work of Hicks and others in terms of their cultural role and manner. The significance attached by Americans to their pictures is the measure of our deprivation, with all its implications for our self image and our relationship to nations around us.

But the sombre nature of these implications need not be transferred backwards onto the works and the artists themselves. Ellis Bryngoch's delightful confidence in his own ability is partially preserved for us in a few prints, drawings and letters. Here he writes to the daughter of Walter Davies, Gwallter Mechain, concerning the loan of a portrait of her father as the source of his own depiction of him in *Oriel y Beirdd*. The original was probably Hugh Hughes's portrait of 1826, which does survive:

> Regarding the Portrait of the immortal Gwallter Mechain, I beg to state that I have commenced operation thereon; not only that I intend taking pains to execute the portrait in a style of masterly superiority, but I am resolved that it shall be presented to the public in the full conviction that it will contain a faithful representation of the departed great in his canonicals . . .

A limited amount of work on Hughes and Roos over the last two years has resulted in the identification, and in some cases recovery from the brink of destruction, of nearly fifty pictures. Given a change of critique where it matters, resources might be made available to repeat this last-minute salvage operation with the works of Edward Pugh and W. S. Chapman (two of the most obvious candidates for investigation), and perhaps others, as yet scarcely known to us. The American example shows that the results of such a change could be very significant for the contemporary culture.

The responsibility for our deprivation lies primarily with the National Museum and its art department, whose business it is to lead in the understanding of the culture whose distinct history is its only justification for existence. That it has never done, because those working there, in particular in the crucial era of Canon-Brookes, themselves had no understanding, and certainly no love, for that culture. Other public institutions, including major art galleries like the Glynn Vivian, the colleges of art, and the University, who have all been in a position to collect, interpret, and encourage research, have failed equally dismally. The National Library has collected,with a kind of instinctive acquisitiveness for *y pethe*, but hampered by the absence of a clear definition of its role, and until the recent arrival of a new visual art specialist, without an appropriate critical framework to understand the work. There is no doubt that the state of mind now exists at all levels in the National Library to address the problem, but the financial means to research, exhibit and interpret the work are pitifully small. There is, for instance, neither a picture conservator nor an exhibitions officer, an astonishing state of affairs for a national art collection. It remains to be seen whether the new people at the National Museum will display a greater commitment to Wales than their predecessors, and turn that commitment into a new hanging and interpretive policy, and into the sponsoring of research.

The pictures of our artisan painters look different from high art pictures because they reflect different aspirations on the part of the artists and different expectations on the part of the patrons, from those at work in high art. It is the closeness of these aspirations and expectations to the mainstream of Welsh life which makes them so important. Whilst I think it a very good thing that we should have a Poussin (or even half a Poussin), the fact is that the acquisition will do nothing to make the culture stronger and more self-confident from within the stream of its own development, which is what matters if we are to continue to assert our particularity. The money spent on that one picture could have put together a fine collection of our own work, and housed it in a building where it could be displayed and interpreted to the public. It is only that kind of major redirection of resources, based on a complete revision of existing critique, which will contribute significantly to the reassertion of a culture able to stand outside that depressing and deceitful epithet, 'British'.

Humming Bird Dunes

MICHAEL DISNEY

From Planet 80, April/May 1990

I was brought up in Pembrokeshire within fifty yards of the sea. Going to sleep at night you could hear the waves rattle and seethe amongst the stones in the cove. Something in the smell and sound of the ocean became such a part of growing up that I cannot endure to be away from it for very long. When I want to think, when I must escape from depression, I have to find a lonely inaccessible beach and commune with the sea. Fortunately my profession as an astronomer takes me to all areas of the globe and I have been able to discover and enjoy beaches in exotic places from Tasmania to Tonga, from Chile to the Bahamas, and from Russia to British Columbia. The best of them remain fixed in the amber of memory. Here is one from Mexico.

I was at the time working at the University of Arizona for two years. It was my first job. We were very poor and my wife was eight months pregnant. Before the baby arrived we decided to snatch a few days away from the heat and bustle of Tucson.

The road to Mexico lies across the Sonorha Desert, misnamed for it is more honestly a cactus forest. Saghuarro cacti, taller than houses, stretch their necks to the blazoned sky like vegetable dinosaurs. Each plant takes two centuries to grow, guarding its bodily fluids with crucifying thorns. It is a local sport to shoot them from the back of a passing truck.

There is no natural border between Arizona and Mexico. The saghuarro stretch away to purple mountains on both sides, but the philosophical transition from north to south is unforgettable, even disturbing. Where Americans colonize and tame the land-scape, Mexicans ignore it. The American bulldozes a road, tows in an enormous silver mobile-home, erects a TV aerial, gets the gen-erator going and fills the prefabricated pool. The yellow school bus calls and the Stars and Stripes fly at full mast. By some miracle of adaptation Hereford cattle turn cactus into beefburgers. Intercontinental ballistic missiles lie waiting in their silos beneath a land where not long ago the Apaches roamed.

South of the border the same landscape is empty, left to the eagles and the dust-devils. Instead, the Mexicans teem together in ramshackle townships of haunting poverty. Hovels of cardboard and tin crowd around the white Spanish missions. Women carry water on their heads. Jeeps give way to donkeys. There are fright-ening numbers of children.

As we drove south, the highway quickly deteriorated into dirt and potholes so that I feared for our little car. Oncoming trucks hurled stones against our windscreen. Driving became hot, dusty and dangerous work. Towards evening we reached the ancient Spanish port of Guaymas and turned off for Bocochibampo Bay. In the darkness we found a very ancient hotel that smelled as if it was somewhere near the sea, but we were too exhausted to do more that evening than crawl into bed.

We were woken in the morning by palm fronds rattling against the wooden shutters. I pushed them aside and we found our-selves on an ancient balcony overlooking the sea. Standing on the balustrade, staring at us rather like a sleepy clown, was a pelican who flapped off in disgust when we laughed at him. We leaned on a balustrade twisted with purple trumpet-flowers and looked down on the bluest water you ever saw, the Sea of Cortez.

The best beaches can be found only with great difficulty; in fact that is no small part of their charm. Little did we know it but the search for our first Mexican beach was going to take all day. Perhaps because of the hot sun Mexicans never build a road unless they really need it. And having built a road they all want to live on it. Thus we found that there were only two types of beach in Mexico: beaches that are wholly inaccessible because there is no track to them and beaches that are crowded with shacks, people, donkeys, garbage and flies.

By mid-afternoon we were desperate. The temperature inside the car was way over 120 degrees whilst my very pregnant wife was queasy from being jolted over the most abominable stone tracks. The map was useless and my Spanish worse. The ruts were so large that one constantly had to get out and get under to see if the engine was still in place.

We reached yet another dead end in the cactus. This time Marie got out to look around for herself. She came back swearing she could smell the sea. I was ready to try anything except another Mexican road so we literally drove off into the cactus while she led the way, prospecting on foot. We struggled between cacti, around trees and in and out of dried arroyos. It was mad, when I look back on it. However we could smell the sea all right and after about a mile we reached a promising grove of palms with a tall white sand-dune on the far side. I parked the car on the soft shell-white sand and we struggled up the enormous dune together. We'd arrived. Below us there curved the most delicious white sand bay with no sign that human beings had ever set foot on it. The arms curved round a mile or more to either side of it finishing in two rocky islets almost directly out to sea. We slid down the face of the dune, threw off our clothes and plunged into the refreshingly cold water.

We pitched camp on the landward side of the dune under an organ-pipe cactus, a vegetable monster thirty feet high, larger even than a saghuarro. Its dozens of pipes were home to a family of gila woodpeckers. Around us, at a safe distance, flourished every variety of spiked and thorny plant. The barrel cacti protected their watery green pulp with close-knit hooked spines fully an inch or more long. Only when they learned how to outwit those spines had the early pioneers been able to assuage their thirst and cross the western deserts. There were ochotillos whose thorned flails were bright with delicate scarlet flowerets, jumping chollas like lethal thistles and palo-verde trees encased in bright green skin in the place of bark. Behind and above us towered pinnacles of sandstone turning blood red in the evening sun.

I took my spear-gun and goggles in search of supper. The colour had gone from the depths by now, apart from a giant incandescent orange goldfish, which we later found out to be a very rare garibaldi perch. I am hopeless with a spear-gun, more likely to shoot my foot than anything edible. But here the fish were entirely tame, even curious. A fat black grouper with swivelling button eyes followed me around like a dog. More than half ashamed I put the spear-gun to his gills, pulled the trigger and despoiled paradise.

Nights in the desert are unforgettable. That night a trillion stars burned right down to the cactus. The heat of the day radiated off into space leaving a coolth that caressed the skin. A hint of dew stole in off the sea. Our fire crackled and popped, orange sparks climbing to die among the blue stars. The grouper sizzled in tin foil while Marie turned the potatoes over in the embers. I was sipping from our demijohn of wine when a coyote howled from not a hundred paces away. We had slipped back another half a million years.

At the first paling of dawn we dragged our sleeping bags out of the tent and made a nest for ourselves among the succulent ice-plants at the summit of the dune. We watched the stars fade, first the Milky Way then the bright constellations. The sun rising from behind the inland mountains burnished their spires first with crimson, then with gold, finally silver, projecting their shadows far out across the bay. Purples and greens stole out upon the sea's cold lapping surface with a night breath from the land. The tips of the organ-pipe cactus were the first to catch the sunlight and cast their own shadows across the mesquite below. The gila wood-peckers stirred from their holes in our cactus and announced the coming of the day.

As the sun rose above the mountains driving the colour out of the desert, so the sea turned into a bowl of liquid cerulean blue. There were so many fish in it that I swear you could smell them. Fishing, I later found, was no sport, for the fish impaled them-selves as soon as the bait was in the water. Indeed we saw children catching small fish in a cove near Guaymas simply by dragging hooks through a shoal and snagging them. We, however, were more interested in sea mammals than fish. Sea-lions were rumoured to live off this shore while the grey whales come to give birth to their young in the Sea of Cortez. Snuggled in my sleeping bag I kept watch through binoculars. Skeins of cormorants passed far out to sea while frigate birds with pointed wings and crescent tails were lords of the high air. But the pelicans, so ungainly on the ground, excited our greatest admiration. A line of perhaps a dozen would pass across the deep, barely millimetres above the surface. The odd syncopated flap seemed to suffice them for a hundred-metre glide.

We saw no whales that first morning, though we were to see them later. We were intrigued, however, by a loud smacking from across the bay. Through the glasses I discovered a huge manta ray hurling itself out of the water again and again to belly-flop back into the sea with a crash. It behaves in that way to rid itself of parasites

Then Marie gasped and grasped my arm. Three feet above us, hovering perfectly still, his tiny head turning inquisitively from side to side was a ruby-throated humming bird. Suddenly the dunes were alive with them, sipping nectar from red flowers opening in the sun. We could hear their whirring before we saw them flash by. There was nothing delicate about their behaviour. They chased one another exuberantly and noisily around the sky. Arrowing upwards like projectiles they would scream down again and pull out inches from the ground. If I couldn't understand, at least I could appreciate, how these same mites were capable of crossing two thousand kilometres of open Caribbean in a single flight. At times there were half a dozen hovering about our heads intrigued by the red tartan patchwork of our sleeping bags. Then, as suddenly as they came, they were gone. Fortunately they returned to visit us every morning.

During the night coyotes had visited our camp, leaving footprints everywhere. Nothing however was damaged and nothing stolen. To protect it from just such a visitation I had left the uneaten half of our grouper on top of the car roof. Despite pawmarks on the sides of the car where they must have stood up to sniff, it remained there unharmed. Unwrapped from its charred foil the remains looked wholly uneatable, but Marie flaked it from the bone, whipped together some mayonnaise *à la* desert, and we feasted on a delicious breakfast.

Having packed some lunch, we secured camp and set off along the margin of the bay to explore. The seaward side of the dune was now bright with purple sea figs, succulents whose flowers open only when the sun is in his zenith. Marie, who collected shells, was pleased with the twisted black-and-purple horn shells found in the shallows, but more delighted with another entirely unfamiliar find. It was flat, almost two inches across, perfectly pentagonal in shape and something like a medallion. Sandy in colour, it was hard, though not as hard as shell. Centred on one surface was a shallow, symmetric five-cornered opening. What was it? The five-sided shape and the colour suggested it had something to do with the echinoderms, perhaps the skeleton of some tropical sea-urchin. Marie took several back for her friends in Tucson who told us they were 'sand dollars'.

From the top of the islet at the far arm of the bay, to which we swam, we had a fine view back over our domain. Protected by the most rugged mountains, our beach was surrounded by a pristine cactus forest. It was hard to see how we could ever have found our way into such a hidden land. There was no sign of man. Even the sea, far out beyond our bay, was empty.

When we cast a line from the rocks, an immediate tug denoted success. The fish wasn't large, but had a parrot's beak, and a formidable array of spines. While I worked out how to remove the hook, it began to swell up alarmingly into a globe. And if that wasn't enough to put us off, he grunted piteously until we threw him back in the water. On our way back to camp, something happened which I still cannot believe. There had been a great deal of aerial activity far out to sea. Lines of pelicans, cormorants and other sea-birds seemed to be milling about in the air over a shoal of fish. Through the glasses you could just see the pelicans diving into the mêlée from the air. The morning wore on and the shoal moved in towards us as the flocks of accompanying birds increased. The pelicans appeared to be working in well-regulated squadrons, driving the shoal into our bay and towards the beach where we stood. About a hundred of them filled the air with a frenzied beating of wings. Climbing to about sixty feet, each bird would take aim, close its wings into a perfect arrow and plummet seawards like a harpoon. The instant before hitting the surface – and we could hear the 'whomp' as they did so – their wings would fold completely and the whole bird would be gone deep in a flurry of spray. Seconds later they would be on the surface again manoeuvring to get a struggling fish out of their beaks and into their mouths. I could see the prey still writhing in their pouches and then in their crops. After a final shake the pelican would thrash its way into the air again for another climb, another dive and another meal.

They came closer and closer. The air was filled with the beating of wings and the cries of gulls and other sea-birds involved in the feeding frenzy. The water in front of us became a seething mass of crashing pelicans and frantic fish. They came right into the shallows, almost at our feet. Suddenly, the sand was alive with a million silvery shapes leaping and flashing in the sun. The pelicans had literally driven the shoal ashore. All around us, within yards, the birds gorged and the fish died. The gulls screamed and fought over the gleaming harvest until they could swallow no more. The pelicans, too heavy to fly, and almost too heavy to swim, paddled sedately off to sea. We, too, joined in that primal feast, collecting enough of the shimmering bodies, turning mauve and green in death, to cook for dinner that night.

Apart from a total lack of fresh water, Humming Bird Dunes remained our paradise for ten days. My home-made still proved unsuccessful and as we had brought with us only a single five-gallon jerry-can, we had to retreat to the nearest village for replenishments, for local oranges and for giant watermelons which somehow remained fresh and cool in the shade. During our stay we had only one visit, but a very strange one. A troupe of Indians dressed in gaudy clothes passed along the beach one morning and disappeared as mysteriously as they came. The men carried heavy packs, the women bore children on their hips. They stared at us without recognition or greeting then passed on their way. We were afterwards told they were exiles from the island of Tiburon which lay just over the horizon. Some years before, the police had been called in to investigate the frequent disappearance of citizens from the mainland shore. It was concluded that cannibals from Tiburon were responsible. The army was sent out, the waterholes were poisoned and the people exiled to the mainland where they still roam the beaches in hope of one day being allowed to return.

When we had packed our tent on the final morning we climbed to the top of the dune for the last time to bid farewell to our kingdom. We christened it 'Humming Bird Dunes' and vowed never to tell another soul how it might be reached. So perhaps it all remains there as pristine as we left it twenty years ago. I would never dare go back to find out.

Inequalities: Caradoc Evans and D. J. Williams

W. J. REES

From Planet 81, June/July 1990

It is not my intention in this article to assess the merits of D. J. Williams and Caradoc Evans as artists. My intention is to examine their work as sociology. In particular, I wish to deal with a problem which arises when their work is placed in its historical and social context. The problem is this. Caradoc Evans portrays a rural community of south Cardiganshire (according to the pre-1973 divisions of local government) as that community existed at the end of the last century. D. J. Williams portrays a rural community of north Carmarthenshire of the same period. These two communities were separated by a distance of some 25 to 30 miles, by an administrative county boundary, and by a low line of hills. In any broad sense of the word 'society', both writers are portraying essentially the same society at the same period in its history. Nevertheless, they present widely different pictures of it. How did it come about that two men possessed of great powers of observation and of an unusual capacity to convey their meaning through the written word, should nevertheless describe the same society so differently?

The only part of their work which I wish to consider here is Caradoc Evans's first collection of stories, *My People* (1915) and D. J. Williams's *Hen Dŷ Ffarm* (The Old Farmhouse) first published in 1953. These, when compared in some detail, show very clearly two things: that these two writers see the same basic features in the society of their time, and that they see them as salient in radically different ways.

We can begin with the general background. It is a basic feature of rural life almost everywhere that its prosperity and stability depend upon the products of the earth and upon animal husbandry. A provident care for the land and its animals is an underlying consideration which guides the greatest part of the activities of daily life. Both writers see this. A preoccupation with crops and pasture, with flocks, herds and draught animals runs as a continuous thread through their pages. But when we turn to the social relationships and to the moral and cultural habits which stand on these foundations, we get from our authors two strikingly different pictures.

In *Hen Dŷ Ffarm* we are presented with a community of free and equal men and women, industrious and provident, lacking indeed in the superficial refinements of a more materialistic civilization, but devout and cultured in a simple and sincere way; a community maintained not by the external trappings of law and order, but by the underlying sympathy and goodwill which free and equal men and women have with and towards one another. Except for the occasional appearance of a policeman or an exciseman, who descends upon the community usually as an intruder, law and government in any official sense seem wholly remote from the life of the society. One of the things which D. J. Williams frequently and deeply deplores is the extension of the authority of central government – 'people in London' – over this community during this century.

In *My People*, on the other hand, we are shown a community of deeply and often savagely individualistic men and women, a community in which a realistic calculation of self-interest overwhelms all feelings of kindness and human sympathy, and in which standards of value, such as they are, are invariably a cloak to cover up the iniquity of the relatively powerful and well-to-do. The state of affairs which appears in *Hen Dŷ Ffarm* as the absence of central government and external authority appears now more positively as a local theocracy in which the ministers of religion and the elders of the chapel wield a pompous and largely self-serving authority over credulous and superstitious minds.

That is how these writers view the general background. Buried in this general background, there are less general features which are worth examining in detail. For example, both in *My People* and *Hen Dŷ Ffarm* the importance of the farm animals is impressed upon us, and there is one thing which is very interesting: in both of them the farm animals are presented as members of the community; they have merit and worthiness and have a social status accordingly. But there the agreement ends.

In *Hen Dŷ Ffarm* the farm animals are members of a community of equals. They are industrious and honoured citizens who co-operate with human beings as human beings co-operate with them. There are painful exceptions to this, as when a pig is being killed or an animal has to be sold, but these are exceptions, and are in any case felt to be painful in a society of this nature. One has also the feeling that although the draught animals are hard worked, they are compensated by an assured supply of fodder and by shelter from hard weather.

In *My People*, on the other hand, the farm animals are members of a hierarchical society, and they have a fairly definite position in that hierarchy. Although a good animal does not enjoy as high a status as its owner, it has generally a higher status than a servant, or even in some cases a wife. The story which brings this point out very clearly is the story 'A Heifer Without Blemish'. At the April fair Tomos of Parcdu finds himself a wife but by mid-morning (by 10.15 a.m. precisely) he is distressed to find that that is all he has so far accomplished. Later in the day (at 5.25 p.m. precisely) he is a happy man, for he has found and bought a heifer without blemish!

Let us now take the status of women. There are few occupations in the world which place more burdensome demands on the labour of women than does peasant agriculture. Both Caradoc Evans and D. J. Williams portray the external facts faithfully. Both leave us with a clear impression that the work of women was endless and burdensome, and that this greatly stunted their physical and mental development. But the two writers part company as soon as they begin to interpret the inner meanings of these facts.

D. J. Williams sees the status of women as honourable and dignified. And this is for an obvious reason. Although men and women alike have to work hard, often extremely hard, nevertheless equality of labour carries with it an equality of status and esteem. In this community, as he describes it, dishonour attaches only to time-wasters and to those who frustrate and obstruct the civilizing toil of others. Honour goes to those who co-operate in constructive work, be they men, women or beasts. That is the ground of the equality which they all enjoy.

Caradoc Evans, on the other hand, depicts a state of affairs in which women are virtually a subject and exploited class. This is true of wives and daughters alike. Society is seen as primitively patriarchal; the commanding voice is that of husband and father. The hard work is done by women who are conditioned to obey male commands. Women who rebel against the accepted custom, women like Betti Lancoch in the story 'The Woman Who Sowed Iniquity', are sluts and Jezebels who inspire the wrath of the big men in the chapel. They come to no good. The men, by comparison, oversee the work on the farm, look after the accounts, and keep up the good name of the family by regular attendance at prayer meetings.

If we turn to the institution of marriage, both writers show us that men and women in this society do not usually set up independent households when they get married. Usually the bride enters the family of the bridegroom and takes with her a dowry in cash or in kind. The young married couple then retain an interest in the inheritance of the farm in due course. For this reason, and since land is not a movable asset, many families remain on the same land for several generations. Both writers concur in their portrayal of these basic facts. They greatly diverge, but without the appearance of formal inconsistency, in their account of the motivations and strivings which underlie the facts.

D. J. Williams dwells on the social aspects of marriage but says little about the economic aspect. *Hen Dŷ Ffarm* has some excellent paragraphs, perceptive and compassionate, on the personal adjustments which have to be made on both sides when a member of one family enters as an equal member of another. In those paragraphs and elsewhere we are made to see that failure to make these adjustments, on either side, can create tensions, sometimes enormous tensions, within a family. In keeping with his general outlook, D. J. Williams highlights the importance of the family (*yr aelwyd*) in the early upbringing of children, and he tells us, time and again, how blessed he was in the *aelwyd* on which he himself was brought up. (The Welsh word *aelwyd* is descriptively equivalent to the English word 'hearth', but when used in social contexts it is more emotionally charged than 'hearth' and has greater overtones of moral worth.)

Caradoc Evans, on the other hand, portrays mainly the economic aspects of marriage and we are left with a more depressing picture. The essential requirement of a good marriage is the possession by bride and bridegroom of material wealth of one kind or another. In addition, there are requirements which bride and bridegroom need to satisfy independently: the bride must be able to milk cows, feed calves, look after hens and work in the fields, while the groom needs to be fervently religious, so as to keep the family in good standing in the chapel. There is much to-do about the dowry which the bride brings with her into the matrimonial home, and it is clear that to marry an only son or daughter is preferable to marrying one who has brothers or sisters. A marriage in which the bride is already pregnant is not wholly respectable but less disrespectable than marriage to a girl who is addicted to finery and self-adornment.

Then there is the question of the plight of the weak and the needy. Both writers are fully aware of the existence of the poor and the destitute, and both recognize that to be poor in this society is to be very poor indeed. But they go beyond that. Both seem to see in operation a dual system of social security, one being official and the other unofficial. One is the system of parish relief administered under the Poor Law. The other is a spontaneous, unorganized, system whereby eccentrics, ne'er-do-wells and the like are invited to stay at a farm for a few weeks and, while there, are given some work to do. When the practice is seen to be founded on mutual self-interest it develops into a custom. When an unfortunate individual has established a relationship of this kind with a farm, he tends to arrive of his own accord, often without much prior warning, stays for a few weeks, and then departs of his own accord, often with as little warning as when he came. We cannot, of course, conclude that there existed a *system* such as I have described. Whether the facts point to the vestigial remnants of an ancient system of social security by then in decline, or whether they point to a strategy of the times designed to alleviate the hardships of parish relief, or to a mixture of both, it is not possible to say without a great deal of research. But what we are concerned with are the facts as these writers saw them. And they seem to see the same basic facts.

Once again, their interpretation of the inner meanings and of the social significance of these facts diverges widely. D. J. Williams

293

says little about parish relief. What de does say conveys the impression that he regards it as niggardly. Nevertheless, he nowhere finds wretched and degrading poverty. Its absence is due not to the provisions of central government but to the natural generosity and goodwill found in a closely-knit community where everyone knows everything about everyone else. That community is like an enlarged family in which the better-placed members come to the aid of those less fortunate than themselves, and in which the latter come to the aid of the former if and when, as a result of the turns of the wheel of fortune, their roles happen to be reversed.

What Caradoc Evans sees, however, are engines of exploitation by means of which the wealthier, albeit hard-pressed, farmers get access to cheap labour. Parish relief is seen as a purchase by the parish of a pauper's labour time. During busy times of the year, such as at hay-making time, a farmer can commandeer a pauper's labour, since that labour is deemed to be the property of the parish. The informal system described earlier seems no better. By this method an able-bodied man is induced to work on a farm with nothing to show for it except food and shelter, while the farmer has had a good deal of work done at very little cost to himself. The two systems of relief which at the hands of D. J. Williams seemed so essentially different, appear at the hands of Caradoc Evans to be essentially similar. Both provide loop-holes and opportunities whereby the comparatively well-to-do profit at the expense of the very poor. In fact, in *My People* all relations between rich and poor are calculating, ambiguous and hypocritical. We could go on to speak about the newly established Board Schools, about the local carriers, courting habits and probably much else. But enough has now been said to show the great gulf which separates these two accounts. The question is how to account for this gulf.

There are some hypotheses which come to mind readily. D. J. Williams was writing near-contemporary history. From time to time he remarks that a certain story can now be told since it cannot give offence to any person now living. He is clearly anxious not to cause offence to anyone still living in his old locality, and, understandably, he would have wished to avoid encounters with the law of libel. This places some limitation – how far we do not know – on what he is prepared to state in print.

Caradoc Evans is writing fiction and is freed from such limita-
tions. He is also far less anxious to avoid causing offence; he may
even have thrived on doing just that. D. J. Williams, in addition,
lived and worked in Wales. He met with considerable antagonism
as a result of his political work and it would have been only
prudent if he tried to avoid arousing further antagonism by his literary work. Evans, on the other hand, lived in England and, not
being involved in Welsh politics, he could better afford to risk
Welsh unpopularity as a result of his literary work. There is
probably some truth in such hypotheses. Even so, they leave
unexplained the massive inner coherence of the two accounts that
we are given.

The more plausible supposition is that both accounts are more
or less true, but true of different communities. This view has
seemed to fail, however, for one obvious reason. That two such
widely different communities could exist within some 25 or 30
miles of each other has seemed incredible. What I now wish to
show is that this assumption is, nevertheless, the correct one. The
eighties of the last century were years of acute depression in
Welsh agriculture. For a number of reasons, the depression
affected the parishes of Llansawel and Troed-yr-aur very differently. The major factors in fashioning the divergent outlooks of
the two men were the different ways in which that crisis was
experienced by them.

The agricultural depression was acute from 1879 until the
middle of the nineties. Between the three-year period 1877–80 and
the three-year period 1894–7, prices of store cattle fell by 20 per
cent and the prices of fattened sheep and pigs fell by 18 per cent.
Between 1879 and 1894 land values dropped by 5.1 per cent.
between 1886 and 1891 there were tithe troubles in various parts
of Wales and these led to rioting in north Wales. In north Wales an
unknown number emigrated to the United States, while in south
Wales an unknown but larger number migrated from the countryside to the coalfield. But more relevant for present purposes are
the ways in which the depression affected different sections of
society and different localities.

In 1893 the Gladstone government set up the Royal
Commission on Land in Wales and Monmouthshire. The
Commission held inquiries for two years and heard evidence from
over a thousand witnesses from all over Wales. It published a full

report of its inquiries in five large volumes. Much of the evidence is loaded in favour of one cause or another and requires careful interpretation. But some matters stand out clearly. Small farmers, whether tenants or owner-occupiers, bore much of the weight of the depression. These, for the most part, were unable to pay their way, were falling into debt and had difficulty in paying their rents or in keeping up mortgage payments. Their anger exploded, however, against tithes. Very interestingly, owner-occupiers on mortgages were generally more hard-pressed than were tenants; mortgagors were less ready to allow postponements or reductions of payments than were the much maligned landlords. The burdens which fell upon other sections of the rural community were mainly consequential upon those which fell on the small farmers. Farm workers, regarded as consumers, stood to gain by the fall in agricultural prices, but for most of them that gain was more than offset by the fact that many were laid off and that wages were depressed throughout the period. Landlords felt the weight of the depression in varying degrees; loss of revenue from defaulting tenants induced many to reduce rents (by up to 20 per cent in some years) while others proceeded to sell off the tenanted holdings. The farmers who felt the depression least were the middle-range holders, tenants or owner-occupiers who held 75 acres and upwards. These were protected by economies of scale and aided by the cheapness of labour (which latter implied that the weight of the depression was being transferred to some extent from farmer to farm worker). Those who had a reserve of capital introduced the new machines which were becoming increasingly available and which enabled them to shed labour and reduce costs in other ways. Farmers in these categories were able generally to tide over the difficulties; the worst that happened was that they carried out fewer repairs, or postponed improvements, or accumulated less than they would otherwise have done.

How did all this affect D. J. Williams? He does say that the times were 'bad enough' for farmers. But he had no real experience of the depression, and there were several reasons for that.

First of all, there was the date of his birth. He was born in 1885, six years after the depression had begun. By the time he was ten years of age the depression was virtually over. It was over therefore before he was able fully to comprehend its significance.

But more important was the nature of the locality into which he was born. The parish of Llansawel was a prosperous place despite the depression. In 1857 the railway from Llanelli reached Llandeilo, connecting the latter with the industrial area of south Wales, and giving the surrounding area an extensive market for its agricultural products. D. J. Williams speaks of the area as 'unrivalled dairy country'; he speaks glowingly of the butter, cheese, eggs and poultry taken to Llandeilo market; his recollections are of 'a land flowing with milk and with the honey of memories'. According to the Census Enumerators' Returns for 1881, the parish also had large holdings. Out of 72 holders of land, holding five acres or more, only 16 (22 per cent) held less than 50 acres each, while 33 (46 per cent) held 100 acres or more. More than half, namely 40 holders (55.5 per cent), held 75 acres or more. Many of the farms were tenancies of the Rhydodyn (Edwinsford) Estate. When the Royal Commissioners met at Llansawel on 19 April 1894, they heard evidence mainly about the Rhydodyn Estate. Complaints were brought against the landlord for raising rents as a result of improvements made by tenants, one complaint being made in respect of improvements made by James Williams (D. J.'s 'Uncle Jemi') of Cilwennau Uchaf (the acreage being given as '499 acres, 3 roods, 39 perches, (or 1 perch under 500 acres)'). In general, however, the complaints did not go beyond the standard complaints made by tenants against landlords, in good and in bad times alike, throughout the nineteenth century. It is scarcely possible to detect in them the overtones of a severe economic depression.

But, above all, there was the social position of D. J. Williams's family. The author's grandfather, Jaci, farmed Penrhiw (a little over 200 acres). He also had a lease on Trawsgoed (300 acres) where he placed his eldest son Josi. Jaci's brother, James (mentioned above) farmed Cilwennau Uchaf (500 acres). His brother, Bili (who did not prosper greatly, largely through faults of his own), at one time farmed Cwm Du Bach (110 acres). There were 'other relatives' at Beili Tew (156 acres). In addition, Mari, a great-aunt of D. J. on his mother's side had married into Yr Esgair (340 acres), a farm bordering on Penrhiw. As to Penrhiw itself, Jaci had bought it outright in 1839 for £1,005. Early on, he had introduced new machinery, and the farm usually employed four servants as well as occasional day-labourers. Jaci deemed that he had given dowries of £200 to each of his daughters, Anne and Let, and he may have given to his son, Josi, 'double what his two sisters got'.

These were large sums for those days. When Jaci died in May 1886, Penrhiw was divided and bequeathed in equal shares to his two remaining sons, of whom our author's father was one. D. J. Williams writes: 'Such was the wonderfully rich world into which I was born, a world in which there was very little anxiety about money beyond paying the way fairly comfortably without running into debt anywhere, and a world, too, so far as I am able to judge, where all, in proportion to their age and experience, were as equal as any human community can be expected to be.'

In the case of Caradoc Evans, however, the position was vastly different. To begin with, he was born in 1878, a year or so before the general depression began. But his experience of it was also heightened by local experience of an earlier depression, the effects of which were still weighing heavily on the community. Before coming to the general depression, we have to look briefly at the legacy of the earlier one.

The roots of the earlier depression lay in the loss of cattle markets, aggravated by shortage of capital and an uneconomic size of land holdings. South Cardiganshire was mainly a cattle-raising and dairy-farming area. Its prosperity, like that of other similar areas, had long depended on the drover practice, whereby professional drovers drove cattle to be sold at markets in England. From the middle of the century onwards, the railways had progressively taken over the work of the drovers. But the railway did not reach Crymych (about a dozen miles from Cardigan) until 1874. It reached Cardigan in 1886 and Newcastle Emlyn (the nearest station to Troed-yr-aur) in 1895. Long before that time, local cattle-raisers had lost whatever advantages they may have had in long-distance markets. For other forms of agriculture, capital was short and investment was low. The sociologist, David Jenkins, failed to trace any mowing machine in the two parishes of Troed-yr-aur and Betws Ifan prior to 1891, or any self-binder prior to 1894. At the turn of the century, mowing was still laborious work done by scythesmen, and binding was done by hand. The low level of investment was partly the cause and partly the result of the small size of holdings. The same sociologist has calculated that, in the parish of Troed-yr-aur in 1900, 64 per cent of holdings were less than 30 acres. Average income per head was extremely low, which implies either that poverty was widespread or else that there was wretched poverty in some cases. In 1875–6 the mean tax on income per head in the County of Cardigan was £8. 4s., which compared with £12 in Wales generally and with £15. 7s. in the counties of England.

The result was a social catastrophe. Relations between land-lords and tenants deteriorated, becoming venomous in many cases. The Royal Commission in its sitting at Newcastle Emlyn on 24 April 1894 was given the names and addresses of 17 tenants in the surrounding area who had been evicted for voting Liberal in the parliamentary election of 1868. It was given the names and addresses of others who had had their rents raised apparently for having stayed at home on the day of the election. It received strong hints that others who had other grievances were not coming forward to state them for fear of reprisals at a later date. The causes of these troubles were as much economic as political. Some landlords, less politically motivated, met the difficulties by putting holdings on the market, but that did little, if anything, to relieve the economic depression. In the main, holdings were bought by tenants with the aid of high mortgages. Many of the new owner-occupiers were saddling themselves with debts which they were unable to repay. Since the mortgagors were usually merchants, tradesmen or auctioneers, the main economic effect of the change of ownership was to transfer capital from agriculture to other branches of the local economy. Relations between small-holders and other members of the community became strained in other ways. In the absence of any officially recognized co-opera-tive organization, most small-holdings continued to function by means of an *ad hoc* arrangement of 'labour debts'. These were debts which were payable in labour, and which might be incurred by one farmer when calling upon the help of another farmer, or by a parishioner when given the facility of a row of potatoes in a farmer's field. Since such debts were inherently imprecise, they were perpetually a source of grievances and quarrels.

The national depression of the eighties lowered still further the level of prosperity. More landlords put holdings on the market, with much the same results as previously in the seventies. The Census Enumerators' Returns for 1881 show that in the parish of Troed-yr-aur only one farmer was employing labour, and that he was employing only one person. Since numerous parishioners gave their occupation as 'farm labourer', one can only conclude either that these were employed in other parishes or that they were employed within the parish only as casual labourers. The opportunities for gainful employment for young people in the parish were clearly very few. Between 1891 and 1901 the parish lost 8 per cent of its population. Much of that percentage consisted of younger members of the community.

About the fortunes of Caradoc Evans's family very little is known. He was the fourth in a family of five children. When his father died in 1882 his mother was thirty-five years of age. How she and the children managed after losing the father's income as an auctioneer is largely a matter of conjecture. The family's only secure source of livelihood was the smallholding of nine or ten acres at Rhydlewis. How much income, and what kind of income, the holding provided, is unclear. How much help the mother received from relatives, what humiliations the family suffered in receiving or in not receiving such help, is also unclear. Caradoc spoke bitterly, in later life, of the poverty which the family endured. But he was reticent on details, and some details which he purported to give have not been confirmed by later research. Even so, it cannot be doubted that, during the years before the children left school and for some time afterwards, the family lived in great hardship. In February 1893, a few weeks after his fourteenth birthday, Caradoc himself joined the 8 per cent of the population that was lost to the parish of Troed-yr-aur. He departed to seek his fortune elsewhere.

It is now possible to arrive at some conclusions. One must be that both writers have given reasonably authentic portrayals of the communities in which, respectively, they were brought up. In fairness to both, neither of them at any time seems to have claimed to be doing more than that. Neither of them claimed to be portraying Welsh rural life or Welsh peasant life in general.

Another conclusion that has to be drawn is that the two communities which they described so differently did exist within some 25 or 30 miles of each other. This sociological phenomenon is adequately explained (1) by the inequalities of land holding, as between the parishes of Llansawel and Troed-yr-aur, (2) by the disparate effects of the railway system which, for Llansawel, created a wider market for its products, and in south Cardiganshire, destroyed an existing market, without creating another, and (3) by the further effects of a country-wide agricultural depression which scarcely affected Llansawel, but which intensified a pre-existing depression in south Cardiganshire. We have here also a classic example of the way in which the railway network, which connected areas of Wales with England, could isolate areas of Wales one from another. Even after the railway had reached Cardigan and Newcastle Emlyn, it was almost as easy to travel from Troed-yr-aur to Rhydcymerau or Llansawel by trap and pony as to travel by rail, and not much easier than it would have been in the Middle Ages.

Another conclusion which is inescapable is that the early experiences of the two writers fashioned their creative work. D. J. Williams's family left Penrhiw in 1891 and, for various reasons, the fortunes of the family declined. Nevertheless, the life at Penrhiw left imperishable memories in the mind of this one son. The days of his early childhood always remained for D. J. Williams the great days of his life: happy, spacious, halcyon days. Through the vicissitudes and triumphs of life, in his labours in the coal-mines of south Wales, in the classrooms and quadrangles of Oxford colleges, among the cells and corridors of Her Majesty's Prison at Wormwood Scrubs, he always remained the child of Penrhiw. In his literary creation, the life at Penrhiw is projected as an ideal for all humanity. Not that it was, or ever would be, an ideal life for all men. *Hen Dŷ Ffarm* gives a fleeting glimpse of Twm Coch (Red Tom) in his final years. Twm Coch had suffered a stroke and we see him on a frosty autumn day lifting swedes on a neighbour's field: he 'would take a swede up out of the drill with his good hand and transfer it to his paralysed hand, which shook so much that the earth among the roots fell to the ground like meal'. Twm Coch had been a man servant of Jaci Penrhiw, and was once known to have carried a huge tree-trunk on his back from a 'deep, wet dingle where not one of the horses could go near it'. But he ends his days in grotesque and grovelling poverty. Jaci meanwhile, and partly as a result of the labour of Twm Coch, had accumulated more wealth and had handed it on to his descendants. The episode has the characteristics of many episodes portrayed by Caradoc Evans. But D. J. Williams was so enchanted by his early upbringing that he could not bring himself to see the element of exploitation in the way of life which he so well described.

Caradoc Evans's response to his own upbringing was more complex. He makes no plea for a different economic or social order. His portrayal of rural exploitation provides ample material for a radical manifesto. But *My People* is not a manifesto on behalf of anything. A certain obscurity about its underlying intentions has lent some support for the view that the author's motivations were almost wholly personal. But there is some evidence also for the view that they were mainly reformist. John Harris, in his Introduction to a recent edition of *My People* (Seren Books, 1987), shows that its author consciously modelled his literary style on that of the Old Testament, seeing in it the best vehicle for his own purpose. This was the style in which the Biblical writers chastised the people of Israel and sought to impel them toward a more upright way of life. This evidence supports the view (which may not be held by John Harris without qualification) that the author's target was not any institution as such, but a hypocritical and self-serving moral code which he sees as corrupting all institutions. On this view, Caradoc Evans was a reformer, but a reformer in the essentially religious tradition, a moralist speaking in parables.

We are on firmer ground, however, if we put on one side all questions about the author's motives, and consider only the nature of the work itself. Few would deny that *My People* has a disturbing moral quality. What it portrays, above all else, is a collapse of nearly all feelings of sympathy, and a consequential distortion of ordinary moral values, under conditions of social deprivation. The portrayal is not a work of pure fancy or imagination; it is plainly a realistic account of life as experienced in a specific place at a specific time. It is one of the few permanently valuable legacies of the prolonged social crisis in south Cardiganshire at the end of the nineteenth century.

Finally, what conclusions can be drawn about the value of these two works for the student of social history? There can be little doubt that both writers have to some extent magnified for literary purposes those aspects of rural life which most intimately affected their own lives, and that the work of each to some extent corrects and complements that of the other. But we cannot conclude that a true portrayal of Welsh rural society in general at the end of the last century must therefore lie midway between these two portrayals. We know that the problems of south Cardiganshire were exceptional. It was to be expected that a portrayal of life as seen from Lanlas Uchaf would be exceptional. But we also know from the Report of the Royal Commission in 1896 that approximately

86 per cent of land holdings in Wales were less than 50 acres. In the light of that fact, the picture of life at Penrhiw seems to bear little relation to the conditions of daily life for the greater part of rural Wales. On a *priori* sociological grounds, it seems highly probable that, if we take Wales as a whole, Caradoc Evans's portrayal is less misleading, and to that extent more helpful, than that of D. J. Williams. Whether that conclusion could be confirmed by detailed research on a nation-wide scale, however, is a question beyond the scope of this article, and must be left unanswered.

People with Problems

ROBIN OKEY

From Planet 84, December 1990/January 1991

Last April I spent the night in the Hotel Central on the main square of the capital of Transylvania, till 1918 a province of the Habsburg monarchy and still perceptibly more 'European' than the rest of Romania. Yet at 10 p.m. not a single water outlet on any floor would work. I reported this to a little group of staff sitting chatting in the foyer and one of them confidently led me to a shower I had already tried. When a doomed gurgle resulted, he turned and said vehemently: 'It's all the Communists' fault. Nothing in this hotel works – because of Communism!'

This bleak little anecdote points the contrast between the glamour attaching to East Europeans' inspiring risings against Communist misrule last autumn and the drab realities of life in the post-Communist aftermath. Briefly, the Western media were awash with images of protesting East Europeans. We saw in turn fleeing East Germans panicking the Communist authorities into opening the Berlin Wall, the key-jingling demonstrators of Wenceslas Square in Prague, finally the turbulent streets and TV studios of Bucharest. Now that East Europeans are struggling to build a new political system, remould shattered moral values and transform tottering economies, the gaze of a fickle world has turned elsewhere. Eastern Europe is again, as it was to Neville Chamberlain in 1938, the 'far away' region of which 'we know nothing'. Yet can we afford to ignore people whose fate is bound, willy nilly, with that of our continent and therefore our own?

The trouble is it is much harder to write interestingly about post-Communist Eastern Europe than about the death of the old regime. That had the natural shape of classical tragedy, as high hopes and much initial idealism, poisoned at source by the taint of Stalinism, spiralled inexorably through the calamities of 1956, 1968 and 1981 and the moral and economic decay of the 1980s to the final denouement. Now, though several features of post-Communist order cry out for comment – its political structures, its mood, its economy, its relation to its pre-Communist, specifically its nationalist, legacy – perspective is lost in the multiformity of events. An old British stereotype provides a yardstick, however. It is of Eastern Europe as the zone of darkness and xenophobia where nothing really goes right. Once the euphoria of last autumn faded and habitual British pessimism reasserted itself, Robert Kilroy-Silk was writing in *The Times* of 9 February: 'Any fool could have foreseen that the consequences of the almost overnight removal of repressive regimes would mean serious disorder verging on anarchy and chaos. Gorbachev has let loose the dogs of war as we will see in the next few months and years in Eastern Europe.' How far do events in 1990 bear out these dire forebodings?

In the first place, alternative political structures have emerged with considerable speed. Those who feared that the collapse of Communism would produce a dangerous void or a hopeless babble forgot Aristotle's dictum that man is a political animal. It is not that anti-Communism has been muted in the interests of continuity. The bust of the Czech Communist leader in 1948, Klement Gottwald, has been carried away in a tumbril, the Polish Communist headquarters is to house the next Warsaw stock-exchange; East German and Polish secret police mutate into taxi drivers, Gorky into Tolkien in Polish set texts and the Bulgarian Red Star into – what else? – a red rose. As Social Democratic parties and the advocates of a 'third way' like East Germany's New Forum collapsed in successive elections and Roger Scruton and the 'Kind Lady' Mrs Thatcher were honoured guests in Prague, it became clear that the moderate left has also, for the time being at least, shared in Communism's discredit. The year 1989 has closed the cycle of revolution to the Left which began in 1789.

What, then, is its message? East European leaders are not Thatcherite clones, though some aspire thereto. Their two most significant thinkers, Václav Havel and Solidarity's Jacek Kuroń, are if anything, centre-left in instinct. But their inspiration is radical liberal rather than socialist, their emphasis on individual responsibility and the traditional freedoms of press, association and conscience as the building blocks of a healthy civil society. This is the lesson of Havel's famous criticism of the shopkeeper who puts up a poster saying 'Workers of the World Unite' not because he believes in it, but to get the secret police off his back. Respect for words and their true meanings is not a fad for intellectuals, but the only way to escape corruption by totalitarian social control. The aspiration to recreate a genuine civil society based on free exchange of views can be read from the very titles of the movements of 1989: New Forum in East Germany, Civic Forum in Czechoslovakia, Democratic Forum in Hungary, the Bulgarian Club for the Support of Glasnost and Democracy, the Romanian Group for Social Dialogue, the Serbian Committee for the Protection of the Freedom of Thought. The forum, front or coalition, too, has proved an effective instrument in the transition to a new political order, amalgamating the proliferating political parties which at first so alarmed disciplined Western observers, as democracy usually does when we observe it in action. In the event, clear-cut parliamentary situations with governing party coalitions facing one or two major opposition groupings have emerged in Hungary, Croatia and Slovenia as well, if less happily, in Bulgaria. Civic Forum and Solidarity, which govern without significant opposition in Czechoslovakia and Poland are widely expected to break up into their component parts, as indeed could already be said to have happened in the rival Walesa and Mazowiecki support groups.

Of course, major and minor distinctions must be made. The minor one is between Poland and Hungary, where the liberal-conservative clash (crudely, national Christian populism versus free-market cosmopolitanism) overshadows weak socialist forces, and Czechoslovakia and the old East Germany, where social democratic elements (not always so-called!) are somewhat stronger. The major distinction is between all these countries and the Balkan lands, where, barring the ex-Habsburg lands of Croatia and Slovenia in Yugoslavia, varieties of ex-Communists still hold the upper hand, not to speak of the unreconstructed Party of Labour of Albania. Does this mean that what has been said above about the demise of Communism has been exaggerated? Not really. Iliescu's National Salvation Front and the re-dubbed social-ists of Bulgaria and Serbia are essentially non-ideological groupings of the old party apparat, which have been able to main-tain themselves by exploiting nationalism and the weak civic traditions of the Balkans. They no longer aspire to a 'third way', as Prime Minister Petru Roman's dream of making Romania the South Korea of the Balkans and the Bulgarian comment on IMF loan conditions – 'we have no alternative' – indicate. What the Balkan states do point up is that the end of totalitarianism is not yet democracy. The bitterness of Romanian students and of the Bulgarians who stormed the Socialist Party headquarters in September lies in a feeling of having been cheated out of their rev-olution, but in the literal sense it is not so much electoral fraud as rural and (in Romania) worker distrust of young urban radicals which has frustrated them.

The gloom of Romanian oppositionists is reflected, to a greater or lesser extent, all over Eastern Europe. What accounts for the undoubted crisis of morale? For one thing, though the new politi-cal process may have delivered potential governments rather well, people are not used to the compromises it entails. Havel's concept of 'living in truth' sits ill with the half truths which most politicians in open societies practise. Politics is more complicated than is suggested in the delightful election poster of the Hungarian Young Democrats – a picture of two embracing couples, one Brezhnev and Honecker, the other two comely young people of opposite sex, with one word: Choose! Apathy is wide-spread. Only 45 per cent voted in the second round of the Hungarian general election, only 42 per cent in the Polish local elections in May, the first nation-wide free poll in the country for sixty years. By September the electoral pendulum was already swinging sharply against the ruling Hungarian Democratic Forum.

But there are deeper-seated reasons for apathy and disillusion. To understand Eastern Europe today we must recognize that, except in Romania, its immediate background was no longer fifties-style Stalinist tyranny but the corrupt, drab, incompetent regimes of the seventies and eighties, when ideologically bank-rupt leaders tinkered capriciously with pseudo-reforms. Only cynicism flourished in this debilitating epoch. The continuing problem of the secret police is a festering reminder, which has so far brought down two East German party leaders, two Czechoslovak cabinet ministers and an East German minister in the very week of unification. Iliescu's plea that Romanians need to trust each other may be self-serving, but still makes sense. I saw something of the intransigence of youth in an intelligent young Transylvanian Hungarian last spring. His lecturer in Marxism-Leninism had told him that she was now teaching an optional course in civics, but would he please come, as her job depended on it, and he must realize she had not meant what she'd said earlier. 'I can tell what a person thinks in their heart and you believed what you taught us,' he reproved her sternly.

If trust is at a discount, what is going up in Eastern Europe is drugs, crime and porn. Everywhere police morale and efficiency are at rock bottom. The Bulgarian police are one-fourth under-strength and their relative wages have plummeted to forty-second in sixty occupations: 1,250 policemen in the old East Germany have been arrested. Those professionally concerned with morals, the clergy, report a decline in church attendance, certainly in Poland. Ironically, controversial measures for religious instruction in schools are being pushed through in a number of countries (and anti-abortion in Poland) at a time when page three journalism is increasingly the only kind which can survive the vastly greater costs of commercial publishing. Western materialism may be more effective in weakening the hold of traditional values than Marxist atheism.

The question of consumerism goes to the heart of the current East European dilemma. It is stupid for prosperous Westerners to chide East Europeans for coveting quality Western products. Yet it is only honest to point out that they know little of the skills and share few of the attitudes necessary to produce them. This may seem a slur, but anyone who's spent some time in Eastern Europe will, I think, know what I mean. For convinced Marxists, East European dissidents' view of the market as embodying human relationships as opposed to the impersonal state may seem perverse, yet it arises from East European experience. Under 'actually existing socialism' you did not have to please the customer or sell a product. One trivial example. To someone used to Western hype it is almost surreal to hear a Romanian tourist official dispose of a request for directions to reach a village recommended for a fine view: 'It's just a village; there's nothing to see; the bus station is miles away.'

East European society is not adapted to provide the goods and services it craves. The crisis of morale centres above all on the crisis of the economy. It is threefold: external debt; an internal structure of uncompetitive industry; and very low wages paid in unconvertible currency. What is a non-economist to make of the disarmingly simple cure to these complex problems which seems to be urged on all sides: privatization?

The problems are vast. There are questions of scale (Poland is pledged to privatize 80 per cent of its industry in three to four years); machinery (no real capital markets, stock exchanges or accounting know-how); legality (who owns what is nominally the 'people's' property?); plausibility (who would want to buy, say, an outmoded metallurgical plant?); and practicality – who, except for the 'red barons' or ex-Comminist apparatchiks and the black marketeers, could afford to buy anyway? Yet allowing foreign capitalists to participate on a big scale risks rip-offs. Should shares therefore be given away, as Czechoslovakia and Romania have recently proposed and *The Economist* is urging? But where does that leave entrepreneurial venture theory? The conundrums seem endless, and so far there has been more talk than action. Poland's first privatization law in July provided for 40 enterprises over the next year; only 7,500 to go! The Czechoslovak law of September, after publicly expressed doubts by President Havel (a closet third-wayer?), applied only to service industries. The first East German privatization supremo resigned in despair after a month. Does privatization belong to the never-never land of monetarist economics, by which a Sir Allan Walters can claim East European real wages are too high – thus casting light on *The Times* report that a Bulgarian female collective farm-worker's wages at 45 dollars a month are inflated fourfold by an artificial exchange rate?

Meanwhile, prices rise and subsidies are cut. Poles now spend 60 per cent of their income on food, as against 40 per cent before; unemployment may reach 2–4 million. A quarter of East Germany's workers were on short-time when the state expired; half a million Romanian chemical workers face prospective redundancy. East European moves to trim their trade surpluses with the Soviet Union, and the resulting rouble mountains, have exposed their industries' dependence on the Soviet market and brought the Hungarian bus giant Ikarus, for example, to the verge of bankruptcy. The Soviets' cut-back of oil supplies has been exacerbated by the Gulf crisis, as nearly all former Warsaw bloc countries had large surpluses with Iraq, which were to be balanced through oil. By September, Czechoslovakia could cover only two-thirds of her industrial energy needs, and Bulgaria, too, had had to introduce petrol rationing. Yet Polish pleas for Gulf compensation and remission of four-fifths of their 40 billion dollar debt have been rejected and there is no sign of a Marshall Plan strategy for Eastern Europe. Orthodoxy holds that the region needs technical know-how and private investment rather than official loans, which overlooks the fact that private capital will await the creation of an adequate infrastructure only institutional funding can provide.

Not everything is equally bleak. Poland and Yugoslavia's bold currency reforms, linking the zloty to the dollar and the dinar to the Deutschmark respectively have stopped galloping inflation in its tracks and have produced unexpectedly large trade and budget surpluses to help tide over bad industrial recession. Joint ventures with Western capital are multiplying in Poland and Hungary – 2,000 in Hungary alone – and Hungarian social scientists have targeted the petty bourgeoisie and the peasants, once they get title deeds to their old lands, as groups that could respond to the new entrepreneurial climate. But in the longer term, inflation will revive and the spirit of enterprise will wither away unless new structures are created to discourage the one and reward the other. We are back to privatization, the great *deus ex machina*, after Communism itself the most unfathomable social experiment ever contemplated in modern times.

The economic question is hanging fire. Not surprisingly, people facing so uncertain a future have taken solace in the past. The son of the last Habsburg emperor has been invited to stand for the Hungarian presidency, to which the 77-year-old appears to have replied, 'Thank you, but not this time'. An enthusiast has located 2,700 pre-war statues in Budapest withdrawn by the Communists from public gaze. Old political parties have been reborn. Does this mean that Eastern Europe is 'reverting to type', as it were, with resuscitation of the national tensions which so worry Kilroy-Silk and other British commentators? Here we must beware of glibness. The old parties have done conspicuously badly in this year's elections, particularly the peasant parties. Social structures have changed fundamentally since the war. As to nationalism, two things should be remembered. Firstly, nationalism is a universal creed in Eastern Europe and in its nineteenth-century origins was unquestionably a positive force, engaging the energies of repressed nationalities in social mobilization and cultural uplift. The territorial disputes which later emerged can be exaggerated; there were only two short wars between native peoples in the notorious Balkans in the century from 1815 to 1914. Secondly, many of the worst sources of discord were removed after 1945, with the expulsion of the Germans from Poland and Czechoslovakia and the cession of Eastern Poland to the Soviet Union. Current tensions owe as much to neo-Stalinism as to nineteenth-century tradition. Marxism-Leninism accepted the nation as a legitimate entity, and identified the national with the anti-imperialist struggle. Rigidified within Marxism-Leninism's dogmatic, self-righteous categories, Communist nationalism, in the hands of Ceausescu, Zhivkov or the Serb Milošević, had the vices but not the virtues of the real thing.

That said, if we except the Slovaks' battle for grammatical equality with the Czechs in Czechoslovakia/Czecho-Slovakia, there are two sources of long-standing nationalist discord in Eastern Europe today. In Transylvania a Magyar minority of two million calls for language rights and for a measure of cultural autonomy from a suspicious, even paranoid Romanian majority. The tragedy of the current impasse is that only Romanian intransigence could provoke the secessionist drive in Transylvania, and the backing for it in Budapest, which Romanians fear. In Yugoslavia, Serb nationalism first whetted by its self-assertion over the Albanian majority in the province of Kosovo now confronts its counterparts in Croatia and Slovenia, Catholic lands which aspire to the Central European Pentagonale orchestrated by the Italian foreign minister De Michaelis. Ruled by non-Communists, they will tolerate only a confederal Yugoslavia, which Serbia would contemplate only on condition that borders were redrawn to safeguard the Serbs of Croatia and Bosnia. In July, intellectuals I met thought these national quarrels an admirable device for diverting attention from the bold economic strategy of Ante Marković's central government. After the Serb-Croat clashes of September such complacency is less likely. But it is still more probable that Yugoslavia will survive rather than fall apart, albeit in a weaker, confederal form.

Until very recently the thought of a hole in the heart of the Balkans would have unnerved the most hard-bitten diplomat. The fact that the Yugoslav crisis has aroused so few alarm bells shows how big a change Gorbachev has brought about in world affairs, and how much Eastern Europe's reputation as a trouble danger zone has owed to great power rivalries rather than the activities of East Europeans themselves. Their own future may be troubled, for reasons given above, but these troubles will not lead to the major international crises some have predicted, so long as both Germany and Russia continue to support the East European emancipation they opposed in 1848–9 and between the wars. Here, however, is the rub: Kohl no doubt speaks for most Germans on the Oder-Neisse line. Who now does Gorbachev speak for?

Churchill once said that the Soviet Union was a riddle wrapped in an enigma inside a mystery. Yet it seems, given half a chance, that Soviet people are not so different from anyone else. With a time-lag they are following their former satellites. National identities are being asserted; radical democracy has won the great Russian cities; a leading ideologist has pronounced that the problem is not just the moustache (Stalin) but the beards (Marx and Engels); and the Communist Party has accepted the case for an unhyphenated market economy. True, all these steps are more fraught for Russia than for Eastern Europe. The Soviet Union is like Yugoslavia on a vaster scale, with an army, like the Serb-dominated Yugoslav army, which might prove the final instrument of exasperated centralism. The issue remains undecided. In opposed idealisms, Mikhail Gorbachev sees the Soviet Union, after successful perestroika, taking its place as a reformed socialist state in the 'common European home', while the Washington analyst Francis Fukuyama sees it breaking up neatly into its component parts without apparently incommoding the liberal democratic work which is coming into its own. Against these perspectives are the claims of Russian *Realpolitik*: for a reconstituted empire, possible without the Balkan states, led by whoever has the stomach for the job; and the Solzhenitsyn compromise: a Slavic state, including the Ukraine and northern Kazakhstan, with the remainder turned loose to fend for themselves, provision being made for the sixty million at present living outside their national homelands. The range of possibilities seems forbiddingly vast. Yet perhaps a hybrid is possible out of the balance of mutually constraining forces: a confederation, yes, no doubt minus the Balts, but one not resting on reform Communist ideology or exclusive Russian nationalism. It seems to be the goal of Yeltsin, but whether his outsize frame and personality are matched by equivalent ability remains to be seen; the prototype is De Gaulle.

One thing is certain. There will continue to be a very large state based on Moscow, whose feelings, whether friendly or sullen, cannot be ignored by the former satellites in their overtures to the European Community. The Community offers these lands at present only associate status and is absorbed in its internal debate over closer union, in part as a means to contain the new Germany. Yet what is more desirable from the standpoint of good relations with Russia – a minimally enlarged Community, proceeding to super-power status as, effectively, a single international entity, or a broader, looser body? Can such a broadening be avoided as EFTA negotiates on entry, Austria presents a strong case and Czechoslovakia, Poland and Hungary wait in the wings, even if the Balkans are fobbed off with Turkey? Western policy shows a lack of urgency about the imbalance which is developing between the two halves of the continent, as the Warsaw Pact and its economic counterpart Comecon fade away, Gorbachev's hopes for an overarching security organ through CSCE (the Conference on Security and Co-operation in Europe) are ignored, and East European states (like Hungary in August) float ideas for regional military alliances. The fate of perestroika, the prospects of Eastern Europe and the powers of the EC can no longer be treated as quite separate issues. That is the meaning of the opening of the Berlin Wall in November 1989.

Nearer home one further lesson can be learnt from Eastern Europe. The collapse of the socialist system there is a harsh but necessary verdict on the difficulties socialism faces when it seeks to turn itself from an aspiration for social justice into a comprehensive political philosophy. In its Marxist form it twisted this aspiration into a fetish of state power for class purposes, and it misunderstood the relation of class and nationality in modern society. Nation-based states have known successes and failures; class-based states only failures. Socialism, *pace* Mrs Thatcher, will survive, but as one strand in plural polities, not as the world historical creed of a prospective new society. The only plausible basis for a world order to hand is the free association of democratic nations, pooling their so-called sovereignty. While applauding the emancipation of the nations of Eastern Europe, as in 1848 and 1918, Welsh people have a further chance, perhaps a final one, to ask themselves if these events hold no message for them, too. As the old proverb has it, *tri chynnig i Gymro.*

A Pistol Shot in a Concert?

GWYN A. WILLIAMS

From Planet 84, December 1990/January 1991

Twelve years ago, I was infuriated by a review of one of my books. This is a regular occurrence, but twelve years ago, the pain was so sharp that I broke a rule and dispatched a prolonged yelp at the offending journal.

It was a review of a book I'd written on the Merthyr Rising of 1831. The reviewer, who apparently intended to be kind, called me a Welsh Edward Thompson. This sent me into a prolonged bout of empathetic mourning for one of those old bottles of quite decent Rioja wine which used to suffer the humiliation of being marketed under the implausible title of Spanish Burgundy. The wretch then went on to call the book a characteristic product of the New Left. I pointed out with some asperity that I was not a member of the New Left, not the Old New Left, the New New Left or the Instant New Left. I was not even a member of the Old Left. I was a member of the Antediluvian Left.

Even a modest historical monograph can make an answer to the question 'Which side are you on?' very difficult. But if controversy over commitment is a familiar feature of the historical landscape, it fades into oblivion once you dip a tentative toe into the acid pool next door – the practice of Literature Proper or writing with a capital R. My most vivid memory of the large and active Department of English at Cardiff was that hardly anybody in it was on speaking terms with anyone else – on doctrinal grounds. And this was even before the appearance of Post-Structuralists and Neo-Deconstructionists.

There is a school of thought which holds that all writing, of whatever kind, is in the last resort political. Certainly, good and necessary work has been done on the political assumptions and commitment which lie hidden in many overtly unpolitical works – Jane Austen, for example. I've had some fun myself trying to filter out what politics there are in the black novels of P. D. James. On the other hand, I was quite astonished to learn that Ruth Rendell is an active supporter of CND and a believer in community government at its most radical. Not something you'd gather from her books, I think. She'd probably be pleased to hear that. Have you noticed, by the way, that the more grisly ranges of that detective-cum-horror genre have been monopolized by brilliant women? I imagine there's some deeply political significance to that. I can't think off-hand what it is, except that it seems ominous.

One could, no doubt, analyse the political commitment in the work of, say, Barbara Pym and Alice Thomas Ellis. And it would be a waste of time. Whatever political commitment there is would be so removed from text and content as to be irrelevant to the experience and assessment of such writing. Its only relevance would be to the set of attitudes which would make such writing possible in the first place. If you are of a radically opposed attitude, of course, you could deny the right of such writing even to exist. Many political regimes have taken this line, by no means only Communist regimes. I take it we want no more of that poison? No, there are great tracts of some of the finest writing to which the question 'Which side are you on?' is either irrelevant or of only marginal significance.

Far stronger has been the opposed dogmatism which asserts that political commitment has no place whatever in literature, which would seem to remove a great deal of human life from it. The most vivid expression of this opinion came from the early nineteenth-century French writer Stendhal, a caustic, brilliant, acrid kind of writer whose works at one stage obsessed me. Reading them was like getting drunk on vinegar. Stendhal was the closest approximation I know to The Nearly Man. He was very bright and was nearly the best student in his class. He idolized Napoleon and was nearly a good Napoleonic diplomat in Italy. He longed to be a warrior, a profession for which he was singularly unsuited, and nearly saw the Battle of Waterloo. He said his books would not be read until 1940 and he was nearly correct. He had many love affairs and, in one, nearly succeeded. He wrote a whole book on the Art of Love and the longest chapter in it is entitled 'The Fiasco'.

At one stage he delivered himself of the ringing declaration that introducing politics into the novel was like firing a pistol shot in the middle of a concert. The supreme irony, of course, is that Stendhal's two masterpieces are both deeply political. *The Charterhouse of Parma* is a merciless exploration of Restoration Europe after 1815, the Europe of Metternich and the clericals. It carries the most vivid account in history or literature of that historic moment when Buonaparte, then a Jacobin general, led his army of sansculottes into Italy in 1796, one of the few genuinely revolutionary campaigns in history. And *The Scarlet and the Black* is actually a celebration and lament for the Napoleonic ideal in a sordid and second-rate society. It has the best description of a battle, seen from the worm's-eye view, I have ever read, better even than Tolstoy.

So where are we? I suppose to quote C. E. M. Joad from the ancient 'Brains Trust', it depends what you mean by politics. Or to cite an even more ancient folk wisdom, 'taint what you do, it's the way that you do it.

We are all painfully familiar with the results when the state politically directs literature. We are no less painfully familiar with the results when, without outside direction, politically driven writers people their pages with homilies, parables, individuals cut from cardboard and characters who are simply mouthpieces for the author. This problem of constriction at the heart of writing of committed people struck me forcibly recently when I tried my hand at turning two political thrillers into film scripts.

The political thriller, spy story, *roman noir* is the characteristic genre of our time, for good reason. Some time back, I was tickled when Pluto Press, declaring that all thrillers were written by right-wingers, launched a competition for a left-wing detective story. The results were mixed, but I thought the exercise futile. The political thriller, often attaining to the qualities of good literature, *has* been colonized by left-wingers. Eric Ambler, master-craftsmen of the good yarn, is outstanding. No one, I think, would call Graham Greene a right-winger, or for that matter, John Le Carré (have you read *A Small Town in Germany*?). The genre, on the European scale, has in fact been dominated by disillusioned ex-Communists, a category of human beings which must by now have numerically eclipsed even its great rival, the communion of ex-Christians.

The two thrillers I've been working on were written by left-wingers acutely aware of contradiction, complexity and irony. Raymond Williams's *The Volunteers* opens with an apparent attempt to assassinate the Minister of Wales in the grounds of St Fagan's Folk Museum. As a Welshman who is a redundant histor-ian, I found this notion deeply attractive. Through the protagonist, a sixties' left-winger turned creep for something which looks very like Sky Television, Raymond Williams dives through multiple levels of deception and self-deception to arrive at the final, un-chosen, forcible redemption of his protagonist in the face of a hidden menace all too familiar from our experience of our own hag-ridden state security system.

It's a good story, but it fails. With his protagonist, Raymond Williams tries to be slick, and Raymond Williams trying to be slick I find a painful experience. In his quite genuine awareness of com-plexity, contradiction and irony, he loads his characters with an endless debate which explores these contradictions and which leads to the argument reaching its climax before the action does – which in a political thriller will just not do. Moreover in that argu-ment, the author explores such depths of nuance, shift and contradiction as to become incomprehensible. This is a recurrent feature of Raymond Williams, most visible in his *Marxism and Literature* – passages of brilliant perception cheek by jowl with pas-sages of impenetrable opacity. He will not be brutal. He will not be vulgar. It is sometimes necessary to be both.

The other was by Jorge Semprun, now Minister of Culture in the Spanish government. During the Civil War, he was evacuated to the Soviet Union and educated there. He broke spectacularly with Communism in the 1960s. He was a script-writer for Costa Gavras films like Z. His own book, *The Second Death of Ramón Mercader* I find extraordinary. It is even more complex than Raymond Williams's. At the heart is an apparent Spaniard called Ramón Mercader – the same name as the assassin of Leon Trotsky. Like Semprun, he was evacuated to the Soviet Union during the Civil War, returned under the agreement of 1956 to become head of the Soviet espionage system in Spain. A senior member of the KGB defects to the Americans while staying in position and betrays him to the CIA (though this is not revealed until some time into the novel). Mercader becomes aware that he has been betrayed and goes to an emergency contact in Amsterdam enjoined upon him by his controller, an Old Bolshevik. The assassination of Trotsky runs as an undercurrent throughout and we are plunged into the world of the Soviet and East German and American intelligence agencies, the Dutch Special Branch, and an American film-maker working on Trotsky's killing. All the Communists have been in Stalinist jails, but remain Communists – an attitude I understand, as indeed should all Catholics; the Americans emerge as absolute bastards.

The author himself intervenes from time to time, in long disquisitions on the *Encyclopedia Britannica*, on the realities of popular usage, on the fact that the trouble with truisms is that they are true, on the tremendous power generated by clichés. He introduces a French academic called Boutor. The point about Boutor is that he is a French academic who can't stand Marcel Proust – which for a French academic is sheer tragedy. There is a whole chapter on him which is very funny. But he's introduced solely to serve as the third-person witness to a killing by the hero or protagonist – and the author spends some time justifying this inclusion. In the end, it is revealed that Mercader is not a Spaniard at all but a Russian Jew. But as a political thriller, it has long since been ruined by its own author.

This book is certainly an acquired taste which probably few will acquire. It is, like most of the best political writing of our time, an elegy for Communism, for the Communism that might have been. I personally find it enthralling, above all, for a character called Aunt Adela who is the personification of Old Castilian Virtue. She might have been a Castilian Saunders Lewis, except that she did not adopt Castile but was bred-in-the-bone in it. She is a good Republican because her unremittingly Castilian family are. In the end, the complications of Jorge Semprun's plot compel this Old Castilian lady to act as a courier for the Communist International, in the cause of her beloved nephew Ramón Mercader, who bears the name of the man who assassinated Trotsky and who is in reality a Russian Jew.

The dominant mode of *The Second Death of Ramón Mercader* is tragic irony. In my opinion, tragic irony has to be the thematic quality in any political writing these days. If it isn't ironic, don't trust it. If the author isn't ironic, he's a liar, above all to himself. I suppose it's what Richard Crossman meant when he said that the Left had to come to terms with Original Sin.

One way through this jungle was opened for me by Albie

319

Sachs's paper delivered recently to a seminar of the African National Congress in Lusaka. Albie Sachs had preached for years that culture should be a weapon of struggle in South Africa. Now he calls for a ban on that kind of talk for five years, because he had totally changed his mind. He had realized that this kind of thinking crippled literature and stifled genuine creativity. He talks about the richness of human experience which is excluded from the dedicated art of militants and explores the multinational mosaic of cultures which is South Africa. He puts in a moving plea for Afrikaans, asks militants not to regard the language itself as a political enemy and looks forward to the day when Afrikaans, as he puts it, will once more become the language of liberty.

One point he makes seems very interesting to me. He says South Africa has not yet produced an *And Quiet Flows the Don*. This, of course, was a novel by a revolutionary about a deeply anti-revolutionary people, the Don Cossacks. It is how a committed writer handles the opposition that makes or mars his or her book as literature. The opposition must surely be fascinating if only because it must seem inexplicable. Even Stalin who in his day could indulge the fancies of what Marx called an Oriental Despot, encouraged and protected a handful of quite reactionary writers in the Soviet Union, because he enjoyed them. It is said his favourite play was Bolgakov's *The White Guard* which he saw twenty-five times, sometimes sitting alone in the theatre. The experience must have added a dimension to the cast's perception of the notion that a critic can axe a play!

Failure to take the opposition seriously, a tendency to diminish them and turn them into caricatures, has seriously weakened most Welsh committed writing this century. It diminishes some of Saunders Lewis's more explicitly political work, for example. His plays *Gymerwch Chi Sigaret?* and to some extent, *Brad* (Treason) are in this respect seriously inadequate in comparison with his *Siwan*. Characteristically, Saunders Lewis is much stronger when he is affirming values rather than denying them and when the politics – and the enemy – are at one remove. *Siwan* is a fine play based on a real event – Llywelyn's marriage to a king of England's natural daughter who became a pillar of strength to him in his precarious ambition. When he discovered she was having an affair with a Marcher lord, in an access of passion he broke all the conventions then operating in such matters and ruined his own diplomacy, because he hanged the lord and banished his wife, only to become reconciled with her later. This makes for very powerful writing and for writing which is effectively committed, because the commitment is mediated through intensely human experience and because an enemy, while present, is not very visible. But I have found this rare in Welsh writing and inadequate treatment of the opposition seems to mar much left-wing Welsh writing as well.

In contrast, consider the astonishing sweep of the writing of Gabriel García Márquez. What dominates much of his writing is the history of his own country in this century – the endless civil wars between Liberals and Conservatives, divided over the Church and clericalism essentially, the desperate pact to share power to avoid total disintegration, the new waves of dissident violence which ensued, climaxing now in the power of the drug barons. García Márquez is without doubt a committed man and the commitment shines through his books. But the political commitment operates at one remove and what seems to obsess him is depiction of his own society in all its multiple and contradictory forces and their play on a myriad human beings. The panorama of *A Hundred Years of Solitude* is breath-taking. And his qualities are no less apparent in his many miniatures, all interlocking – *No One Writes to the Colonel*, for example, about an old man on the losing side waiting for the pension promised by the pact which never comes and vesting his hopes in the fortunes of a clearly doomed fighting cock, in the end living on what, at the close of the story, he calls shit.

When I reel out of García Márquez, I tend to find myself asking, God in Heaven, how could anyone treat the experience of the Welsh people in this century on this scale and to this depth? I can find no answer. Robert Minhinnick in his introduction to the Academi Gymreig conference, noted not only that most writers are odd, problematical, slightly damaged people who are only on their own side, but that much political comment in recent Welsh writing has been oblique to the point of invisibility. He wondered whether this can continue in our own problematical times.

I take his point, but as far as I can see, committed writing works best when the commitment operates at one remove, when the writer is concerned less with, say, politics, than with the play of politics on people, whether those people are themselves political or not. This often takes the form of the panoramic sweep. Think of

321

Primo Levi's remarkable *If Not Now, When?* on Jewish partisans in the chaos of wartime Eastern Europe. I do not know how Howard Spring's now ancient book, *Fame is the Spur*, stands with critics, but it certainly bowled me over when I was young, so much so that I can still remember whole tracts of it. Technically, it is the life of a Labour politician who follows the trajectory of Ramsay MacDonald, but it is much richer than that – and much better, I think, than Upton Sinclair's schematic Lanny Budd series. Outstanding in this field, I think, is Victor Serge's *The Case of Comrade Tulayev*, which is the best exposition of Stalinism I know, peopled with a myriad individuals and families, all brilliantly stitched into a crowded canvas. These panoramic sweeps can operate within the exploration of a single life, as in Arthur Koestler's *Darkness at Noon*, and they inform the context in the best miniatures in the style of *No One Writes to the Colonel* or *Siwan*.

What strikes me about works like this is that they operate at the point where hope and despair are in painful balance. Edward Thompson once made the same point about Wordsworth. He was at his best, Thompson thought, at that moment when he had lost faith in Jacobinism but had not yet slurped over into the populist cant of current Toryism. Thompson called this the Jacobinism of despair. The parallels with our own day are obvious. The characterization is certainly true of Arthur Koestler, for example, of Victor Serge, and indeed of Primo Levi as well. I suspect it may be true of Gabriel García Márquez. I suppose it signals the degradation and death of a once great movement of hope which embraced millions and whose cataclysm now engulfs much of the world's population.

That crisis, as we know, is now assuming world-historical significance in a Europe which is itself being driven on the one hand into a process of unification which transcends the polity known as the nation state, on the other into deeper and deeper regionalism, a Europe which has to open up to, and radically rethink, its relationships with the desperately poor but vividly alive peoples of Africa and Asia and South America, and which lives on a planet which is being destroyed, paradoxically, by our own efforts to make it more comfortable. On the western rim of this Europe lies our rich and powerful island under a regime I find cantankerous and catastrophic but appallingly deep-rooted; and on the western rim of that, Pobl y Cwm, with a problematical past confronting an even more problematical future. What will the response of committed Welsh writers be to a predicament which demands a small regiment of Gabiel García Márquez to interpret it?

To put it briefly, I haven't a clue. Neither, I suspect, has anyone else. Committed Welsh writers, I assume, will commit themselves to Wales. But there's the rub. It's easy to love Wales. It's the bloody Welsh are the problem.

All I can do is throw out a few ideas which came to me when I was trying to resolve the personal crisis inflicted on me by the terrible year 1979, *blwyddyn y pla*, the year of the plague. The elections of that year seemed to call in question the whole basis on which Welsh history had hitherto been written and I was literally hag-ridden into an attempt to write a history of Wales without preconceptions. I failed, of course, but I was left with a handful of governing notions.

Firstly, the necessity of a Pascal Wager. Pascal made a wager on the existence of God. He made a bet that God existed, in order to give his life meaning. If he lost the bet, he'd find out in due course. Marx made a wager of that kind, that human history had a meaning which was accessible to human reason. For two thousand years, people inhabiting these two western peninsulas of Britain had called themselves or had been called Cymry or Welsh. But from the moment of their appearance in history, the identity of this people so defined had been highly problematical. There are ways of looking at their history which ignore the concepts Wales and Welsh – and these ways seem as historically valid as any others. For reasons probably beyond reason, I made a Pascal Wager that Wales had existed and did exist. On that wager I base my work. I suspect all Welsh writers will have to make a Pascal Wager of some kind.

Secondly, it was obvious that something called Wales had had some kind of existence. It became clear that the Welsh invented Wales or Cymru because they had to. They had no choice. Of course, all nations have been invented, but the Welsh operated in peculiar circumstances. In all reason, we ought to have disappeared centuries ago. We didn't because we re-invented ourselves as the Welsh on a radically altered base in generation after generation, through crisis after crisis. Wales has been an artefact which the Welsh have repeatedly reproduced. In our present predicament, the question whether the Welsh or a sufficient number of them will re-invent Wales yet again, must I think be a problem which, consciously or unconsciously, Welsh writers will have to face.

Thirdly, it became clear that until the late eighteenth century, Welsh culture, in both languages, however British it considered itself, had in fact been much more European, continental as opposed to insular, than the culture of its giant neighbour which was drenching it. This was certainly true of Welsh writing in Welsh, but it was also true of Welsh writing in English from the days of John Dee and the Tudor humanists, whether Protestant or Catholic, right through to the days of Iolo Morganwg. That London-Welsh circle in the late eighteenth century is visibly a branch of the contemporary European or at least French–Low Countries–Italian intelligentsia – far more so than their much more numerous and influential English contemporaries. It was during the eighteenth century that this offshore island of Europe pulled away into those two hundred years of overarching world imperial power which radically changed the nature of the culture of its peoples – above all that of the Welsh. Now this island has shrunk back to being an offshore island of Europe once more. Whether in these circumstances, the Welsh or a sufficient number of them will rediscover or reinvent the European character of Wales in a Europe which is changing out of all recognition must surely be a matter which will concern committed Welsh writing.

This is a matter of identity, in some respects of the naming of names. Here I think Welsh writers have not fully got to grips with the style of living of a people which is essentially subordinate and has been through most of its life. We have certainly tackled some aspects of this permanent subordination, what Gramsci would have called the subaltern nature of Welsh life, notably those which touch on oppression and resistance. Other aspects have not figured so prominently, or even at all, perhaps because they are uncomfortable. Our history until the early twentieth century was very similar to that of the Czechs. In fact, the similarities are so close as to be uncanny. A parallel and comparative history of Czechs and Welsh would be a meaningful exercise. Both peoples were and are regarded by outsiders as servile. Clearly this offends us, notably those of us whose image of Wales is of a noble miner making a heroic stand. Both Welsh and Czechs retort that it is not servility at all but the instinct for survival of a threatened people.

This is without doubt true, but some of the more negative

aspects of survival techniques have largely escaped treatment. We were the land of the white gloves, with no serious crimes. Our crimes were as petty as our bourgeoisie and our ambitions were as petty as our spites. There is one neglected force in Welsh history, that sly, mild, levelling malice which has been so characteristic a feature of our gallant little nation. The malice is levelling, as it is among the Czechs, and at particular times can be a political power. We know about it, we all experience it, but we rarely enter it into the literary account — and there we differ from the Czechs.

I think it is a product of permanent subordination, as are other more genial features of our life. We cultivate inwardly a certain Welsh populist style. It dates ultimately from the Wales of the *gwerin* and didn't suffer much of a change when the *gwerin* mutated into the working class. It has been remarkably persistent. When the legendary Welsh brain surgeon meets the legendary Welsh bricklayer in London, a populist style is still *de rigueur*. It's like an unconscious conspiracy in front of strangers. One feature of it, I think, is precisely the naming of names. In the Welsh media these days, nobody seems to have any surnames. Given the range of surnames available to us, that may be understandable, but the result is that you feel you're being swept into a wild Druidic dance of pseudo-bardic names.

I have been astonished and appalled to find that I've been swept into it, too. I never expected to be known as Gwyn Alf. I am now Gwyn Alf even in official contracts. This is not my name of course, but my initial attempts at feeble resistance have now settled into a morose resignation. If I do go into history at all, I assume it will be as Gwyn Alf, which I find devastating. Because whatever identity or range of identities Gwyn Alf is meant to convey, they are not mine. Whoever Gwyn Alf is, he's not me.

I don't know whether others are in the same predicament, but I think this is a minor and comic symptom of a general condition I find less and less comic. Whether we speak English or Welsh, we seem to feel the need to people our own felt Wales with a range of easily recognizable types and styles which, in total, are diminishing. They are self-diminishing. We seem to want to create a cosy Welsh world in a Wales whose predicament is singularly uncosy. We are a very small people, but I think this is a badge of subordination. To me it represents the diminishing and sometimes

325

debilitating shorthand of a subordinate people cultivating a reassuring self-indulgence in the interstices of subordination.

My final thought stems from my gloomy efforts to discover why I was saddled with that dread middle name in the first place. I was named after my grandfather, Alfred Williams, a collier and one of the characters of Dowlais, known as Alf Gordon because of an alleged resemblance to General Gordon of Khartoum. He got it from his own father. My great-grandfather was a sailor in Briton Ferry who later kept The Tap there. He claimed that he used to hunt whales from Briton Ferry. I believe him. I'd believe anything of anybody from Briton Ferry. He was a Chartist and a believer in the Norman Yoke theory of history – that this island had been a democracy before the coming of the base and brutal Normans, ruled by a real people's king, good King Alfred. This was a wide-spread belief in the early popular and labour movements. Several newspapers named themselves after this populist hero. One was called *The People's Alfred* and an edition came out in Swansea. Hence the dread descent to myself.

My grandfather was in my case a figure in his own right, the first working man to be elected to the Board of Guardians. Half of Dowlais used to turn out to see him off, with watch chain and gold-tipped cane, to the meetings in Merthyr. He never recognized British summer time. 'By God's time,' he'd say with scorn, 'it's half-past-ten, but *by Labour Party time . . .*' This was grotesquely unfair since summer time was introduced by Lloyd George, to cut down the drinking. My grandfather hated the Labour Party, a sentiment which was cordially reciprocated. At election times, the early Labour Party would gather around his house. If they'd won, they'd content themselves with the 'Red Flag'. If they'd lost, they'd try to break the door in. My grandfather and his sons would stand by in the passage, armed with pick handles. Since those sons had by then joined the Labour Party, this served to introduce me early to the Marxist concept of the dialectic – that history advances through contradiction.

In Merthyr I was not known by my own name, not even by my father's – I was Alf Gordon's Grandson. I suspect that if I'd been a teacher in Merthyr, I'd never have got a headship.

When I complained about this to a friend in the Labour Party, he replied somewhat morosely, 'Well, men are more like their grandfathers than like their fathers.' When I reported this comment in turn to my old tutor in Aberystwyth, he replied with what was evidently a well-known aphorism – 'Men are more like their times than like their fathers.' I don't know whether, in male style, women are included in this generalization or whether they have a distinct pathology of their own in such matters.

That, however, does capture a truth, I think. Men *are* more like their times than their fathers. But thinking about these recent manifestations of subordination led me to a more disturbing thought – that men might be more like their times than like themselves. Men or people more like their times than themselves – that, I do believe, opens an area of discourse in context which committed Welsh writers will seriously have to explore.

A Local Institution: The Ladies of Llangollen

CERIDWEN LLOYD-MORGAN

From Planet 91, February/March 1992

In early December 1831, Sarah Ponsonby, born into an Irish Ascendancy family, died at Plas Newydd, Llangollen, her home since 1780. So came to an end one of the most remarkable phenomena in the history of Llangollen, still vying today with the International Musical Eisteddfod to keep this small Welsh town on the tourist map. Sarah had outlived by only two and a half years her 'Beloved' and inseparable companion, Lady Eleanor Butler, with whom she had shared her life since the two women's famous 'elopement' from Ireland. Despite their longing for a life of 'sweet and delicious retirement', they had found themselves leading a busy social life. Not only did they move in local aristocratic circles, but there was a constant stream of visitors to their door. They quickly became celebrities, and no tour in Wales by the genteel, or those aspiring to gentility, was complete without a visit to their home. Sometimes they would hide in the house, watching from the upstairs windows as their unwanted guests gawked around the gardens.

When Sarah Ponsonby died, a local man, John Morris, was paid 1s.6d. (7½p) per night 'for sitting up 9 nights during the time the corpse was in the house . . . defending the property in and out of the house'. This was a generous sum, but Llangollen had become used to generosity at Plas Newydd. Their diaries and account books record regular gifts to local people when in need: 'Thomas Owen's wife for their unfortunate daughter – 2 shillings' is typical. It was only fitting that the same generosity should be continued on their behalf after their deaths.

Eleanor Butler had naturally left the bulk of her estate to Sarah when she had died at the age of 90; Sarah, being left alone and perforce childless, had little choice but to leave their combined worldly goods to one of her relatives back in Ireland. She chose her 'beloved kinswoman' Caroline Hamilton, wife of Charles Hamilton of County Meath. As a married woman, however, Caroline had to leave the administration of the affairs at Llangollen to her husband.

The contents of the house, reflecting the taste and idiosyncrasies of the Ladies, were auctioned six months after Sarah's death, in a sale lasting seven days and providing plenty of scope for the inquisitive. Furniture, books, ornaments and personal treasures were dispersed, but the Hamiltons did take back with them to Ireland some of the best china, some framed views of landscapes in England and Wales, and also the personal papers preserved by the Ladies. Only a small group of letters remained, and those were mainly from famous persons or reflected some of the more momentous chapters in the lives of Sarah Ponsonby and Eleanor Butler, which suggests that they themselves had already decided what should be kept. The vast numbers of surviving letters from them to friends and relatives give some idea of the amount they must have received and destroyed. Apart from such letters as they chose to keep, the archive included their journals and various note-books, which together provide a commentary both on their life together and also on life in north-east Wales in the late eighteenth and early nineteenth centuries.

The Hamiltons, to their credit, kept the archive intact, and it came to be known as the Hamwood Papers after their family home. And in Hamwood they remained until 1990, when they were acquired by the National Library of Wales, and were brought back to Wales close on 160 years after they had first left it.

The lodge at Hamwood might have been designed by the Ladies themselves, for its neo-Gothic decoration evokes the Strawberry Hill excesses of Plas Newydd itself, though the American mailbox installed just outside the front door tends to undercut the old-fashioned charm of the cottage-garden flowers. The gate onto the drive sticks a little, the drive has that slightly unkempt look of great Irish houses in privately-owned decline: no well-raked gravel and carefully pruned shrubs here. The house itself comes as a shock: a solid, square Georgian box, but the windows replaced with Edwardian single-paned sashes, giving it the half-blind look normally brought on by double-glazing. I entered through the kitchen door, greeted by the present head of the family, and by a bevy of dogs of assorted breed. A smell of dogs and damp pervaded the rooms. I found myself installed in the drawing room, a huge room, perhaps originally two, with a handsome fireplace at each end. The warmth of the July sun did not penetrate here. I was surrounded by generations of family portraits, and noticed a miniature of Sarah Ponsonby painted before her exodus to Wales. The hand-painted nineteenth-century wallpaper was stained with damp and in places hung limply from the walls.

As I unpacked loose papers from their boxes, squinting at the Ladies' tiny handwriting, a dog nuzzled my knee, then tripped on a hole in the carpet. From across the hallway came snatches of conversation: the Major regaling the agent from Dublin with hunting anecdotes. Strong tea, chocolate biscuits and a tumbler of gin were brought to fortify me. The scale of this house is vast. No wonder that the Ladies, brought up in similar mansions, thought of Plas Newydd, for all the grand name they bestowed on it, as a humble cottage. A trek upstairs and down a long, long corridor off which numberless rooms tantalizingly opened, brought me at last to the loo, a marvel of unspoilt Victorian plumbing . . . Back in Aberystwyth, reading the Hamwood Papers in a modern office seems almost inappropriate. There is a conflict, too, between a sense of voyeurism inherent in reading the letters and diaries of others, and the fascination of the story that unfolds, but at least in this case the papers were carefully preserved by their owners, apparently with a consciousness of their value as documents and an eye on posterity, although whether they had posterity in mind when writing is more uncertain.

Most of the diaries, kept by Eleanor Butler for periods between 1788 and 1821, veer from the lyrical evocation of shared moments of peaceful happiness, or physical description of fields and gardens at their most picturesque, to a highly colloquial style, including mordant personal comments. Certainly, had the diaries been published immediately after the Ladies' deaths, they could have caused offence or hurt to many individuals. Nearly 200 years on, however, the Hamwood Papers provide a remarkable window onto everyday life, for they give us precisely that humdrum detail which reveals how people lived, and yet is normally taken for granted by contemporary writers because of its very ordinariness. Much of this information emerges indirectly, especially from anecdotes or lists of expenses.

Most modern accounts of the Ladies of Llangollen have tended to emphazise the romantic story of their 'elopement' and to investigate the nature of their relationship, to the extent that the specifically Welsh dimension of their lives has been somewhat undervalued. Yet it should be noted that they made a conscious choice to come to Wales, although Wales was only just beginning to attract aristocratic visitors making a tour. But this was probably part of the attraction. When they first crossed from Ireland in May 1778, they spent some time wandering through Wales in search of a possible home. From Milford Haven as Sarah Ponsonby recorded in the first of the journals, they wandered up through Pembrokeshire towards Cardiganshire then through Montgomeryshire and up to the north-east, keeping firmly on the Welsh side of the border apart from the odd sortie into Shropshire. Once settled at Llangollen their visits to England were restricted to day excursions to places of interest, as part of a group of friends from among the local gentry.

At Plas Newydd they rapidly became a local institution, and apart from putting Llangollen on the map for outsiders they made a considerable contribution to the local economy. They were not well off by the standards of their class, and their financial problems were exacerbated both by their tendency to overspend and by the delays in the arrival of their private income. But they clearly gave priority to paying their bills to local traders: 'Paid . . . some other small bills in the village and cleared ourselves, thank God, in this district.' Most of their needs were supplied locally, including flower pots, cheese, 'repairs to a sieve and a new milking can', a whip from Davies the saddler, tape and thread for carpets, emetics from the apothecary, and oil for painting. Their bill at the Lion Inn included not only wine and carriage of parcels but also oats and, more unexpectedly, a load of manure.

Since Plas Newydd had limited space for guests, visitors often slept at the Hand Inn, and over the years the sheer numbers who came to Llangollen to see the Ladies, whether friends, relatives, or simply curious strangers, must have injected substantial sums into the local economy.

331

The Ladies' interest in gardening and, increasingly, small-scale farming did mean that they became less dependent on local suppliers for some of their provisions. References to their garden in their journals, letters and commonplace books reveal what a staggering variety of both vegetables and fruit were grown at Plas Newydd. Apart from basics such as potatoes, cabbages and peas, apples, plums and gooseberries, they succeeded in growing more exotic items such as melons, peaches, apricots, walnuts and figs. By 1785 they were growing at least a dozen different varieties of gooseberry, whose characteristics they carefully noted: 'fine tasted, large red gooseberry and great bearer', 'green, wretched bearer'. By 1788 they had acquired a 'watering machine' for the garden, and paid a shilling to a local wood-turner for making a new handle for it. Some of their plants they bought in, others were presents or exchanges with other keen gardeners. Thus they acquired cucumber plants from Chirk Castle, and seeds and cuttings for flowers from such friends as Mrs Wingfield, wife of the vicar of Ruabon.

The Ladies planned the garden themselves, but they also undertook much of the actual gardening, such as planting bulbs, or potting up cuttings. For heavier work they employed a series of gardeners, notably Moses Jones, whose fondness for the bottle led to his being fired (and later reinstated) on several occasions. Once the Ladies had acquired more land, by renting an extra field, they were able to grow hay for winter fodder for their cows, such as their beloved Margaret, who often accompanied them on their dignified walks around Llangollen. They even began to grow barley, which enabled them to brew their own ale. As a result of this expansion in their activities, their need for local labour increased, and the Ladies employed both men and women for seasonal agricultural tasks such as ploughing, liming, cutting thistles, haymaking and harvesting. And they drew again on the local labour force for work such as building a new dairy, or a wall around the dunghill, for the annual whitewashing of the house, and chimneysweeping. Gifts of money are recorded for small services unexpectedly rendered: tuppence to a boy who brought them some white foxgloves, roots and all, and a shilling to another lad for 'guarding us from the bull'.

Their interest in the local people as individuals cannot be doubted, nor can the mutual affection which grew up between them. Where known, they consistently refer to the humblest neighbours by their names, and both Llangollen inhabitants and strangers are described in all their human dignity as well as eccentricity. Thus we meet Davy the miller, and hear news of his infirm father and 'Shanette the reputed witch of the village [who] brought us a new year's gift, a large parcel of apples', as well as the 'thin old man who came to the door and sang a Christmas Carol in a melodious, solemn voice', or 'a very old woman with pictures to sell. Told us she was from Carnarvonshire, had a blind daughter whom she supported by the sale of these pictures which she purchased in Chester and vended about the country'. Under Eleanor Butler's pen, everyday sights come into view with startling clarity: 'a comfortable well clad old woman rode up the field with a pipe of tobacco in her mouth, the puffs from which softened the keenness of the air and must make her journey over the mountains delectable'; 'Evan Williams [the weaver] and his wife walking slowly and pensively round their hanging field, examining the thread which lies there for bleaching, and counting the lambs'.

It would be unfair to the Ladies to conclude from such peaceful vignettes, that they held an idealized view of the life around them. That is belied by their evident distress at the poverty which drove people they knew to the workhouse, at semi-starvation in bad winters, infanticide by desperate single mothers, the dangers of 'numerous vagabonds . . . under the appearance of maim'd sailors . . . pedlars etc.' who mugged travellers and broke into houses, having first poisoned the watchdogs, the countless untimely deaths from disease and accident – none of these are glossed over but presented as an integral part of daily life, and victims of such misfortunes are referred to with sensitivity as well as sympathy. In fact, Lady Eleanor's more cutting remarks are reserved for the better-off members of society: the curate who preaches 'dreadfully', unwanted and ill-bred visitors, or Mr Edwards, landlord of the Hand, with whom they quarrelled.

Although there is no evidence of their learning Welsh, it seems unlikely that they could have avoided acquiring at least some passive knowledge of the language; certainly their spelling of Welsh place-names is far more accurate than that found in the most popular modern biography of the Ladies. Sarah Ponsonby and Eleanor Butler were also very much aware of, and indeed interested in, Wales as a country with its separate history and culture. The catalogue of books in their library, which enables us to reconstruct its contents shelf by shelf, includes such important works as David Powel's *Historie of Cambria* and Sir John Wynn's *History of the Gwedir Family*. They refer to eisteddfodau, and were quick to share Llangollen's pride and pleasure when a local man, Jonathan Hughes, won a major eisteddfod chair in 1789. They invited him to Plas Newydd, 'a tall venerable figure [who] can speak very little English'.

Welsh traditional music delighted them too. The journals contain many references to singers and musicians, including people singing unselfconsciously whilst about their work, and they describe the difficulties in trying to get someone who could write music to note down a tune they had heard being played in an inn, for no sooner had the man reached the inn than the drink would interfere with the task in hand. It is tempting to think that this tune might be 'Mentra Gwen', a version of which Sarah Ponsonby copied out so beautifully in her commonplace book.

By birth Eleanor Butler and Sarah Ponsonby were aristocratic Irish ladies, but by adoption they became indisputably a part of north Wales. It is true that they occasionally reveal attitudes often characteristic of modern incomers – as in their determined efforts to put a stop to things they personally disapproved of, such as anything that might spoil the view – but in general they display a humility, and a sympathetic interest in even their humblest neighbours, unusual in women of their class. Far more than the catalogue of all their aristocratic visitors, whether English, Irish, French or Welsh, it is above all their account of the day-to-day activities, joys and sorrows of these Welsh neighbours which breathes life into the Hamwood Papers.